SOCIAL POLICY

Visit the *Social Policy* Companion Website at **www.pearsoned.co.uk/bochel** to find valuable **student** learning material including:

- Weblinks to original documents, government and other offical publications, statistical sources
- Links to social policy information from the devolved assemblies and Eire
- Annually updated Key Issues and other information for each other

SOCIAL POLICY: ISSUES AND DEVELOPMENTS

Hugh Bochel

Department of Policy Studies,
University of Lincoln

Catherine Bochel

Department of Policy Studies,
University of Lincoln

Robert Page

Institute of Applied Social Studies,
University of Birmingham

Rob Sykes

School of Social Science and Law,
Sheffield Hallam University

PEARSON
Prentice
Hall

Harlow, England • London • New York • Boston • San Francisco • Toronto • Sydney • Singapore • Hong Kong
Tokyo • Seoul • Taipei • New Delhi • Cape Town • Madrid • Mexico City • Amsterdam • Munich • Paris • Milan

Pearson Education Limited
Edinburgh Gate
Harlow
Essex CM20 2JE
England

and Associated Companies throughout the world

Visit us on the World Wide Web at:
www.pearsoned.co.uk

First published 2005

ISBN 0 130 87009 9

British Library Cataloguing-in-Publication Data
A catalogue record for this book is available from the British Library

Library of Congress Cataloging-in-Publication Data
A catalogue record for this book is available from the Library of Congress

10 9 8 7 6 5 4 3 2 1
09 08 07 06 05

Typeset in 10pt Book Antiqua by 3
Printed and bound in China
GCC/01

The publisher's policy is to use paper manufactured from sustainable forests.

Short Contents

Part IV European and international developments

Contents

Part III Theorising social policy

Part IV European and international developments

Companion Website resources

Visit the Companion Website at
www.pearsoned.co.uk/bochel

For students
- Weblinks to original document, government and other official publications, statistical sources
- Links to social policy information from the devolved assemblies and Eire
- Annually updated Key Issues and other information for each chapter

About the contributors

Robert Adams is (part-time) Professor of Social Work at the University of Teesside.

Alex Bryson is a Principal Research Fellow at the Policy Studies Institute.

Dee Cook is Professor of Social Policy and Director of the Regional Research Institute at the University of Wolverhampton.

Tony Fitzpatrick is Reader in Social Policy at the University of Nottingham.

Brian Lund is Principal Lecturer in the Department of Sociology at Manchester Metropolitan University.

Stephen McKay is Deputy Director of the Personal Finance Research Centre at the University of Bristol.

Karen Rowlingson is a Senior Lecturer in the Department of Social and Policy Sciences at the University of Bath.

Preface

Social policy affects all of us, featuring in our everyday lives effectively from the cradle to the grave, through our use of services, our payment for them, whether directly or through taxation, and our discussions about topics such as asylum seekers, housing, education, healthcare or pensions.

The subject is taught in many universities and other higher education institutions in the United Kingdom, either on its own or as part of a wide variety of other degree programmes. This book is intended to support the study of social policy and in particular to provide a focus on social policy primarily for the period since 1997. It attempts to explain and explore the nature of contemporary social policy, examining both theoretical dimensions and key policy areas.

The authors have set out to make this presentation of the subject thorough but accessible, through the use of text, boxed examples and tables and cartoons. Each chapter begins by identifying the key issues with which it deals, uses a variety of examples (labelled as 'policy eye' and 'briefings') and ends with a chapter summary, followed by review questions, suggestions for further reading, useful websites and references.

Students will naturally develop their own way to use the book: some may seek to read it through from start to finish, others will be concerned to develop more specific knowledge, and will therefore focus on certain chapters, or even parts of chapters. However, the nature of the subject is such that there will inevitably be links that can be made between the contents of the different chapters and these will strengthen your understanding of social policy. We hope that you find it useful.

Hugh Bochel
Catherine Bochel
Robert Page
Rob Sykes

Acknowledgements

Author's acknowledgements

We are grateful to Andrew Taylor, Anita Atkinson and Emma Travis at Pearson, and to Helen Baxter, our copy editor, for their encouragement and forbearance. They recognised the range of commitments and pressures that exist for many writers, but at the same time they helped to ensure that the book remained on our list of priorities. We would also like to thank Kelly Meyer and Michelle Morgan for their input into the design of the book.

Publisher's acknowledgements

We are grateful to the following for permission to reproduce copyright material:

Child Poverty Action Group for an extract from *Poverty, Crime and Punishment* by D. Cook (1997); Her Majesty's Stationery Office for an extract from the White Paper 'The New NHS. Modern. Dependable' by the Department of Health (1997); Cambridge University Press for an extract adapted from *Practical Ethics 2nd* edition by P. Singer (1993); Open University Press/McGraw-Hill Publishing Company for an extract adapted from *Managing Scarcity: Priority Setting and Rationing in the National Health Service* by R. Klein and P. Day (1996); and Palgrave Macmillan for an extract from *Political Ideologies: An Introduction* by A. Heywood (2003).

Cartoons on pages 6, 24, 53, 70, 92, 112, 138, 158, 184, 207, 230, 257, 282, 295, 329, 346 www.CartoonStock.com; Table 3.2 from *Financial Statement and Budget Report 2001*, Crown copyright material is reproduced under Class Licence

Number C01W0000039 with the permission of the Controller of HMSO and the Queen's Printer for Scotland (H M Treasury 2001); Tables 5.1 and 5.2 from *Social Trends*, 33, Crown copyright material is reproduced under Class Licence Number C01W0000039 with the permission of the Controller of HMSO and the Queen's Printer for Scotland (Central Statistical Office 2003); Table 6.1 from *Department of Health, Health and Personal Social Services Statistics*, Crown copyright material is reproduced under Class Licence Number C01W0000039 with the permission of the Controller of HMSO and the Queen's Printer for Scotland (Department of Health 2003); Figure 8.2 redrawn from http://www.nhs.uk/england/aboutTheNHS/default.cmsx, 2nd September 2004, © NHS Information Authority; Figure 9.2 redrawn from *US Housing Review 2002/2003*, pub Chartered Institute of Housing/Council of Mortgage Lenders in association with Joseph Rowntree Foundation, reprinted by permission of Chartered Institute of Housing (Wilcox, S. 2002); Figure 10.1 redrawn from *Ethics: The Heart of Health Care*, Copyright 1998, © John Wiley & Sons Limited, reproduced with permission (Seedhouse, D. 1988); Figure 10.2 redrawn from *Ethics: The Heart of Health Care*, 2nd Edn, Copyright 1998, © John Wiley & Sons Limited, reproduced with permission (Seedhouse, D. 1998); Figure 11.1 redrawn from graphic Who benefits from transport spending? in *The Guardian* 21.5.04, Copyright © The Guardian, reprinted by permission of Guardian Newspapers Ltd.; Briefing 11.2 redrawn from *Tackling Obesity in England*, Crown copyright material is reproduced with the permission of the Controller of HMSO and the Queen's Printer for Scotland (National Audit Office 2001); Table 12.1 from Poverty and social security: What rights? Whose responsibilities? in *British Social Attitudes: The 18th Report* edited by A. Park *et al.*, reprinted by permission of Sage Publications Ltd. (Hills, J. 2001); Tables 15.1 and 15.2 from *The Social Situation in the European Union 2003*, reprinted by permission of the European Communities (European Commission/Eurostat 2003); Figure 16.1 redrawn from Mapping global governance in *Governing Globalization* edited by D. Held and A. McGrew, reprinted by permission of Polity Press Ltd. (Koenig-Archibugi, M. 2002); Figure 16.2 redrawn from *Inequality of world incomes: what should be done?*, www.open democracy.net, reprinted by permission of openDemocracy (Wade, R. H. 2001).

In some instances we have been unable to trace the owners of copyright material, and we would appreciate any information that would enable us to do so.

Part I

The context for social policy

Introducing social policy

1

Hugh Bochel

Issues in Focus

Social policy is one of the social sciences, along with subjects such as politics or sociology. It is sometimes studied on its own and sometimes as part of another subject. It is also often taken as part of professional training, such as in nursing or social work. This chapter seeks to provide a consideration of the subject of social policy and what it means to be studying it. It therefore:

- explores the nature of the subject, including the way in which it has developed as an academic discipline over time

- provides a very brief overview of the development of the welfare state

- outlines the structure of the remainder of the book.

What is social policy?

The almost inevitable starting point for a book such as this is the question 'what is social policy?'. While this is perhaps equally likely for a book on other social sciences, there is perhaps a greater importance for social policy, in part because the subject itself has developed and changed direction considerably from the 1980s and in part because these considerations continue to have significant resonance within the subject as it and its subject matter evolve further.

Social policy is clearly related to other social science disciplines, such as economics, politics or sociology, but it also has a resonance with professional courses, such as those focusing on social work, housing or nursing. As such, the study of social policy often draws on concepts and insights that come from these areas, but at the same time it brings its own distinctive approach to the understanding and analysis of the world. In the same way, a subject such as criminology, which has largely emerged in UK higher education from the 1990s, also draws on a range of subjects, including social policy, but is itself developing and debating its boundaries.

Social policy as an academic discipline can be seen as differing from others in a number of ways: for example it is different from sociology in its focus on the formulation, implementation and delivery of policies that affect the circumstances of individuals, groups and society; it differs from politics in its focus on welfare and well-being; and it is different from economics, because it is less concerned with the production of goods and services and again because of its emphasis on social or welfare policies and their outcomes. This is not to say that there are not sometimes closely related interests and there may be social policy academics in other university departments, while social policy departments may in turn contain individuals who draw heavily on or who originate from other subjects. There are also many institutions where social policy is in a department jointly with one or more other subjects, such as criminology, politics, social work or sociology.

This introductory discussion notwithstanding, the nature of the subject has changed considerably over time. For much of the 20th century social administration, as it was then called, was strongly associated with the **Fabian** tradition, itself linked to social democratic thought including the Labour Party (see Chapter 13). Many social administration academics were therefore seeking not merely to study social policy, but also to influence it in a generally Fabian direction, often using their research and analysis to support their political arguments. These could roughly be characterised as a belief in the role of the state as a central pillar of welfare provision (the 'welfare state') and a commitment to research and analysis that was concerned with the identification of needs and the impact of state welfare in attempting to meet those needs. However, in the second half of the 20th century a more critical approach emerged within the subject and, by the 1970s and 1980s, it was possible to identify a number of theoretical challenges to the association of Fabianism and the study of social administration and social policies linked to the welfare state. These included:

● The *New Right* – one of the most significant attacks on state provision of welfare (see Chapter 12) came from the right and, in particular, from think tanks such as the Adam Smith Institute, the Centre for Policy Studies and the Institute for Economic Affairs. These critiques took a number of forms but could generally be seen as arguing that: the welfare state was a burden on the economy and that it demanded too high levels of public expenditure and an excessive tax burden on entrepreneurs and citizens; that it damaged individual choice, in contrast to the market, which promotes it; and that it weakens the family and encourages dependency. The strategies that the New Right put forward as alternatives typically involved cuts in income tax, a shift away from state provision to individuals providing for themselves and their families through the private market, direct charging for services such as education and health and the replacement of most of the benefits and services provided by the state with alternatives from the private and voluntary sectors.

- *On the left* there also emerged a number of criticisms – some began to accept that the role of the state remained problematic in the provision of welfare and while in some instances state intervention had been valuable in changing social conditions, in others it had not always been so beneficial. Some argued that one answer was the injection of more resources to help tackle problems more successfully, while others favoured alternative approaches, such as the decentralisation of power and the encouragement of self-help for particular groups. One view, associated with a Marxist approach, suggested that in reality state welfare reflected the needs of capitalism for an educated, healthy workforce, and that this explained the failure of the welfare state to solve social problems.

- *The centre* – critiques of the welfare state also emerged from centrist positions, often focusing on the view that the large bureaucratic organisations that were often responsible for delivering welfare were inefficient and inflexible and were remote from the needs of consumers and that they tended to be run in the interests of professionals and administrators rather than users or citizens; from this perspective proposed solutions generally involved a shift towards a pluralistic, decentralised and more participative pattern of provision, including a much greater role for the voluntary sector.

- Other critical perspectives (see Chapter 14) – for example, *feminists* pointed out that there were a number of assumptions behind the provision of many services, including education, healthcare and the personal social services, such as that it was 'natural' for women to provide care for children, disabled people and older people and that they would often provide this care free at home while men went out to work and earned the household income. The state therefore could be seen as exploiting and encouraging the 'caring role' of women. Even when women did work (often in the 'caring services') there was a tendency for them to do so in the less-well paid jobs, while men dominated the higher status better paid positions. In a similar manner, it could also be pointed out that many welfare services failed to recognise particular needs of minority ethnic groups, disabled people and others.

In addition there were other developments that encouraged reflection within the subject. These included other New Right critiques, in particular of bureaucracies, which have been important in the delivery of state welfare. New Right thinkers have argued that bureaucrats are primarily concerned with promoting their own interests and that they do this at the expense of the public interest. In addition they suggest that political control of state bureaucracies is often ineffective. From the perspective of the New Right these combine to increase the pressure for higher levels of public expenditure, which itself is seen as problematic and a drain on the economy.

From the 1970s there also came to be a much greater awareness of the comparative dimension of social policy. In part this resulted from the United Kingdom's membership of the European Union, which inevitably focused greater attention on Europe and other European states. However, increasingly this interest spread to other areas of the world and in particular sought to learn from the experiences and policies of other states. For some, the Scandinavian states provided models for state welfare founded in a social democratic approach. For others, the more market-oriented approach of the United States appeared to present a more appropriate path for the United Kingdom. Whatever the approach, it became apparent that there was a great diversity of forms of welfare provision, with very different mixes of provision by the public, private, voluntary and informal sectors. The comparative approach to social policy has developed greatly in recent years and is now a major strand within the subject. In addition, there are many examples of **policy transfer**, with governments drawing on ideas and policies from other countries, such as the establishment of the Child Support Agency by the Conservatives (see Dolowitz 2000), and elements of New Labour's New Deal, which drew on the experience of the United States.

The impact of all these developments inevitably affected the subject of social policy. Over a period of time it came to reflect and respond to these debates, arguably becoming broader and in some respects at least more critical. It is therefore not surprising that during the 1980s there was considerable debate

Source: www.CartoonStock.com

about the nature of the discipline. However, the subject has not entirely lost its traditional links, with a number of university departments and awards continuing to use the term social administration, while the government bodies that fund and oversee much of higher education, such as the Higher Education Funding Council for England and the Quality Assurance Agency for Higher Education (QAA), often refer to social policy and administration. Indeed the QAA's subject benchmark statement (Policy eye 1.1), which seeks to outline the nature and characteristics of the subject and the attributes and capabilities that an honours graduate in social policy should possess, is for social policy and administration. As illustrated elsewhere in this book (for example, Chapters 11 and 16), the boundaries and relevance of social policy and its insights continue to evolve.

However, attempts to define the subject also need to recognise that social policy exists outside the academic world and that much of what governments

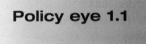 **Policy eye 1.1**　Social policy and administration subject benchmarks: defining principles

Social policy and administration is about the study of the distribution of welfare and well-being within societies. Its focus is on the ways in which different societies meet the basic human needs of their populations. In doing this it follows these principles:

1　The study of social policy requires the rigorous linking of theoretical analysis with empirical enquiry.

2　The study of social policy involves the identification, and understanding, of different value positions.

3　The study of social policy requires students to acquire the skills and qualities that will enable them to become active and informed citizens, capable of participating effectively in the policy process and equipped for a dynamic labour market.

4　The study of social policy will draw on the intellectual traditions and perspectives of social science disciplines.

5　Students will appreciate the interaction and interdependence between theory and the operation and impact of social policies.

　Interestingly, consideration of this demonstrates both the academic and applied nature of the subject, since the benchmark statement attempts to set out academic characteristics but is doing so in response to a policy imperative in the form of pressure from governments to measure and maintain standards in higher education (see Chapter 5).

Source: Quality Assurance Agency for Higher Education (2000)

and other bodies *do* is social policy. Policies can be designed to help people, although even those that are intended to do so may not, for a variety of reasons. Others may be 'technocratic' in nature – designed to improve a mechanism, perhaps to achieve something more efficiently or economically. And social policies can be used to control people, as we have seen in recent years with demands to control or deter asylum seekers. One of the things that students and analysts of social policy need to do therefore is to examine policies critically – to look at their intentions and impacts and consider the extent to which they do actually achieve their goals and the reasons why and why not this might be the case. We must therefore sometimes try to set aside our personal views and opinions. In addition, it can be useful to try to see things from the perspectives of others, for example, we can seek to understand why some people feel strongly about individual choice and others favour collective provision, or why managers and health professionals in the National Health Service may clash over the best way to meet particular goals. We can try and put ourselves in the place of politicians who have to make sometimes difficult decisions about the level of resources that should be spent on welfare (and other areas of activity) and how the money for this should be raised; or in the place of the people who then have to deliver services, or those who are recipients. Each of these may provide us with very different perspectives on social policies. However, we also have to recognise that we all have our own values and attitudes, our own visions of what a good society should be like and that the study of social policy is likely to involve us in both seeking to be objective and in maintaining our beliefs and that at times there is likely to be a tension between the two.

Development of the welfare state

Although the discussion so far has illustrated that we cannot simply equate welfare or social policy with state welfare, it is worth considering the development of the British welfare system and, in particular, the system as it emerged following the Second World War, as this helps establish the context for much of the remainder of the book.

Prior to the First World War the Liberal governments of 1906-1914 introduced a series of reforms to welfare. These included the Old Age Pensions Act 1908 and the National Insurance Act 1911. The former introduced non-contributory means-tested pensions and the latter contributory, but not means-tested, National Insurance for sickness and unemployment for some groups of workers. Contributions were paid by employees, employers and the state. In 1918 an Education Act was passed that abolished fees in elementary schools and raised the school leaving age to 14 and the Housing and Town Planning Act of 1919 allowed subsidies to local authorities to provide housing for the working classes. In subsequent years the scope of much of this legislation was expanded, with unemployment benefits being provided for additional categories of claimants and local authority house building being supported by further subsidies.

However, it was the Labour government of 1945–1950, led by Clement Attlee, that fundamentally shaped the post-war welfare state. The economic depression of the 1930s and the high levels of unemployment and poverty of the period, together with the desire for a better society following the war, provided the opportunity to establish a more comprehensive level of state provision. The Beveridge Report of 1942 set out a blueprint for the development of state welfare. While intended to focus primarily on social insurance, Beveridge took the opportunity of setting out a vision for welfare provision more generally. He argued that governments should seek to manage the economy to ensure that mass unemployment would not occur again and that a complete system of social protection should be created to support those who were not able to provide for themselves. The Education Act 1944, passed by the coalition government, reflected the trend towards greater acceptance of state welfare, allowing for universal free state secondary education. The 1944 White Paper on Employment Policy was also important, providing official acceptance of **Keynesian** economics and a commitment to the maintenance of full employment. The Labour government therefore legislated to provide a system of welfare provision 'from the cradle to the grave' (Policy eye 1.2).

By the late 1940s there was a general consensus in favour of the new system. This was aided by the apparent success of Keynesianism and the establishment of full employment, which helped increase government revenues from taxation and reduce government expenditure on welfare benefits and services.

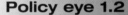

Policy eye 1.2   Legislative foundations of the welfare state

1944 Education Act – made free secondary education available to all, with an 11-plus exam to establish selection for grammar schools

1945 Family Allowance Act – provided family allowances

1946 Housing Act – provided central government subsidies for local authority housing

1946 National Insurance Act – introduced unemployment benefit for insured men (and their wives) and women, and pensions for old age

1948 National Assistance Act – introduced means-tested income support for those not covered by National Insurance

1948 National Health Service Act – created the National Health Service

1949 Housing Act – sought to designate council housing as not just for the working classes and extended subsidies for local authority housing

However, it is worth noting that the welfare state did not attempt to provide universal high-quality provision across the board. For example, while the NHS did seek to provide good-quality healthcare, regardless of the ability of individuals to pay, social security benefits were paid at low levels.

Nevertheless, for almost three decades the welfare state did appear to work and was a central element of British politics and society. In the mid-1950s the term 'Butskellism', an amalgam of the names of Butler, the Conservative Chancellor, and Gaitskell, the Labour shadow Chancellor and later party leader, was coined to illustrate the closeness of the two main parties' policies. Under successive Conservative governments from 1951 onwards, an increasing proportion of public expenditure was devoted to the welfare state. However, by 1964, when Labour returned to power, the UK's economic position was weakening and while the government continued to spend on capital projects, such as hospitals, housing and schools, plans to expand a range of benefits were not all carried through.

By the 1970s welfare had become the major area of expenditure in the national budget and, as noted earlier in this chapter, the system was coming under criticism from across the political spectrum, particularly from the right. After 1975, when Margaret Thatcher became leader of the Conservative Party, New Right thinking increasingly began to affect the political mainstream and from 1979 it is possible to identify the impact of their ideas on social policy, including privatisation, the greater stress on the use of markets in welfare provision and the emphasis on consumers or customers of services. However, it is important to recognise that even under the Conservatives, while there were significant changes, New Right ideas were not implemented to the extent that their supporters would have wished, in part because even within the Conservative Party there remained some support for a role for the state in welfare and in part because of the continuing commitment of public opinion, particularly for the mass services such as healthcare and education.

Structure of this book

While the discussion so far has outlined the complexity of the study of social policy, this book is written on the assumption that most students of social policy have little or no knowledge of the academic subject, even if all have inevitably come into contact with social policies. It is intended to provide a contemporary perspective, rather than one that covers the historical development of social policy. The following chapter deals with the government and politics of social policy, for, while politics may be an academic discipline of its own, students of social policy need to have some understanding of the way in which politics and government work as these are inevitably major influences over social policies.

There follows a series of chapters that can be characterised as focusing primarily on the principal service areas of social policy. While inevitably reflecting the legacy of previous governments and policies, these examine the development of social policy under Labour from 1997. These are followed by discussions of two areas that illustrate the breadth of social policy and its relevance to contemporary society, with considerations of the growing emphases on ethical ideas and the concept of risk and a more general discussion about the importance of social policy perspectives to areas that have sometimes been termed the 'new' social policy.

The book then progresses to consideration of some of the theoretical perspectives that have been outlined briefly in this chapter and that influence both our academic understanding of social policy and the making and implementation of social policies.

The book concludes with an examination of European and international developments, focusing on the European Union and its impact on social policy development and on globalisation and its implications for social policy.

Each chapter provides direction to additional sources of information, both written and via the internet, to allow students to follow up areas in which they have a particular interest.

Summary

This chapter has outlined the development of the subject of social policy and provided a brief history of the welfare state in the United Kingdom. It has shown that:

- the academic study of social policy has moved away from a focus on the welfare state towards a much broader consideration of provision by the public, private, voluntary and informal sectors

- theoretical debates have been and continue to be important, not only in increasing our ability to understand and explain social policy, but also in influencing the decisions of policymakers, as was reflected in the move away from the post-war consensus over the social democratic state towards a view that has been more influenced by New Right thinking

- our understanding of social policy has been affected further by the growth of an international dimension, which itself has been affected by the greater awareness of the range of modes of welfare provision (and different systems of payment for welfare) in different states and by the United Kingdom's involvement in the European Union

- the extent of political support for state welfare has varied significantly over time, with the post-war consensus perhaps representing the zenith of commitment by the political mainstream
- the practice of social policy under successive governments from the 1980s has seen a shift in emphasis away from the state as a provider of services towards a new role, whether as an enabler, a regulator, paying for or subsidising provision.

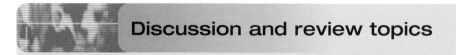

Discussion and review topics

1 What is social policy?

2 In what ways do social policies affect your everyday life?

3 How useful is the concept of the 'welfare state'?

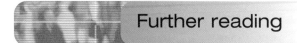

Further reading

Alcock, P., Erskine, A. and May, M. (eds) (2002) *The Blackwell Dictionary of Social Policy*, Blackwell, Oxford – a useful source of definitions of a range of ideas relevant to social policy

Alcock, P., Erskine, A. and May, M. (eds) (2003) *The Student's Companion to Social Policy,* Blackwell, Oxford – contains a number of useful discussions including over what social policy is, approaches to social policy, resources and careers

Fraser, D. (2002) *The Evolution of the British Welfare State*, Palgrave Macmillan, Basingstoke – this book provides a comprehensive history of welfare policy in Britain

Glennerster, H. (2000) *British Social Policy since 1945*, Blackwell, Oxford – concentrating on the period since 1945, outlines the development of social policy and the major influences on it

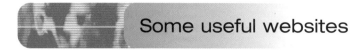

Some useful websites

www.direct.gov.uk – provides links to government departments and other organisations responsible for social policy and services throughout the United Kingdom www.oecd.org - the Organisation for Economic Cooperation and Development site contains considerable amounts of information relevant for comparisons across countries

www.qaa.ac.uk/crntwork/benchmark/socialwork.pdf – despite the use of the term social work in the address, this is the QAA benchmark statement for both social policy and administration *and* social work

References

Dolowitz, D. (2000) *Policy Transfer and British Social Policy*, Open University Press, Buckingham

Quality Assurance Agency for Higher Education (2000) *Social Policy and Administration and Social Work*, QAA, Gloucester

The politics and government of social policy

2

Catherine Bochel

Issues in Focus

Both social policy and politics are closely tied to decisions about the make-up of society and the distribution of resources (including income and wealth) within it. Each is therefore concerned with the appropriateness of social arrangements and the means by which these are determined. Within the political system there are a variety of forces that impact on social policy – changes of government inevitably bring different policy priorities and approaches, pressure groups lobby governments to achieve their aims and the media also seek to influence government and to highlight issues. In addition, recent years have seen significant changes in the mechanisms of social policy formulation and implementation, with devolution to Scotland, Northern Ireland and Wales being a clear instance of this and these also have implications for social policy.

This chapter examines:

- the role of political parties, pressure groups and the media with regard to social policy

- developments in approaches to the government of social policy under both Conservative and Labour governments.

Politics and social policy

Attempts to define 'politics' can develop into complicated debates in the same way as can occur with definitions of social policy. However, for present purposes we can adopt a simple view. Politics can be seen as the arena within which conflicts and differences are expressed and, to a greater or lesser extent, resolved. If politics is sometimes defined as 'who gets what, when and how', this illustrates well the inevitable link between politics and social policy.

Similarly, given the centrality of social policy concerns in contemporary society, with issues such as education, employment, health and pensions frequently at the core of political debate, this is clearly a two-way relationship.

There are, of course, many aspects of politics that could be considered in relation to social policy. For present purposes the concentration will be on political parties, pressure groups and the media, as these can be seen as having a direct impact on social policies. Later in this chapter some of the institutions and mechanisms of government will also be examined. However, a glance at any major politics textbook will show that there are many other concepts, ideas and structures that could be considered in relation to social policy.

Political parties

Perhaps surprisingly, there is a relative paucity of literature on political parties and social policy and in looking at this area, students of social policy are therefore often reliant on more general literature drawn from political science. This section draws out some of the key characteristics of parties as they might be seen to relate to social policy. However, it is perhaps worth noting that Jones and MacGregor (1998) provide one relatively recent example of a linkage from the social policy perspective, focusing particularly on the 1997 general election.

Functions of parties

The functions of political parties can be categorised in a number of different ways, many of which can be seen to have some relationship with social policy, although for some the connection is more apparent and perhaps more important. If we examine three of these, the nature of the links with social policy can be illustrated:

1   *representation* – political parties seek to organise within the electorate and to provide meaningful choices that enable voters to elect governments. In reality, most voters cast their vote for a party rather than for an individual candidate. These votes may encapsulate a number of reasons, such as judgements on their policies (including those that relate to social policy), the parties' likely effectiveness as governments, and, perhaps increasingly, their leaders

2 *participation* – parties also provide one significant form of participation, varying from voting at general elections (including on the basis of the type of choice just outlined) to membership and working for a party through attending meetings, campaigning and even standing for election

3 *elaboration of policies* – parties develop programmes and policies to present to the electorate as part of their attempts to achieve office. These may range from fairly general statements of intent to much more detailed policy proposals. Any examination of political debates or party manifestos over the post-war period demonstrates that social policies have been a fundamental part of this function.

The close relationship between politics and social policy is further illustrated by the importance of ideologies to parties and the impact that these have had on their policies. Chapters 12 and 13 examine this in part in relation to the impact of 'New Right' ideas, in particular on the Conservative Party and the varying impacts of socialism and social democracy on the Labour Party. If we examine the post-war period it is quite apparent that ideology has impacted on social policy, although not always as extensively as might be supposed.

The Labour government elected in 1945 is often depicted as creating the welfare state in the United Kingdom, or at least with doing so on the foundations created by previous governments, and in particular the Liberal government of 1906–1914. Whichever of these views is accepted, there can be little doubt that Clement Attlee's Labour government, itself influenced by the Beveridge Report of 1942, did fundamentally shape the welfare state as it developed in the post-war years. Importantly however, while it was the Labour Party that became associated with the creation of the welfare state, the very idea appeared to have widespread support so that even when Labour were defeated at the general election of 1951 there followed a period that has often been described as one of 'consensus'. This implied a general acceptance of broadly **social democratic** ideals that included a commitment to the welfare state and to a continued expansion of state welfare provision as the economy grew as well as to the role of government in maintaining low levels of unemployment through **Keynesian** economic policies.

While the extent and basis of this 'consensus' might be questioned, for the next 30 years the reality was that there was a maintenance and expansion of the role of the state in the provision of welfare. However, by the mid-1970s a number of challenges had emerged to the welfare state, including practical problems, such as reduced economic growth and oil price rises and political and ideological questions about the extent to which the welfare state had been successful and whether it was the most appropriate way of meeting needs. From the mid-1970s the Conservative Party began to move more to the political right, influenced by 'New Right' ideas and, when it returned to power in 1979 under the leadership of Margaret Thatcher, it had a commitment to the free market and the private sector and to reducing state intervention in society. The period from 1979 to 1997 saw attempts to roll back and reshape the frontiers of the state, including welfare provision, using a variety of instruments such as privatisation (for example sales of council homes), increased use of **means testing** (in social security), restructuring (including the NHS and local government), greater use of **performance measurement** (school and hospital 'league tables') and the introduction of **internal markets** (such as in health and social care).

Following the election of Tony Blair as leader of the Labour Party in 1994, many commentators have suggested that the Party shifted to the political right and that the creation of 'New Labour' included acceptance of some of the ideas that had emerged from New Right critiques of the state, and of the welfare state, and the continuation of policy trends that had originated under the Conservatives, such as means testing and encouragement of private sector provision. However, it is also possible to argue that there have been some changes that contrast with the position under the Conservatives, with, for example, significant increases in public expenditure and some evidence of a general redistribution from the rich to the poor. Many of these issues are dealt with in this book (see in particular, Chapters 3 to 9 and Chapter 13). It is also possible to argue that following their election defeat in 2001 the Conservative Party in turn began to adapt its policies, seeking to develop itself as a more inclusivist party, with successive leaders at least paying lip service to the recognition that the United Kingdom had changed and that some of the Party's perceived political excesses during the 1980s and 1990s were no longer appropriate.

Party leaders

From the 1960s onwards, it has frequently been argued, British government has been moving towards a 'prime ministerial' or even 'presidential' style of government, with the prime minister occupying an increasingly powerful position. This has arisen at least in part from the increasing emphasis on the party leaders in the media and thus in the eyes of the public, not only at election time but continuously as part of the political debate, a shift that has been intensified by the greater role of television as a means of communication. The apparent dominance of prime ministers such as Harold Wilson in the 1960s and 1970s and Margaret Thatcher in the 1980s helped reinforce this impression.

It is clear that prime ministers can bring significant influence to bear on welfare policies. It was Margaret Thatcher's commitment to New Right ideas and her use of right of centre **think tanks**, such as the Adam Smith Institute and the Institute for Economic Affairs, that encouraged the adoption of policies such as the 'right to buy' council houses, the creation of internal markets in health and social care and the use of league tables of performance in education. However, the example of Margaret Thatcher also serves to demonstrate that even dominant prime ministers rely on the support of their members of parliament and if they lose that they risk being removed from office by their own parties.

One of the characteristics of the first Blair government that was much commented on was the strengthening of government within the Prime Minister's Office and the role of key individuals, such as the chief of staff, Jonathan Powell, and the press secretary, Alistair Campbell. However, despite this apparent strengthening and Blair's attempts to define and develop a 'Third Way' (see Chapter 13), in many respects the government was not dominated by the Prime Minister alone, but also by the Chancellor of the Exchequer, Gordon Brown. While the Prime Minister did make occasional forays into the social policy arena, the government also saw the Treasury, under Gordon Brown, developing an almost unprecedented role in social policy, ranging from initiatives such as Tax Credits, largely designed to help the 'working poor', to **public service agreements** requiring other government departments to establish targets for delivery of services.

Pressure groups

A central feature of liberal democracies such as the United Kingdom is that it is often argued that power is widely distributed among different groups (sometimes called **pluralism**) and that at any one time there are a variety of

---

Briefing 2.1   Examples of pressure groups

Child Poverty Action Group (CPAG) – a cause group that campaigns for the abolition of poverty among children and young people in the UK and for the improvement of the lives of low-income families. Its membership consists of individuals and organisations. It is funded predominantly from membership subscriptions, sales of CPAG publications and grants and donations.

Amnesty International UK – a cause group launched in 1961, with a membership of 195,000 in the UK. The UK section of Amnesty International, it works to improve human rights worldwide. It is funded predominantly through membership subscriptions, appeals and donations, events and community fundraising and from legacies.

Action on Smoking and Health (ASH) – a cause group working for the reduction and elimination of health problems caused by tobacco in society. It works through advocacy and lobbying, by working with organisations interested in health and welfare and through challenging the tobacco industry over what it sees as misleading information. Some of the ways it is funded include: donations, subscriptions and sales of merchandise.

British Medical Association (BMA) – a sectional organisation founded in 1832, the BMA is a professional association of doctors, representing their interests and providing services for its 128,000 members. It is funded through membership subscriptions.

National Union of Teachers (NUT) – a sectional organisation that represents teachers, the NUT has a membership of 232,000. It is represented on national education bodies and makes representations to government on all matters affecting teachers and schools, particularly education policy at national and local level. It is funded through membership subscriptions.

interests competing to influence decision making. Outside the party political arena there exists a huge number of pressure or interest groups. These can usually be differentiated from political parties by the fact that they generally seek to influence government, rather than to govern themselves. They can range in size from small, ad hoc groups, such as those that sometimes form to campaign against the closures of local schools or hospitals, or to fight for or against particular local forms of provision, to the large, well-known groups that feature regularly in the media (Briefing 2.1). Pressure groups are an alternative and important form of participation, with the membership of pressure groups far exceeding that of the political parties.

While pressure groups can be characterised in a number of ways it is perhaps useful to consider them as 'cause' and 'sectional' groups:

- *cause groups* – those organisations that seek to promote causes that are based on particular values or beliefs, such as the Child Poverty Action Group, Age Concern and Shelter. It is this category that would normally include the ad hoc groups just mentioned

- *sectional groups* – those bodies that represent the interests of particular groups in society, such as trade unions or professional organisations, such as the British Medical Association or the British Association of Social Workers.

Groups are also often described as 'insider' or 'outsider', a terminology that refers to their relationship with government. Insider groups are those that are seen by government as legitimate, are consulted with and that are most likely to have their voices heard. Outsider groups either do not have, or in some cases do not wish to have, a close relationship with officials and policy-makers.

In relation to social policy it is apparent that there are a whole host of pressure groups that campaign on a wide variety of issues at both central and sub-central government levels. Following the 1997 general election the emphasis on 'partnership' under Labour appeared to offer a greater prospect for consultation and partnership with regard to policymaking and implementation for some groups, although the extent to which this occurred in practice was sometimes questionable. Indeed, it is difficult to assess the impact of pressure groups in social policy as their influence may vary with a whole variety of factors including the proximity of their ideas to governments' policy proposals, the resources available to the group, the acceptability of their views to the media and the public and the external economic and political environment. Nevertheless, the continued existence and activity of pressure groups in the social policy field itself requires some consideration of their role.

The media

The media have become a key part of British society. Whether newspapers, magazines, radio, television or the internet, there are myriad sources of information available to us. However, it is important to recognise that the role of the media is not confined to the provision of information; the media also have the potential for influencing the way in which we interpret issues and debates and perhaps even setting the agenda for decision makers and influencing decisions themselves.

Despite the potential importance of the media to social policy there has been relatively little research into this relationship. Yet there remain a number of important questions, including: what is the role of the media in setting the agenda? what influence do the media have on those who make policies? and what might this tell us about the exercise of power in contemporary society?

One of the best-known examples of media coverage of social issues is Cohen's (1987) study of Mods and Rockers in the 1960s, which highlighted the role of the media in creating and amplifying what he termed 'folk devils' and 'moral panics' (Briefing 2.2).

Briefing 2.2   Folk devils and moral panics

Societies appear to be subject, every now and then, to periods of moral panic. A condition, episode, person or group of people emerges to become defined as a threat to societal values and interests; its nature is presented in a stylised and stereotypical fashion by the mass media; the moral barricades are manned by editors, bishops, politicians and other right-thinking people; socially accredited experts pronounce their diagnoses and solutions... Sometimes the panic passes over and is forgotten, except in folklore and collective memory; at other times it has more serious and long-lasting repercussions and might produce such changes as those in legal and social policy or even in the way the society conceives itself.

Source: Cohen (1987) p. 9

From roughly the same period, another well-known example of the role of the media is that of the television drama, *Cathy Come Home*, which has frequently been credited with leading to the creation of the charity, Shelter, and having a substantial impact on the issue of homelessness and the introduction of legislation in the 1970s. More recent examples of media coverage and involvement range from largely negative coverage of asylum seekers to the role of the *Daily Mail* in campaigning for an inquiry into the death in 1993 of the black teenager, Stephen Lawrence, leading ultimately to the Macpherson Report that highlighted the issue of institutional racism. Given the variety of media and the complexity of their roles and influences, the remainder of this section seeks to provide some framework through which we can seek to analyse and understand the relationship with social policy.

The media and public opinion

There is perhaps a general assumption by both the media and by many commentators, that the media are important in bringing issues to public attention and that they are, to some extent, influential in changing attitudes and perceptions, even in affecting policy. However, the extent to which this might be the case is not easy to gauge. For example, there are major differences, not just between, say TV and the press, but also within the press (and with the advent of satellite and digital broadcasting increasingly within TV), for example between the tabloids and the broadsheets or between left- and right-leaning papers. The public also make distinctions, with the evidence suggesting that they are generally much more ready to say that they believe that TV news reporting is truthful than newspaper coverage.

The media are often accused of trivialising or distorting issues, either to make headlines or as a form of entertainment. Sometimes this may be positive, as a way of bringing an issue to public attention, but often it can create or reinforce misconceptions or stereotypes or may personalise or individualise what could be seen as *social* issues or problems. However, this may not entirely be the media's fault – for example, many agencies view the media as being in a position of power, able to influence public opinion and policymaking. They may thus seek to attract media interest and this in turn may mean accepting media agendas and a subsequent modification of their messages and concerns. Journalists may therefore use crude and stereotypical images of, say, homeless or disabled people as a way of making good copy, attracting attention or making a point; but, importantly, some agencies may collude with these images to attract coverage (or in the case of some charities coverage and potentially funds).

In terms of seeking to assess the overall impact of the media on public opinion there have been a number of perspectives on this:

- *direct effects* – the view that the media have a direct impact on public attitudes is now largely discredited – the public do not form a passive audience which unquestioningly absorbs and accepts whatever they are fed by the media

- *reinforcement* – this perspective argues that the media do not create or mould public opinion so much as reinforce pre-existing opinion. It is now widely accepted that the public select and interpret media messages in accordance with their existing viewpoints – in other words, we actively interpret the information that the media provide; in addition, it is mainly those media messages that reinforce what we already believe that we select. The same media coverage can therefore be interpreted very differently by different members of the public

- *agenda setting* – the argument from this view is that the media do not determine what we think, but that they *can* influence what we think *about*.

In general, this view accepts that the public has its own agenda, but that the media can influence its priorities, especially on matters about which the public knows relatively little

- *framing* – progressing from the agenda-setting standpoint, this view suggests that the media are able to affect political life (including social policy) and the way in which people see and understand it. This may happen in different ways: *interpretation* – so that the same event may be presented in different ways to give it a completely different meaning and the effect may be both unintentional and unconscious; *bad news* – the mass media concentrate on bad news, conflict and violence because these sell newspapers and attract TV audiences, but negative news can create cynicism, disillusion, distrust of politicians and professionals, and apathy; the *'fast forward syndrome'* – news and reaction to it now spreads so rapidly that policies can be launched in the morning news, criticised at lunchtime and buried by the evening and at the same time there is so much 'news' that the public cannot cope with or understand such a flow of events; *personalisation and trivialisation* – the mass media concentrate not on problems, issues or policies but on personalities and appearances, so that politicians and others may sometimes be less concerned with policy options than with looking and sounding right.

Whichever interpretation we accept, for social policy one of the important abilities of the media is the potential to reach millions of people who may not otherwise be involved or interested in an issue.

The media and policymaking

So, to what extent can the media impact on policymakers? Does coverage of issues such as immigration, homelessness or hospital waiting lists influence either their agendas or decisions? Again, these are difficult questions to answer because relatively little is known about this – such influence is hard to identify or measure. However, it is possible to consider a number of points:

- It is perhaps at the stage where issues may be coming onto the agenda (for example, through pressure group activity) that the media may be most likely to have an impact; it is certainly the case that many pressure groups make great attempts to get the media on their side or depend on the media to get issues onto the public and politicians' agendas.

- Despite this, it is difficult to identify many concrete examples of the media having an impact on social policy; indeed, it is arguable that the media have most impact when the ideas they are pushing are compatible with the general socio-economic and political environment; at the same time, and related to this, the transmission of ideas may not be a one-way process, so that government views and interpretations can themselves permeate into mass media accounts.

- The media may have only a limited impact on policymaking, but they can perhaps play a role in setting the parameters for policy debates and in framing policy discussions and in some cases media coverage and campaigning can be an important factor in attempts to change policy.

Ownership and regulation

While freedom of the press is often presented as one of the central tenets of liberal democracy, at the same time, one of the major concerns of many academics and others has been the ownership and control of the media and the impact of this. While initially concerns were often focused around the power of press barons directly to influence politics, for example through persuading people to vote for particular parties or candidates, others have argued that the major influence of newspapers has been their 'cumulative support for conservative values' (Curran and Seaton 1991: 61) and the status quo. In addition, it is clear that newspapers are able to select particular issues for discussion and to marginalise or ignore others. This last point is perhaps of significance to social policy as it is sometimes said that it is radical or progressive voices that receive least space in the press.

As with the press, the broadcasting media, and particularly television, have also seen a concentration of ownership, with News International's dominance of satellite broadcasting within the United Kingdom being seen as problematic by many (especially when combined with its strong press presence). One difference here is the existence of the state-funded BBC, with its responsibility to provide public service broadcasting, although it has been argued that this has been, and will continue to be, undermined by the pressure to maintain audiences and the increased choice available to viewers. In addition, at least for party politics, the terrestrial broadcasters have a statutory duty to provide 'balanced' coverage, although this does not necessarily apply to the satellite broadcasters, which it would clearly be difficult for a national government to control in any case.

For the written media, in reality, control and regulation has rested largely with the media themselves. While there have been debates about the extent to which parts of their coverage are acceptable, for example in relation to privacy, particularly of public figures, or to coverage of some particular issues, as with the *Daily Mirror*'s publication of photographs in 2004 (later accepted as fakes) alleged to be of British soldiers mistreating Iraqi prisoners, and there have been calls for greater regulation, the primary responsibility continues to lie with individual newspapers and with the Press Complaints Commission rather than there being firmer legal or statutory controls.

Recently the debate over the role and control of the media has become further complicated with the widespread availability of the internet. This has created new opportunities for the collection and dissemination of ideas and information but raises new questions over the regulation of content. In addition, the internet is already being used to campaign in both old and new manners, for example by anti-globalisation protesters (see Chapter 16). In other respects there is clearly potential for a whole range of individuals and groups to have much wider

"If we're going to keep this quiet,
we'll need a public enquiry"

Source: www.CartoonStock.com

access to a great variety of information and potentially for more inputs into policymaking; but at present much of this is speculation. However, there are already fears that existing inequalities might be reinforced by unequal access (see Chapter 11). While the government therefore seeks to provide more and more of its services online, it will therefore be important to monitor the ability of different social groups to use this new facility.

Government of social policy

While the preceding section has demonstrated the importance of politics to social policy (by and large, *politics matters*), this section seeks to illustrate that the mechanisms by which policies are made and implemented can also be significant. If we reflect over the period since 1979 it is possible to identify not only major shifts in policy under Conservative and then Labour governments, but also changes in the way in which social policy is 'governed'.

The remainder of the chapter seeks to discuss the governance of social policy under the Conservatives from 1979 to 1997 and to consider the extent to which there is continuity or change under Labour and the implications of this for social policy in the future.

Government under the Conservatives, 1979–1997

Butcher (1995) has described the traditional mode of operation of government in the social policy arena as 'the public administration model of welfare delivery ... in which the five core social services ... were delivered by a combination of national and local governmental organizations' (p. 155). However, from 1979 to 1997, styles of governance can be seen to have moved through two main phases: up to 1988 the emphasis was largely on *'managerialism'*, reflected in the focus on initiatives that drew on what the government perceived to be 'private sector values' and based on the belief that business performance tools from the private sector could be transferred to the public sector to make it more efficient and effective at both central government and local government levels. From around 1988, there was a shift towards a style of governance based on 'the *new institutional economics*' (Hood 1991) with concepts such as markets and consumer choice being central to this (Rhodes 1997). At the same time there were attempts by the government to encourage a greater range of service providers across public, private and voluntary sectors, making the organisation, implementation and delivery of services more complex and dependent on a much wider network of organisations. Many of these changes were encapsulated in the term 'the new public management', a concept that encompasses features such as devolution of responsibility towards lower level agencies, budgetary limits, incentives to collaborate with the private sector, competition between providers, concentration on core services and privatisation of non-essential functions, use of performance measurement and greater consumer choice.

The programme of management reforms introduced by Margaret Thatcher in 1979 was to stretch for 18 years and resulted in significant change to both the structures and styles of governance over that period. These included the introduction of **internal markets** such as those in the NHS and education, privatisation, greater use of performance measures and standards, the increased use of arm's length government including **quangos** and **Next Steps agencies**, centralisation of power, reform and residualisation of local government and the introduction of a variety of mechanisms designed to give consumers a greater say in the operation and delivery of services.

Changes to local government were largely imposed by central government. Up to the late 1980s the managerialist style of governance focused on structures such as the imposition of performance measures and the downsizing of existing functions, through for example, privatisation, thus reducing the power of local authorities and consequently their ability to operate across a variety of areas. From the late 1980s the style changed to that of the new institutional economics, which introduced a more radical approach to governance, at the heart of which were structures such as markets and consumer choice. This shift to local authorities acting as enablers rather than providers can be seen in the removal of functions from local authorities, often through legislation, including the Education Reform Act 1988, the Housing Act 1998, the Local Government Act 1988 and the Local Government Act 1992. The influence of local government was further reduced by the reorganisation of local government in 1996, resulting in the abolition of a number of large Labour-controlled counties such as Humberside, Cleveland and Avon. In addition, attempts to give consumers greater control over services were implemented through the introduction of charters and other methods of redress.

An important feature of governance under the Conservatives, including social policy, was the use of structures of 'macro-governance' to devolve a variety of functions previously undertaken by local and central government to organisations such as quangos, non-departmental bodies and Next Steps agencies. Between 1979 and 1997 the Conservative governments created 109 agencies and increased the number of special purpose bodies to well over 5,000 involving 70,000 government appointments and the responsibility for £52 billion of public expenditure. Here the concept of 'governance' can be seen to involve the devolution of 'non-essential' functions such as policy implementation and service delivery, while allowing the centre to retain control over core functions such as policy formulation.

The very nature of 'governance' of social policy, particularly after the Conservatives' emphasis on the creation of a mixed economy of welfare, involves a broader range of organisations from all sectors, public, private and voluntary, becoming involved in service implementation and delivery. This creates multiple networks of organisations each of which needs to form links with others. As a result highly complex networks of relationships develop and a key aspect of this is the extent to which they are dependent on one another. Yet, for much of the 1980s and 1990s, the government's approach could be seen to equate much more to the traditional model of central–local government relations, with local government being viewed merely as the agent of central government and existing to carry out its wishes. For social policy such a model was arguably inappropriate, because the essence of governance in the field involves delegation and cooperation between a wide range of welfare agencies.

There are a variety of issues that arise from this approach. One of the most important is that the actual process of governing becomes more complex because of the number and variety of organisations involved and this raises issues such as: the extent to which these organisations are accountable to the state and the public; the relationship between the state and these organisations; and the interdependence and fragmentation created by the complexity of organisations and the structures of governance.

Government under New Labour

The changes to the mechanisms of policymaking and implementation that took place under the Conservatives may have been substantial, but in the early years of the Labour government the pace accelerated further, with constitutional reforms, new emphases, such as on partnership and 'joined-up government' and continued use of measures such as performance 'league tables' that had been introduced under the Conservatives. While some commentators characterised Labour's social policies as displaying a high degree of continuity from those of the Conservatives, the same could not be said about the government's approach to the **policy process**.

The Labour government demonstrated a commitment to improving the quality of policymaking (Policy eye 2.1). The notion of 'joined-up' government – that each department is aware of what is going on within other departments and can take account of the work each is undertaking – served to reinforce this approach. The use of public and pressure group consultations and the incorporation into legislation (DETR 1998) of a duty for local authorities to consult with local communities can be seen as further dimensions of this. However, the extent to which this apparent commitment to different modes of decision

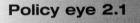

Policy eye 2.1   Professional policymaking for the 21st century

A series of high-level 'features', which, if adhered to, should produce fully effective policies:

- Three 'themes' – vision, effectiveness and continuous improvement;

- Nine core 'competencies':

1   Forward looking – takes a long-term view of the likely impact of policy

2   Outward looking – takes account of factors in the national, European and international situation and communicates policy effectively

3   Innovative and creative – questions established ways of dealing with things and encourages new ideas; open to comments and suggestions from others

4   Using evidence – uses best available evidence from a wide range of sources and involves key stakeholders from an early stage

5   Inclusive – takes account of the impact on the needs of all those directly or indirectly affected by the policy

6   Joined up – looks beyond institutional boundaries to the government's strategic objectives; establishes the ethical and legal base for policy

7   Evaluates – builds systematic evaluation of early outcomes into the policy process

8   Reviews – keeps established policy under review to ensure it continues to deal with the problems it was designed to tackle, taking account of associated effects elsewhere

9   Learns lessons – learns from experience of what works and what does not

Source: Cabinet Office Strategic Policy Making Team (1999)

making, evidence-based policy and participation has been realised in practice remains a matter for debate.

More specifically there have been a number of other changes in policy-making under Labour. One has been the greater role for the treasury, which under Gordon Brown as Chancellor of the Exchequer, played a significant part in directing social policy through the **Comprehensive Spending Reviews** and public service agreements, as well as the use of the tax system to deliver credits such as the Working Tax Credit (see Chapter 3).

Partnership has been seen by Labour as one of the key mechanisms for the implementation and delivery of policy and while this approach was used by the Conservatives, it was to a more limited extent. Under Labour there have been a wide range of attempts to encourage partnerships across the public, private and voluntary sectors in health, education, housing, crime prevention and so on. These were viewed by the government as appropriate for tackling particular social problems and in improving the quality of public services. The **Private Finance Initiative** (PFI) is one of the more controversial initiatives, with the private sector building schools, which have then been leased to local authorities, and hospitals, which have been leased to the NHS, before these revert to the public sector after a set period. Critics have claimed that such initiatives have proved more costly than if they had been undertaken wholly by the public sector.

The revolution in ICT has also been seen by the government as opening up opportunities for electronic service delivery and the government made a commitment to provide all government services electronically by 2008, in much the same manner as electronic banking services. While this does appear to have a number of benefits for citizens there remain concerns about a number of issues, including equality of access (see Chapter 11).

Since 1997 there have also been other developments relevant to social policy. One of these was the increase in the number of women elected to the House of Commons and the devolved administrations. In Westminster the proportion of female MPs rose from 9 per cent in 1992 to 18 per cent in 1997. The advent of devolution resulted in significant female representation in the Scottish Parliament (40 per cent) and the National Assembly for Wales (50 per cent). This led some to anticipate different approaches to decision making, with perhaps a more consensual and less adversarial approach, and different policy emphases, such as a greater stress on family-friendly policies.

Overall, many of the issues that can be identified with the Conservatives' approach to the governance of social policy are also applicable to Labour. The complexity of networks continues to pose questions about the mechanisms that governments seek to use to implement policy, as does the contradiction between centralising and devolving tendencies that have been particularly apparent under New Labour. And, despite the apparent commitment to improving the quality of policy making, questions remain over the extent to which this is being achieved in practice.

Constitutional and structural change

Immediately after coming into office in 1997 Labour introduced or outlined a number of changes that had significant implications for the government of social policy. These included devolution, incorporation of the European Convention on Human Rights into UK law and acceptance of the Agreement on Social Policy (originally signed at Maastricht in 1992 by the then other 11 members of the European Union). This section will consider the nature and impact of some of these reforms, while the Agreement on Social Policy is discussed (in part) in Chapter 15.

Devolution

It is important to note that the different constituent parts of the United Kingdom have always possessed some social, economic, legal and political features that have distinguished them from each other. These were to some extent recognised by the existence of the Northern Ireland Office, the Scottish Office and the Welsh Office as part of the governmental machinery, seeking to take account of at least some of these differences. However, until recently these differences were not reflected in terms of elected legislative bodies.

Following referenda in the autumn of 1997 the Scottish Parliament and the National Assembly for Wales came into being on 1 July 1999. In Northern Ireland, as part of the ongoing peace process, an Assembly came into existence on 2 December 1999, although it has had a rather on–off existence, reflecting the vagaries of the peace process. Devolution therefore played a major part in Labour's attempts to modernise government.

Each of the new devolved administrations possessed some powers over social policy (Policy eye 2.2), arguably greatest in the case of the Scottish Parliament and least in the case of the Welsh Assembly. While some have been critical of what they have seen as a lack of radicalism in the new bodies, and in general they could be seen as following the same path as Westminster (perhaps not surprisingly given that Labour were also in power in both Scotland and Wales and the on–off nature of the Northern Ireland Assembly), it is nevertheless possible to identify a number of areas where they could be seen to be diverging from the path taken at Westminster. In Scotland early examples included the early repeal of Section 28, which banned the promotion of homosexuality, and a decision in 2001, in contrast to the government at Westminster, to accept the recommendation of the Royal Commission on Long-Term Care of Older People that long-term care should be free. Across the United Kingdom we now have an even greater variety of approaches to social policy, including differences on foundation hospitals, funding of higher education, prescription charges, testing of school pupils and the use of tables of school performance. It seems likely that in future the diversity of policies and methods of policy implementation and delivery will continue, particularly as political control in the different administrations will be likely to change over time. Devolution will therefore provide different models and approaches to social policy within the United Kingdom.

Policy eye 2.2   Social policy and the devolved administrations

Responsibilities

Scottish Parliament	National Assembly for Wales	Northern Ireland Assembly
Local government	Local government	Education
Education	Education	Health
Health	Health	Social services
Housing	Housing	Social development
Social work	Social services	
Transport	Transport	
Police and fire services		
Prison and prosecution systems		
Criminal law		

Powers

Primary legislative power and tax-varying powers	Secondary legislative abilities but no tax-varying powers	Primary legislative and executive authority for devolved matters

Human Rights Act and the European Convention on Human Rights

Although the United Kingdom ratified the European Convention on Human Rights (ECHR) in 1951 successive governments refused to incorporate it into UK law. Citizens who felt that their human rights had been infringed were therefore not able to use the domestic courts, although they *were* able to appeal to the European Court of Human Rights in Strasbourg, an expensive and time-consuming process. The Court found against the UK government on many occasions, on issues varying from censorship of prisoners' mail to different ages of consent for heterosexuals and homosexuals and, although the UK was not bound to comply with the decisions of the Court it consistently did so and UK law was changed to reflect its judgments. However, the Human Rights Act 1998 finally incorporated the ECHR into UK law, thus making it possible for individuals who believe that their human rights have been infringed to pursue this in the domestic courts, speeding up the timescale and reducing the costs. While much of the early media coverage of the impact of the Act involved the rights (or otherwise) to privacy of often high-profile individuals, the effects of the Act have already been seen in a number of areas of social policy, including mental health, where patients detained under the Mental Health Act do not now have to demonstrate that they should no longer be detained, but it is now incumbent on those detaining them to demonstrate that they have a case. Similarly, many public authorities have been forced to change some of the ways in which they operate and interact with the public because of the requirements of the Act and the ECHR.

Local government

Many of New Labour's changes have also affected local government. Local government in the United Kingdom has always been subservient to central government. It has no independent right to exist and all its functions and activities can be changed by parliament. Despite this relative weakness, and constant reforms over recent decades, local government has retained a significant role in social policy. Even following 18 years of Conservative government that saw large-scale restructuring of local government in England, Scotland and Wales, a reduction in its ability to raise its own income and a reduced responsibility for the direct provision of services, it retained a significant role in social policy. At its most basic it is possible to identify a number of services that clearly relate to social policy for which local authorities have a responsibility, including education, the personal social services, housing and planning. While from the 1980s there has been a shift away from the direct provision of services by local government to a position where councils play a much greater role in the strategic planning of services and the enabling of provision, in many instances they continue to be significant providers. When these responsibilities are added to those for planning, highways and passenger transport, sport, environmental health and libraries, the continued importance of local government for social policy is clear.

Following Labour's return to power in 1997 the new government produced a plethora of policies and proposals that not only outlined potential reforms of local government but also dealt directly with many of the services for which it is responsible. Among the most important of the government reforms have been those that have sought to 'modernise' local government. These included:

- *New decision-making structures* – it was clear from the early days of the 1997 Labour government that they wanted to see new political management and decision-making structures introduced into local government in an attempt to provide greater democratic accountability and more effective policy-making. By the late 1990s many local authorities had shifted away from the traditional model of services overseen by committees of councillors towards a cabinet model, with, in most cases, a cabinet with a leader, and other councillors having primarily a responsibility for scrutinising the decisions of the cabinet. In a smaller number of instances authorities chose to go for a directly elected mayor and a cabinet. These changes were supposed to result in more efficient, transparent and accountable local government.

- *The creation of the GLA and the election of a Mayor of London* – while the Conservatives had abolished the Greater London Council in 1986, Labour recreated a London-wide tier of local government with an elected Mayor of London and a Greater London Authority. However, they had little power over social policy with the emphasis being primarily on strategic economic and to some extent transport policy. In common with other local authorities, the London boroughs retained responsibility for local government's social policy commitments.

- *Best Value* – from 2000 Labour replaced the system of compulsory competitive tendering (CCT), which had been introduced under the Conservatives, with a new scheme called Best Value. While critics suggested that there was little change, the government argued that, where CCT was concerned only with the cost of a service, emphases on quality, continuous improvement and public consultation made Best Value a very different and more comprehensive system. However, if a council is deemed to be failing in its duty to secure Best Value, the secretary of state has the power to intervene and even to impose an outside provider.

In addition, local government was affected by many other initiatives emanating from central government, ranging from tackling social exclusion, through the use of testing of school pupils and performance measures for schools and the provision of accommodation for asylum seekers, to attempts to tackle anti-social behaviour and to reduce crime. Although these developments ranged across the spectrum of local government responsibilities, it is possible to identify a number of key features. First, they followed the approach of the previous Conservative governments in continuing to stress the role of local authorities as enablers of services rather than as providers. Second, as with other areas of social policy, there was an emphasis on 'partnerships' and collaboration across public, private and voluntary sectors as a way of tackling problems and meeting needs. Third, there was continued use of mechanisms of external audit and inspection as a major driver, from the government's perspective, of improving standards and quality. While there may have been a rather less critical view of local government than before 1997, the government's attitude nevertheless showed an unwillingness to trust local government to deliver improvements on its own.

Finally, it is worth noting that as well as the tiers of government addressed here (central government, the devolved administrations and local government), the Labour government had proposals to introduce regional assemblies in parts of England dependent on the results of referenda intended to be held in the autumn of 2004. In addition, as is discussed in Chapter 15, the European Union has a limited, but growing influence on social policy. The concept of 'multi-level governance' is perhaps therefore now appropriate in the United Kingdom, emphasising the number of levels of government and the overlapping networks across them.

Summary

This chapter has outlined a variety of features of politics and government in the United Kingdom and related these to the making and implementation of social policy. It has suggested that:

- there are a variety of ways in which social policy can be affected by politics, not only directly through political parties and the process of governing, but also by influences such as pressure groups and the media

- under the Conservative governments of 1979–1997 there was an emphasis on what were seen as the virtues of the private sector and in particular markets and marketisation, with the 'consumer' at the centre, and this was reflected in social policy through initiatives such as privatisation, compulsory competitive tendering, attempts to create 'internal markets', greater managerialism and use of quangos and 'Next Steps' agencies for the delivery of some services

- the New Labour government elected in 1997 demonstrated a significant degree of radicalism in its approach to the policy process, most notably through the introduction of devolution to Northern Ireland, Scotland and Wales, the passage of the Human Rights Act and an emphasis on 'better' policymaking and implementation, making terms such as 'joined-up government', 'evidence-based policy', 'partnership' and 'modernisation' part of the social policy lexicon

- the role of the European Union (discussed in Chapter 15) in social policy should not be neglected here.

Discussion and review topics

1 How do political parties and pressure groups differ in their attempts to influence social policy?

2 What is the role of sub-central government (the devolved administrations and local authorities) in the making and implementation of social policy?

3 What are the principal differences between the Conservative governments of 1979–1997 and the Labour governments that followed in their approaches to the government of social policy?

Further reading

Bochel, C. and Bochel, H. (2003) *The UK Social Policy Process*, Palgrave, Basingstoke – this book examines the policy process and social policy, drawing on both theoretical and practical ideas and examples

Budge, I., Crewe, I., McKay, D. and Newton, K. (2004) *The New British Politics*, Pearson, Harlow – one of the big current politics textbooks, which provides a thorough introduction to British politics

Hill, M. (1997) *The Policy Process in the Modern State*, Prentice Hall/Harvester Wheatsheaf, Hemel Hempstead – provides a discussion and evaluation of the policy process and the exercise of power in contemporary society

Newman, J. (2001) *Understanding Governance*, Sage, London – this book is a comprehensive exploration of the shifting agendas of governance under New Labour

Some useful websites

The main political parties throughout the UK each has its own website, including:

www.conservatives.com, www.labour.org.uk, www.libdems.org.uk, www.snp.org.

www.direct.gov.uk – this site provides access to a huge amount of information about government and services, with links to most central and local government sites, including those in the devolved administrations of Northern Ireland, Scotland and Wales

www.europa.eu.int – the gateway to the European Union – provides access to information on the institutions and policies of the EU

References

Butcher (1995) *Delivering Welfare: The Governance of Social Services in the 1990s*, Open University Press, Buckingham

Cabinet Office Strategic Policy Making Team (1999) *Professional Policy Making for the Twenty First Century*, Cabinet Office, London

Cohen, S. (1987) *Folk Devils and Moral Panics*, Blackwell, Oxford

Curran, J. and Seaton, J. (1991) *Power Without Responsibility: The Press and Broadcasting in Britain*, Routledge, London

Department of the Environment, Transport and the Regions (1998) *Modern Local Government: In Touch with the People*, Stationery Office, London

Hood, C. (1991) 'A public management for all seasons?', *Public Administration*, 69, 3–19

Jones, H. and MacGregor, S. (1998) *Social Issues and Party Politics*, Routledge, London

Rhodes, R. (1997) *Understanding Governance: Policy Networks, Governance, Reflexivity and Accountability*, Open University Press, Buckingham

Part II

Developments in services

Income maintenance and taxation

3

Karen Rowlingson and Stephen McKay

Issues in Focus

Virtually all of us will, at one time or another, receive money from the social security system and pay money in the form of taxes. Both are fundamental parts of the role of the state in contemporary society. However, there remain significant differences over both taxes and income maintenance, including over their respective levels. In an attempt to make themselves more electable, prior to their election in 1997 New Labour pledged not to increase levels of income tax. This chapter analyses some of the key debates focusing on:

- defining what is meant by social security and taxation and considering the aims of the two systems

- outlining the sizes and structures of the two systems

- a comparison of the dominant neo-liberal discourse on social security and taxation with the collectivist discourse

- reviewing recent changes made to taxation and social security systems.

The social security and tax systems can, to some extent, be seen as two sides of the same coin. One collects in money for government, the other distributes it to people – sometimes straight back to the same people, sometimes to the same people at a later date and, quite often, to others. Virtually all of us will, at one time or another, receive money from the social security system and pay money in the form of taxes.

This chapter compares and contrasts the social security and tax systems. It begins by setting out the dominant neo-liberal discourse on social security and taxation. Within this discourse, taxation is seen as a burden and social security as a waste of money. The dominance of this view explains why governments of all political persuasions have, in recent decades, tried to maintain or reduce levels of taxation and control social security expenditure. An understanding of neo-liberalist discourse also helps to explain why 'tax expenditures' receive such little attention and why benefit fraud is treated far more severely than tax fraud. An alternative, more collectivist discourse is also set out, which argues that the tax and social security systems can be seen as a means of securing social justice by reducing levels of inequality and insuring against risk. The chapter then goes on to outline the size of the two systems, showing how they have both grown dramatically since the Second World War. It considers what is meant by social security and taxation, pointing out there are different ways of defining both systems and that some state provision, such as Tax Credits, blurs the boundary between social security and taxation. The various possible aims of the systems are discussed, since at any one time, different parts of the systems may be aiming to achieve a range of, and sometimes competing, aims. The chapter then describes the structures of the social security and taxation systems, which are huge and complex, affecting most people most of the time. Finally, recent changes in the taxation and social security systems are reviewed, concluding that, from 1997 onwards, these systems have, to some extent, been used to redistribute income from the rich to the poor.

Context: Cultural assumptions and socio-economic inequality

Debates about each major political party's commitments to tax levels have figured strongly in recent elections, from allegations of 'tax bombshells', to commitments not to raise income tax rates, to the concept of **'stealth taxes'**. The increase in National Insurance rates announced in the 2002 Budget – mostly to pay for additional spending on the National Health Service – represented a watershed, to the extent that direct tax rises were used to fund public spending; but they represented political business as usual in that income tax rates were regarded as sacrosanct.

For social security, the main political discussions in recent years have arguably been concerned with how punitive the government should be in tackling fraud and reducing spending on the unemployed. Tony Blair has consistently referred to social security spending as representing economic failure elsewhere, declaring in 2001 that Labour were 'cutting the costs of economic failure; with real terms social security spending falling for the first time in decades' (speech to the Confederation of British Industry, 5 November 2001).

Cultural assumptions

Cultural assumptions form a crucial underpinning of the current systems of social security and taxation. These assumptions play a powerful role in setting the political agenda for the reform of social security and taxation. It is all too easy to portray spending on benefits as a 'burden' and to regard tax cuts as giving people 'their money' back. Only rarely does the system of tax exemptions figure in discussion (see Briefing 3.1).

The idea that taxation is a burden and, furthermore, that social security is a waste of money fits in with a free market or neo-liberal economic philosophy (see Chapter 13). This philosophy, stemming from the work of the 18th-century thinker Adam Smith and championed in the 20th century by writers such as Hayek and Nozick, is that state intervention should be minimal. Nozick (1974)

Briefing 3.1   **Public attitudes to taxation**

In their study of attitudes towards taxation, Hedges and Bromley (2001) found that people's responses to the tax system were based on both ignorance about the system and strong emotions. The public generally believed that the level of taxation was constantly increasing and was far heavier than that in the rest of Europe. The vision of the tax system as a 'burden' or even 'highway robbery' as one respondent termed it (2001: 8), illustrates the deeply negative attitudes towards taxation. People generally saw tax as a penalty rather than a payment for services. They did not feel that they gained value for money from their payment of taxes and they were generally confused by the complexity of the system. When respondents were told that most tax revenue was spent on social security benefits they were particularly annoyed and felt that this confirmed their view that much of 'their' money was being wasted – on 'scroungers' and the 'workshy'. Respondents assumed that most social security expenditure went on the unemployed, but when they were informed that most of the social security budget was spent on pensioners, they were happier to have 'their' money spent on pensioners than other groups. This attitude towards social security expenditure is confirmed by successive waves of the British Social Attitudes Survey which have asked respondents about the acceptability of spending more on different groups of social security recipients (Bryson 1997). Pensioners are generally seen as far more 'deserving' than other groups. This notion of 'deserving' and 'undeserving' groups is another prevailing, and longstanding, cultural assumption surrounding the benefit system.

famously declared that: 'Taxation of earnings from labor is on a par with forced labor' (1974: 169). From this perspective it is argued that taxes and benefits should be kept very low, because if they are set too high people will face disincentives to work. Underlying this philosophy is the idea that people who engage in paid work are 'independent', while those who receive social security benefits are 'dependent'. Wages from paid work constitute an individual's own money, to which they have an inalienable right. Such a philosophy suggests that those who put individual effort into earning wages should therefore be able to keep as much of 'their' money as possible.

These cultural assumptions are very strong in the United States. They are also strong in the United Kingdom. The Conservative governments from 1979 to 1997 broke the tentative post-war consensus over the welfare state as Thatcherism sought to 'roll back the frontiers of the state' and to allow the market to flourish unhindered by regulation and taxation. After successive defeats at the ballot box, 'New' Labour distinguished itself from 'Old' Labour precisely on this point.

An alternative way of looking at tax and social security stems from what might be called a social solidarity or collectivist philosophy. Underpinning this approach is the idea that the role of the state is a positive one, as it creates the conditions under which people can flourish and social justice can be achieved. People are not divided into those who are 'dependent' and those who are 'independent'; rather, all are seen as interdependent on each other. The emphasis here is on **social inclusion**, interdependency and solidarity, rather than individual freedom. This broad philosophical approach encompasses

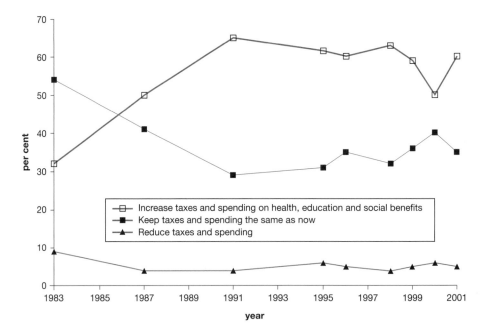

Figure 3.1 Views on what governments should do about taxes and benefits

Source: Based on Taylor-Gooby and Hastie (2002) Table 4.1

elements of socialism and social democracy, with implications for social policy as outlined in Chapter 13.

Although the neo-liberal perspective appears the most common way of seeing tax and social security, evidence from the British Social Attitudes surveys has shown high, if variable, support for higher taxes to pay for higher public spending (see Figure 3.1). In 1983 the balance of opinion was to maintain levels of tax and spending. In each subsequent year the policy of taxing and spending more (on particular social areas) has proved the more popular view. There was a sizeable dip (to 50 per cent) in 2000 and a decline over much of Labour's first term, before rising to 59 per cent by the 2001 survey.

Nevertheless, Labour remain committed to maintaining rates of income tax, leading to charges of having introduced or increased so-called 'stealth taxes' instead. This has included such changes as increases in stamp duty, extension of employer National Insurance contributions to all benefits in kind, increases in Insurance Premium Tax and so on (see Briefing 3.2).

Socio-economic inequality

The social security and tax systems should also be considered within the context of the dramatic increases in inequality that took place in the United Kingdom during the 1980s and early 1990s. Between 1979 and 1994/95, incomes for the richest one-tenth of the population grew by between 60 and 68 per cent, while those of the poorest one-tenth showed only a 10 per cent increase before housing costs or a fall of 8 per cent when housing costs were taken into account (Hills 1998). Families with children were much more likely to be poorer at the end of the 1980s than they had been at the beginning and, by 1990, roughly one child in three was living in poverty. There are a number of explanations for this rise in inequality: for example, tax cuts in the 1980s favoured those on higher incomes, with the result that the taxation system did

Briefing 3.2	Summary of neo-liberal and collectivist discourses on tax and social security

Neo-liberal discourse	Collectivist discourse
State intervention is problematic and should be minimised	State intervention is vital to securing equal opportunities and social justice
Taxation is a burden	The taxation and social security
Social security is a waste of money	systems are mechanisms for ensuring
Workers are independent	that everyone has enough to live on
Benefit recipients are dependent on the state at best, scroungers at worst	We are all interdependent and may, at different times of our lives, pay taxes and/or receive benefits

not restrain rising inequality in the way that it did in other countries; a decision to link a number of social security benefits to the prices index, not to increases in earnings, meant that those who stayed on benefit fell behind as earnings grew; there was also a rise in the number of people out of work (either unemployed or economically inactive); and for those in work, there was an increasing division between those in well-paid jobs and those in low-paid jobs. As a result, inequality grew faster in Britain between the mid-1980s and the early 1990s than in any western nation for which comparable data are available.

In the mid-1990s Britain became more equal in terms of incomes. Falling unemployment and the abolition of the **Community Charge** (Poll Tax) were among the factors that helped those with the lowest incomes to make up some of the lost ground. But the divide between rich and poor that had widened so dramatically during the 1980s was only narrowed to a limited extent and income inequality has remained much greater than in any previous decade since the Second World War (Hills 1998).

Importance of social security and taxation

We will all spend most of our lives either receiving or paying for social security – frequently both at the same time. However, the systems themselves are far

---

Policy eye 3.1   Size of the social security and taxation systems

- Total government tax receipts were forecast to be £398 billion in 2001–2002 or 40.2 per cent of UK GDP. This was equivalent to £6,600 per person.

- About 27 million people pay income tax and this tax raises just over one-quarter of all government income.

- Government spending on social security benefits in the UK in 2001 was around £100 billion per year – about one-third of all government spending and more than was spent on health, education and social services combined. This represents about £2,000 each year for every man, woman and child in the country and in many years exceeds the total raised through income tax.

- Three-quarters of British households now receive at least one social security benefit, with one-fifth of working-age households receiving one or more means-tested benefits (cash benefits dependent on a family's level of income) or Tax Credits.

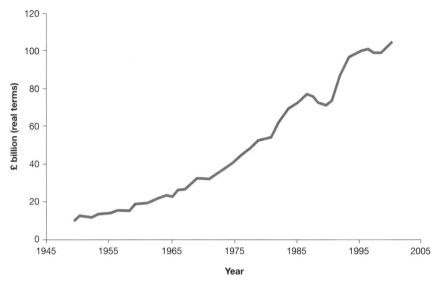

Figure 3.2 Spending on UK social security (in real terms, 2002 prices)

from simple and most of us understand very little about what they aim to do, how they operate and what their effects are. Policy eye 3.1 illustrates the importance of these systems in Britain.

Since the Second World War, spending on social security has risen almost continuously. Figure 3.2 has been adjusted for price inflation and hence shows the 'real' growth in total spending in this area. There has been a tenfold increase over the period, with only occasional dips generally associated with times of falling unemployment. This illustrates the way in which social security has come to take on roles that were not anticipated in the post-war Beveridge plan, such as growing levels of economic inactivity (for example, rising spending on disability benefits), increases in life expectancy (affecting pensions spending) and changes in family forms (such as more lone parents receiving benefits in their own right). Until the 1980s benefit rates also tended to increase more rapidly than price inflation, more closely matching growth in the economy as a whole.

Over the same time period, the number of people paying direct taxation has also increased to some 27 million, compared with fewer than 5 million before the Second World War (Figure 3.3). Income Tax used to be paid by higher earners, but is now paid by most workers (whether as employees or as self-employed). It is also paid by some people not in work, including pensioners with significant occupational pensions.

The combined effects of taxes and benefits include providing some degree of equalisation of income between rich and poor in any given year. In 2001–2002 the incomes from employment, self-employment and investments of the best-off 10 per cent of the population were nearly 35 times as great as those of the worst-off 10 per cent (Lakin 2002). After taking into account taxes and benefits, they were 'merely' 13 times better off. If we also include the

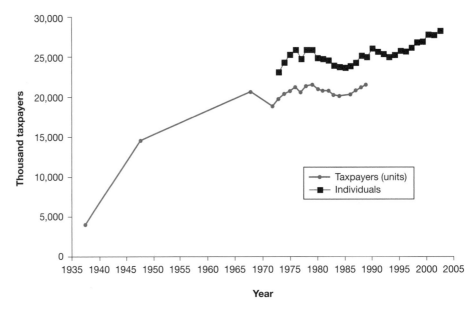

Figure 3.3 Number of Income Tax payers, 1938–2002

Source: Based on Inland Revenue Statistics (2002) Table 1.4

benefits provided by the state in kind (health, education, housing subsidies) then the disparity falls to 5:1 (see Figure 3.4).

Defining 'social security' and taxation

Social security and taxation clearly play a central role in people's lives. But what is meant by these terms? There is no universally accepted neat definition of 'social security' or 'taxation' and this section discusses possible definitions.

Social security

Starting with the widest definition, social security is sometimes used to refer to all the ways in which people organise their lives in order to ensure access to an adequate income. This wide concept includes securing income from all sources such as earnings from employers and self-employment, financial help from charities, money from a family member and cash benefits from the state. So in the area of welfare related to maintaining income there are different means by which this may be achieved. Of foremost importance is the private sector, for example earnings from employment and profits from self-employment are the chief source of income for most people of working age and pensions in retirement are often based on such earnings.

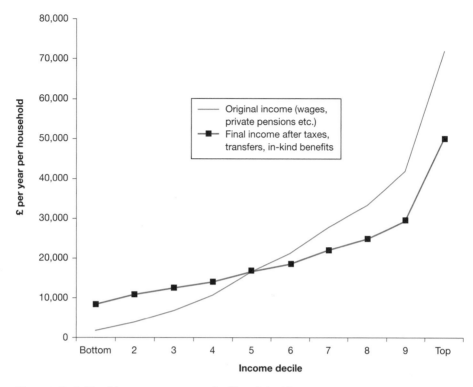

Figure 3.4 Final income compared with original income

Source: Based on Lakin (2002) Table 14

A slightly narrower definition of social security would include all types of financial support *except* those provided by the market system. In this way, reliance on the immediate or extended family would still be classed as helping to achieve social security. However, it is increasingly usual to adopt an even narrower definition and to regard social security as those sources of immediate financial support provided by the state.

The definition of 'social security' as the system of cash benefits paid by the government to different individuals appears to be fairly simple and unproblematic. But it is inadequate or, at least, does not include the same range of activities that most people would regard as being social security. This is because some 'benefits' are not paid for by the state or need not be. For example, statutory sick pay used to be paid by government but, while it remains a legal entitlement, it is now a cost met mostly by employers. There are also occupational schemes for sickness, widowhood and retirement that are similar to state benefits and that have a similar function, but which are organised by employers. In addition, it is possible to envisage governments finding ways to 'privatise' what are currently state benefits or instigating new compulsory private provision, perhaps for pensions. So, both voluntary employer schemes and some programmes mandated by government may also be classed as social security – neither of which neatly fits the definition given earlier.

Taxation

Taxation can be defined as the different sources of government revenue. This definition is quite wide and includes not only those sources known specifically as 'taxes', but also those sources known as insurance 'contributions' as well as 'duties', 'royalties', 'levies' and so on. Revenue from interest and dividends can also be included in a very wide definition of taxation and it is such a definition that is used for this chapter.

The British Income Tax system is an individualised system whereby people within a couple are treated independently (for example, in having their own personal allowances and not having their income combined for tax purposes). In contrast, the social security system treats couples as couples, operating a couple-based means test for income-related benefits and allowing additions for 'dependants' in the case of contributory benefits. In general, Income Tax liabilities are based on annual gross incomes and the payments that are due depend on income over the whole tax year, whatever increases or decreases in weekly amounts take place over the year. Again, by contrast, many means-tested benefits are based on income over a relatively short period – if you have no money in a particular week, it is important you receive payment promptly. Income Tax bills – and rebates – may therefore be considered at a more leisurely pace.

A relatively new and growing feature of the tax system are 'Tax Credits'. They started their life, however, as part of the social security system. Working Families Tax Credit (WFTC) was introduced in 1999 to replace Family Credit, a benefit to top up the wages of low-paid families. Although WFTC was termed a 'Tax Credit' it was very similar to the benefit it replaced, as it acted to top up people's wages. It was not assessed annually or on individuals, as with the Income Tax system. But the government generally prefers to see Tax Credits as standing apart from social security benefits – in particular, because they are received by those in work, rather than those not in work.

There are also reasons related to national accounting practices for preferring to treat Tax Credits as part of the tax system. A Tax Credit is treated as negative taxation rather than a positive expenditure on social security benefits. When WFTC was removed from the social security budget and placed, instead, within the taxation system, it looked as though social security spending had reduced overnight. This sits well with a free market neo-liberal philosophy where social security spending is seen as a waste and taxation should be kept as low as possible. What could be better than negative taxation!

Some Tax Credits are, however, more properly counted as part of the tax system. Child Tax Credit and Working Tax Credit were introduced in April 2003. They have some features that make them align much more closely with the tax system, so, for example, the amounts are based on gross incomes over the whole year – like Income Tax. However, amounts are based on family incomes, whereas as noted earlier Income Tax is an individual system. Moreover, Child Tax Credit is paid directly to the person most responsible for childcare in a way akin to Child Benefit, rather than first reducing any tax liability – which resembles more closely the benefits system. Amounts are also designed to be paid into bank accounts, rather than being collected in cash, or being credited to payslips. So, while the new Tax Credits take financial support more closely into the tax system – and are being delivered by the Inland Revenue – there are still good reasons for seeing some of the new Tax Credits as very similar to social security benefits.

The new state Pension Credit for pensioners, by contrast, is very clearly a renamed social security benefit with no closer linkage to taxation than the benefit it replaced. It remains within the remit of the Department for Work and Pensions.

Tax expenditures

Most forms of taxation have systems of allowances, reliefs, credits, deductions and so on, which comprise exemptions from the general applicability of the tax. For example, some income is exempt from taxation – such as gross income spent on private pension contributions and interest received on special savings accounts, currently called individual savings accounts. It may be argued that tax allowances are similar to subsidies and so should properly be seen as public expenditure, rather than deductions from tax. Why should direct payments to pensioners appear as a cost while tax concessions for private pensions show up – if at all – simply as lower tax? For this reason, the term 'tax expenditures' has been coined for such exemptions, although in popular parlance the term 'loophole' might be equally apt. The existence of such exemptions is one means of pursuing tax avoidance – legal ways of reducing tax liability.

The value of tax expenditures varies widely across OECD countries and often appears to benefit better off families. Many poorer families are not subject to tax measures that attract such exemptions and hence cannot gain from certain tax expenditures. Conversely, some specific tax expenditures are said to be targeted at poorer households, such as a lower rate of Value-Added Tax (VAT) on domestic fuel and on children's clothes, than on most other goods and services. However, since richer families spend more on these items than poorer households, the cash gain is actually smaller for poorer families than for the rich, although the proportionate gain for poorer households may be greater.

Tax expenditures remain an important part of government policy, although the value of some of them has been reduced in the last ten years, including removal of Income Tax reliefs for married couples and for mortgage interest payments. The costs of tax allowances and exemptions are only periodically subject to close scrutiny, although regular figures on their size are produced in government reports. The cost of a tax exemption is inevitably an estimate, since people might behave differently if the exemption were removed. The estimated value of tax expenditures is vast. Inland Revenue estimates of the value of some particular tax exemptions include those shown in Table 3.1.

Table 3.1 Value of selected tax expenditures, 2001–2002

Tax expenditure	Value
Tax relief for approved pension schemes	£14.4 billion
National Insurance contracted-out rebate for occupational schemes	£6.9 billion
Capital Gains Tax: exemption of gains arising on disposal of main residence	£5.7 billion
National Insurance contracted-out rebate for personal pensions	£3 billion
Inheritance Tax: exemption of transfers on death to surviving spouse	£1.2 billion
First £30,000 of redundancy payments	£850 million
Individual Savings Accounts	£650 million
Personal Equity Plans	£625 million
First £8,000 of reimbursed relocation packages provided by employers	£300 million
Foreign service allowance paid to Crown servants abroad	£80 million
Inheritance Tax: quick succession relief	£10 million

Aims of social security and taxation

Having defined taxation and social security, we now ask what are the aims of these systems? The answer is complex. As in other countries, the system in Britain has evolved over time and as a result is not necessarily what would be designed if policymakers were starting from scratch. Furthermore, different parts of the system have different aims, making it impossible to identify one aim and it is even arguable as to what the main aim of the system is. With these reservations in mind, some of the possible objectives of social security include:

● insuring against the risks of particular events in life, such as unemployment and short-term sickness

● relieving poverty or low income

● redistributing resources across people's lifecycles, especially from working age to retirement

● redistributing resources from rich to poor

● 'compensating' for some types of extra cost (such as children, disability)

● providing financial support when 'traditional' families break down.

Within these general aims, the British social security system has been designed to achieve the following:

- maintain incentives for self-provision (such as through earning and saving)
- keep non-take-up of benefits low
- counter possible fraud
- ensure that administrative costs are low.

The aims of the British system have traditionally been more limited than those of systems in Europe, if wider than in some parts of the rest of the English-speaking world. The importance of relieving poverty in the British system explains the considerable reliance on **means testing** in Britain. Receipt of means-tested benefits depends on a person or family's having resources (typically income and perhaps savings) below a certain level in order to receive benefits. Means testing is also common in America, New Zealand and Australia but much less so elsewhere, especially in continental Europe, where social security tends to be less centralised and more concerned with income maintenance and compensation.

As with social security, it is possible to identify a variety of aims of taxation, including:

- raising money for war and defence
- enabling people to save against future risks
- paying money to people on very low incomes
- paying for local or central services
- reducing people's consumption of certain goods
- redistributing income and/or wealth.

Throughout history, one of the main reasons for taxation was to raise money for war. Indeed, this was the rationale for the introduction of Income Tax during the Napoleonic Wars. With the growth of the welfare state, however, the tax system has taken on rather different aims, such as enabling or compelling people to save money in case they experience unemployment, sickness or retirement. Taxes are also used to pay money to people who do not have sufficient to live on. The tax system also aims to raise money for local and central government services such as health and education. A rather different possible aim of the tax system might be to reduce people's consumption of particular goods. For example, tobacco is generally considered to be harmful and so it is argued that high taxes on tobacco will reduce people's consumption of this substance. Similarly, taxes on petrol may reduce car journeys, which lead to pollution and so are detrimental to the environment.

A final possible aim of the tax system is to redistribute income and/or wealth from rich to poor. If the rich are most heavily taxed and most of the money is then given out either in cash or services to poorer groups, then the tax system is performing a 'Robin Hood' function. But the extent to which this occurs in practice is debatable, as the poor pay a large proportion of their income in taxes (such as VAT) and wealthier groups actually take a great deal of advantage of welfare state services (such as education and pensions, for example, as they stay in education for longer and they live longer thus receiving more in pensions).

As outlined in the following section, a distinction is generally made between direct taxes (such as those on income) and indirect taxes (such as those on personal spending). A tax system that takes a higher proportion of tax from the income of richer than poorer people is known as a progressive system. Under a regressive system, the poor pay a higher proportion of their income in taxes than do the rich. Generally speaking, direct taxes on income tend to be progressive, while indirect taxes tend to be regressive – partly because poorer groups spend a higher proportion of their incomes and partly because spending on some taxed goods does not rise much with income. Those who argue for greater emphasis on direct taxation are often doing so from a collectivist perspective, since direct taxation tends to be more progressive than indirect taxation.

Overview of the current system

Social security

The social security system today is highly complex, having evolved considerably over time. Very few people, perhaps none, understand it in all its detail. For every possible generalisation about the system there are myriad caveats. It is therefore difficult to give a brief overview without oversimplifying the system and therefore possibly misleading (see Ditch 1999 and McKay and Rowlingson 1999 for further details). Nevertheless, this section attempts to provide such an overview. There are various ways of classifying the different benefits in the UK system. For example, benefits can be categorised into two dichotomies: universal versus means tested and contributory versus non-contributory. If we use the rules of entitlement as our yardstick, social security can be divided into three main components: contributory benefits (benefits which rely on having paid contributions); means-tested benefits and Tax Credits (benefits which depend on income); and contingent benefits (benefits which depend on your position or category), as follows.

Contributory benefits

The roots of the current social security system lie in the Beveridge Report published in the early 1940s, although insurance-based and other benefits had been introduced well before this time. At the heart of the Beveridge approach

Source: www.CartoonStock.com

– of contributory benefits or 'social insurance' – is the idea that people face a range of risks that might lead to severe reductions in living standards. These include the risk of unemployment, being incapacitated and unable to work, retiring or losing the main income earner in a family. Some risks are rather uncommon and relatively unrelated to economic circumstances, such as widowhood. Other risks, such as retirement, are much more widespread and predictable.

The main issues that arise with social insurance include:

- Why should the state provide this service, rather than private insurance? What relationship should there then be between state and private insurance?

- What risks should be covered?

- On what basis should contributions be made or be deemed to be made?

Social insurance benefits have entitlement based on having paid National Insurance contributions and being in a risk covered by these benefits (such as unemployment or retirement). These benefits are individualised in that the earnings of a partner do not generally affect entitlement. The main benefit in this group is the state retirement pension. Other benefits are the contributory parts of Incapacity Benefit and contribution based Jobseekers Allowance.

Means-tested benefits/Tax Credits

Entitlement to means-tested benefits depends on the level of 'family' resources, particularly income and savings. The four main examples in the British system are Income Support, Working Tax Credit, Housing Benefit and Council Tax Benefit. As argued earlier, Working Tax Credit can be seen as part of the taxation system but here it is counted as an example of means-tested public support.

The system of benefits based on means testing, particularly for those on low incomes, is sometimes known as 'social assistance'. In Britain, social assistance is almost synonymous with the benefit Income Support (the equivalent means-tested benefits for pensioners are the Minimum Income Guarantee (MIG) and the Pension Credit) and income-based Jobseekers Allowance for unemployed people. These benefits are paid to those whose income and savings are below defined levels, taking into account the size and type of family.

Countries differ a great deal in the extent of this type of provision. In Australia and New Zealand, almost all benefits include an element of 'means testing'. This does not mean that only the poorest may receive benefits – in some instances the aim is to exclude the richest rather than to include only the poorest. In much of northern Europe, social assistance plays a much smaller role, picking up those not covered by the main social insurance system. In addition, such schemes are often administered locally, with local organisations having some discretion about the precise rules of entitlement.

Additional conditions are often attached to receiving social assistance. People of working age, without sole responsibility for caring for children or disabled adults, must be able to work, available for work and actively seeking work. In past times, they may have had to enter a workhouse to qualify.

Contingent benefits

These are sometimes referred to as categorical benefits or as non-means tested and non-contributory. Entitlement depends on the existence of certain circumstances (or contingencies) such as having a child (Child Benefit) being disabled (Disability Living Allowance, Severe Disablement Allowance) or, at least until recent changes, being a lone parent (One Parent Benefit, now abolished).

In the British social security system, some benefits effectively recognise that certain groups of people face extra costs which the state will share. The clearest example is benefits for dependent children and Child Benefit. There is no test of contribution, and the family's level of income is not taken into consideration. There are, however, certain tests of residence that must be satisfied. Disability benefits provide another example, where some elements are purely contingent and reflect neither means nor previous contributions.

It is worth emphasising that this division into three groups is something of a simplification of differences between benefits (see Briefing 3.3). Means-tested benefits do not just depend on financial resources; they tend to also rely on some combination of being in a particular situation or a particular family type. For example, able-bodied single people may only claim Income Support if they meet conditions relating to being unemployed. And it is possible for certain sources of income to affect contributory benefits, for example Jobseekers

Briefing 3.3	Main types of benefit/Tax Credit and examples of each

Main types of social security benefit	Main examples of these types
Contributory (insurance-based) benefits	State retirement pension
	Incapacity Benefit
Means-tested benefits	Income Support/Minimum Income Guarantee
	Housing Benefit
	Council Tax Benefit
Tax Credits	Working Tax Credit
	Child Tax Credit
Contingent benefits	Child Benefit
	Disability Living Allowance

Allowance and Incapacity Benefit (both contribution based) can be reduced if a person receives income from a personal or occupational pension.

Taxation

The tax system is often divided into 'direct taxes' such as Income Tax and National Insurance contributions and 'indirect taxes' such as Value-Added Tax

Briefing 3.4	Main types of tax and examples of each

Type of taxation	Main examples
Direct taxes on income	Income Tax, National Insurance contributions
Capital taxes	Capital Gains Tax
	Inheritance Tax
Indirect taxation	Value-Added Tax (VAT)
	Duties on petrol, alcohol and tobacco
	Vehicle excise duty (road tax)
Taxes on company profits	Corporation Tax
Local government taxes	Council Tax
Other sources of revenue	Taxes on savings

(VAT) that applies to most goods and services and duties on petrol, alcohol and tobacco. But government revenue is more complex than that and a different categorisation is offered in Briefing 3.4.

Table 3.2 shows that Income Tax is the largest single source of government revenue, but that this most prominent form of tax still only accounts for just over one-quarter of revenue. National Insurance contributions are the second most important source of government income, followed by VAT and then Corporation Tax.

Some of the categories in Table 3.2 are amalgamations of a number of different taxes. For example, 'other indirect taxes' includes a range of different sources of revenue, but by far the largest of these is petrol duties. Petrol duties account for 46 per cent of all 'other indirect taxes'. Duties on tobacco and alcohol combined account for a further 29 per cent. Within the category of 'capital taxes', stamp duty forms the major component (63 per cent), followed by Capital Gains Tax (20 per cent) and then Inheritance Tax (18 per cent).

Direct taxes on income

'Direct taxes' include both Income Tax and National Insurance contributions. Income Tax is, perhaps, the most politically sensitive tax and the Labour Party committed itself to maintaining (or reducing) levels of income tax during the 1997 and 2001 election campaigns. Not all income is subject to Income Tax. The main sources of income that are taxed include earnings from employment and

Table 3.2 Main sources of government revenue, 2001–2002 (forecasts)

	Forecast 2001–2002 (£bn)	Percentage of total
Income Tax (net of Tax Credits)	104.1	26.1
National Insurance contributions	62.6	15.7
Capital Taxes	12.8	3.2
Value-Added Tax	61.3	15.4
Other indirect taxes	49.0	12.3
Corporation Tax	57.5	14.4
Council Tax	14.7	3.7
Other sources of revenue	36.2	9.1
Total revenue	**398.2**	**100**

Source: HM Treasury (2001)

Table 3.3 Income Tax rates, 2003–2004

Gross income	Rate of Income Tax
Less than personal allowance (£4,615 for under 65s)	0
Personal allowance plus £1,920 (lower rate band)	10
From lower rate band to £29,900 + personal allowance (basic rate band)	22
Higher rate band (gross income above £29,900 + personal allowance)	40

self-employment, pension payments during retirement and some social security benefits (such as Incapacity Benefit). People do not pay tax on all their income from these sources. They each have a personal allowance and if their income (from taxable sources) falls below this personal allowance, they pay no Income Tax at all. The level of personal allowance depends on age, with those aged 75 and over having the most generous level (at £6,260 in 2001–2002) and those aged 65–74 having a personal allowance of £5,990. Those under 65 had a personal allowance of £4,535.

Until April 2000, married couples had an extra allowance. This was often used by the man in the couple, particularly if the woman stayed at home to look after children. The Labour government abolished this allowance for all but those born before 1935. This reform was criticised by the Conservative opposition as penalising marriage, while the Labour government's main aim was to redistribute from married couples (who may or may not have children) to people with children (who may or may not be married).

For those with taxable income above their personal allowance, there are different rates of tax depending on their level of income. Table 3.3 shows these different rates of tax and the current levels of the tax bands.

This looks relatively simple compared with the social security system. But people nevertheless get confused about how the tax system works in practice. For example, people earning over £29,900 do not pay 40 per cent tax on the whole of their income. The 40 per cent tax rate is only paid on the income over £29,900 plus the personal allowance. So in practice, someone of working age would have to earn above £34,515 to come into the higher rate band. And they would only pay 40 per cent tax on their income above this amount (or a tax rate of about 22 per cent of total gross income, at least initially).

National Insurance contributions (NICs) may be considered as another form of direct taxation. They were initially introduced in the early part of the 20th century to pay for retirement pensions. NICs are sometimes portrayed as different from taxation because they are supposed to be contributions to one's own pension or other insurance benefits. However, the revenue from this source has never been invested in the way that private pension contributions are invested. Instead, today's National Insurance contributors are paying towards the benefits of today's recipients.

The vast majority of revenue from NICs comes from 'Class 1' contributions. Employees pay these as a tax on their earnings and employers as secondary contributions on those they employ. Employees pay NICs at a rate of 10 per cent on any earnings between the primary threshold (£89 per week in 2003/4) and an upper earnings limit (£595 a week in 2003/4). Employees pay no contributions on earnings above the upper earnings limit. Employers pay contributions at a rate of 11.9 per cent on all earnings above the secondary threshold (£89 a week in 2003/4). The existence of an upper limit on NICs reduces the 'progressive' aspect of this tax.

Capital taxes

There are three main capital taxes: Capital Gains Tax; Inheritance Tax; and stamp duty of various kinds. Capital Gains Tax is levied on gains from selling assets by individuals or trustees. The first £7,500 of an individual's gain is exempt currently. The amount of tax paid depends on how long the asset has been held and whether or not it is a business asset. For assets held for less than a year, 100 per cent tax is charged above the exempt amount.

Inheritance Tax is paid when people receive an asset on or shortly before someone's death. Asset transfers below £242,000 in 2001–2002 are exempt from inheritance tax. If the asset is transferred on death then the rate of tax above the exempt amount is 40 per cent.

Stamp duty is paid on transfers of stocks and shares, land and property. All transfers of stocks and shares are taxed at 0.5 per cent, but there are different rates depending on the value of land/property and exemptions for properties in some deprived areas.

Indirect taxation

VAT is the main form of indirect taxation and this can be divided into four categories, as follows (Adam and Frayne 2001):

- a standard rate of 17.5 per cent on most goods and services (accounting for 56 per cent of consumer expenditure)

- a reduced rate of 5 per cent on domestic fuel and power, women's sanitary products and children's car seats (accounting for 3 per cent of consumers' expenditure)

- exempt goods have no VAT levied on the final good sold to the consumer but firms cannot reclaim VAT paid on inputs

- zero-rated goods (including food, construction of new homes, public transport, children's clothing, books, medicines on prescription etc.) have no VAT levied on the final good or on the inputs used in its creation.

During the 1980s VAT was raised from 8 to 15 per cent and the money raised enabled the government to reduce the basic and higher rates of income tax. The rate was increased again in 1991 to pay for a reduction in the Poll

Tax/Community Charge. The Conservative government at the time would have argued that a shift from direct (income) tax to indirect tax (VAT) would reduce tax-induced disincentives to work but, as argued earlier, this is not necessarily the case.

Other indirect taxes include duty on petrol, which sparked an explosive protest in the late 1990s. Protestors against high levels of petrol duty blockaded the movement of petrol and the petrol pumps began to dry up. In 2001–2002, almost 80 per cent of the cost of petrol and diesel went in taxation. A similarly high percentage of the price of cigarettes goes straight to the government. Wine is taxed less heavily than cigarettes and beer even less (at about 29.3 per cent of the price going in taxes) (Adam and Frayne 2001).

The existence of high duties on petrol, alcohol and tobacco can provide incentives to evade taxes. For example, in 2002, it was claimed that there was a significant incidence of people illegally using sunflower oil to run their cars on rather than buying diesel. Similarly, people may cross the Channel to stock up on tobacco and alcohol and this is perfectly legal for personal consumption, but it is illegal to buy such goods with the intention of selling them on.

Vehicle excise duty (often referred to as Road Tax) is another indirect tax in this category. So too are Insurance Premium Tax, air passenger duty, landfill tax, climate change levy and betting and gaming duties etc.

Corporation taxes

Corporation taxes are charges on profits made by UK companies. The standard Corporation Tax is currently 30 per cent, with a reduced rate of 20 per cent for companies with profits less than £300,000.

Council Tax

The system of local taxation was a major problem area for government in the 1980s, leading to the introduction of the hated Poll Tax (or Community Charge as it was officially known). In 1993, the Council Tax was introduced, based on property price levels rather than on individuals. Properties are put into one of eight bands depending on their value and then individual councils set the amount of Council Tax to be paid by people living in each of the properties. Council Tax provides about one-fifth of local authority revenue.

Other sources of revenue

Other sources of revenue include the taxation of income from saving. Certain forms of saving have received more favourable treatment under the tax system than others. For example, personal and occupational pensions received tax relief on contributions and no tax on fund income. These reliefs were introduced to encourage people to save in such schemes, but wealthier groups were much more likely to take advantage of these schemes than poorer people and so the tax system had an inbuilt advantage towards better off groups. In recent years, various tax-privileged schemes have been introduced (such as individual savings accounts) to benefit people with varying levels of income.

These ISAs however, have still been mostly taken up by wealthy people and government is piloting new schemes such as the Saving Gateway, which will only be available to working-age people on relatively low incomes.

Tackling fraud in social security and taxation

A key issue in relation to the administration of taxes and benefits is the extent and nature of fraud. Cook (1989) was one of the first to point to the considerable differences between the treatment of benefit fraud and tax fraud. Benefit fraud has traditionally received much more attention from the state and those suspected of committing benefit fraud have been treated much more harshly by investigators, prosecutors and sentencers. These differences relate back to the prevailing assumptions about tax and social security discussed at the start of this chapter. For example, those committing tax fraud are generally seen to be merely trying to keep hold of 'their' money, whereas benefit fraudsters are seen as receiving even more money than they should be entitled to. A collectivist perspective might be more sympathetic to some benefit fraudsters, as it would consider the very low incomes of people on benefit (and most benefit fraudsters) compared with the very high incomes of tax fraudsters.

Grabiner's (HM Treasury 2000) report on the informal economy discusses both of these types of fraud but, in common with previous work, devotes far more of the discussion to benefit fraud. The report, however, points to the harsher penalties for benefit fraud and so recommends that new legislation is introduced to bring in a new statutory offence of fraudulently evading income tax, to be tried in magistrates' courts.

Recent reforms and future prospects

The social security and taxation systems are in a period of change. The Labour Party made a manifesto pledge in 1997 to:

> [E]xamine the interaction of the tax and benefits systems so that they can be streamlined and modernised, so as to fulfil our objectives of promoting work incentives, reducing poverty and welfare dependency, and strengthening community and family life (Labour Party 1997: 13).

In the field of social security, the government has sought to differentiate those above and below working age and to further differentiate between those of working age who are in paid employment and those who are not. The mantra 'work for those who can, security for those who cannot' has been the main guiding principle. In the field of taxation, reforms have been redistributive in practice even if the government has not announced its intention to channel resources from rich to poor or trumpeted some reforms that have done just that. The major changes during the first Labour term are shown in Table 3.4.

The overall effect of the reforms of the tax system has been to the financial benefit of 36.1 million people, with almost 8 million people losing out (Clark, Myck and Smith 2001). In general, the reforms have been redistributive, with people in the bottom half of the income distribution gaining more than those in the top half. If the effects of the social security reforms are added to this calculation, we find an even more progressive effect. Those in the poorest 10 per cent of incomes have seen their incomes rise by 18.5 per cent due to the reforms, whereas those in the wealthiest 10 per cent have seen their incomes drop slightly (Brewer, Clark and Wakefield 2002).

There has also been redistribution between different family types, with the main 'winners' being people with children and pensioners. Among people with children, the main 'winners' have been those with no earners in the household.

One of the main reforms in this field is the increasing use of Tax Credits and, thereby, the increasing integration of the tax and benefit systems. From April 2003 two new Tax Credits were introduced: Working Tax Credit (WTC) and Child Tax Credit (CTC). Working Families Tax Credit disappeared and WTC is available to anyone in work who is a parent or is aged over 25 (and who satisfies particular conditions in terms of hours of work and level of income). This tax credit is often paid through the wage packet. CTC is paid to the main

Table 3.4 Major reforms, 1997–2001

Social security changes	Tax changes
Cuts to lone parent benefits	Married couple's allowance abolished for people born after 1935
Various New Deal programmes (e.g. for young people, lone parents etc.)	Introducing 10% starting Income Tax rate
Work-focused interviews for all benefit claimants (the ONE programme)	Basic rate cut by 1% to 22%
Substantial increases in levels of Child Benefit and child components of Income Support	Primary earnings threshold on NI raised
Working Families Tax Credit introduced (now Working Tax Credit)	Upper Earnings Limit for NI raised from £525 to £575 per week
Child Tax Credit introduced	MIRAS abolished
Winter fuel payments introduced	

carer of children, regardless of whether they are in work or not. It replaces the child components of all means-tested benefits and many contributory benefits. The system extends financial support higher up the income ladder than was previously the case. By 2005/6, the planned expenditure on Tax Credits will have risen to £14.6 billion a year.

The new system is a significant step change from the previous system of Tax Credits as needs are assessed according to annual income. This places the system more on a par with the current tax system rather than the benefit system (where weekly changes in income need to be reported when claiming certain means-tested benefits). Every year, a reconciliation will be made to see if people are owed more Tax Credits or, conversely, need to pay back any over-payments. This could lead to major problems for people who need to pay back overpayments, although a certain amount will be disregarded. The system will, however, assess income jointly for couples – a system more common to the benefit system than the current tax system. The introduction of these new Tax Credits does bring the tax and benefit systems closer together for families with children but falls far short of total integration even for this group.

Summary

This chapter has identified some of the key elements of discourse around social security and taxation and has outlined a number of significant themes.

- The dominant neo-liberal discourse sees a minimal role for the state with both levels of taxation and social security kept low. An alternative collectivist discourse takes a more positive role of state intervention, seeing higher levels of taxation and social security as essential for achieving social justice and solidarity within society. These discourses have a major impact on policy in this area. The neo-liberal discourse justifies tax cuts and restrictions on entitlement to benefit, with the social security system becoming a residual system to target those in greatest need. The collectivist approach calls for a fair system of tax and more universal benefits for all citizens rather than targeting the very poorest.

- Despite the dominance of the neo-liberal discourse since 1979, the size of the social security budget has actually increased (largely due to an increase in the numbers of people out of work). But poverty and inequality have also increased, because of reluctance to raise taxes and redistribute resources to those with least. Since 1997 there has been some redistribution from rich to poor, but this has taken place fairly cautiously and very quietly.

- It is not straightforward to define the social security and taxation systems. At their simplest, social security is about the cash benefits that people receive and taxation is about government revenue. But these definitions can be challenged. There are also two types of provision that do not fit easily into this framework. For example, the government effectively gives out money to people in the form of tax allowances and other types of 'tax expenditures'. These are rather hidden but constitute a huge subsidy, often to the advantage of better off families. The dominance of the neo-liberal perspective explains why this form of expenditure is much less visible and seen much more positively than expenditure on social security benefits.

- The introduction of Tax Credits has also caused difficulties in defining the tax and social security system. Tax Credits have some features that align them with the tax system (such as being based on gross annual income) but they are also similar to the benefits system (e.g. they are based on *family* income rather than individual income). A Tax Credit can almost be seen as a reduction in taxation for people rather than a benefit 'handout'. This sits well with the neo-liberal approach.

- The aims of the two systems can vary considerably from very ambitious aims, such as major redistribution from rich to poor, to more limited ones, such as targeting help on those most in need. Both systems are incredibly complex and have been revised through a series of largely piecemeal reforms since the Second World War. This complexity is sometimes cited as a cause of error and abuse in the systems. Fraud is another problem within these systems, although benefit fraud is often much more vigorously pursued and prosecuted than tax fraud.

- There have been a number of fairly major reforms to the system since 1997, leading to a redistribution of wealth from working-age families without children to pensioners and working-age families with children. There has also been a general redistribution from rich to poor. But this collectivist approach to social security and taxation has been relatively cautious and has been undertaken very quietly so as not to upset the perceived neo-liberal views of the swing voters of middle England.

Discussion and review topics

1 Is a neo-liberal approach incompatible with a high level of state involvement in the provision of a social security system? What are the implications of an approach grounded in social solidaristic and collectivist thinking?

2 How useful is the system of Tax Credits in alleviating poverty?

3 What role should there be for the private sector in the provision of social security?

4 What emphasis should the social security and taxation systems give to combating fraud?

Further reading

Benefits – a journal that provides a valuable means of keeping up to date on developments in and research on the benefits system

Ditch, J. (ed.) (1999) *Introduction to Social Security*, Routledge, London – a collection of useful chapters on a variety of aspects of social security by different authors

Hills, J. (1998) *Income and Wealth: The Latest Evidence*, York Publishing Services, York – an authoritative account by one of the acknowledged experts in the field

McKay, S. and Rowlingson, K. (1999) *Social Security in Britain*, Macmillan, Basingstoke – the authors provide a comprehensive coverage of the social security system while maintaining a generally clear approach

Millar, J. (ed.) (2003) *Understanding Social Security*, Policy Press, Bristol – this book provides a relatively recent review that takes account of reforms to the social security system

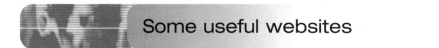

Some useful websites

www.cpag.org.uk – the Child Poverty Action Group campaigns against child poverty and its website provides articles and other information on this and related topics

www.dwp.gov.uk – the site of the Department for Work and Pensions contains official information on a wide range of benefits available to potential claimants and to publications and statistics

www.hm-treasury.gov.uk – the Treasury site and that of the Office of National Statistics (www.statistics.gov.uk) are useful sources on the budget and public expenditure

www.ifs.org.uk – the Institute for Fiscal Studies produces timely commentaries on tax and benefit reform, from an economic perspective, as well as other aspects of social and public policy

www.inlandrevenue.gov.uk – the Inland Revenue website provides a good range of information on taxation and the statistics section is a source of up-to-date figures, including on topics such as tax expenditures covered in this chapter

www.poverty.org.uk – established by the New Policy Institute and supported by the Joseph Rowntree Foundation, this site monitors levels of poverty and social exclusion in Britain

References

Adam, S. and Frayne, C. (2001) *A Survey of the UK Tax System*, Briefing note no. 9, Institute for Fiscal Studies, London

Brewer, M., Clark, T. and Wakefield, M. (2002) *Five Years of Social Security Reforms in the UK*, Working Paper W02/12, Institute for Fiscal Studies, London

Bryson, C. (1997) 'Benefit claimants: victims or villains', in Jowell, R., Curtice, J., Park, A., Brook, L., Thomson, K. and Bryson, C. (eds) *British Social Attitudes: The 14th Report*, Dartmouth, Aldershot

Clark, T., Myck, M. and Smith, Z. (2001) *Fiscal Reform affecting Households, 1997–2001*, Institute for Fiscal Studies, London

Cook, D. (1989) *Rich Law, Poor Law, Different Responses to Tax & Supplementary Benefit Fraud*, Open University Press, Milton Keynes

Ditch, J. (ed.) (1999) *Introduction to Social Security*, Routledge, London

Hedges, A. and Bromley, C. (2001) *Public Attitudes towards Taxation*, Fabian Society, London

Hills, J. (1998) *Income and Wealth: The Latest Evidence*, York: York Publishing Services

HM Treasury (2000) *The Informal Economy: A Report by Lord Grabiner QC*, HM Treasury, London

HM Treasury (2001) *Financial Statement and Budget Report*, www.hm-treasury.gov.uk/Budget/Budget_2001/Budget_Report/

Inland Revenue Statistics (2002) www.inlandrevenue/gov.uk/stats

Labour Party (1997) *New Labour: Because Britain Deserves Better*, Labour Party, London

Lakin, C. (2002) 'The effects of taxes and benefits on household income 2000–01', *Economic Trends*, Office for National Statistics, London

McKay, S. and Rowlingson, K. (1999) *Social Security in Britain*, Macmillan, Basingstoke

Nozick, R. (1974) *Anarchy, State and Utopia*, Basil Blackwell, Oxford

Taylor-Gooby, P. and Hastie, C. (2002) 'Support for state spending: has New Labour got it right?', in Park, A., Curtice, J., Thomson, K., Jarvis, L. and Bromley, C. (eds) *British Social Attitudes: the 19th Report*, Sage, London

'Working off welfare'

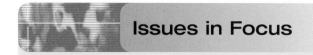

4 Alex Bryson

Issues in Focus

'Work is the best form of welfare' (Department for Work and Pensions 2002a). It pays better than welfare. There is a string of psychological studies testifying to the fact that workers are psychologically better off than non-workers and it is the chief means by which families can break out of poverty. It follows that increasing the proportion of the adult population in work should be a central tenet of government policy. However, this is easier said than done and there are many difficult questions. What do you actually do to get people into work – and make sure they stay there? Who do you prioritise for this assistance and who should you leave out? What should we expect from recipients in return for assistance? Anyway, is it really the case that work is better for all? For example, there is some evidence that children's education can suffer if their mothers work (Ermisch and Francesconi 2000); many people have crucial caring roles in the home that limit their job opportunities; and, while some disabled people may benefit from working, others clearly do not. Answering questions like these posed involves ethical, moral, political, and economic judgements which are the stuff of social policy and which have faced all governments, here and elsewhere, when devising programmes designed to help people off welfare and into work.

This chapter covers key issues around work and welfare through:

Issues in Focus continued

- an examination of the history of welfare-to-work in Britain up to the point at which Labour entered government in 1997, a history that depicts the relationship between the state and those lacking paid work

- consideration of theories that inform policymakers' understanding of the underlying causes of unemployment and how these are linked to the policy options that New Labour faced on entering government

- a description of the underlying philosophy of New Labour's approach to paid work and an assessment of New Labour's policy initiatives in this area since 1997.

While work and employment have always been a key area of concern for social policy in the United Kingdom, their importance has been highlighted over the past 25 years. Under the Conservatives in the 1980s (see Figure 4.1) high levels of unemployment resulted in large increases in expenditure on welfare benefits and debates over different explanations for unemployment. From 1997 the Labour government effectively placed work at the centre of its social policies, with initiatives aimed not merely at increasing employment or reducing unemployment, but also at using work to tackle social exclusion. This chapter begins with a consideration of the development of 'welfare-to-work' programmes in the UK, noting the different emphases apparent since the 1940s. It moves on to

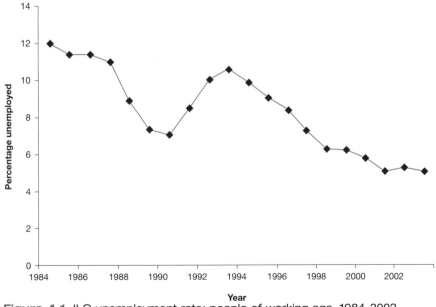

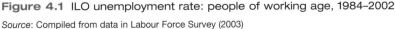

Figure 4.1 ILO unemployment rate: people of working age, 1984–2002

Source: Compiled from data in Labour Force Survey (2003)

an examination of explanations of the causes of unemployment and the implications that these have for the policies that have been used by governments in their attempts to tackle the problem. However, it becomes apparent that not only are the causes of unemployment complex but that at any one time there are a number of influences acting on levels of employment and unemployment, while the position is further complicated by relationships with and impacts of other government policies. The chapter progresses to a discussion of the Labour government's approach, in particular to welfare to work, together with an evaluation of the extent to which its policies have been successful. It concludes with a brief examination of prospects for the future.

Brief history of welfare and work in Britain

Welfare-to-work policies are intended to move those reliant on the state for financial support (on welfare) into a position of relative financial independence through paid work (into work). Their origins may be traced back to the poor relief offered to 'paupers' by local communities under the provisions of the Poor Law in the 17th century. The system was governed by the principle of 'less eligibility' whereby, to discourage dependency, one must ensure that any assistance offered to the unemployed individual must fall short of the benefits derived from work. In addition, eligibility for assistance was dependent on stringent work tests. These principles governed the system until the beginning of the 20th century when the first bricks were laid in the construction of an entitlements-based system based on National Insurance contributions which gave entitlement to pensions and unemployment insurance. Since then there has been a hotly contested debate about the weight to attach to entitlement, on the one hand, and conditionality, on the other.

As President of the Board of Trade responsible for setting up Britain's first Labour Exchanges, Winston Churchill was firmly of the belief that **work tests** were necessary, not only to weed out 'loafers and vagrants' but in order to protect the unemployment insurance system from unnecessary claims. The Act setting up labour exchanges institutionalised the dual function of **benefit policing**, on the one hand, and job placement service, on the other, which characterised the British system until the early 1970s when job placement and benefit administration services were separated. As early as 1943, the then Minister of Labour, Ernest Bevin, had criticised the system for compelling claimants to participate in training programmes, arguing that training was only of value where the person concerned was a 'willing collaborator'. Furthermore, he believed that employers would not cooperate in schemes where they were expected to train those who were 'industrially least effective'. On these grounds he rejected Beveridge's proposals, contained in the Beveridge plan of 1942, for claimants to train or work for their benefits. But it was only in the 1960s that there was real policy interest in transforming the system that was viewed predominantly as a means for paying unemployment benefits into an economic agency devoted to employment. The foundations for this were laid with the separation of jobcentres and benefit offices in the early 1970s, ushering in a decade in which the service focused on:

- encouraging employers to increase vacancy notification

- encouraging jobseekers to use the service when changing jobs

- broadening the service's clientele from the unemployed and low skilled to all jobseekers

- improving the service's knowledge of the labour market and labour market trends.

This period coincided with concern about the contribution of poor training to the demise in Britain's international competitiveness, a brief that the Manpower Services Commission focused on, together with the public job placement services. However, with the arrival of mass unemployment in the early 1980s the new Conservative government refocused energies on the unemployed and, in particular, training for unemployed people. The primary mechanisms for this were a reintegrated employment service combining job placement and benefit administration, as recommended in the Rayner Review of 1982 and, during the 1990s, training and enterprise councils, run by employers, to deliver training for the unemployed. During the governments of Margaret Thatcher and John Major there was a substantial rise in the number of unemployed claiming benefits, a dramatic increase in expenditure on training for the unemployed, a shift in the system away from contributory towards means-tested routes into unemployment-related benefits, increased emphasis on the conditionality of benefit receipt and the penalties attached to non-compliance, a big decline in the real value of out-of-work benefits as benefits were indexed to prices rather than earnings and an extension of wage supplementation policies (see the discussion of social security in Chapter 3). Some argue that the system was consciously remodelled along the lines of 'workfare' programmes being developed at that time in the United States: indeed, there is some evidence of wholesale policy transfer from the US to Britain (Dolowitz 1998). However, the period was also notable for what successive Conservative governments did not do. They did not extend work tests to benefit recipients other than the unemployed, they did not cut the duration of means-tested unemployment-related benefits and they did not make working or training an absolute condition for benefit receipt – other than in specific instances, such as in the case of 16–18 year olds.

Causes of unemployment and construction of policies to tackle them

Broadly speaking, three views of the causes of unemployment and worklessness have influenced the development of welfare-to-work policies in Britain: economic, behavioural and institutional.

Economic theories identify deficiencies in the demand for labour, on the one hand, and the supply of labour available to employers, on the other, as key factors generating unemployment. More people may be desirous of jobs than there are jobs in the economy, resulting in unemployment. There may be an absolute dearth of jobs in the economy as a whole or differential rates of growth across regions can produce a mismatch between jobs generated and locally available labour. Deficiencies in demand can be cyclical, arising during downturns in economic activity, as occurred in the early 1980s and the early 1990s. Even when the economy picks up, recession can leave its mark on individuals who become unemployed because employers prefer to recruit those with no unemployment history. This results in periods of extended unemployment for some, producing rising long-term unemployment, as experienced in the mid-1980s. There are also secular trends in economic development that have resulted in a gradual decline in employers' demand for unskilled labour and manual labour more generally. This, coupled with pressures from international compe-

"You'll have to look harder than that to find a job, son."

Source: www.CartoonStock.com

tition to shed labour in efforts to raise productivity, has led to the disappearance of many jobs traditionally undertaken by those leaving unemployment.

Since the 1970s, it has become unfashionable for governments to respond to these problems by seeking to manage industrial development or to influence the demand for labour by injecting money into the economy to generate job-creating growth. Even if a government were minded to do this, it is by no means certain that employers would welcome demand management by government and governments' room for manoeuvre would be severely limited by the dictates of European monetary union and responses from investors and the stock market. Direct subsidies to declining industries are usually prohibited under EU rules.

Instead, New Labour and governments before it have adopted a **supply-side** approach developing means by which governments can assist individuals and employers to overcome some of the shortfalls in the economy. These include:

- subsidies to reduce the cost of recruiting the unemployed – including direct **wage subsidies**, grants to meet (re-)training costs, reduced payroll taxes

- training unemployed people in the skills employers require

- **'make work'** schemes giving the unemployed work experience which they might not otherwise receive in the open market

- efforts geared to improving the number of job offers received by the unemployed, including job search assistance and employer placements.

It is not only the dearth of jobs that economists point to as a cause of unemployment. A second issue is the nature of jobs created since the demise of the fabled 'male breadwinner' jobs that permitted families to prosper as single-earner households. The rise of the service economy and increased international competition in the trading sector has resulted in more flexible labour practices since the 1970s, with an increased proportion of jobs being low paid, often offering part-time or temporary contracts with limited career prospects and poor non-wage benefits. At the beginning of the 1980s, earnings-related supplements to benefits and benefits which rose with earnings meant that these deficiencies in the labour market created real incentive problems since, for many, work did not pay. Consequently, the unemployed did not enter employment as quickly as they might otherwise have done. The problem of financial incentives has spawned a number of policies since then including:

- widening the gap between out-of-work benefits and in-work income through more generous in-work wage supplementation and reductions in the real value of out-of-work benefits

- lowering hours thresholds governing entitlement to wage supplements

- alterations in rules governing how much workers can earn before their benefits are affected ('earnings disregard' rules) which help workers smooth their incomes during dips in earnings

- assistance with expenses incurred on entering work, such as single payments for work-related expenditures, help with travel and childcare costs and delays in the withdrawal of out-of-work benefits covering housing costs.

Moving from economic to *behavioural* theories regarding the roots of unemployment, these come in two varieties. First, there are those that hold that unemployment is a reflection on the character of the unemployed. It is not that jobs are unavailable: rather, the unemployed are unprepared to take those jobs that are available. The problem becomes the unemployed themselves, who hold unrealistic expectations about their job prospects. Their moral fibre is called into question. In the language of the 19th century they were regarded as 'feckless'. In the late 20th century they were described by some as an '**underclass**', dependent on the state for their survival. Mead (1986 and 1997) contends that the unemployed are 'incompetent', in the sense that they wilfully refuse to do what is in their best interests, namely participate constructively in society by taking work.

The policy implications of this behavioural diagnosis of the unemployment problem are clear cut and have informed the design and implementation of policy in respect of unemployment for centuries. To discourage dependency, one must ensure that any assistance offered to the unemployed individual must fall short of the benefits derived from work. In the language of the New Poor Law of 1834, the recipient's condition must be 'less eligible' than that of the poorest labourer. In addition, the unemployed should be required to perform certain activities in return for assistance. In its more liberal form, compulsion is confined to activities that are intended to improve the claimant's job prospects, such as attendance at work-focused interviews, job search, training or supported employment. In its less liberal form, these activities encompass character-forming activity which may not directly improve the claimant's job prospects but, by building the moral fibre of the individual, will help the individual into a position of independence. The objective is to change the character and behaviour of the unemployed.

The second type of behavioural theory points to the demotivating effect of longer term unemployment on the individual arising from the debilitating effect it has on the individual's morale, material resources and social contacts. This motivational problem emanates directly from long-term unemployment, rather than from the character of the unemployed. However, the policy prescriptions required to tackle the problem are similar to those stemming from other behavioural diagnoses, with the onus on the state coaxing individuals back to work using sticks as well as carrots, if necessary.

The *institutional* view points to the role of welfare state institutions in creating and sustaining unemployment and worklessness. Some argue that the emphasis on entitlement, rather than conditionality, creates perverse incentives for benefit claimants that are 'responsible for the loss of key civic values of work, honesty and thrift' (Field 1997: 61). Again, this leads to consideration of increased conditionality of benefit payment and improved work testing. More fundamentally, some maintain that the welfare system is beyond reform and should be abolished. Others blame the system for spending too much time on work-testing and too little time on servicing employers: these analysts argue the primary purpose of a job placement service should be to serve employers efficiently by focusing attention on offering suitable candidates to employers on terms which increase claimants' chances of job entry. Policies congruent with this analysis include active engagement with employers – along lines similar to those adopted by private employment agencies – offering 'sweeteners' to employers in the form of wage subsidies, training grants and tax or National Insurance contribution breaks and policies allowing employers to 'sample' claimants' suitability without making a long-term commitment (for instance, through work trials). Seen in this way, work testing may be counter-productive, since it signals to the employer that candidates from the public job placement service are unwilling applicants.

These different definitions of the problem of unemployment and workless-ness thus lead to different sorts of policy prescription. However, these are not necessarily *alternatives* for policy. Unemployment may arise from any or all of these causes in combination and so policies may seek to address a number of these different factors. There may also be a wider policy agenda including con-cerns about poverty and social exclusion, equal opportunities in employment and concern for the most disadvantaged groups in the labour market. And there will often be tensions in policy, whereby the achievement of one aim can make it difficult to achieve another. For instance, benefit sanctions designed to ensure claimants attend job interviews may increase levels of claimants' job search activity but will do nothing to improve their job prospects if employers believe that they are 'workshy' and not attending of their own volition. Or, more broadly, policies may succeed in getting individuals into work but not in ensuring that they have adequate incomes to keep themselves and their fam-ilies out of poverty.

Labour and welfare-to-work

On coming to power in 1997 Prime Minister Tony Blair proclaimed: 'This will be the welfare-to-work-government' (Blair 1997) and Policy eye 4.1 summarises the key measures that have been introduced. Labour's analysis of the problem linked economic, behavioural and institutional factors. For example, the new govern-ment's first welfare reform Green Paper (DSS 1998) argued that the existing system of support was 'too passive', offering cash payments and expecting little in return. Thus behavioural outcomes (unemployed people lacking the motiv-ation to seek work) were linked to institutional structures (the system failing to create the conditions for active engagement with the labour market).

The government wanted to devise a system that was more 'active', offering claimants 'a hand up, not a hand out' (Harman 1997). In practice, this meant making benefit payments more conditional on undertaking activities geared to labour market (re-)entry. In recent times, this approach can be traced back to

Policy eye 4.1   Welfare-to-work in Britain: main measures since 1997

1997   New Deal for Lone Parents introduced as a voluntary programme offering advice on jobs, benefits, training and childcare through personal adviser. Target group is lone parents with children of school age.

1998   Labour's welfare reform Green Paper offered 'a new welfare contract between the citizen and the state with rights matched by responsibilities. We will rebuild the welfare state around the work ethic: work for those who can; security for those who cannot . . . It is the responsibility of government to provide positive help; it is the responsibility of the claimant to take it up.'

New Deal for Young People introduced as a compulsory programme for those aged under 25 after 6 months unemployed – flagship for New Deal programmes: initial intensive job search assistance followed by one of four options (subsidised employment, environment taskforce, work in voluntary sector or full-time education/training).

New Deal for Long-term Unemployed introduced – compulsory for those aged 25 plus and unemployed for 12 or 18 or 24 months (depending on the area).

New Deal for Disabled People introduced – voluntary programme offering advice and information.

Prototype employment zones set up providing more intensive support for the most disadvantaged jobseekers in high unemployment areas.

Work-based training for young people available to 16–18 year olds not in full-time education or a job.

National Childcare Strategy aims to provide quality and affordable care for all children aged 0–14.

1999   Introduction of the statutory National Minimum Wage.

Replacement of Family Credit and Disability Working Allowance by Working Families Tax Credit and Disabled Person's Tax Credit respectively: more generous and usually paid direct from employer.

New Deal for Partners of the Unemployed extends job search assistance and training opportunities to partners of unemployed people, on a voluntary basis.

New Deal 50 for Over 50s, on a voluntary basis, offers information

Policy eye 4.1   continued

and advice and in-work Tax Credits and training grants to those aged 50+ on benefits.

Work-based Learning for Adults provides vocational and prevocational training to adults after 6 months' unemployment.

2000   Welfare Reform and Pensions Act 1999 comes into force requiring attendance at work-focused interview; full family benefit sanction.

The ONE pilot integrates benefit claiming and institutes work-focused caseloading for all claimants of working age.

Target set that 70% of lone parents should be in employment by end of the decade.

2001   Introduction of joint claims for childless couples requiring both satisfy benefit receipt conditions.

Learning and Skills Councils replace TECs as bodies responsible for post-16 training.

2002   Jobcentre Plus created: 'will provide a single point of delivery for jobs, benefits advice and support and help, using a personal adviser system' (DWP 2002b).

Compulsory work-focused interviews required for new claimants to Income Support.

New Deal 25+ replaces NDLTU, conforming more to the NDYP model.

Extension of joint claims to childless couples aged under 45.

2003   Child Tax Credit and Working Tax Credit introduced.

Source: House of Commons (2000)

1986 when periodic work-focused interviews were introduced for the longer term unemployed. These interviews, known as 'Restart' interviews, were compulsory in the sense that individuals' benefits could be reduced or withdrawn if they continually refused to attend without good cause. Attendance at work-focused training courses such as employment training also became a condition of entitlement. Labour chose to emphasise these elements of the Conservative legacy, with organisations such as the OECD also identifying active labour market policies as a key ingredient for non-inflationary economic growth.

Under compulsory New Deal programmes, greater powers of sanction (including the 'full family sanction' in which all benefit can be reduced) were introduced. Claimants such as lone parents, disabled people and partners of unemployed people are now required to attend work-focused interviews and can also be sanctioned for non-attendance at these. There has also been an increase in the intensity with which review interviews are used: continual review is the hallmark of **caseloading**, a method for dealing with claimants which seeks to create a personal relationship between the state official (often referred to as a 'personal adviser') and the claimant (the 'client').

Underpinning this approach was a shift in the way government perceived the relationship between the state and the claimant. Labour described this as a change in the contract between the state and the individual: a new settlement would involve new rights for the claimant in return for an acceptance of new responsibilities. Those rights included the right to expect government to guarantee the availability of good-quality training places for those required to take these up. In effect, the government was underwriting a guarantee to be the 'employer of last resort' for some groups of claimants, which represented a break with previous Conservative policy. Claimants could also expect access to good-quality job search advice and training provision offered directly by the state or by private providers under contract to the state.

The government also sought to guarantee a minimum rate of pay in the marketplace through the introduction of the statutory National Minimum Wage. The minimum wage is the only far-reaching welfare-to-work policy that Labour has adopted which seeks to tackle deficiencies in labour demand, and is motivated by a belief in '**making work pay**' because benefit claimants would only take work if there was sufficient financial incentive to do so. This consideration also explains the enhanced system of wage supplementation introduced with Tax Credits (discussed further in Chapter 3). Tax Credits sought to strengthen financial incentives to enter work by increasing the generosity of payments, offering substantial assistance for those with childcare costs, reducing the rate at which the credit was removed with higher earnings and paying the credit direct through the employer to emphasise the link with working.

The New Deal for Young People, the government's flagship welfare-to-work programme, exemplifies the new approach. It targets young people in the belief that early intervention in individuals' careers can enhance long-term job prospects by eliminating the early scarring effects of long-term unemployment. After an initial intensive period of job search and assistance with overcoming immediate barriers to employment, it offers some choice to claimants in the form of four options (subsidised employment, environmental work, voluntary work and full-time education or training) guaranteeing minimum quality standards. As the Chancellor of the Exchequer put it, there is 'no fifth option' (Brown 2000) of non-participation. Those who do not leave the programme after their option return to the intensive job search and assistance element of the programme and may enter new options. The programme effectively abolishes long-term unemployment for young claimants outside the programme by requiring continued participation until leaving benefit.

The different measures and provisions used to achieve the policy goal of helping people move from welfare to work are very diverse and include a wide range of different types of support targeted on different groups. Policy eye 4.2

identifies nine areas of welfare-to-work provision, each tackling the perceived causes of unemployment, but from different angles. All these policies coexist, reflecting government recognition of the complex causes of unemployment. Some (the minimum wage, tax credits, work-focused interviews for lone parents and the sick and disabled) mark new departures, while others build on past experience and that of other countries.

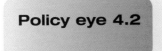

Policy eye 4.2   UK welfare-to-work measures and programmes

Job search assistance

New Deals; Jobplan workshops; Jobfinder Plus; programme centres (previously Jobcentres); job interview guarantee scheme; Jobfinder Grant; travel-to-interview scheme

Training provision

New Deals; Work-based Training for Young People; Advanced and Foundation Modern Apprenticeships; Work-based Learning for Adults; career development loans; in-work training grants

Job sampling

New Deal employer option; New Deal voluntary sector option; work trials

'Make work' schemes

Environment taskforce under New Deal for Young People; New Deal for Long-term Unemployed; StepUp

Review/caseloading

ONE pilots; New Deals

Employer assistance

Work trials; wage and training subsidies under New Deals for Young People and Long-term Unemployed

'Making work pay'

Working Families Tax Credit; Disabled Person's Tax Credit; childcare payments; statutory National Minimum Wage; in-work training grant for lone parents; earnings disregard

Community-based initiatives

Employment zones; New Deal for Communities; action teams for jobs

Assistance with caring responsibilities

National Childcare Strategy; in-work credits covering childcare costs; improved maternity rights, introduction of paid parental leave

Evaluating welfare-to-work policies

On entering government, Labour signalled its concern that welfare-to-work programmes ought to be judged by their ability to get claimants into work, rather than simply moving them off benefits. Here we consider how three strands of policy have fared on this criterion: compulsion; making work pay; and the New Deals.

Compulsion

Since 1997 many of Labour's welfare-to-work initiatives have been characterised by the more liberal form of compulsion described earlier, involving activities that are intended to improve the claimant's job prospects, such as attendance at work-focused interviews, job search, training or supported employment.

There were indications from the Restart evaluation in the late 1980s that periodic work-focused interviews, supported by benefit sanctions for non-attendance, increased the rate at which unemployed claimants left benefit and lowered the time they spent unemployed on leaving benefit *and* increased the rate at which claimants entered jobs. Labour took encouragement from this evaluation since it showed that making benefit receipt conditional on active programme participation could assist in speeding claimants' exit from unemployment. However, subsequent studies have shown that the value of compulsion depends on the nature of the intervention, the target group, labour market conditions and the way in which the programme is delivered. For instance, recent evidence on the effects of regular review interviews suggests the positive effects are most apparent when the interviews are a condition of benefit receipt. Voluntary reviews under ONE (Green et al. 2001) had little impact. But, since ONE interviews became a condition of benefit receipt, the programme has had a small effect in increasing the rate at which lone parents leave benefit (Kirby and Riley 2001). However, there was no effect on JSA claimants or the sick or disabled. Furthermore, the effect for lone parents is confined to delivery through jobcentres and is not apparent where ONE is delivered through call centres and the private sector.

There is other evidence that 'threat' effects can encourage claimants to sign off. Long-term unemployed claimants participating in the Project Work programme (which has informed the design of the New Deal for the Long-term Unemployed) signed off benefits at a much faster rate than a comparator group of non-participants as they approached a 'make work' scheme after an intensive period of job search. However, they were no more likely to move into jobs than non-participants (Bryson, Lissenburgh and Payne 1998). A threat effect was also discernible in the evaluation of joint claims with some couples in the stock of claimants ending their JSA spells to avoid converting to a joint claim which would have extended job search and availability requirements to both in the claimant couple. However, there was no effect on job entry (Bonjour et al. 2002).

Compulsion is counterproductive when employers believe claimants have been compelled to make job applications or attend interviews and when it results in employers being flooded by unsuitable candidates simply wishing to satisfy benefit eligibility requirements (Bryson and Jacobs 1992). It also proves ineffectual when administrators view requirements as unfair or unethical: in these cases, administrators refuse to enforce them, so they become a 'dead letter' (Bryson and Jacobs 1992).

Making work pay

Low pay is invariably cited as the main reason for claimants refusing job offers so 'making work pay' policies would seem to be important in easing claimants' entry to work. Certainly, the expansion of wage supplementation policies since the early 1990s has coincided with a modest increase in lone parents' likelihood of working (Blundell 2001). Family Credit made recipients financially much better off in work than they would have been on out-of-work benefits (Marsh and McKay 1993) but its incentive effect was blunted somewhat by uncertainty surrounding eligibility for it and its interaction with other income sources (Kempson, Bryson and Rowlingson 1994). However, it encouraged lone parents to take short-hours work, matching their earnings from work with Family Credit income (Marsh and McKay 1993). Early evidence on the operation of the Working Families Tax Credit confirms a positive incentive effect for lone parents (Blundell 2001).

In-work benefits can also increase employment levels by helping workers stay in work during a dip in earnings, thus extending the time they stayed in work and reducing the likelihood of re-entering unemployment in the future (Bryson and Marsh 1996). However, there are two negative aspects to wage supplementation through in-work benefits or Tax Credits. First, wage supplementation can limit earnings progression in the medium term, trapping employees in long-term reliance on state assistance while in work (Bryson 1998) by creating disincentives to train, seek promotion or work longer hours due to the withdrawal of the wage supplement as earnings rise. Second, the evaluations of both Family Credit (Marsh and McKay 1993) and WFTC (Blundell 2001) show wage supplements are a disincentive to two-earner status among couples and discourage work by the non-recipient.

The statutory National Minimum Wage also helps work pay. There appear to have been no adverse employment effects on those whose wages would have needed to be raised to comply with the minimum (Stewart 2002) and the availability of higher wages has drawn previously economically inactive people into the labour market.

The New Deals

The New Deals mark something of a departure from previous welfare-to-work programmes. First, they are multifaceted, offering different things to participants as they move through the programme. Second, claimants have some – albeit constrained – choice as to which option to take up if they are still out of work after the initial intensive Gateway stage. Third, benefit receipt is conditional on participation for those claimants within the eligible group. So, has the approach been successful in getting claimants into work? Evaluations of most of the New Deals are yet to be published, so we focus on the New Deals for Young People and the Long-term Unemployed. As far as the New Deal for Young People is concerned, the answer appears to be yes. The programme appears to have increased the rate at which young men leave unemployment for jobs (Blundell 2001). Some of the effect is due to intensive job search assistance at the beginning of the programme (Blundell 2001). It is not obvious why this has worked when previous job search programmes have not. One possibility is that caseloading clients results in better quality advice and increased trust between adviser and claimant. Another is the prospect of the Options phase of the programme looming after four months on the programme: if claimants do not like the look of any of the options, this may increase their desire to leave the programme. The remainder of the effect is accounted for by the job subsidy element of the programme (Blundell 2001; Dorsett 2001). There are some parts of the programme that appear to have worked less well, notably the full-time education and training option. This was least effective in getting claimants into work, but it was effective in ensuring people continued in education or training on leaving the programme.

Evidence on the impact of the New Deal for the Long-term Unemployed is more mixed, perhaps because the target group is more difficult to place. However, the subsidised employment component has improved participants' job entry rates (Winterbotham, Adams and Hasluck 2001).

Prospects for the future

Many of the problems identified by Labour on entering government in 1997 persist today – work rates among lone parents and women with unemployed partners remain low, the quality of labour available to employers is not sufficient to meet the demands of available jobs and low pay is endemic in low-skilled occupations. Other government policies can help, not least the compulsory education system and higher education. Nevertheless, a lot is riding on the success of welfare-to-work policies. The New Deals are having a positive, if small, effect on groups like young people and Tax Credits have led to a substantial transfer of income to poorer working families. However, some big policy departures have yet to be fully evaluated, while the fact that the programmes are relatively recently established means that it is difficult to appraise what the longer term effects of these policies might be. The real test will come when the economy faces a downturn.

Prospects for the future success of welfare-to-work policies therefore remain uncertain. One major source of uncertainty is the changed nature of the clientele that the system, and Jobfinder Plus in particular, is dealing with. Traditionally, welfare-to-work has been focused on those classified as unemployed 'jobseekers', that is, people who are not employed but who are required to be available for, and seeking, employment as a condition of benefit receipt. But in the last few years the government has widened the target group to include non-working claimants receiving other benefits (Income Support, some invalidity benefits) who are not required to be available for, or seek work, as a condition of benefit receipt. This new group of clients for Jobfinder Plus, which includes lone parents and the sick and disabled, dwarfs the traditional client group. From the perspective of service delivery, the widening of the client group raises two key issues. First, what will work for this new 'less active' group of clients? And, second, how do we manage the resource implications of a sudden twofold increase in our customers? In particular, Jobfinder Plus is facing a thorny issue: what is an appropriate level of resources to devote to these more 'hard-to-place' clients given the difficulties placing them in jobs?

A second source of uncertainty arises from the rate of policy change that Jobfinder Plus and other agencies are managing. Table 5.2 illustrated the rate of change in welfare-to-work policies since Labour came to power in 1997. Jobfinder Plus came into being towards the end of this period and is responsible for the majority of the measures identified. This responsibility stems directly from the government's belief in the need to 'provide a single point of delivery for jobs, benefits and support and help, using a personal adviser system' (DWP 2000b). It is not simply which welfare-to-work policies are used, but how they are implemented, that determines how successful they are. Studies show wide variation in the success of a single policy across areas (eg. Evans, McKnight and Namazie 2002) and there is evidence from the United States that the quality of provision and the nature of delivery are critical (Evans 2001). However, there is little evidence on which delivery mechanisms work in Britain and why. In future, government will need to spend more time and money on the evaluation of alternative delivery mechanisms.

Welfare-to-work landmarks, 1601–1996

1601	Poor Law Act
1834	Poor Law Amendment Act introduced principle of less eligibility and requirement to be confined in workhouse
1909	Labour Exchanges Act
1911	National Unemployment Insurance (numbers eligible increased with Acts of 1920 and 1921)
1921–1932	Genuinely seeking work requirement resulted in denial of nearly 3 million claims. Eventually repealed after opposition from trade unions
1946	National Insurance Act enacted main elements of Beveridge Report of 1942. Recommendation for unlimited period of benefit receipt if recipient attends work or training centre was not enacted

1966	Earnings-related unemployment insurance benefits and contributions introduced
1971	*People and Jobs* recommends separation of benefit administration and job placement
	Family Income Supplement: in-work benefit (forerunner of Family Credit)
1973	Opening of first Jobcentre separate from unemployment benefit office. Creation of the Manpower Services Commission
1981	Derek Rayner's Review (*Payments of Benefit to Unemployed People*) recommends reintegration of job placement and benefit administration
1980	Benefits uprated by prices index rather than earnings index
1982	Abolition of compulsory registration for employment at jobcentres. Abolition of earnings-related supplements to unemployment benefits
1986–1988	Fowler review leading to Social Security Act 1986 which, in 1988, resulted in the replacement of Supplementary Benefit by Income Support and introduction of Family Credit, an in-work benefit for those with children working 24+ hours
1986–	Restart interviews: beginning of periodic review. Compulsory Restart courses for long-term unemployed. Travel to interview scheme. Wages councils abolished
1987	Reintegration of jobcentres and unemployment benefit offices announced
1988	Social Security Act required young people's participation in YTS with refusal resulting in benefit loss. Employment Act disqualified unemployed from unemployment benefit if they withdrew from training without good cause. Jobcentres and unemployment benefit offices reintegrated into a single Employment Service. Abolition of the Manpower Services Commission
1989	Social Security Act: actively seeking work requirement; permitted period in which to restrict availability for work
1996	Social Security Act replacing Unemployment Benefit and Income Support for the unemployed with Jobseekers Allowance, a single benefit with very similar rates whether eligible through contributory or means-tested route. Contributory entitlements cut from 12 to 6 months

Summary

This chapter has covered a range of debates relevant to the relationship between work and welfare and has identified a number of key areas for consideration:

- While there has been a long-standing link between work and welfare in Britain, debates about the extent of entitlement to benefits, on the one hand, and conditionality, on the other, remain significant in discussions about policies towards unemployed people.

- There are a number of perspectives on the causes of unemployment that have impacted on the development of welfare-to-work policies in the United Kingdom and the policies of governments can be seen as grounded in the extent to which they draw on these different approaches.

- Since 1997 the Labour government has emphasised the importance of work to individuals and to society and has stressed that individuals have rights in return for responsibilities, one of which is to be willing to work. The impact of these ideas can be seen in the examination of New Labour's 'welfare-to-work' policies.

- Evidence on the success of the government's policies in tackling problems of unemployment and low pay is mixed and analysis is complicated by the interaction with other areas of government activity, perhaps most notably education, although it is possible to identify a number of areas in which there have been some successes, albeit in a time when the economy has been performing relatively well. Nevertheless, on the basis of the evidence of the first six years of the Labour government, it remains difficult to make sound judgements on the prospects for the future of welfare-to-work programmes.

Discussion and review topics

1 How useful are economic, behavioural and institutional explanations of unemployment in leading us towards policies to tackle unemployment?

2 To what extent is it appropriate to argue that the principle of 'less eligibility' continues to dominate debates over benefits for unemployed people?

3 How successful have New Labour's welfare-to-work policies been in improving levels of unemployment among vulnerable groups?

Further reading

Deacon, A. (ed.) (1997) *From Welfare to Work: Lessons from America*, Institute for Economic Affairs Health and Welfare Unit, London – contains an introduction to American thinker Mead's views on welfare and welfare reform, together with commentaries from a number of British writers

Peck, J. (2001) *Workfare States*, Guildford Press, New York – traces the development of welfare-to-work policies in the United States and the way in which they were taken up in the UK and Canada

Philpott, J. (ed.) (1997) *Working for Full Employment*, Routledge, London – a collection of analyses of the nature of unemployment and the range of different policy responses

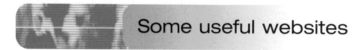

Some useful websites

www.dwp.gov.uk – the site of the Department for Work and Pensions contains information and links to a variety of publications including on government policies and statistics

www.employment-studies.co.uk – Institute for Employment Studies provides access to a variety of publications concerned with employment

www.lowpay.gov.uk – established by the government in 1998 the Low Pay Commission provides annual reports on the impact of and advice on the rates of the National Minimum Wage

www.oecd.org – the site of the Organisation for Economic Cooperation and Development gives access to a range of information including statistics on standardised unemployment rates for OECD member countries

www.theworkfoundation.com – the Work Foundation undertakes research, consultancy and campaigning activities and this site has links to a number of relevant publications

References

Blair, T. (1997) 'The Will To Win', speech as Prime Minister, Aylesbury Estate, Southwark, 2 June 1997

Blundell, R. (2001) 'Welfare-to-Work: Which Policies Work and Why?', Keynes Lecture in Economics, UCL and IFS

Bonjour, D., Dorsett, R., Knight, G. and Lissenburgh, S. (2002) *Joint Claims for JSA – Quantitative Evaluation of Labour Market Effects*, report to the Working Age Evaluation Division of the Department for Work and Pensions

Brown, G. (2000) 'Chancellor of the Exchequer's Budget Statement', 21 March 2000

Bryson, A. (1998) 'Lone mothers' earnings', in Ford, R. and Miller, J. (eds) *Private Lives, Public Responses: Lone Parenthood and Future Policy in the UK*, Policy Studies Institute, London

Bryson, A. and Jacobs, J. (1992) *Policing the Workshy: Benefit Control, Labour Markets and the Unemployed*, Avebury, Aldershot

Bryson, A. and Marsh, A. (1996) *Leaving Family Credit*, Department of Social Security Research Report No. 48, HMSO, London

Bryson, A., Lissenburgh, S. and Payne, J. (1998) *The First Project Work Pilots: A Quantitative Evaluation*, report to the Employment Service and Department for Education and Employment

Dolowitz, D. (1998) *Learning from America: Policy Transfer and the Development of the British Workfare State*, Sussex Academic Press, Brighton

Dorsett, R. (2001) *The New Deal for Young People: Relative Effectiveness of Options in Reducing Male Unemployment*, PSI Discussion Paper No. 7, Policy Studies Institute, London

DSS (Department of Social Security) (1998) *New Ambitions for Our Country: A New Contract for Welfare*, The Stationery Office, London

DWP (2002a) Department for Work and Pensions Service Agreement, *http://www.dwp.gov.uk/publications/dss/2001/dwp-psa/psa.pdf*

DWP (2002b) 'Budget help for lone parents', press release EMP1704 – BLP, 17 April, DWP Press Office

Ermisch, J. and M. Francesconi (2000) *The Effect of Parents' Employment on Children's Education*, ISER Working Paper, 2000–31, *http://www.iser.essex.ac.uk/pubs/workpaps/pdf/2000-31.pdf*

Evans, M. (2001) *Welfare to work and the organisation of opportunity: Lessons from abroad*, CASE Report 15, Centre for the Analysis of Social Exclusion, London School of Economics, London

Evans, M., McKight, A. and Namazie, C. (2002) *The New Deal for Lone Parents: First Synthesis Report of the National Evalution*, Department for Work and Pensions Report No. 116, *http://www.dwp.gov.uk/waed/esr116rep.pdf*

Field, F. (1997) 'Re-inventing welfare: a response to Lawrence Mead' in Deacon, A. (ed.) *From Welfare to Work: Lessons from America*, Institute for Economic Affairs, London

Green, H., Connolly, H., Marsh, A. and Bryson, A. (2001) *The Medium-term Effects of Voluntary Participation in ONE*, Department for Work and Pensions Research Report No. 149

Harman, H. (1997) 'New Deal for Lone Parents is welfare reform in action', DSS press release, 23 October

House of Commons (2000) *Employment and Training Programmes for the Unemployed*, House of Commons Research Paper 00/81, House of Commons, London

Kempson, E., Bryson, A. and Rowlingson, R. (1994) *Hard Times: How Poor Families Make Ends Meet*, Policy Studies Institute, London

Kirby, S. and Riley, R. (2001) *The Employment Effects of ONE: Interim Findings from the Full Participation Phase*, Report for the Department for Work and Pensions

Labour Force Survey (2003) *www.statistics.gov.uk/STATBASE/tsdataset. asp?vlnk=429&more=y*

Marsh, A. and McKay, S. (1993) *Families, Work and Benefits*, Policy Studies Institute, London

Mead, L. (1986) *Beyond Entitlement*, Free Press, New York

Mead, L. (1997) 'From welfare to work: lessons from America' in Deacon, A. (ed.) *From Welfare to Work: Lessons from America*, Institute for Economic Affairs, London

Stewart, M. B. (2002) *The Impact of the Introduction of the UK Minimum Wage on the Employment Probabilities of Low Wage Workers*, Conference Paper presented at the European Association of Labour Economists, Paris, 19–22 September 2002

Winterbotham, M., Adams, L. and Hasluck, C. (2001) *Evaluation of New Deal for Long-term Unemployed People Enhanced National Programme*, Employment Service Research Series

Acknowledgement

The author would like to thank the Regent Street Polytechnic Trust for financial support.

Education

5

Hugh Bochel

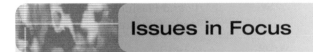

Issues in Focus

Education has for long been viewed as a key feature of social policy, whether for its role in enabling individuals to fulfil their potential, as an influence on equality and inequality or through its importance in providing an appropriate workforce to meet the economic and other needs of the country.

Before the 1997 general election New Labour placed education at the centre of its agenda, a position perhaps best summed up in Tony Blair's mantra 'Education, education, education'. However, education has always raised difficult questions for governments and, as this chapter illustrates, these have been clear in the years since 1997 with debates focusing on issues including:

- the level of resources available to schools, colleges and universities, including how higher education in particular should be funded

- how to measure and improve levels of performance, both of educational institutions and of individuals

- questions over the relationship between inequality and education and the role of education in reducing or mitigating inequality.

New Labour's concern to reshape the education system has been one of the major features of the Blair governments. Yet such attention to education is not new, with governments frequently having sought to adapt the education system to meet their perceptions of priorities at particular times. This apparently constant desire for reform is perhaps a result of education generally being seen as providing a variety of benefits, individual, social and economic, which governments seek to interpret and affect as part of their wider goals, as well as the costs to the state, with education accounting for around 5 per cent of GDP. For each individual, education can be portrayed as offering opportunities for personal development and the realisation of potential; at a social level it has frequently been viewed as having the potential for reducing social inequality and for contributing to social unity and development; and for the economy its purpose can be argued to be providing a skilled workforce ready to enter employment, as well as having other attributes such as flexibility, self-responsibility and time keeping relevant to the world of work. The importance of education is such that the temptations for governments to 'reform' education may therefore be almost overwhelming.

This chapter begins by outlining the development of the education system and, in particular, the ways in which, during the post-war period, it has been affected by the differing concerns of governments, including its perceived importance to the United Kingdom's economic competitiveness. It moves on to examine the reforms introduced by the Conservative governments of 1979 to 1997, including the introduction of the National Curriculum, standardised attainment tests and the growth in higher education. The chapter then considers the further changes to education, from pre-school to higher education under New Labour. While the focus of much of this chapter is on education in England and Wales, it is important to recognise that this is one area of social policy where there are significant variations across the constituent elements of the United Kingdom and some of these are highlighted in the following discussion.

Education up to 1979

Up to 1870 education was largely limited to those sections of the middle and upper classes who were able and willing to pay for the limited provision available through church, private and voluntary schools, although there was some education for poor children in schools associated with workhouses. However, in 1870 the Elementary Education Act was passed which created elected school boards to establish non-compulsory education provision for 5 to 13 year olds, funded from the rates, where existing provision was inadequate (in Scotland, where by the mid-19th century a considerable proportion of the population was literate, through the provision of schools by large towns, individuals and societies, the Education (Scotland) Act of 1872 similarly made education the responsibility of school boards). The next 50 years saw a series of extensions of the state's role in education: compulsory education up to ten was introduced in 1880, fees for elementary education for most children were abolished in 1891 following which the school leaving age was raised to 11 in 1893 and 12 in 1899. In 1902 the Education Act made local authorities responsible for schools, including church schools, a position which laid the basis for the organisation of education for the remainder of the century. Then in 1918 the school leaving age was raised to 14 (this had occurred in 1901 in Scotland). However, while the role of the state was developing gradually, private education, in the form of the independent **public schools**, was left largely untouched.

The next most significant developments in education came with the appointment of R. A. (Rab) Butler as Minister for Education in 1941. At that time most children left school at the age of 14, with the majority leaving with no formal qualifications. While there had been proposals for reform from the end of the First World War, economic recession meant that the status quo had remained despite a widespread recognition that the education system served only to reinforce privilege and did not meet many of the nation's needs.

Butler proposed a radical review of the education system and the Education Act of 1944 saw the creation of a tripartite settlement:

- *grammar schools*, to cater for academic 'highfliers', who might be expected to progress to university or enter professional careers, business or management

- *technical schools*, for children who might go on to work in engineering or crafts

- *secondary modern schools*, which would take those children who did not appear to fall into either the 'academic' or 'applied' categories.

Entry into each of these schools would be through one common examination, the eleven-plus. This tripartite structure would cater for children aged from 11 to the new school-leaving age of 15. Although the Act proposed that the leaving age be raised to 16 as soon as practicable this did not happen until 1972.

The Education Act made central government (the Ministry of Education and the treasury) responsible for the provision of financial support for local authorities, while the latter were given responsibility for managing the schools and for the strategic planning of education in their areas (including primary, **secondary** and further education, to which part of **higher education** was added when polytechnics were created in the 1960s). In relation to this the Act also reinforced the divisions within education between primary education, secondary education up to 16, tertiary education from 16 and university education. The role given to local authorities allowed them to make different decisions about which elements they sought to develop, with some emphasising the primary sector while others placed greater stress on expenditure at secondary level.

The Act ensured, for the first time, the provision of free education for all children and, through the abolition of fees combined with the eleven-plus, gave bright working-class children the opportunity to progress to grammar schools. Butler also intended that the creation of technical schools would ensure that Britain did not lag behind its economic competitors in technical education, a desire that was followed up by the Labour governments of the 1960s with the expansion of vocational education and the establishment of polytechnics.

However, despite its radical nature and the administrative, structural and educational changes that it introduced the Butler Act has been criticised for failing to tackle a number of issues. In particular it left the private 'public schools' untouched and, according to some, actually further institutionalised the ethos of privilege through the creation of state grammar schools.

The Act also institutionalised the role of religion and the Church within state education, a development which has periodically been an area of tension and which rose to the fore again in the late 1990s and early 2000s through the increasing multi-faith identity of the United Kingdom and in particular the issue of Muslim and other faith schools. Despite Butler's hopes, the Act also failed to raise the profile of technical education in Britain as local education authorities tended to focus on the provision of academic education through grammar schools and 'practical' education through secondary moderns, often seeing the question of technical education as primarily for employers to address through the system of apprenticeships.

Following the 1944 Act there was a period of relative consolidation of the education system. The primary area of conflict was over the eleven-plus examination which was increasingly seen as serving to distinguish between those who 'passed' and progressed to grammar schools and those who 'failed' and went to the secondary modern, a view given greater credence by the lack of development of the third type of school, the technical school, in many areas and by the higher levels of funding given to the grammar schools. For many children and parents attendance at secondary moderns was viewed as failure. In contrast, supporters of the system argued that grammar schools gave able working-class children the potential to progress to grammar schools on merit and that the higher level of resourcing for those schools was appropriate in order to allow the most able to be able to develop their full potential. This became an important part of the debate over equality and inequality during the 1960s and 1970s.

The Labour Party increasingly took the view that a move towards a system of **comprehensive** schooling, already adopted by some local authorities, would help reduce inequalities and in 1965 the Secretary of State for Education, Tony Crosland, requested all local authorities to submit proposals to move towards local secondary schooling on a comprehensive basis. However, this was not a requirement supported by an act of parliament and it was not until the 1976 Education Act that the government sought to use legislation to ensure the reorganisation of education on comprehensive lines. This Act also restricted the ability of local authorities to continue to fund grammar school places. However, like the Butler Act before it, the 1976 Act did not really address the role and position of private education. Table 5.1 provides an illustration of the changes in pupil numbers arising from attempts to introduce comprehensive education.

Table 5.1 School pupils: by type of school (United Kingdom)

	1970/71	1980/81	1990/91	2000/01
			(thousands)	
Public sector schools				
Nursery and primary	5,952	5,260	5,060	5,450
Secondary				
Comprehensive	1,313	3,730	2,925	3,340
Grammar	673	149	156	205
Modern	1,164	233	94	112
Other	403	434	298	260
All public sector schools	9,507	9,806	8,533	9,367
Non-maintained schools	621	619	613	626
Special schools	103	148	114	113
Pupil referral units				10
All schools	10,230	10,572	9,260	10,116

Source: Central Statistical Office (2003) Table 3.3

During the 1950s the Conservatives established a number of new universities, creating some from scratch and upgrading others from university college to university status. In 1963 they also established the Robbins Committee on Higher Education, which recommended a doubling of student numbers. With the election of the Labour governments of the 1960s concern over higher education was reinforced by anxiety over Britain's perceived failure to keep up with the rest of the world in industry and innovation. The government sought to develop a new, more vocational and technologically oriented form of higher education delivered through new 'polytechnics' which would deliver degree-level educational programmes in practical and technical subjects, rather than the arts subjects which had previously dominated university education. As with schools and **further education** colleges, the polytechnics were placed under the control of local education authorities, which then had a strategic overview from **nursery**, through **primary** and **secondary** schools through to higher education within their areas. The other major development in higher education under Labour in the 1960s was the creation of the Open University, aiming to provide degree-level education to adults who had missed that opportunity earlier in life. This education was radically different from the existing model, being delivered primarily through distance-learning techniques supported by well-resourced, good-quality teaching materials and supplemented by television and radio programmes. In this way, delivery in classrooms was to be much reduced, although some level of classroom support was maintained and supplemented through 'summer schools'.

By the mid-1970s education had returned to the policy agenda as a significant issue, in part again due to concern over the UK lagging behind its competitors, with the technical expansion of the previous decade seeming to have had little effect, but also with the emergence of a new issue, evidence of high levels of illiteracy and innumeracy among school leavers. Some critics sought to blame this on the creation of comprehensive schools and the bias against grammar school education and argued that these had driven down standards of education for all children.

Education, 1979–1997

The Thatcher governments of the 1980s placed at least part of the blame for Britain's economic ills on 'trendy' educators whom they perceived as having emphasised equality and new teaching methods at the expense of providing a solid educational foundation for children. In line with their emphasis on individual choice and the role of the market they sought to use these mechanisms to raise academic standards. The Education Act 1980 removed the requirement

Source: www.CartoonStock.com

for local authorities to pursue comprehensive education (see Table 5.1) and introduced the Assisted Places Scheme to allow 'high ability' children of poorer parents to attend fee-paying schools.

However, it was not until the 1988 Education Reform Act that the Conservatives undertook radical reform of education. This piece of legislation allowed for the creation of **grant-maintained** schools, for local management of schools, the introduction of the **National Curriculum** and standardised testing. The Conservatives argued that allowing grant-maintained schools to opt out of local education authority control would enable them to develop their own policies, including on entry and selection. These schools would be funded directly by the Department of Education and Science (later the Department for Education and Employment) and would be managed by their head and deputy head teachers together with the school's governing body. Other schools would also be able to become locally managed, controlling the bulk of their budgets, including teachers' salaries and other staffing costs, equipment, books and internal maintenance, although local authorities would remain responsible for capital costs and providing services such as careers advice.

The 1988 Act offered schools the choice of remaining under LEA 'control' with their budgets being 'top sliced' for central administrative and service costs or becoming grant maintained and receiving their entire budget directly from the Funding Agency for Schools, thus having no formal relationship with the LEA. Schools were able to move to grant-maintained status through a vote by governors followed by a vote by parents, with a simple majority of those voting being needed for acceptance. Using grant-maintained schools and locally managed schools the Conservatives hoped to create a 'market', with schools competing for pupil numbers. As resources would be allocated on the basis of the number of children enrolled in a school it was argued that schools would have an incentive to perform well to attract pupils, while those that performed badly would lose income and, ultimately, risk closure. By 1997 680 secondary schools (15 per cent of the total) had grant-maintained status, along with 514 primary schools (2 per cent of the total), overwhelmingly in England (DfEE 1988).

In order to develop market mechanisms further and to allow parents to make decisions about which school to choose, the government encouraged the production of 'league tables' of school performance which would allow parents to make comparisons of schools in their area. However, despite being widely publicised in the media, critics argued that, in reality, these league tables have merely reflected the class backgrounds of children attending different schools and say little or nothing about the extent to which the schools themselves make a difference to their pupils' achievements.

As another part of the response to the criticism that standards of basic literacy and numeracy were falling and that children were leaving school unable to read, write and do basic arithmetic the government introduced the National Curriculum in an attempt to emphasise the teaching of basic skills across England and Wales. This provided a standard syllabus and gave the Secretary of State the power to determine how much time each week would be spent on particular subjects. The Secretary of State was also given power over the content of the curriculum, although in practice this was largely allocated to the

National Curriculum Council. There were a variety of criticisms of this innovation including the danger of reducing time available for children to learn subjects such as drama, music and even sports and games (the last sometimes combined with concern over the impact on children's health of a reduction in the time available). Other criticisms were centred around the idea of a 'national curriculum' in a multicultural and multi-faith society with children of a wide variety of backgrounds and abilities. Indeed, the first version of the National Curriculum was revised in 1995, allowing greater discretion for schools over non-core subjects, reducing the level of targets and monitoring and giving greater flexibility of options for 14 to 16 year olds to encourage more vocational routes for some students.

In order to measure educational standards the Education Reform Act also introduced **standardised attainment tests** (SATs), to be applied across a range of subjects at various stages in a child's school life (the original suggestion was for testing at 7, 11, 14 and 16 although the last was dropped). Supporters argued that the National Curriculum and SATs would place a new emphasis on traditional values and help make parents aware of the information that they needed to choose a school for their children. Critics feared that this was a return to selection and that children might be labelled as 'failures' at an early age.

The 1988 Act also allowed introduced significant change to the realm of higher education, allowing polytechnics to leave LEA control and become free-standing corporations. One of the aims of this was to end the 'binary divide' between the polytechnics and the more traditional universities, a division that was arguably already in the process of diminishing as there was increasing commonality of courses taught between the two notionally different types of institution. Shortly after, the status of polytechnics was changed and they became universities, which, together with colleges of higher education, received funding from the Higher Education Funding Councils. Finally, under the Act, local planning and funding of vocational training was transferred to employer-led training and enterprise councils.

One other significant feature of higher education under the Conservatives was the growth in the numbers of students, with an increase from 473,000 in full-time undergraduate education in 1980/1 to 664,000 in 1990/1 and 1,052,000 in 1997/8.

Under Margaret Thatcher's successor as Prime Minister, John Major, the Conservatives continued to seek to develop both consumerist and quality-control approaches to education. The 1992 Education (Schools) Act abolished Her Majesty's Inspectors of Schools and created the Office for Standards in Education (OFSTED), with the remit of improving standards and achievement through regular inspection, public reporting and advice. Under Chris Woodhead, the Chief Inspector for Schools from 1994 to 2000, OFSTED became a major force in monitoring and influencing school-age education. The Act also legislated for the annual publication of school performance tables, with the intention of informing parents' choice of schools for their children. Also, from 1992 Further Education Colleges followed the path of incorporation previously undertaken by polytechnics and became independent from LEAs and responsible for their own management and finance.

However, despite the Conservatives' claims to be undertaking change to improve education and to raise standards, a rather different interpretation can be put on many of the educational reforms of the late 1980s and early 1990s, based on the arguments that they were as concerned with reducing the power of local authorities as with improving educational standards and that the attempts to create markets in education were as much for ideological as for educational reasons. This view is buttressed by the fact that many of the government's actions in education mirrored those in other areas of public services, such as health and social care, with the emphasis on the consumer and accountability through the market rather than the traditional pattern of services accountable to the public through elected representatives in local government.

Education since 1997

New Labour were famously elected in 1997 to the echoes of Tony Blair's commitment to 'Education, education, education' (see Policy eye 5.1). This emphasis was not limited to education on its own, but the role of education was seen as important for another of the government's flagship policy areas, the New Deal, which aimed to provide every adult with the opportunity to find employment. Education was also portrayed as vital to tackling social exclusion and creating an opportunity society. The government therefore sought to emphasise the provision of basic skills, including literacy and numeracy.

This concern with education continued into the second Labour term and following the party's second general election victory in June 2001 a new

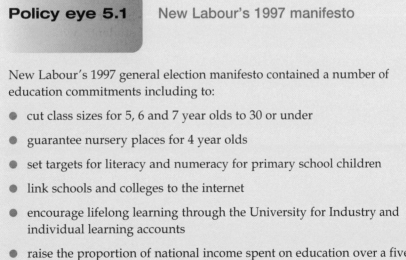

Policy eye 5.1   New Labour's 1997 manifesto

New Labour's 1997 general election manifesto contained a number of education commitments including to:

- cut class sizes for 5, 6 and 7 year olds to 30 or under

- guarantee nursery places for 4 year olds

- set targets for literacy and numeracy for primary school children

- link schools and colleges to the internet

- encourage lifelong learning through the University for Industry and individual learning accounts

- raise the proportion of national income spent on education over a five-year period.

Department for Education and Skills was established under a new Secretary of State, Estelle Morris, herself a former teacher.

Following her resignation in 2002 Charles Clarke became Secretary of State. Where expenditure on education was concerned, after a period of fluctuation and then decline under the Conservatives, falling to 4.5 per cent of GDP in 1996/7, levels of spending began to grow again to a projected 5.0 per cent of GDP in 2002/3.

Nursery places and pre-school education

Britain has often been differentiated from many other countries by the commencement of compulsory education at five years of age, compared with six or seven in some other countries and by the perceived lack of development of public pre-school provision, so that for example in 1970/1 only 21 per cent of three and four years olds were in such provision. However, there was a growing level of provision during the 1990s so that by 1999–2000 64 per cent of three and four year olds were spending at least some time in pre-school education (Central Statistical Office 2001) and shortly before their general election defeat in 1997 the Conservatives had introduced a voucher system which parents could use to purchase provision from the private or public sector. However, the new Labour government scrapped this scheme and instead sought a significant increase in the number of places to meet its promise of places for all four year olds and two-thirds of three year olds. Together with a significant increase in the level of resources for such provision it required LEAs to establish plans for early years development and childcare, including the provision of places for all four year olds. As a result by 2000/1 63 per cent of three and four year olds were making use of pre-school provision. During their second term Labour undertook to provide free nursery places for all who wanted one by September 2004. Reflecting government's continuing concerns for ensuring quality in education, from September 2001 OFSTED became responsible for inspecting all early years' childcare and education in England.

Reflecting the frequent complexity of social policy, the Sure Start programme was introduced as part of Labour's attempts to tackle social exclusion, seeking to work across government departments to ensure that children and families in disadvantaged areas had access to services, opportunities and help for young children. As such it formed a significant part of the government's ambitious drive to eradicate child poverty in 20 years and to halve it in ten. It was intended to involve both parents and a range of agencies in a variety of initiatives designed to give children in disadvantaged areas a better start in life, including increasing the number of childcare places available and a number of other programmes associated with education.

Primary and secondary education

Education under the 1997 and 2001 Labour governments was frequently characterised as dominated by flows of initiatives from central government, some of which are outlined in the following sections. Indeed, there were frequent accusations from teachers and others that the sheer volume of initiatives emerging from central government was such that it was adding substantially to the workload and stresses of teachers and itself undermining the prospects for achieving significant change and quality education. While not exhaustive, the developments now outlined illustrate the pressures for reform of school-age education from the Labour governments.

Class sizes

One of Labour's main pledges prior to coming to power was to reduce class sizes for five to seven year olds to give a maximum class size of 30, using money freed up by the scrapping of the Assisted Places Scheme to do this. While there were disagreements over the value of such a policy this was fairly rapidly achieved allowing the government to claim a significant manifesto success.

National Grid for Learning

Labour also emphasised the role of technology in teaching with the National Grid for Learning, promising to connect every school in the country to the internet and while 17 per cent of primary schools and 83 per cent of secondary schools had links to the internet in 1998 by 2001 this figure had reached 96 and 99 per cent respectively.

Standards and the National Curriculum

Despite the changes under the Conservatives, including the introduction of the National Curriculum and standard national assessments using SATs, there remained a widespread belief that educational standards were continuing to fall. The White Paper, *Excellence in Schools* (1997), set out some of the challenges facing education. As a result, in school-age education there was considerable emphasis on getting 'the basics' right, from attempting to ensure literacy and numeracy (for example, through the literacy and numeracy hours introduced in 1998) to the continuation of external monitoring of the standards of individual schools and local education authorities. As part of their attempt to achieve this, Labour maintained and even increased the emphasis on 'standards' and 'performance' from the Conservative years, including the use of testing. For example, by 2002 new, higher targets had been set for performance in English and Maths at Key Stage 2 of 85 per cent of pupils achieving level 4 or higher in English and mathematics with 35 per cent achieving level 5 or higher in both subjects (see Table 5.2). Following the Conservatives, the Labour government used OFSTED to exercise pressure for much of this activity, including identifying schools and even local education authorities that were 'failing' and setting targets for national as well as schools' educational performance.

Table 5.2 Pupils reaching or exceeding expected standards: by key stage and sex, 2002 (England)

	Teacher assessment		Tests	
	Males	**Females**	**Males**	**Females**
Key stage 1				
English	81	89	—	—
Reading	81	88	81	88
Writing	79	88	82	90
Mathematics	87	90	89	92
Science	88	91	—	—
Key stage 2				
English	67	78	70	79
Mathematics	74	75	73	73
Science	82	83	86	87
Key stage 3				
English	59	75	58	75
Mathematics	69	72	67	68
Science	66	69	66	67

Source: Central Statistical Office (2003) Table 3.7

The debate about standards and performance under both Conservative and Labour governments has frequently encompassed the publication of information on individual schools. Perhaps inevitably, there has been much debate about the value of 'school league tables' and, in particular, about what information they actually usefully provide: they apparently provide data on the achievements of individual schools, but since much educational attainment is determined by factors outside the control of schools they can be misleading – for example, some schools may be adding little value to the performance of students who might be expected to perform well largely arising from their socio-economic backgrounds (for example, in 2000, 74 per cent of children of parents classified as 'higher professional' received 5 or more GCSE grades A to C, compared with 61 per cent of those from 'lower professional backgrounds', 51 per cent 'intermediate', 36 per cent 'lower supervisory' and 29 per cent of those whose parents were in 'routine' groups), while others might be adding considerably to pupils who might be expected to perform less well and such achievements do not generally emerge in 'league tables'. Critics have also noted that there is an incentive here for schools to try to attract pupils who might do well and that, for example, 'Filling up a school with "able" children and keeping children with SEN [special educational needs] to a minimum is the cheapest and most labour-efficient way of enhancing league-table performance' (Gewirtz, Ball and Bowe 1995: 186).

One of the apparent contradictions much noted under the Conservatives was the contrast between the devolution of some powers to schools through local management and the unprecedented centralisation of overall control of education through the National Curriculum, standardised assessments, the publication of 'league tables' of school performance and the expansion of school inspection through OFSTED. Similarly, Labour showed a willingness to exercise control from the centre. This included the introduction of the literacy and numeracy hours, which some critics argued not only reflected a low level of trust of the teaching profession, but also through going beyond prescribing not only the time that should be spent to how it should be used, added a further dimension to central control. Another example of the government's willingness to become more directly involved in school-age education came with the passage of the School Standards and Framework Act 1998 which gave the government the power to intervene where it considers that a local authority has failed to carry out its duties correctly, whether this is at the level of an individual school or a whole LEA. The first use of these powers was seen in 1999 when parts of the work of Hackney LEA were given to private contractors and in 2000 there was further use of private sector contractors in Leeds, Rotherham and Sheffield.

Under Labour there were also a number of changes and adjustments to the National Curriculum, one of which not only reflected the government's multi-faceted approaches to education, but is also particularly apposite to social policy: Citizenship was introduced as part of the secondary curriculum from September 2002 to encourage political literacy and understanding of topical issues, to help young people to learn about rights and responsibilities and to encourage active involvement both in school and in the wider community. Other changes included revised syllabi across a range of subjects, including English, History, Mathematics and Science.

Yet another government initiative was that around 'beacon schools', which were recognised as providing good quality education and high standards and which could provide advice and guidance to other schools. By September 2001 there were around 1,000 beacon schools of which about one-quarter were at secondary level.

Diversification

Perhaps somewhat ironically, given that one of the problems identified by some critics of the Conservatives' attempts to develop a market in education was the lack of diversity of provision, Labour's approach to comprehensives has largely been to accept the diversification of educational institutions that took place under the Conservatives and the open enrolment approach of allowing parents to choose the most appropriate school for their children.

Notably, in contrast with the Labour governments of the 1970s, selection by state schools was not opposed by the Labour governments, the status of the remaining grammar schools could be changed following ballots of parents in feeder schools and the public schools have been left alone. The Green Paper, *Schools Building on Success* (Department for Education and Employment 2001), focused on secondary schools and set out Labour's proposals for extending diversity through the creation of more specialist schools (in areas such as technology, language, arts, business and enterprise, science and sport), faith-based schools, city academies and enabling external sponsors to take over 'underperforming' schools on fixed-term contracts. It also set further targets for performance for 14 year olds.

The subsequent White Paper, *Schools Achieving Success* (Department for Education and Skills 2001), reiterated much of New Labour's aims including diversity of schooling, the role of standards and targets and flexibility of the education system and qualifications. It also re-emphasised the commitment to vocational education and attempts to raise the status of the vocational route through secondary school. It was followed by the Education Act 2002, which again promoted the government's vision of flexibility and innovation including a degree of deregulation, further possibilities for the creation of new state-funded schools with sponsorship from private, voluntary or faith groups, continued pressure to tackle 'failing' schools and greater freedom for the best-performing schools. In addition the Act also allowed for the fairly widespread reform of existing legislation, for example, to reduce the necessity for education matters to be dealt with by parliamentary bills.

Relations with teachers and local education authorities

The Labour governments' relations with teachers were dogged by criticisms relating to the teaching profession, whether these related to difficulties of recruitment and retention, the administrative workloads created by the many initiatives emanating from central government or critical remarks about the teaching profession, including from the Chief Inspector for Schools up to 2002, Chris Woodhead, and from some ministers. The role of teaching assistants has also been debated following the huge increase in their numbers over the past decade and the need for training and qualifications for this group. The General Teaching Council for England and the General Teaching Council for Wales were established in September 2000 following the Teaching and Higher Education Act 1998 and became responsible for the regulation of the profession from 2001 when the registers of teachers were established, although they have no role in determining pay and conditions. In Scotland a General Teaching Council had been established in the 1960s. These developments were intended to help raise the status of the profession and to ensure and improve the standards of teaching.

In terms of the management of teaching it is quite clear that the past 20 years have seen a shift away from a position where management provided the framework, with teachers as professionals determining the nature of their teaching, through an attempt to manage through markets, to a position where there is largely management by targets and performance, a situation which has arguably been mirrored in others areas of social policy, such as healthcare and social care.

The government also set out its view of the role of local education authorities (DfEE 2000), making clear that 'schools that are good schools manage themselves' (2000: 7) and that LEAs should only intervene in schools where there were problems, particularly 'failing' schools. It saw the remainder of the role of LEAs as being concerned with functions unsuitable for individual schools, such as planning the supply of places across the authority, ensuring that all children have access to a school place or suitable alternative provision.

Education action zones and Excellence in Cities

One of the features of the first Labour government was an attempt to focus on key areas through a series of geographically oriented initiatives such as health action zones and education action zones. Education action zones (EAZs), established in the School Standards and Framework Act 1998, were intended to raise educational standards and tackle social exclusion in some of the worst performing areas of the country. Initially, 25 EAZs were established with a further 48 following in the second round from September 1999 to April 2000. They were initially established for three years but all of the first-round zones were extended to the maximum of five years. The zones were overseen by education action forums made up of the main partners, such as the LEA, parents, representatives of the local community, voluntary organisations, businesses and other organisations, as well as representatives from the schools themselves. The forums were required to draw up an action plan to raise educational standards in their area, including targets for each school and the zone as a whole, and these were then approved by the Secretary of State. The round-one zones were able to receive up to £750,000 a year in funding from the DfES and in return were expected to attract up to £250,000 a year in cash or kind contributions from private sector partners.

Round-two zones were able to receive up to £500,000 a year from the DfES with up to another £250,000 available on the basis of matching private sector contributions. However, early evaluations suggested some weaknesses in the EAZs, including a lack of progress in raising standards in secondary schools and a failure to innovate, as well as some problems with financial management. In addition to EAZs, some non-statutory zones were established as part of the Excellence in Cities initiative, designed to bring additional resources to some urban areas, with three-year lives. These had fewer powers than EAZs and more limited access to government funding, with a maximum of £300,000 available each year.

Other changes

Although outside school education the government made further reforms affecting the secondary age group. These included the creation of the Connexions Service, which draws on the work of a number of government departments to provide advice and guidance for 13 to 19 year olds on topics ranging from careers to homelessness and drug abuse, and the establishment of the Learning and Skills Council in April 2001 which sought to develop greater links between education for 14 to 19 year olds and employers. It also brought responsibility for all post-16 learning to one body for the first time. Also in 2001 the role of OFSTED was expanded further when it took over responsibility for inspecting all 16–19 education in sixth form and further education colleges.

Lifelong learning and higher education

Under Labour there has also been emphasis on 'lifelong learning', reflecting the perceived requirements of a flexible, skilled labour force able to adapt to the needs of the information age and the changing demands of employers. Labour made much of the commitment to lifelong learning, perhaps reflecting both the party's traditional concern with social justice and opportunity and New Labour's particular concern with economic efficiency and a skilled and flexible labour force. Education and training can be seen as central to both of these through removing barriers to employability (and hence potentially lessening some aspects of social exclusion), through investing in human capital and thus creating greater flexibility. Making the link from school education the White Paper, *Excellence in Schools* (DfEE 1997) made clear the government's aim of broadening A levels and giving greater status to vocational qualifications while at the same time seeking to ensure the achievement of key skills and high standards.

While higher education had already seen a great expansion in the age participation rate under the Conservatives, Labour's key target was that 50 per cent of young people should progress to higher education by the age of 30 by 2010. Among the tools intended to achieve this were education action zones and Excellence in Cities initiatives (outlined earlier) focused on areas where participation rates were often very low and strands of targeted funding for HE institutions to encourage them to meet targets for widening participation.

However, progress was arguably slower than the government would have wished in relation to both lifelong learning and widening participation. In addition, critics have pointed out that the very aim of lifelong learning contrasts with the ending of free tuition, the introduction of fees for students in higher education and the phasing out of student grants (although Labour-led administrations in Scotland and Wales had both reversed some parts of this policy by 2002).

In terms of lifelong learning, two of the government's main initiatives were the University for Industry (UfI) and individual learning accounts (ILAs). The UfI was seen as a way of making education and training more widely available through acting as a broker for the delivery of high-quality, flexibly delivered learning with a target for initial operation of autumn 2000. By 2001 it was offering education in England and Wales through the learndirect network. However, early evaluations, while recognising that there were real gains to learners, questioned the extent to which learndirect was achieving some of its objectives, such as engaging with employers and enhancing productivity.

An even more problematic area, which has arguably been one of Labour's greatest policy failures to date, was the introduction of individual learning accounts. These were intended to make a government contribution of up to £200 for some courses prices at £250 for individuals in England seeking to develop their knowledge and skills, which it was hoped would be topped up by employers and employees. However, while coming into effect on 1 September 2000 and reaching the initial target of one million ILAs by May 2001, almost a year ahead of schedule, ILAs were closed by 23 November 2001 following a perception that their growth had outstripped their anticipated cost to public funds and suspicions of widespread fraud and abuse of the scheme (see Policy eye 5.2). A highly critical report by the House of Commons Education and Skills Select Committee identified a whole series of weaknesses with the approach taken by the government (Education and Skills Select Committee 2002).

The Committee concluded that there was a need to provide a system of expanding adult learning, both for individuals and for the nation as a whole, and that any future development would require stronger quality assurance and security mechanisms, a full business model, information on unscrupulous providers and stronger and clearer contract management arrangements with the private sector.

Reflecting the emphasis on standards in school-age education, higher education has also seen attempts to measure and ensure quality, encompassing both teaching and research. From the 1990s higher education institutions have been subject to a number of external judgements including assessments of the

Policy eye 5.2	Individual learning accounts – a policy failure
May 1997	Labour Party manifesto
28 July 2000	Learning and Skills Act 2000 received Royal Assent
1 September 2000	Individual Learning Accounts Regulations come into effect
20 October 2000	DfES caps ILAs at £200 – 80 per cent of £250
March 2001	Interim target date for opening half a million ILAs
May 2001	Government announces one millionth ILA
24 October 2001	Secretary of State for Education and Skills announces that ILAs will be closed on 7 December
23 November 2001	Closure of ILAs in England
March 2002	Original target date for one million ILAs

quality of teaching in individual subjects and research assessment exercises to judge the quality of research undertaken. From the 1990s however it has been the research assessment exercise that has had the most significant influence on the level of funding received by institutions, leading some critics to claim that it has tipped the balance away from a concern with teaching towards research. During Labour's second term there were significant debates over the extent to which research funds should be concentrated on a relatively small number of 'elite' institutions, rather than being dispersed more generally across the sector.

However, during the second Labour term in office much greater consideration was given to the funding of higher education and, particularly, how to meet the government's aspirations of Britain's possessing world-class universities and of achieving 50 per cent participation rates in higher education. Although in Scotland the Scottish parliament had already made a decision to abolish tuition fees, the calls from some universities to be allowed to charge 'top-up fees', with costs of up to £15,000 per year being mentioned in some cases, made this a national issue. The government had already initiated a review of higher education under the then Secretary of State, Estelle Morris, but her resignation and replacement by Charles Clarke allowed a delay for further reflection and debate. By early 2004 the debate had moved on to the point where the government was proposing that universities be able to charge 'top-up' fees of £3,000 per year, but there remained significant opposition to this in universities and in parliament.

Education and devolution

As noted at the start of this chapter, there have historically always been some differences in the education systems of England, Northern Ireland, Wales and particularly Scotland, and these have been accentuated in the past 20 years. As with some other areas of social policy, responsibility for education has become even more fragmented with the introduction of devolution under Labour, with the devolved administrations in Northern Ireland, Scotland and Wales having responsibility for some or all parts of their own systems, while in England it is under the remit of the Department for Education and Skills.

Among the differences that have previously existed between Scotland and England, for example, have been that Scotland took a different approach to comprehensive schools in the 1970s with a much more uniform move towards comprehensive education. Similarly the examination system has historically been based on the system of 'highers', with school students having typically taken five subjects at that level at the age of 17, although recent years have seen a shift towards greater depth of study. In addition, in Scotland a General Teaching Council came into being in 1966, 35 years before those for England and Wales. At degree level Scotland has awarded honours degrees after four years, with students potentially being admitted at 17 years of age. Even under four successive Conservative governments in the 1980s and 1990s, Scotland retained significant differences, with no National Curriculum and no development of specialist schools.

The period since 1999 has seen further differences emerging across the United Kingdom, with among the most significant divergences being the decisions by the devolved administrations of Scotland and Wales to abolish tuition fees for undergraduate students, while in Northern Ireland publication of league tables of school examination performance has been ceased. Given the extent of diversity emerging so soon in the life of the devolved governments, it seems likely that education systems will demonstrate further diversity as political control of both Westminster and the devolved administrations changes and develops.

Education landmarks, 1979–2002

1979	Education Act
1980	Education Act
1981	Education Act
1985	*Better Schools* White Paper
1986	Education Act – actually two!
1988	Education Act
1992	*Curriculum Organisation and Classroom Practice in Primary Schools* report
	Education (Schools) Act
1993	Dearing Report
	Education Act
1994	Education Act
1996	Nursery Education and Grant-Maintained Schools Act
1997	Education Act
	Excellence in Schools White Paper
	Connecting the Learning Society National Grid for Learning
1998	School Standards and Framework Act
2001	*Schools Building on Success* Green Paper
	Department for Education and Skills created
	Education and Skills: Delivering Results – A Strategy to 2006
2002	*Schools Achieving Success* White Paper
	14–19: Extending Opportunities, Raising Standards Green Paper

Summary

This chapter has outlined the historical development and some of the most significant recent changes in education in the United Kingdom. Reflecting over the period since 1979 it is possible to identify a number of themes:

- There has been a steady shift towards the marketisation and diversification of school-age education, with Labour largely accepting the reforms made by the Conservatives in terms of open enrolment and variation among schools; indeed, while they reversed the move towards schools opting out of LEA control using the School Standards and Framework Act 1998 (although these schools were allowed to become 'foundation' schools under the supervision of the LEA but with a significant degree of autonomy), some have viewed Labour as taking unprecedented steps towards the use of markets and the involvement of the private sector, giving examples of private involvement in education action zones and as potential managers of failing schools and LEAs.

- The issue of 'standards' has been at the fore of governments' attempts to reform education, resulting in a range of proposals designed to maintain and raise standards including the National Curriculum, OFSTED, testing of children at set stages in their school careers, the introduction of the literacy and numeracy hours and the use of performance measures for schools.

- One of the significant criticisms of Labour's approach to education, particularly for primary and secondary schools, has been the sheer volume of initiatives and guidance directed at schools and teachers, leading the government to be accused of both increasing central direction and prescription and of overloading those responsible for implementing policies.

- Overall, there has been a movement towards a position where, in general, schools are responsible for their budgets and performance, where the role of LEAs is generally about strategic management and where central government has enhanced its control through a range of mechanisms including central direction and performance measurement.

- The profile of 'lifelong learning' has been raised by governments, particularly in relation to the creation of a flexible labour force and the needs of the economy. However, attempts to increase the levels of involvement, whether through the University for Industry and individual learning accounts or through widening participation in higher education, have demonstrated that governments can face considerable difficulties in implementing policies in this area.

- Reforms to higher education have seen an increasing squeeze on the level of resources available to universities and colleges which, together with attempts to increase the level of participation in higher education, have led to major debates about the way it should be funded and who should pay.

Discussion and review topics

1 What role should the private sector play in the provision of education?

2 How successful have Conservative and Labour governments been in raising standards in school-age education since 1979?

3 Discuss the principal arguments for and against selectivity in education.

4 To what extent do changes to education under Conservatives and Labour mirror governments' approaches to social policy more generally?

Further reading

Department for Education and Skills (2001) *Schools Achieving Success*, The Stationery Office, London – one of the series of Green and White Papers dealing with education that have emerged from the Labour government, it seeks to lay out a vision for the development of secondary education

Tomlinson, S. (2001) *Education in a Post-Welfare Society*, Open University Press, Buckingham – this book provides a thorough coverage of the development of education since the 1944 Education Act, including the different philosophical perspectives that have impacted on education

Trowler, P. (2002) *Education Policy*, Routledge, London – taking a rather different approach, the second edition of this book examines education policy from a perspective grounded more in the policy process

Some useful websites

www.dfes.gov.uk – the site of the Department for Education and Skills contains and has links to a great deal of government information, including publications and statistics from pre-school provision to higher education

www.education.guardian.co.uk – *Education Guardian*, together with the two *Times* sites given in this section, this provides ready access to contemporary debates and an archive of past articles

www.northernireland.gov.uk – Northern Ireland Executive, through which site it is possible to access information on the education system in Northern Ireland

www.ofsted.gov.uk – Office for Standards in Education – provides information about the role and activities of OFSTED together with access to reports and other publications

www.scotland.gov.uk – Scottish Executive makes available a significant amount of information on current developments in education in Scotland, together with some useful historical background

www.tes.co.uk – *Times Education Supplement* site is concerned with school age and further education and contains much to interest students including news and analysis

www.thes.co.uk – *Times Higher Education Supplement* covers higher education in a fashion similar to the sister site, which precedes it

www.wales.gov.uk – National Assembly for Wales, through which site it is possible to access information on education and training in Wales

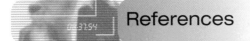

References

Central Statistical Office (2001) *Social Trends 31*, The Stationery Office, London

Central Statistical Office (2003) *Social Trends 33*, The Stationery Office, London

Department for Education and Employment (1997) *Excellence in Schools*, The Stationery Office, London

Department for Education and Employment (1999) *Education and Training Statistics for the United Kingdom*, The Stationery Office, London

Department for Education and Employment (2001) *Schools Building on Success*, The Stationery Office, London

Department for Education and Skills (2001) *Schools Achieving Success*, The Stationery Office, London

Education and Skills Select Committee (2002) *Third Report – Individual Learning Accounts*, House of Commons, London

Gewirtz, S., Ball, S. J. and Bowe, R. (1995) *Markets, Choice and Equity in Education*, Open University Press, Buckingham

Personal social services

6 Robert Adams

Issues in Focus

Since the early 1970s the personal social services have acquired, some-what unjustifiably but perhaps in some respects inevitably, the image of a stigmatised and stigmatising service for stigmatised people. This has much to do with the fact that the social services form a key part of the central and local government apparatus for delivering public welfare, yet in contrast with other universal services such as education, they grapple with some of the more intractable, private and often literally insoluble problems arising in some people's lives.

The personal social services occupy a pivotal space between indi-vidual people's widely differing perceptions of their wants and needs and the services provided by society. This chapter outlines some of the key issues in relation to their role including:

● these services reflect the values of the state, yet are intended to safeguard individual rights and maximise human potential. There is therefore an inevitable tension between the role of the personal social services as they intervene in people's lives, control, manage and try to minimise or prevent problems of mental health, confusion among older people, offending by young people, abuse of children and adults and seek to empower citizens and encourage autonomy and independence

Issues in Focus continued

- arguments about how best to achieve these aims range from the technical and financial in terms of costs and benefits, through the organisational in terms of how to structure and manage the services, to the political and ethical in terms of what is best and what is right

- the complexity of these issues ensures that the personal social services remain a controversial aspect of public services and social policy.

Add to these the unhappy history of underfunding, poor management, deficient decision making, failures of services and harm to, and sometimes deaths of, clients and many of the reasons for the problematic status of the personal social services become apparent. This chapter sets present-day social services in historical and policy context and examines the three main aspects of their functions: family and childcare, community care and youth justice.

The social services department was conceived in the mid-1960s in a spirit of idealism about what it would achieve. In 1965, Richard Titmuss had a vision of 'a structural reorganization which places the emphasis on *social service* rather than on biological or sociological criteria – like the family – or on one element in the pattern of needs – like health or rehabilitation. We need departments providing *services*; not departments organized around categories of client or particular fragments of need' (Titmuss 1979: 90 [italics in original]). This observation came at a historical moment of great significance. The Seebohm Committee on Local Authority and Allied Personal Social Services was about to begin its deliberations and the resulting Seebohm Report (1968) was the most important report in the history of the personal social services, leading directly to the creation of social services departments in England and Wales under the Local Authority Social Services Act 1970. However, Titmuss made his statement at a time when universalistic provision by the welfare state was a widely shared aspiration. Since then, this goal has been eroded by successive governments, initially being affected by the fiscal crisis of 1973/4, then by the attitudes of the Conservative governments of 1979 to 1997 and the subsequent Labour governments (1997 onwards). But the Labour government's plans, announced in 2003, for the reshaping of the personal social services around trusts and specialist agencies designed to encourage organisations to delivering services together tailored to meet people's needs, in at least that respect echoed the ideal expressed by Titmuss.

In the relatively short timescale of their existence, social services departments and the provision of the personal social services have been constantly reviewed and reformed by central government. This chapter outlines some of the most significant of those developments, emphasising particularly the period since 1997 and examining the changing shape of the personal social services. As with several of the aspects of welfare policy covered in this book, the personal social services have developed differently in the constituent parts of the United Kingdom, a situation which the introduction of the devolved administrations for Northern Ireland, Scotland and Wales in the late 1990s is likely to exacerbate. This chapter does not attempt to do justice to that diversity, focusing mainly on England, with some references to Northern Ireland, Scotland and Wales, although the further differentiation of policy and practice will clearly bring with it important implications for the personal social services.

Historical and policy context

The story of the personal social services could be written from the viewpoint of progressives and liberals within the caring agencies as one of fairly continuous progress, as social services departments in England and Wales evolved and grew rapidly from their birth in the Local Authority Social Services Act 1970 (in Scotland social work departments were established following the Social Work (Scotland) Act 1968, while in Northern Ireland health and social services provision was brought under one organisational umbrella and administered by health and social services boards). But from a more critical perspective, despite the massive expenditure, the personal social services could be judged to have failed to provide the decent, consistent and reliable welfare services that people – notably children, lone parents, poorer people, vulnerable people who are older, disabled and mentally ill – deserve, want and need. For example, the first ever survey by the Department of Health of experiences of personal social services in England by people receiving services, found that more than half (51 per cent) of respondents from black and minority ethnic groups said that social services staff did not take note of any important matters relating to their race, culture or religion (DoH 2001: 4, Table 2).

In the early 1970s the original reforms brought about following the Seebohm Report were supported by a widespread optimism that the resulting **generic social services** would command more power in local authorities and hence more resources than had hitherto been the case. There was an expectation that bringing a broad continuum of services together would make them less stigmatising and more accessible and a belief that the new species of generic social workers could deliver comprehensive social work and care services to adults, children and families. In addition, the recommendations of the Seebohm Report formed a central plank in a much wider programme of related policy changes in family and childcare and youth justice promulgated by the Labour governments of 1964–1970.

After 1964, the Labour Party under Harold Wilson presided over an optimistic and widespread consensus between social democratic (with a significant Fabian presence) politicians, civil servants and professionals that new childcare legislation and organisational reform would transform the existing childcare, mental health and welfare services. Two main areas of reform were prioritised. First, arguments such as those presented in the Ingleby (Home Office 1960) and Longford (Labour Party Study Group 1964) reports led to debates over what needed to be done to meet the needs of problem families and culminated in the Children and Young Persons Act 1969. Second, there was a widespread wish to advance what the government, in a significant metaphor, described as the 'war against crime' (Home Office 1964), with measures to combat delinquency being central to this. In a third area, change had gathered pace under the Conservative government of the late 1950s, leading to the Mental Health Act 1959. This shaped a programme of the progressive closure of large mental hospitals and their replacement with **community care** – albeit a process which 40 years on is not yet complete, so that more than a dozen institutions from the days of former lunatic asylums still remain entirely or partly open.

Personal social services, 1970–1979

For several years after their establishment it seemed as though the new generic social services would win over their critics, who mourned the loss of the specialist childcare, mental health and welfare officers of the generation before the 1970s. For example, the numbers of staff employed by social services departments rose, expenditure increased, and the Children and Young Persons

"Thank goodness you're a witch!
We were afraid we'd stumbled on a social worker."

Source: www.CartoonStock.com

Act of 1969 provided the justification for common ways of treating children deemed to be at risk and in trouble.

Enthusiasm for the liberal treatment of children and young people in trouble waned under the Conservative government of 1970–1974 with, for example, calls for tougher treatment of offenders. The inquiry into the death in 1973 of Maria Colwell (Department of Health and Social Security 1974), a seven-year-old girl beaten to death by her stepfather, raised concerns about the need to improve joint health and social services interventive and preventive work with children and families considered at risk.

Simplistic analyses of changes in social policy can sometimes characterise the pre-Thatcherite years as 'spend, spend, spend' and the years from 1979 onwards as inaugurating cuts in public services. However, this is not entirely accurate. While the 1980s may have seen an increased scepticism and a commitment to non-public sector solutions, in significant respects, the turning point was the mid-1970s when the financial squeeze on local budgets following the dramatic Middle East oil price rise of the winter of 1973/4 was followed by widespread retrenchment in the spending plans of the Labour government, between 1974 and 1979, and the personal social services were not immune from this.

Personal social services, 1979–1997

Three main themes dominated policies on the personal social services under the Conservative government: the growing importance of privatisation; the contribution of the voluntary sector and the promotion of self-help and self-care partly through the informal sector; and the introduction of internal markets and compulsory competitive tendering (CCT) under the Local Government Act 1988. Through CCT, local authorities were required to create the necessary budgetary and administrative apparatus in the 1980s for the spread of private contracting for services, from such areas as catering in schools and colleges and waste collection to community care. Paradoxically, just as in education policy Thatcherism combined devolution of budgets and privatisation with increased control through the National Curriculum (see Chapter 5), in the social services, while the welfare state was in retreat, central government control over standards of services was given an unprecedentedly high profile through the setting up of the Social Services Inspectorate (SSI) in the early 1980s and the Audit Commission alongside it, under the Local Government Finance Act (1982). The drive for the extension of entrepreneurialism and enterprise to the public sector was driven not just by the neo-classical, laissez-faire economics of the New Right, but also by the traditional Conservative urges to cut government spending and make services cost effective. The forcing ground for the extension of the model of devolving budgets, compulsory commissioning, contracting, purchase and provision of services was the new internal market, contract culture or mixed economy, for community care, recommended by the Griffiths Report (DHSS 1988) and legislated for under the NHS and Community Care Act 1990.

Private sector involvement has grown since the late 1980s, mainly in areas of child minding and nursery provision for children under five, residential and nursing homes for older people, residential and day care for people with disabilities, sheltered housing and community care. Yet, while direct provision by local authorities was being run down, they and central government retained responsibilities for regulating, inspecting and registering facilities and services.

As with the private sector, from the 1970s, charities and the wider voluntary sector have become inextricably part of the policymaking process and also essential contributors to service delivery. Many voluntary organisations – especially those with a self-help or user-led component – have memberships involving people receiving services. Organisations of disabled people and survivors of mental health treatment such as Survivors Speak Out have become increasingly influential. Under the Conservatives the voluntary sector was viewed as an important alternative to local authority provision, often being praised for being more flexible, responsive and innovative.

However, there were real problems with the development of the mixed economy of care. In particular there was the development of a 'contract culture', with both purchasers and providers of services tending to conform to contractual requirements, thus stifling the very diversity that the government had sought to introduce. At the same time, expenditure on the personal social services was increasing, doubling in cash terms for England from £4.7 billion gross in 1990/91 to £10 billion gross in 1997/98 (see Table 6.1).

Table 6.1 Gross local authority personal social services expenditure (England)

Year	Amount (£ billions)
1990/91	4.7
1991/92	5.1
1992/93	5.5
1993/94	6.3
1994/95	7.5
1995/96	8.4
1996/97	9.3
1997/98	10.0
1998/99	10.8
1999/2000	12.0
2000/2001	12.8

Source: Department of Health, Health and Personal Social Services Statistics (2003) Table E4

Personal social services since 1997

Decentralisation, popular in social work and social services in the 1980s, has found renewed favour in post-1997 Labour policies, for example, with the devolution of powers to Northern Ireland, Scotland and Wales and proposals for the introduction of regional assemblies in England and, from 2002 onwards, an initiative to establish foundation hospitals, owned and managed by local people. Advocates of the controversial foundation hospitals maintained that they would empower patients and local communities, while critics argued that they would be divisive, reintroducing competition and reinforcing hierarchical differentiation between a relatively small number of privileged institutions and the rest.

Such initiatives symbolise what some have seen as the Janus-faced nature of welfare policies of the Labour government. That is, they are oriented simultaneously towards the right and left, reflecting a pragmatic concern with sustaining support from traditional left-wing voters and strengthening support from middle class and business interests. Similarly, Labour's *New Contract for Welfare* (Department of Social Security 1998) promised work for those who could and social security for those who could not. Such policies go with the grain of conservatism by including an individualistic and punitive element, combined with an element responding to traditional Labour thinking and campaigns by long-established pressure groups such as the Child Poverty Action Group (CPAG), focusing on the alleviation of poverty and associated aspects of social exclusion through the Social Exclusion Unit.

From 1997 Labour set out to tackle social exclusion, including reducing dependence on the welfare state, shifting people from 'welfare to work' and replacing the so-called 'handout' culture with a 'hand-up' culture. These policies have the advantage of enhancing people's rights to jobs through acknowledging their responsibilities as citizens, but may be criticised for reducing people's entitlements to benefits that formerly were universalistic rather than means tested and selective.

The concept of **modernising government** in general, and welfare in particular, has been much used by Labour. In general, it is hard to object to the word 'modernisation'; it seems synonymous with progress and reform. In reality, the concept is contested and is used to justify a broad swathe of diverse policy changes in different parts of the public services, including education, health and social services. The modernisation agenda of government places the personal social services at the heart of a political and policy-based contradiction between the satisfaction of individual needs and wants and the achievement of social goals. It has brought the most significant shake-up to social services departments since their inception in the 1970s. Much of the impetus for proposed reforms to the social services was their poor reputation in the light of the huge number of inquiries and investigations of shortcomings in the quality of services, including highly emotional areas such as childcare and an apparent inability to learn lessons (see Policy eye 6.1). In April 2000 a new performance assessment system for social services functions was introduced, based on performance monitoring, review and inspection and was reported on a year later by the annual report of the Chief Inspector of Social Services Inspectorate, which noted the persistence of many shortcomings in services (Department of Health, Social Services Inspectorate 2001). At the same time the increases in expenditure seen under the Conservatives continued (Table 6.1).

The main vehicle for central policy formulation, control of implementation and research funding is the Department of Health, through legislation, quality assurance programmes such as Quality Protects, and management mechanisms and practice procedures to promote 'best value'. Quality assurance is now

Policy eye 6.1   Deaths of children

Among the highest profile criticisms of the personal social services have been those associated with the deaths of children. Four major reports from the past three decades serve as examples.

Maria Colwell – in 1973 seven-year-old Maria Colwell was beaten to death by her stepfather in Brighton. The incident triggered national debate over the care of children. The formal inquiry identified failure of communication and liaison between the agencies involved, with a lack of coordination and passing on of information. In addition, her social worker was blamed for a lack of knowledge and for mistaken decisions, with training being identified as an issue.

Jasmine Beckford – in 1984 Jasmine Beckford died after having been starved and battered to death by her stepfather in Brent. The inquiry blamed social workers for focusing on the parents rather than on children in their own right and for giving in to parents. Jasmine herself had been seen by a social worker only once in ten months.

Kimberley Carlile – in 1986, only two years after the Jasmine Beckford case, four-year-old Kimberley Carlile was starved and beaten by her stepfather in Greenwich. The inquiry found that her death should have been avoidable and concluded that four key social work and health staff in Greenwich had failed to apply the necessary skill, judgement and care.

Victoria Climbié – in 2000, eight-year-old Victoria Climbié died, after having been tortured and starved by her great-aunt, Marie-Therese Kouao, and Carl John Manning in Haringey. The inquiry heard that Victoria was seen by dozens of social workers, nurses, doctors and police officers before she died but all failed to spot and stop the abuse. The report of the inquiry described Victoria's death as a 'gross failure of the system' and made 108 recommendations designed to improve the situation.

geared to an ongoing programme of specifying and publishing standards in each service and monitoring and inspecting performance against them.

In his speech to the 2002 Labour Party annual conference, the Labour Prime Minister Tony Blair argued that: 'Just as mass production has departed from industry, so the monolithic provision of services has to depart from the public sector. Out goes the big state. In comes the enabling state' (*The Guardian*, 12 October 2002: 13). The 'modernised' and 'enabling state' has seen a significant shift away from the traditional social services department. Healthcare trusts, voluntary agencies and private businesses now provide most residential and community care. From the late 1990s local authorities have used reorganisations to abolish social services departments and to merge them with other departments such as housing. Symbolically, in 21st century-Department of Health statistics, the local authority social services department of the 1970s and 1980s is increasingly replaced by the euphemistic title of Council with Social Services Responsibilities. The social services workforce is changing and new roles are being taken on and shed, in areas such as work with young children, now shared with education departments, and community care, carried out jointly with health services. Yet social services retain the lead role in work with children and families: fostered and adopted children, those looked after by local authorities and children considered in need of protection, as well as vulnerable older people, people with physical and learning disabilities, people with mental health problems and young offenders.

Standards of social care are regulated by central government through the General Social Care Council (GSCC), following the Care Standards Act 2000. The Act also established a new National Care Standards Commission (NCSC) that began work in 2002 and which was intended to prevent future failures in care services. The widespread development of evidence-based practice in the health and social services, as well as in the criminal and youth justice systems, has been promoted using research and literature reviews of 'what works' to encourage excellence in evidence-based practice.

Labour has also sought to develop a restructuring of personal social services based around the individual, rather than in terms of the categories of need defined by agencies. This effectively implies:

- organising services around the needs and expectations of the service user rather than starting with a large bureaucracy providing services

- professional and organisational boundaries to be secondary to meeting these needs

- the creation of trusts mirroring healthcare trusts and jointly planning and delivering services across health, local authority education and social services

- care trusts bridging health and social services in offering services for adults and children's trusts

- further reliance on financing and resources linking the state with the voluntary and private sectors.

Aspects of social services

While it is arguable whether the achievements of the personal social services are outweighed by their chronic and widespread shortcomings, it is undeniable that in the decades since the inquiry into the death of Maria Colwell in 1973, social services and social work departments have presided over hundreds of catastrophic failures, often involving the deaths of children and other vulnerable people. The continued failure of social services departments to prevent further scandals in childcare, mental health and treatment of older and disabled people has been the subject of repeated public inquiries and attracts much adverse attention from the mass media. Concerns about defects in the quality of provision are often voiced by the two main bodies in England and Wales concerned with quality assurance in the social services: the Audit Commission and the Social Services Inspectorate (SSI). A joint review team was set up in 1996 to combine the working practices of the Audit Commission and SSI and to 'explore how the different components of a department's work contribute to successful outcomes for service users' (Audit Commission 2002: 2). In Wales, the Audit Commission works in partnership with the Social Services Inspectorate for Wales (SSIW) under the aegis of the National Assembly. The target is to complete 30 reviews a year in England and four or five annually in Wales.

People receiving services, such as mental health users and disabled people, have also criticised the failings of social services to take adequate account of their views and experiences, when taking decisions about the shape, nature and direction of current and future services. Critics of particular services argue that the welfare state has failed to reach specific groups of people, notably older people, lone parents, children and disabled people.

Policy in the personal social services in the 1970s was concerned with identifying and supporting 'problem' families; the provision of services for children in need; providing community care for disabled, mentally ill and older people formerly 'warehoused' in less than ideal residential, often institutional, settings; and reducing youth crime by developing effective ways of working with children and young people 'in trouble'. In future, it remains to be seen whether these categories of people with problems will lose their stigma. Current policy trends can be grouped around the three 'client-based' categories of services: family and childcare, community care and youth justice.

Family and childcare

About one-fifth of children in Britain live in poverty, that is, in a household with income below 60 per cent of the prevailing median income, which, in the absence of an official 'poverty line', might act as a reasonable index of poverty. By such measures, poverty rates among children in the UK remain among the highest in western Europe.

The Labour government's National Child Care Strategy aims to contribute to the long-term aim of abolishing child poverty by 2020. Part of the strategy aims to get lone parents back to work, offering Tax Credits to reduce and prevent poverty and reducing unemployment through the New Deal's incentives to work. Proneness to poverty in households is linked with unemployment of the adults, debt, poor housing, gender, race and disability. Combinations of these multiply a child or adult family member's chances of being poor. Poverty is associated also with social exclusion, social need, neglect and various forms of harm and abuse, all of which the government is attempting to tackle. To this end, there has been massive investment in family support and services for pre-school children, through the **Children's Fund** and **Sure Start**, although this is not followed by comparable services for parents with older children. About one child in 30 is officially defined as in need or neglected, one in 160 is being 'looked after' (the term which replaced 'in care') by a local authority and one in 400 is on a child protection register. The responsibility for all of these areas lies with social services.

Arguably, the family remains the foundation of welfare policy and for nearly half a century, social policy has been designed to preserve and support the traditional family form. Since the mid-1960s, Labour and Conservative governments have retained policies based broadly on traditional assumptions about the 'ideal' family, comprising heterosexual couples and children and the need to defend marriage. Despite the massive influence of feminist and social research on more critical social work and social services theories and practice, only in 2002, following strenuous parliamentary debates in both Houses, did the Labour government break with tradition and ensure that unmarried couples, including same-sex couples, could adopt children (Adoption and Children Act 2002).

The so-called 'problem family' also remained a target for social services for several decades, until the advent of consumerism and user empowerment from the late 1980s. 'Problem families' emerged in the 1960s as a prime target of childcare and family services. The 'problem family' was a term used by the Ingleby Committee, examined critically in three Fabian essays (Donnison, Jay and Stewart 1962) and embraced enthusiastically in the Longford Committee report which argued that whether a child was treated as depraved or deprived was often a matter of chance and that delinquency could be viewed as a particular form of deprivation (Labour Party Study Group 1964: 17). The new family-based service proposed by Longford was supposed to target social work at problem families, the apathetic and the ignorant and those maladjusted people who had fallen through the net of universalistic welfare provision. The essence of this argument fed into White Papers for England and Wales in 1965 and 1968 seeking to tackle the 'war on crime', the Kilbrandon Report for Scotland (Scottish Home and Health Department/Scottish Education Department 1964) and the Social Work (Scotland) Act 1968 and, in England and Wales, the Children and Young Persons Act 1969, which legitimated a welfare approach to the quasi-medical treatment of children deemed 'at risk' and 'in trouble'.

However, the landmark legislation for children remains the Children Act 1989, a notable success of Margaret Thatcher's Conservative government, for the way it brought together disparate strands of previous legislation and promoted children's interests. The Children Act 1989 gave legal status to the principle that children have the right to make their own choices and raised hopes that its comprehensiveness would safeguard children's interests. However, scandals over shortcomings and errors in childcare services continued. Continued concerns about failings in child protection led to Sir William Utting being commissioned to assess the adequacy of child protection measures under the Children Act (Utting 1997). The Children (Leaving Care) Act 2000 attempted to improve the support of children making the transition from residential care to living in the community. Yet within three years, the Laming Inquiry (Department of Health/Home Office 2003) into the death of Victoria Climbié confirmed continuing multiple failures of child protection management and practice in many agencies and made 108 recommendations aimed at raising the priority of child protection in police and social services and other agencies, improving standards of care for children, management, procedures, training and resourcing of services.

It is perhaps questionable whether any of the many inquiry reports, including the voluminous lists of recommendations by Waterhouse and Laming, will in the long run achieve as much significant change as the reorganisation of childcare services into childcare trusts, intended not to serve the interests of any organisation but to prioritise the interests of the child. Without this change, responsibility for children's policies and services would have remained even more stubbornly resistant to joined-up thinking. The Home Office, Transport, Education and Health departments plus local government (overseen by the Office of the Deputy Prime Minister) all retain responsibilities for children. However, in future, multi-professional collaboration and teamwork between different agencies and professions perhaps offer the probability rather than the certainty of major improvement in this aspect of child protection.

Community care

The NHS and Community Care Act 1990 was the single most influential piece of legislation affecting policy and practice in the personal social services passed by the Conservative governments of 1979 to 1997. It established a new market- and contract-based culture for commissioning, contracting and delivering services and created a template for involving local groups and interests in developing and regularly reviewing authority-wide community care plans. It also sought to stimulate managers and practitioners to develop more client- and carer-based approaches to care planning and community care provision.

However, many debates, problems and shortcomings have pervaded the implementation of community care. Fundamentally, in the face of restricted resources in local authority budgets, the much vaunted principles of partnership with people receiving services – widely called 'service users' – and the empowerment of citizens, espoused by governments since the inception of community care legislation in 1990, both remain intrinsically problematic goals.

In addition, one of the factors driving governments to develop community care policies is that residential care is relatively expensive. Yet policies driven by costs do not reflect on the relative quality of services or their benefits to clients and carers. Not every residential establishment is a total institution and not all community care is good-quality care. One person can live enjoyably and fulfilled in residential care; another can become institutionalised in a bed-sit in unsuitable, unsupported accommodation in the community.

It is also known that community caring impacts unequally on women. Despite legislation to improve the situation of carers (the Carers (Recognition of Services) Act 1995), they are more often than not women looking after relatives or young people who care for relatives with little prospect of adequate recompense or relief, especially if they live in a rural area remote from the nearest respite services.

Over and above these general concerns, particular issues arise in relation to services for disabled people, older people, people with mental health problems and mentally disordered offenders.

Disabled people

Policy has been influenced greatly by concepts such as normalisation (Wolfensberger 1972), asserting the right of disabled people to live a normal life, and by social role valorisation (Wolfensberger 1982), emphasising revaluing disabled people through their performance of socially valued roles. But this still implies that disabilities are deviations from the norm and that the disabled person is restricted by the disability and not just by social barriers. Shakespeare summarises the view of critics of disability policies that 'not only has the welfare state failed disabled people, but [. . .] the academic discipline of social policy has added insult to injury' (Shakespeare 2000: 52). He notes two divergent roots of the growing disability movement since the 1970s: first, among social policy academics in the Disability Alliance; and second, involving radical grass roots members of the Union of Physically Impaired Against Segregation. It has taken years of activism by the disability movement to establish more critical perspectives on policy and practice, but these are now starting to impact on a number of areas. One example of a significant power shift resulting from direct campaigns by disabled people is the Community Care (Direct Payments) Act 1996, enabling the handing over of responsibility for direct cash payments for services to specified categories of people entitled to community care, who are then able to make their own decisions about how best to use the money.

Older people

Since the late 20th century, there has been a dramatic increase, in absolute and proportionate terms, in the numbers of older people in society. Research makes it clear that not only children need protection. Older people are disproportionately likely to be abused and to suffer cumulative problems of being poor, badly housed, disabled and living alone. Yet, with an ageing population and restraints on public expenditure, services for older people have been under increasing pressure and the quality of services has been variable. The National Care Standards Commission (NCSC) published new national standards for care homes in 2001, with a view to enabling residents and caring relatives to know the minimum standards of care they could expect.

Policy eye 6.2   Long-term care for older people

In December 1997 the Labour government established a Royal Commission on Long-term Care for Older People, chaired by Professor Sir Stewart Sutherland. The Royal Commission's report was published in March 1999. The Commission concluded that the existing system required reform, being both overcomplex and failing to provide clarity about what people might expect. It recognised that the existing funding models often caused people to move into residential care when this might not be the best outcome and that, while financial aid was available to the poorest people, the system led to the impoverishment of people who had moderate assets before they received any help. The two main recommendations were:

● The costs of care for those individuals who need it should be split between living costs, housing costs and personal care. Personal care should be available after an assessment, according to need and paid for from general taxation: the rest should be subject to a co-payment according to means.

● The Government should establish a National Care Commission which will monitor longitudinal trends, including demography and spending, ensure transparency and accountability in the system, represent the interests of consumers, encourage innovation, keep under review the market for residential care, nursing care, and set national benchmarks, now and in the future.

However, after a long period of consideration the Westminster government agreed only to fund nursing care and even then only that given by a qualified nurse, rather than, say by a healthcare assistant. Personal care (help with eating, dressing, washing or using the toilet) would remain subject to means testing and would still have to be paid for by people judged to have sufficient money to do so.

In contrast, the Scottish executive agreed that for people living in Scotland personal care would be provided free, as well as nursing care.

The increasing cost of providing residential and nursing homes through the 1990s led many private residential establishments to close. There was continuing debate as to whether, and if so to what level, such care for less-well-off people should continue to be funded through social security. Controversies about how continuing, including long-term, care for older people should be paid for were heightened by the Report of the Royal Commission on Long-term Care for the Elderly (Sutherland 1999) (see Policy eye 6.2). This was not popular with the Westminster government for advocating that the state should fund all care of older people, while in contrast that recommendation was taken up by the Scottish Executive for implementation north of the border.

People with mental health problems

One in four families will include a person with mental illness at some point in the lifetime of current family members. Yet mental health legislation is only updated once in every generation (Mental Health Act 1959; Mental Health Act 1983). The emphasis of policy over the past 25 years has been on replacing hospital provision with mental health support for people in the community. People who have been treated as mentally ill, especially those in mental hospitals, have become increasingly vociferous since the late 1980s, through self-advocacy, pressure groups such as MIND and former hospital patients' organisations such as Survivors Speak Out, in advocating for their own rights to be safeguarded and needs met.

Mentally disordered people

Shortcomings in the supervision and support of mentally disordered offenders in the community have been documented in several well-publicised inquiries following cases such as that of Jonathan Zito, where a person discharged from a mental hospital has committed a serious criminal offence. A loophole in the treatability clause of the Mental Health Act 1983 means that while it contains legal powers for compulsorily detaining people with treatable mental disorders, people who are a known risk but who are classified as suffering from untreatable mental disorders, including those suffering from personality disorders, may be discharged.

There was controversy over government proposals in the mental health bill debated in parliament in 2002, which set out procedures whereby such people may be detained as a preventive measure, before they display further symptoms of illness or engage in any (further) criminal behaviour, on the basis of judgements by mental health professionals. The bill demonstrated the tension between protecting the public and the unwarranted criminalising of the individual. On one hand, there is the issue of the rights of people with mental disorders, opposing the extension of compulsory treatment, widening the definition of who should be locked up, resisting the incarceration of people purely on the grounds that they 'might' commit a violent or sex offence and creating and sustaining adequate treatment of them. On the other hand, there is the question of how to protect the community by ensuring compulsion and detention of the small proportion of mentally disordered people who present a genuine and serious risk to their own and other people's safety. This conflict is not easily resolved.

Youth justice

The youth justice system reflects official and public ambivalence towards offending juveniles. The Children and Young Persons Act 1969 straddled the twin goals of treating children in trouble by diverting them from the criminal justice system according to their welfare needs and curbing their problem behaviour through the punishment of the court. Britain is relatively punitive in terms of attitudes and responses to youth crime. Domestic physical chastisement of children by their parents is illegal in many countries, such as the Scandinavian states, but is still permitted in Britain. What is illegal for one adult to do to another is legal for an adult to do to a child. The age of criminal responsibility in also lower than in many other countries in western Europe – ten in England and Wales and eight in Scotland.

About one-quarter of all detected crimes are committed by young people under 17 and, since the early 1970s, social services departments have been involved in responding to the significant problems created by youth crime. High perceived levels of youth crime in some communities feed fears about people's safety in the community and increase pressures on policymakers to create tougher, including custodial, sanctions, despite public inquiries exposing abuses in residential regimes. There is also research evidence that custodial sentences are generally ineffective in reducing the likelihood of future criminal activity (Goldson 2000).

Among the significant volume of criminal justice legislation introduced by the Labour government have been measures aimed at tackling and, where possible, preventing youth crime, linked with wider programmes of community protection, urban regeneration and inclusion, this last under the aegis of the new Social Exclusion Unit. The Crime and Disorder Act 1998 introduced a centralised Youth Justice Board (YJB) overseeing 154 youth offending teams supplying youth justice services, consisting of about 10,000 members of multidisciplinary teams of practitioners, including social workers and other staff employed by social services agencies. The YJB introduced about 70 Youth Inclusion Programmes (YIPs) in 1999 on urban estates with high levels of crime. One of the government's aims is for YIPs to achieve a 70 per cent drop in arrest rates among 13 to 16 year olds at risk. Other measures introduced by the 1998 Act include a custodial detention and training order for children and young people aged 10–17.

The Youth Justice and Criminal Evidence Act 1999 brought in a referral panel aimed at first-time offenders and overseen by a youth offender panel. All existing sentencing options were codified by the Powers of Criminal Courts (Sentencing) Act 2000. The Criminal Justice and Police Act 2001 extended curfews to children under 16, empowering courts to impose secure remands on boys of 15 to 16 to prevent further offending. Such measures heightened criticism that Labour were merely extending the punitive, often custodial, sanctions policy of the previous Conservative government.

The initiative launched by the YJB in 2002 to identify 8 to 13 year olds considered at risk and target them for additional support for them and their families, while in some respects praiseworthy, can be criticised for lowering the age of criminal consent and sucking more young people into the criminal justice system. Such tensions and dilemmas are familiar in youth justice and generate questions with no easy answers: should offenders receive treatment matched to their needs or sentences reflecting simply the seriousness of their offences? Should custody and community safety or the treatment of the offender in the community be the first option?

Future policy in youth justice is likely to reflect government priorities for criminal justice as a whole, emphasising the three themes of crime reduction, tougher sentences for serious offenders and putting victims first. However, the dilemma will remain of convincing a generally punitive and intolerant press and public that sufficiently tough custodial, deterrent sanctions are in force against young offenders, while minimising the use of custody in the interests of effectiveness and extending the more positive use of penalties in the community in the interests of improving the life chances of the offender.

Drug misuse

Since the late 1980s, drug taking has increased sixfold among 14 to 15 year olds (Balding 1998), mostly among poorer and disadvantaged young people (Marlow and Pearson 1999). This has become an increasingly major concern for law enforcement, especially as rising levels of violence and crime are often attributed to the increasing incidence of drug addiction and, although no causal link is proved, about 70 per cent of young people on supervision have been reported to have taken illegal substances (Audit Commission 1996). Arguments for legalising use of **Class A drugs** such as heroin often rest on the assumption that this will reduce the level of criminality. Advocates claim that this would be a fast, cheap and practicable solution to the problem of rising crime, especially youth crime and 'gun crime'. In the late 1990s the Labour government set out to halve drug abuse through tougher policing and punitive criminal justice policies. In 2002 a major revision of policy took place with the emphasis shifting from punishment to treatment. Hard drugs would be available on prescription for registered addicts. Government spending up to 2005 would be increased by 50 per cent, with an additional £500m to be spent on treatment. Whether this would work was doubtful. Young black people, for instance, are not likely to take up drug services because of distrust of white agencies (Pearson and Patel 1998). However, drug treatment and testing orders (DTTOs) were introduced in 2000 for 16–17 year olds.

There are three main criticisms of government policy in this area: it responds to symptoms rather than tackling the social and environmental causes, such as the likelihood that young people experiencing social and economic deprivation are more than two dozen times more likely to become addicted to drugs; treatments such as counselling and cognitive-behaviourally based therapies can be accused of offering a revolving door, with about 90 per cent of drug users relapsing after 'harm minimisation' and behavioural and medical treatments that do not affect the material circumstances of their lives; there is a need for policies to be more 'joined up', with Home Office criminal justice policies linked with the government's initiatives to combat social exclusion, including linking drug treatment agencies with employment services, education and training opportunities and regeneration agencies.

Summary

This chapter has shown how, in a time of rapid change for the personal social services, some striking continuities run through the period. However, it also suggests that it would be a mistake to overplay either of these two dimensions of change or continuity. It has also demonstrated the range and difficulty of many of the areas with which the personal social services are involved. Overall it is possible to argue:

- The inception of the social services department in the early 1970s was not a revolution. It united separate strands of existing activity and made them more visibly connected. Subsequent history has deconstructed them again, a development entirely consistent with the fragmentation of other public services into independent agencies, private trusts and public private partnerships (PPIs), in the guise of making them more effective. Whether this evolution towards more dispersed models of funding, organisation, management and service delivery is an improvement remains to be evaluated in the light of implementation.

- The shape of social services is changing. Health and childcare trusts contribute to the blurring of organisational boundaries between health and social services as conceptual boundaries shift between treatment and care, therapy and intervention and practitioners such as social workers, district and community nurses and occupational therapists engage in more collaborative work and joint professional training. There are continued moves towards multi-agency arrangements to tackle key areas of practice such as child protection, using the model of the national Youth Justice Board and local youth offending teams. This may go some way towards the ideal of creating seamless multi-agency working by enabling policy and practice to become the shared responsibility of many agencies rather than solely that of social services departments. In the process, such centrally imposed models of organisation highlight the contradiction between government aspirations to enhance citizen control of services by local people and the centralisation of policy.

● A concern to safeguard and promote human rights, a genuine commitment to empowering the person receiving services and an ethic of care and an emancipatory politics may offer the best hope of developing a more critical basis than hitherto for delivering personal social services. History suggests that policies shaped exclusively by politicians and others who hold power and delivered by professionals remain unlikely to deliver adequate care services. People growing older, those with HIV/AIDS or suffering mental health problems and experiencing disability are unlikely to be satisfied with social policy responses to their circumstances, which continue to regard them as problems, subordinating, excluding and treating them as victims rather than as capable of self-empowerment and independent living.

Discussion and review topics

1 Why did generic social work fail to live up to the promises of its early days in the 1970s?

2 How successful have attempts been to create a greater role for the private and voluntary sectors in the provision of community care?

3 To what extent does the fact that much policy on the personal social services is made by central government and implemented by local government affect the development of services?

4 Is the tension between the controlling role of the personal social services and their attempts to empower people an inevitable barrier to their success?

Further reading

Adams, R. (2002) *Social Policy for Social Work*, Palgrave Macmillan, Basingstoke – provides an overview of the relationship between social policy and social work and the impact of policies as they affect professionals in the personal social services

Cavadino, M. and Dignan, J. (2001) *The Penal System: An Introduction*, Sage, London – gives an introduction to the penal system in England and Wales, including comparisons with those of other states

Fox Harding, L. (1997) *Perspectives in Child Care Policy*, Longman, Harlow – this book focuses on policies and values as they affect children

Orme, J. (2001) *Gender and Community Care: Social Work and Social Care Perspectives*, Palgrave Macmillan, Basingstoke – draws on feminist perspectives to analyse and understand community care policies, including exploring the uses of 'community' and 'caring'

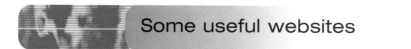

Some useful websites

www.communitycare.co.uk – *Community Care* magazine is a leading publication in the social care field. Its website provides a considerable range of information, including the ability to search for articles

www.doh.gov.uk – the Department of Health's website contains information on its work and responsibilities with regard to social care and links to other relevant sites

www.elsc.org.uk – the Electronic Library for Social Care, administered by the Social Care Institute for Excellence (*www.scie.org.uk*) provides links to other organisations, user groups and specialist services and to general social services information

www.ncsc.gov.uk – the National Care Standards Commission is responsible for the regulation of social care in England

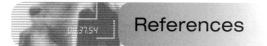

References

Audit Commission (1996) *Misspent Youth. Young People and Crime*, Audit Commission, London

Audit Commission (2002) *Tracking the Changes in Social Services in England: Sixth Overview Report of the Joint Review Team*, Audit Commission, London

Balding, J. (1998) *Young People and Illegal Drugs in 1998*, Schools Health Education Unit, London

Department of Health (2001) *Personal Social Services User Experience Survey 2000–2001*, Bulletin 2001/30, Department of Health, London

Department of Health (2003) *www.performance.doh.gov.uk/HPSS*

Department of Health/Home Office (2003) *The Victoria Climbié Inquiry: Report of an Inquiry by Lord Laming*, The Stationery Office, London

Department of Health, Social Services Inspectorate (2001) *Modern Social Services: A Commitment to Deliver, The 10th Annual Report of the Chief Inspector of Social Services 2000/2001*, Department of Health, London

Department of Health and Social Security (1974) *Report of the Committee of Inquiry into the Care and Supervision Provided in Relation to Maria Colwell*, DHSS, London

Department of Health and Social Security (1988) *Community Care: Agenda for Action*, HMSO, London

Department of Social Security (1998) *A New Contract for Welfare*, The Stationery Office, London

Donnison, D., Jay, P. and Stewart, M. (1962) *The Ingleby Report: Three Critical Essays*, Fabian Society, London

Goldson, B. (2000) *The New Youth Justice*, Russell House, Lyme Regis

Home Office (1960) *Report of the Committee on Children and Young Persons*, HMSO, London

Home Office (1964) *The War against Crime in England and Wales*, HMSO, London

Labour Party Study Group (1964) *Crime – A Challenge to Us All*, Labour Party, London

Marlow, A. and Pearson, G. (1999) *Young People, Drugs and Community Safety*, Russell House, Lyme Regis

Pearson, G. and Patel, K. (1998) 'Drugs, deprivation and ethnicity: outreach among Asian drug users in a northern English city', *Journal of Drug Issues*, 28, 199–224

Scottish Home and Health Department/Scottish Education Department (1964) *Children and Young Persons: Scotland*, HMSO, Edinburgh

Shakespeare, T. (2000) 'The social relations of care' in Lewis, G., Gewirtz, S. and Clarke, J. (eds) *Rethinking Social Policy*, Sage, London

Sutherland, Professor Sir S. (1999) *With Respect to Old Age: Long Term Care – Rights and Responsibilities*, Report of the Royal Commission on Long-term Care for the Elderly, The Stationery Office, London

Titmuss, R. M. (1979) 'Social work and social service: a challenge for local government' in Titmuss, R. M. (ed.) *Commitment to Welfare*, Allen & Unwin, London

Utting, Sir W. (1997) *The Report of the Review of the Safeguards for Children Living Away from Home*, The Stationery Office, London

Wolfensberger, W. (1972) *The Principle of Normalisation in Human Services*, National Institute of Mental Retardation, Toronto

Wolfensberger, W. (1982) 'Social role valorisation: a proposed new term for the principle of normalisation', *Mental Retardation*, 21, 234–9

Acknowledgement

The author would like to acknowledge the critical comments by Wade Tovey on an earlier draft of this chapter.

Crime and criminal justice policy

7

Dee Cook

Issues in Focus

In 1993, Shadow Home Secretary, Tony Blair promised that a future Labour government would be 'tough on crime, tough on the causes of crime'. Following on from that famous soundbite, this chapter will examine the extent to which criminal justice and social policies implemented since 'New Labour' was elected in 1997 have fulfilled that promise.

This task invariably raises the problematic question of the relationships between criminal justice and social justice: put simply, being tough on crime calls for the former and being tough on its causes evokes the latter. But it also raises questions about whether government policies in the 'criminal' and 'social' spheres are coherent, mutually supportive and 'joined up'.

This chapter will therefore:

- consider what is meant by the concepts of 'criminal justice' and 'social justice'

- examine inequality *of* justice – focusing on the operation and outcomes of the criminal justice system

- look at inequality *and* justice – focusing on social inequality and the broader social, economic and political context within which the criminal justice system functions

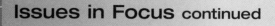

Issues in Focus continued

● examine the relationships between criminal justice and social policies under New Labour, focusing on varying interpretations of what constitutes 'the justice gap' in contemporary Britain.

Crime and criminal justice have long been a topical social and political issue. In the 1970s 'law and order' were an important part of the campaign that brought Margaret Thatcher into power with an agenda and policy responses that were largely punitive in nature. The emphasis for much of the 1970s and 1980s was primarily concerned with seeking to catch and punish offenders, rather than with attempts to rehabilitate them or to prevent offending. Little attention was paid to the social conditions which some argued were the source of much crime.

From the 1990s this concern with crime has remained high on the agenda, perhaps with particular emphasis on areas such as youth crime and 'anti-social behaviour'. Yet, this chapter suggests that there is a need to recognise that there are important links between the concept of 'criminal justice' and that of 'social justice' and in order to achieve the former it may be necessary to take account of the implications of the latter.

Defining criminal and social justice

Criminal justice

What do we mean by 'the criminal justice system'? In the context of England and Wales (in Scotland, the criminal justice service differs fundamentally and the bulk of this chapter deals with the system in England and Wales) the criminal justice system consists of:

● the Police Service: comprising 43 police forces

● the Crown Prosecution Service (CPS)

● the Courts Service: magistrates' courts, Crown Courts and appeal courts

● the Prison Service

● the National Probation Service

● the Criminal Injuries Compensation Service

● victim and witness care services.

(See also the discussion in Chapter 6 of youth justice.) According to the Home Office (*www.homeoffice.gov.uk/rds/cjschap1.html*), these agencies share two common aims, which are summarised in terms of:

● reducing crime and the fear and costs of crime

● dispensing justice fairly, thereby enhancing confidence in the rule of law.

But the extent to which the criminal justice system can meet these overarching aims is inevitably limited by broader structural and social inequalities, such as poverty, poor housing and education, ill health, unemployment and environmental decay, all of which have long been associated with both high crime rates and the likelihood of being a victim of crime. This has resulted in crime being seen as both an indicator and a cause of many of these negative features: in this way crimes such as burglary, theft, criminal damage and drug abuse are seen to indicate social exclusion and a limited 'quality of life' in many poorer neighbourhoods while, at the same time, they are also seen as part of the cause of those neighbourhoods' decline. Such areas thus become a key target for the interventions of both criminal justice and social policies (as will be discussed later).

In this social and spatial context, 'dispensing justice fairly' is also problematic because of the ways in which decisions are taken on who (and where) is policed and the consequences in terms of patterns of **criminalisation**. Criminal justice agencies, both directly and indirectly, tend to use stereotypes of crime-prone individuals, families, localities and ethnic groups which can lead to patterns of policing and punishment that are perceived as 'unjust' by local communities. And so, when policing resources are targeted on individuals, groups and localities who are defined by the police as 'a problem', arrests may well result. But these individuals and communities may well be alienated and tend to lack confidence in the CJS as a consequence (see later). In this way, the aim of 'dispensing justice fairly, thereby enhancing confidence in the rule of law' may be subverted by the routine working assumptions of criminal justice agencies about who and where is crime prone and where the deployment of their resources can yield best 'results'.

Social justice

Moving on to define the concept of 'social justice', one starting point could be the work of T. H. Marshall (1950), which sees social justice involving everyone enjoying the rights and duties of full citizenship. But, as is illustrated later, these rights can be illusory for many of the poor in contemporary Britain. While poverty itself is often defined as an outcome of 'lack of disposable income', social exclusion is a more dynamic and multifaceted process and is directly related to that of citizenship as it involves a 'breakdown of the major social systems ... that should guarantee full citizenship' (Berghman 1995: 20).

According to Marshall, citizenship comprises three essential elements: the civil; the political; and the social. The first is associated with the rule of law and includes freedom of speech and the right to justice. The second concerns the ability to participate in politics (by voting or standing for public office). The third includes: 'the whole range from the right to a modicum of economic welfare and security to the right to share in the full social heritage and to live the life of a civilised being according to the standards prevailing in the society' (Marshall 1981: 10). By examining the meaning of full citizenship we gain an insight into the links between poverty, citizenship and social exclusion. Briefing 7.1 indicates the ways in which full citizenship can effectively be denied by a range of inequalities that stem from a lack of civil, political, social and environmental rights. For example, criminal victimisation, restrictions in legal aid, unemployment, low pay, welfare benefit cuts, water debt, illness (mental and physical) and geographies of despair can all serve to deny the poor the experience of full citizenship.

But poverty is not the only condition that leads to social exclusion. For instance, many British citizens are excluded from full civil, political and social

---

Briefing 7.1   Citizenship: dimensions and denials

Dimensions of citizenship	Denials of citizenship
Civil and political: rights to	
Freedom of speech and association	Criminal victimisation
Freedom from discrimination	Racial harassment
Protection of the law	Public order laws and civil liberties
(for self and property)	Limited political participation
	Erosion of legal rights (to silence, to counsel, to fair trial, to trial by jury)
Social and economic: rights to	
Education	Inequalities in the provision and
Housing	quality of: education, healthcare,
Healthcare	housing, transport and social amenities
Own property	Unemployment
Consume goods and services	Underemployment and low pay
Work and participation in	Erosion of benefit levels
economic life	Restricted access to welfare benefits
An income (welfare 'rights')	Policing of (and for) the family
Environmental: rights to	
The benefits, in amenity and in	Poverty, sickness, mortality and disease
health, of a safe and clean	Geographies of despair
environment	Urban and rural pollution

Source: Adapted from Cook (1997: 30)

participation through institutional racism. The growing incidence of **racial harassment** and attacks (particularly since 11 September 2001) shows that for many black and Asian subjects, even the basic 'negative' right to walk the streets freely, without fear or harassment, is illusory. In 1999/2000 there were 47,814 such incidents reported to and recorded by the police. But, in the same year, the British Crime Survey estimated that 280,000 such incidents took place.

Following on from Marshall, another perspective on social justice was offered by Rawls (1971) who proposed that 'justice as fairness' could be represented by deciding on how to divide up a cake without knowing how big a slice you would get yourself. More than two decades on, the independent Commission on Social Justice was established (under the auspices of the Institute for Public Policy Research) to document the extent of social inequality in Britain and to set out a vision of social justice. It acknowledged that the term itself involved ideas about equality, need, entitlement, merit and desert and that although most people said they believed in social justice, their ideas were complex and indeterminate (Commission on Social Justice 1993). It went on to outline some basic principles which help to flesh out what social justice would actually mean, at the levels of both the individual and wider society. These principles of social justice can be seen in Briefing 7.2.

If we return to the basic aims of the criminal justice system as outlined earlier, they too depend on very similar foundations, both having their roots in the concepts of citizenship and legitimacy. Without ensuring the equal worth of all citizens, mutual and self-respect and the meeting of basic needs, we cannot ensure that all have an equal stake in abiding by the law and so cannot 'dispense justice fairly' and enhance confidence in the law. In this respect criminal and social justice are inseparable.

Briefing 7.2   Principles of social justice

The foundation of a free society is the equal worth of all citizens.

All citizens are entitled, as a right of citizenship, to be able to meet their basic needs – for income, food, shelter, education and health.

Self-respect and personal autonomy are inherent in the idea of equal worth, but their fulfilment depends on the widest possible spread of opportunities and life-chances.

Inequalities are not necessarily unjust – but those which are should be reduced and where possible eliminated.

Source: Commission on Social Justice (1993: i)

Inequality of justice

How does the criminal justice system work in practice?

If we envisage the criminal justice system as a set of filters located at various stages of the process (from decisions to police, arrest, prosecute, sentencing choice and ultimately to the 'hard end' of imprisonment), then the ways in which it operates can be seen to filter in certain individuals and groups, while it filters out others. These processes are evident in, for instance, the differential treatment of what could be termed **'white-collar' offences** and 'traditional' offences (including 'street crime', assaults, theft and handling stolen goods, burglaries etc.) and the ways in which they are (or are not) processed through the system.

First, there are differences in the visibility of these two types of offence, with many 'traditional' crimes taking place in public spaces or with the chance of observation by victim or bystander and with evidence in the domestic or public domain. This also shapes policing practices (as we have already seen), which focus on those areas and communities perceived as crime prone. By contrast, white-collar offences are hidden within private (or cyber)spaces and even the victims are unaware of their commission (as in the case of recent investment and pension fund scandals) and crucial evidence is held by the offenders themselves.

Second, the 'letter of the law' differs: when it comes to regulating business and commerce the law itself is extremely complex, which raises difficulties in proving cases. Consequently, regulators often opt for 'compliance strategies' that aim to persuade the offender to comply with legislation in future, often by using warnings, penalties and informal justice, as opposed to seeking redress through the criminal justice system.

Third, the decision to prosecute (or not) can also be influenced by the offender's ability to pay for their crime. Business and white-collar criminals may 'pay' through informal justice (particularly as many companies do not want the adverse publicity accompanying a court case). In the unlikely event that they are prosecuted, such offenders can afford expert legal advice and their counsel may argue that they are of good character and so have 'paid' enough because of their shame at being brought before the court in the first place. The same means of 'filtering out' of the criminal justice system are not available to many poorer offenders, who are seen (almost by definition) to be of bad character and thus have 'nothing to lose' except their liberty.

Finally, poorer and 'traditional' offenders are likely to be seen by the police, courts and the public as more of a threat to society than their richer counter-parts. A range of negative social indicators may apply to them: young and male, unemployed, living in a 'bad' estate, 'bad' family connections, a 'bad' (often lone) mother. All these indicators may be compounded where the alleged offender is from a visible ethnic minority group.

Taken together, the logic and decisions of criminal justice agencies prove decisive in filtering the traditional offender in and the white-collar offender out of the criminal justice system. Consequently, many would argue that there is still 'one law for the rich, another for the poor' in 21st-century Britain, even when the crimes committed are of a similar nature. To take one example, there are differing outcomes when relatively rich taxpayers defraud the public purse through tax evasion and when the poor commit benefit fraud. In 2001 there were 11,000 prosecutions for benefit frauds, compared with just 70 for tax fraud (of these, almost half referred to internal Inland Revenue frauds and just 27 prosecutions referred to what most of us would understand by tax evasion – making false statements on tax returns. The remainder were for offences relating to thefts of cheques, forged exemption certificates etc.). Ironically, in the previous year, Lord Grabiner's influential report on regulating the (illegal) hidden economy had concluded that 'for tax evasion, the current system seems to work well' (Grabiner 2000: 24). Given the chances of being investigated and prosecuted, it seems that the system does indeed work well – for tax evaders!

But, at the same time, 'the system' works less well for the poor who are much more likely to be (welfare) policed, investigated and prosecuted. Moreover, while high-profile publicity campaigns target the evils of benefit fraud (see, for example, *www.targetingfraud.gov.uk*), there is little official recognition that up to £4 billion in benefits goes unclaimed each year (Office of National Statistics 2001).

The case of 'race' and criminal justice

The outcomes of differential CJS practices are not just a matter of unequal economic status – being 'rich' or 'poor': they are also vividly illustrated through an examination of the treatment of individuals from minority ethnic groups as they are processed through the CJS.

As mentioned earlier in this chapter, negative social indicators are compounded where suspects and offenders are from visible ethnic minority groups, particularly when they are black. (Ethnicity categories, as used by the 2001 Census are: 'White', 'Mixed', 'Indian', 'Pakistani/Bangladeshi', 'Black Caribbean', 'Black African', 'Chinese', 'Other'.) Not surprisingly, recent surveys on the extent of confidence in the criminal justice system indicate a falling off of public confidence, particularly in the police, which is markedly so in the case of black and minority ethnic communities. This may be partly due to bad experiences of contact with the police, particularly in relation to their responses to racial harassment (often seen as inadequate) and to stop and searches (often seen as too frequent and intrusive). In the London Metropolitan police area in 2001 the number of recorded stop and searches rose by 8 per cent for white people, but increased by 30 per cent for black people and 40 per cent for Asians. Disproportionate use of stop and search is also evident at national level. A total of 714,000 stops and searches were recorded by police in 2000/1: 12 per cent were on black people and 6 per cent on Asian people (Home Office 2002a: 13–14). Lack of confidence in the criminal justice system may also be partly due to relatively low recruitment of minority ethnic officers in key agencies such as the police, courts and prisons.

Where the relationship between ethnicity and imprisonment is concerned, the data also show worrying disparities. The latest figures on the ethnic breakdown of the prison population in England and Wales (in December 2002, when the population totalled 69,612) focus on 'British nationals' in prison and so omit numbers of non-British prisoners. The breakdown of British nationals in prison in England and Wales, compared with their representation in the overall population, is shown in Policy eye 7.1.

Source: www.CartoonStock.com

Policy eye 7.1   Minority ethnic prisoners, December 2002

75 per cent were 'white', compared with 95 per cent in the general population.

12 per cent were 'black', compared with 1 per cent in the general population.

3 per cent South Asian (that is, Indian, Pakistani or Bangladeshi), compared with 3 per cent in the general population.

2 per cent Chinese or other ethnic groups, compared with 1 per cent in the general population.

Source: Home Office (2003a: 18)

From these figures, it is clear that at the end of 2002, 'black' Britons were 12 times overrepresented in the prison population, while 'white' Britons were statistically underrepresented. As already argued, this disparity cannot merely be explained by different offending patterns of the groups concerned and the implications of this are acknowledged by the Home Office:

> A modern, fair effective criminal justice system is not possible whilst significant sections of the population perceive it as discriminatory and lack confidence in it delivering justice ... We need to get behind the numbers to understand the process through which discrimination may be occurring in the CJS.
>
> Home Office (2002a: 1)

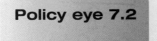

Policy eye 7.2   Race and the criminal justice system

Indian, Pakistani and Bangladeshi people are more likely to be victims of crime.

People from minority ethnic communities are more likely to be victims of racially motivated offences.

The police are less likely to identify suspects for homicides involving black victims.

Ethnic minority victims are less likely to be satisfied with the police response rate.

People from minority ethnic groups are more likely to be stopped and searched.

They are more likely to be arrested.

Black people are less likely to receive a caution than Asian or white people.

People from minority ethnic communities are more likely to be remanded in custody.

They are more likely to plead not guilty.

They are also more likely to be acquitted.

Black people are less likely to be sentenced to fines or a discharge and more likely to receive a community penalty.

Partly as a result of the above (proceeding through the possible/available sentences more quickly than their white counterparts), black people represent a disproportionate proportion of the prison population.

For violent offences, the rate of custody is higher for black and Asian offenders.

Minority ethnic prisoners are less likely to be released on parole.

But they have lower re-conviction rates than their white counterparts.

Source: Home Office (2002a: 2–10)

Nevertheless, Policy eye 7.2 (which summarises the finding of this document in relation to the issue of race and criminal justice) makes these processes fairly clear to the reader.

As argued earlier, the underlying assumptions and the working practices of policing, prosecution, sentencing and custodial regimes, when taken together, disproportionately filter poor, urban dwelling, young (and often black), males through to the hard end of the system – and into custody.

Inequality and justice

This section considers the broader social, economic and political context within which the criminal justice system operates.

What (and who) is the crime problem?

We need to start by asking how the problems of crime and social disorder (as they are increasingly being linked) are being framed within popular and political discourses. Most obviously, the 'crime and disorder problem' in contemporary Britain is often defined in terms of the characteristics of those offenders who have been detected, prosecuted and ended up in prison. However, this is extremely limited, not least because the British Crime Survey estimated that the majority – 58 per cent – of crimes are not reported to the police. Of those crimes that are reported and then recorded, only 23 per cent were detected by the police in 2001/2 (Simmons et al. 2002). Clearly then, the characteristics of the minority of offenders whose crimes are detected, successfully prosecuted and then sentenced is hardly a sound basis for extrapolating what constitutes the crime problem and its source. Nevertheless, politicians, the criminal justice system and the media all produce and reproduce stereotypes of who and what is the crime problem, dubiously based on the characteristics of known offenders.

Politics of imprisonment

The prison population has risen dramatically over the past ten years (and the last five in particular). In June 2003 this population stood at 73,627, consisting of 71,472 males and 4,924 females, housed in accommodation certified as 'normal' for 66,493 (despite an unprecedented prison-building programme, overcrowding remains). This steep rise is evidenced in the snapshot figures in Table 7.1. But the reasons for this increase are not directly related to any upsurges in the crime rate. Rather, it is the logical consequence of penal politics: policies which call for tougher and longer (sometimes mandatory) sentencing better explain and sustain this increase in the prison population, independent of any changes in patterns of crime and offending outside the prison walls.

Table 7.1 Prison population, selected years 1993–2003 (England and Wales)

Year	Number in gaol
1993	44,570 (average)
1997	61,114 (average)
2001	66,300 (average)
2003	73,627 (at 27 June 2003)

Source: Adapted from White (1998) and Home Office (2003b)

An increase in imprisonment is not therefore simply a result of more crimes being committed and more criminals being caught – and it is not politically neutral. To put this into a wider (European) policy context, we can compare the use of custody in England and Wales with that of our European Union partners. If the use of custody in England and Wales were at the European median (the rate most frequent within the EU, which stands at 84 per 100,000 of the population), this would have given us a prison population of under 49,000 in 2002, the year when it actually exceeded 70,000 for the first time (Sparks and Spencer 2002: 54).

Some criminologists have argued that imprisonment may ultimately serve to manage and control what may be termed 'problem populations', so that: 'These "problem populations", unrequired by the productive process, but actually or symbolically threatening it, become perceived as nuisances eligible for state intervention' (Box 1987: 129). In turn, these problem populations may be seen as 'social junk' in need of management (the old, sick, mentally ill) or 'social dynamite', in need of control (the unemployed, lone mothers, young people in general and young men and women from minority ethnic groups in particular) as they are seen to present 'an acute problem of social control because they are actually or potentially ... troublesome' (Box 1987: 130). Certainly, these groups are overrepresented in the prison population.

Moving on to the characteristics of prisoners, some of the characteristics of 'problem populations' begin to emerge. As we have already seen, 'race' or ethnicity is one key factor that serves to filter people into the CJS. The Home Office acknowledges other kinds of risk factor that are likely to propel the vulnerable poor towards imprisonment and to repeat offending when they confirm the following summary research finding (see Policy eye 7.3).

Vulnerability may also take the form of mental ill health and here, too, there is overrepresentation within the prison population. A survey for the Office for National Statistics in 1997 (Singleton et al. 1997), found that:

- 10 per cent of men who were remanded in custody, 7 per cent of sentenced men and 14 per cent of all women prisoners had suffered from a functional psychosis (such as schizophrenia and manic depression) in the past year

- 40 per cent of male sentenced prisoners suffered from a neurotic disorder (such as anxiety, depression and phobias), compared with 14 per cent in the general population

- 59 per cent of remanded men and 76 per cent of remanded women had a neurotic disorder.

If these findings were applied to the prison population in 2001, they would have meant that around 5,300 prisoners were suffering from functional psychosis and 30,000 from a neurotic disorder (with some of those suffering from both conditions). Once again, this raises issues concerning the 'justice' of imprisonment, particularly for the significant proportion of inmates who suffer from mental illness and who are likely to be in need of treatment rather than punishment.

But, it is argued, punishment does not stop with the end of a term of imprisonment: the legacy of being a prisoner shapes life on the outside. The Institute for Public Policy Research (Sparks and Spencer 2002) noted that having a criminal record does not only make it difficult to get a job, but also

Policy eye 7.3   Risk factors – of custody and of reconviction

Unemployment doubles the chances of criminal reconviction.

Homelessness increases the likelihood of reconviction by two and a half times.

Almost three-fifths of those sent to prison are unemployed when they are sentenced; 90 per cent are estimated to leave prison without a job.

Around a third of prisoners lose their homes when they go to prison.

Two-fifths will be homeless on release.

In turn, homelessness is associated with risks around the sex industry and drug abuse.

Between 25 and 33 per cent of rough sleepers have been 'looked after' in local authority care.

'Looked after' children [see Chapter 6] are themselves disproportionately likely to end up in prison and as teenage parents.

Source: Cabinet Office (2001); Home Office (2001)

makes it difficult to open bank accounts, get a mortgage and even home contents insurance and frequently automatically leads to a poor credit rating. The Chief Executive of NACRO (the National Association for the Care and Resettlement of Offenders) persuasively argues that: 'There is something fundamental about the need for a system which is claiming to be a system of justice to operate justly itself.' Not only is injustice demonstrated by discrimination in the operation of the CJS, but 'double or triple punishment' after prison is also fundamentally unjust (*Safer Society*, 13, Summer 2002, 20).

So, what *is* 'the crime problem'?

Criminal justice (and, increasingly, social) policies are driven by political imperatives that deploy a very particular definition of what actually constitutes 'the crime problem'. For instance, the criminal justice priorities outlined in the 2002 Queen's speech indicated that legislation would follow on the 'problems' of anti-social behaviour (litter, graffiti, spray painting and dangerous use of fireworks), but there was no mention of the legislation that had been expected on domestic violence and corporate killing. Overwhelmingly, for this government (as its predecessors), 'the crime problem' appears to be seen in terms of the behaviours of the poor – and particularly the young poor – who inhabit the most deprived neighbourhoods.

Days after his success in the 2001 general election, the Prime Minister, Tony Blair, announced his intention to take action against persistent offenders whom he regarded as 'the core of the crime problem in this country'. He argued that many were under 21, were users of hard drugs, out of work and that more than one-third were in care as children. He also noted that many had no educational qualifications and that nearly half had been excluded from school. However, others would ask, 'what is the problem here'? Is it the criminal behaviours of individual persistent offenders or the conditions within which it is possible for (young) people to 'slip through the net' and suffer such appalling multiple deprivations as these? Policy action – in terms of both criminal justice and social policies – is geared far more to the former than the latter.

Taking these known risks of crime and reoffending seriously would not be a cheap policy option – for example, it would involve developing well-funded national strategies for residential care and housing for young people. But instead of acknowledging the linkages between social and criminal justice policies, the current focus is almost entirely on the criminal justice system – low police detection rates, slow and ineffective court procedures, conniving solicitors and defendants – as the source of what is now termed 'the justice gap' (see later) rather than the inequities of the wider society.

Vexed issue of the 'causes of crime'

Contemporary images and assumptions about crime and offenders continue to tap into a rich historical vein – from the 'dangerous classes' of the 19th century to the 'underclass' of the late 20th, the poor have been portrayed as a threat to both law and social order. But it is important to stress that the 'poverty causes crime' argument is an over-simplistic one. Poverty may indeed be one source of crime: for example, women who engage in prostitution overwhelmingly do so because of poverty and the 'narrowing options' available to sustain themselves and their families (Carlen 1988; Phoenix 1999) and the same is the case for most offences of social security fraud (Cook 1989). But poverty in itself is not a sufficient explanation for crime – not least because the majority of the poor are not criminals and much crime is committed by non-poor individuals and by wealthy corporations. What research evidence *does* indicate is that the extent of social inequality – the gap between 'the haves and the have-nots' – does relate to the commission of crime, both by the rich and the poor alike (Box 1987; Cook 1997).

Similarly, unemployment cannot be seen to 'cause' crime, although it may lead to criminalisation: Stephen Box argued that while unemployment and imprisonment were linked, we should not look at crime and conviction rates, but instead it was essential to critically examine the *nature* of that link: 'the *belief* that "unemployment causes crime" and how this belief directly or subtly affects judicial sentencing practice, probation officers sentencing recommendations, and police deployment, apprehension, arrest and prosecution policies' (Box 1987: 158 [emphasis in original]).

In addressing the causes of crime, then, it is not enough to look for monocausal explanations because the 'causes of crime are multiple and complex'. It is also essential to address issues of subjectivity – how people perceive and interpret their situation – which is itself produced within an economic and social context, as this quote indicates:

> A 'me first' selfishness has been driven by a social system that produces not just deprivation, but also a situation in which those who are deprived are being told they are worthless in a society which is linked very strongly to materialism . . . If you've got a social and economic system that produces deprivation then that increases the risk of higher crime rates; if you have a social and economic system that produces deprivation plus greed then that virtually guarantees higher crime rates.
>
> Paul Cavadino, Chief Executive of NACRO, *Safer Society* (2002: 13, 18)

Once again, inequality is a key factor in driving crime, but how this inequality is internalised and 'felt' is important too. The importance of all of these issues is usefully summarised by Jock Young:

> [T]he crime rate is affected by a large number of things: by the level of deterrence exerted by the criminal justice system to be sure, but also by the levels of informal control in the community, by patterns of employment, by types of child-rearing, by the cultural, political and moral climate, by the level of organised crime, by the patterns of illicit drug use etc. etc. And to merely add together all these factors is complicated enough but insufficient for it does not allow human assessment and

reflexivity – the *perceived* injustice of unemployment, for instance, or the *felt* injustice of bad policing or imprisonment.

Young (1997: 33 [emphases in original])

Clearly, the multiple and various 'causes of crime' add up to more than just the 'sum of its parts' and there is an additional and pressing need to take human reflexivity into account. At the same time it is important to recognise that the 'deterrence' exerted by the criminal justice system is not something we can be 'sure' of at all. Even if we are persuaded by the logic of deterrence, it may operate very variably in practice. Deterrence theory is rooted in a rational calculation of risks – risks of detection, prosecution and subsequent punishment. But, as we have seen, such risks are not only perceived very differently by certain individuals and groups within our society, but are very differently experienced too.

Redefining the 'justice gap'

Crime, disorder and social exclusion

Criminal justice and social policy at the onset of the 21st century remains focused on the themes and imagery of the past two centuries – problem populations and the problem neighbourhood. But the vocabulary has changed: policy now focuses on the language of social inclusion and neighbourhood renewal as key means of addressing crime. The principle means through which policy is implemented is through (allegedly) 'joined-up' and partnership working of (local)-based community safety strategies and the (national) neighbourhood renewal unit. The government's own social inclusion strategy has indicated the need for integration of these strategies, both at local and national levels, to tackle problems such as crime, drug misuse, unemployment and poor schooling and to replace them with a 'virtuous circle' of regeneration where improvements in employment, crime, education, health and housing would reinforce one another (Social Exclusion Unit 1998).

Crime, various aspects of what is termed 'anti-social behaviour', and social exclusion are fused within these discourses. Not only do criminal justice and social policies become intertwined, but so also do the objects of those policies: the lexicon of criminal justice, crime reduction and community safety policies have effectively been extended to encompass a range of (non-criminal) activities under the umbrella of 'anti-social behaviour'. But while criminal justice and social policies have been 'shackled' together, it is notable that a higher degree of influence is accorded 'to crime prevention – as opposed to poverty prevention' (Crawford 1998: 121).

What is the 'justice gap'?

Bringing offenders to justice is the best way of demonstrating to criminals that their crimes will not go unpunished, and to victims that the criminal justice system is acting effectively on their behalf. But there is a justice gap.

Home Office (2002b)

The gap that is being referred to here in the government's framework document for criminal justice (itself entitled *Narrowing the Justice Gap*) is that too few offenders are being caught, brought to court and punished. The taskforce that produced this framework sought to identify the causes of the justice gap and ways of addressing it. The strategy for achieving this focuses on three aims, namely to:

- overcome weaknesses in the overall criminal justice process – encouraging better practice and interagency coordination at local levels

- tackle particular types of offence – such as the street crime initiative

- tackle particular types of offender – in particular the Persistent Offender Scheme that was due to commence in 2003.

But it is possible to present an alternative view of what constitutes the 'justice gap' in contemporary Britain. This would consist of two strands: first, the unequal application of the law, policing and punishment which, when taken together, serve to filter the poor and vulnerable into the criminal justice system while filtering out the rich and the successful; and second, the bigger issue of how it can be possible to achieve criminal justice in the absence of social justice, itself entailing the elimination of unjust social inequalities.

If the New Labour government which, in opposition in 1993, promised to be tough on crime and its causes is serious about this aim, it needs to acknowledge the longstanding evidence that high levels of inequality are positively related to crime and go on to tackle widening income, wealth and social inequalities. As inequality creates the conditions within which crime (committed by the rich and the poor) flourishes, then we have to realise that British social and criminal justice policies have to be reconciled. Thus far, they have been pulling in very different directions.

For example, in relation to economic inequalities, not only does the UK have the most regressive personal tax regime in Europe, but the Prime Minister has been dismissive about the redistribution of income and wealth. For example, speaking on television before the 2001 general election, Tony Blair stated that: 'It is not a burning issue for me to make David Beckham earn less money.' But if Blair were serious about social justice and reducing social inequalities (which are associated with crime), this is exactly the kind of policy response that would be required to narrow the justice gap.

As outlined in Chapter 3, since 1997 Labour in government has used the tax and social security systems to achieve a measure of redistribution of wealth

Policy eye 7.4   Monitoring poverty* and social exclusion: selected findings

In 2000/1 there were 12.9 million people below the poverty threshold (after deducting housing costs). This marks a fall of 1 million since 1996/7.

Although this fall has brought the numbers in poverty back to those of 1995/6, the number of people below the low-income threshold is still almost double that of 20 years ago.

Nearly half of those with incomes below the threshold were in households where someone was in paid work (low pay remains a deeply problematic issue, particularly for women).

The depth of poverty among non-working households was severe: 2.5 million people were more than £50 per week short of the threshold and four out of ten of them were £100 short.

One in five of the poorest households does not have any type of bank or building society account (the same as in 1994/5).

Two-thirds of heads of households in social housing do not have paid work (the same as a decade ago).

People in low income households are twice as likely to say that the quality of their life is significantly affected by the fear of crime.

While numbers of burglaries reported to the police continues to decline, lone parents and households headed by young people (aged 16–24) are three times more likely to be burgled.

*Here 'poverty' is defined by the UK government and the EU in terms of low income, that is, income which falls below 60 per cent of median income.

Source: Joseph Rowntree Foundation (2002)

from the rich to the poor, but those not in work have continued to suffer greatly from inequality. Thus, while the dual-mega-income Beckhams were doing very nicely, around 85 per cent of lone mothers on Income Support were struggling to repay social fund loans.

The latest data available to monitor the government's social inclusion strategy (for 2000/1) indicate some improvement in relation to income poverty. This may be partly due to the initial impact of two important policy measures: Working Families Tax Credit (WFTC) and the establishment of a National Minimum Wage (introduced in 1998). But there is still a very long way to go, as Policy eye 7.4 indicates.

How to narrow the gap?

To address the 'gap' in both criminal and social justice we need to examine the nature of the problem, initially of criminal justice. According to one influential policy group, the IPPR, it surrounds the nature and scope of the criminal law itself:

> There is an inherent contradiction between the relentless extension of the criminal law and social inclusion. NO society should be criminalizing one third of adult men, nor children as young as ten. WE know that the factors leading to crime, and the factors deterring offending behaviour, bear little relation to the impact of the criminal law. Its time to look for alternative strategies.
>
> Sparks and Spencer (2002: 60 [emphases in original])

The IPPR report (Sparks and Spencer 2002) suggests a range of policy options which include:

- changes to criminal law and the use of innovative new and civil remedies

- limiting the introduction of new criminal offences

- the need to restore confidence in the CJS

- encouraging shared responsibility in addressing crime (which entails greater public and corporate involvement)

- to recognise that imprisonment should be a last resort (as it is clearly the antithesis of social inclusion)

- a dramatic reduction in the use of imprisonment

- fundamental to all of the above, a respect for human rights and the rights of the child.

Summary

This chapter has considered the concepts of criminal justice and social justice and the relationship between them. It is evident that many of the issues have roots that go back for long periods of time, but that, in general, responses to 'the crime problem' have neglected the social justice dimension. Nevertheless the chapter has suggested that:

- The criminal justice system acts as a system of filters that draws some individuals and groups in while others are deflected out and this has a strong tendency to differentiate between 'traditional' and 'white-collar' offenders.

- 'Race' is a major influence on the workings of the criminal justice system, with people from ethnic minority groups, and particularly black people, being more likely to be involved with the system at stages from those such as 'stop and search' to imprisonment; they are more likely to be the victims of racially motivated crime; and those from some groups are more likely to be the victims of crime.

- The use of imprisonment is not politically neutral. The United Kingdom jails more people than other EU states. An examination of the characteristics of the prison population raises significant questions over the justice of imprisonment.

- If we really expect people – rich or poor – to obey the law and respect the rights and property of others, we should demonstrably provide them with laws that protect people equally, laws which are equitably applied to all; penalties for lawbreaking which are both justified and appropriate; and penalties that are equally applied to all.

- To narrow the *real* justice gap we should acknowledge that social and criminal justice are inseparable: fully social citizenship means that we *all* should enjoy the rights and duties of full citizenship – civil, political, social, economic and environmental. Thus far, New Labour policy has focused on trying to raise the 'floor' of poverty but has rejected the possibility of reducing the 'ceiling' of income and wealth. Until the wide disparities of income, wealth and rights of social and legal citizenship are seen as '*the* problem', the real justice gap will remain.

Discussion and review topics

1 How true is it that there is 'one law for the rich and another for the poor' in the 21st-century United Kingdom?

2 Why is 'race' such a significant factor in the criminal justice system?

3 Is it possible to consider the criminal justice system without reference to some notion of social justice?

4 What might governments usefully do to help tackle the 'justice gap'?

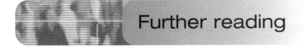

Further reading

Bowling, B. and Phillips, C. (2002) *Racism, Crime and Justice*, Pearson, Harlow – brings together a range of ideas and evidence to illustrate the impact of race and racism in the criminal justice system

Cook, D. (1997) *Poverty, Crime and Punishment*, Child Poverty Action Group, London – this book critically examines the relationship between poverty and crime, including the reasons for committing crimes and the punishment of crime

Croall, H. (2001) *Understanding White-Collar Crime*, Open University Press, Buckingham – takes a broad approach to the concept of white-collar crime, including definitions, extent, regulation and punishment

Maguire, M., Morgan, R. and Reiner, R. (eds) (2002) *The Oxford Handbook of Criminology*, Oxford University Press, Oxford – a substantial work, this book contains a wide variety of chapters looking at different aspects of crime, justice and punishment

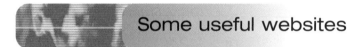

Some useful websites

www.cjsonline.gov.uk – the Criminal Justice System website is intended to provide access to information about the criminal justice system on the internet. It also provides links to many other relevant organisations

www.homeoffice.gov.uk – the Home Office provides information and links to a number of websites dealing with crime reduction, community safety, policing, the Prison Service and more

www.nacro.org.uk – NACRO is a charity that aims to reduce crime and the NACRO website provides information about the work of the organisation and access to publications

References

Berghman, J. (1995) 'Social exclusion in Europe: policy context and analytical framework', in Room, G. (ed.) *Beyond The Threshold: The Measurement and Analysis of Social Exclusion*, Policy Press, Bristol

Box, S. (1987) *Recession, Crime and Punishment*, Macmillan, London

Cabinet Office (2001) *Raising the Educational Attainment of Children in Care*, consultation letter

Carlen. P. (1988) *Women, Crime and Poverty*, Open University Press, Milton Keynes

Commission on Social Justice (1993) *The Justice Gap*, IPPR, London

Cook, D. (1989) *Rich Law, Poor Law*, Open University Press, Milton Keynes

Cook, D. (1997) *Poverty, Crime and Punishment*, CPAG, London

Crawford, A. (1998) *Crime Prevention and Community Safety: Politics, Policies and Practices*, Longman, London

Grabiner, Lord (2000) *The Informal Economy*, HM Treasury, London

Home Office (2001) *Criminal Justice: the Way Ahead*, Home Office, London

Home Office (2002a) *Race and the Criminal Justice System*, Home Office, London

Home Office (2002b) *Narrowing the Justice Gap*, Justice Gap Taskforce, Home Office, London

Home Office (2003a) *Prison Population Brief: England and Wales December 2002*, Home Office, London

Home Office (2003b) *The Prison Population in 2001: A Statistical Review: Research Findings No. 195*, Home Office, London

Joseph Rowntree Foundation (2002) *Monitoring Poverty and Social Exclusion 2002*, Joseph Rowntree Foundation, York

Marshall, T. H. (1950) *Citizenship and Social Class and Other Essays*, Cambridge University Press, Cambridge

Marshall, T. H. (1981) *The Right to Welfare and Other Essays*, Heinemann, London

Office of National Statistics (2001) *Take Up of Income Related Benefits for 1999/2000*, HMSO, London

Phoenix, J. (1999) *Making Sense of Prostitution*, Macmillan, Basingstoke

Rawls, J. (1971) *A Theory of Justice*, Clarendon Press, Oxford

Simmons, J. et al. (2002) *Crime in England and Wales 2001/2*, Home Office, London

Singleton, N., Meltzer, H., Gatward, R., Coid, J. and Deasy, D. (1997) *Psychiatric Morbidity Among Prisoners: Summary Report*, Office of National Statistics, London

Social Exclusion Unit (1998) *Bringing Britain Together: A National Strategy for Neighbourhood Renewal*, The Stationery Office, London

Sparks, C. and Spencer, S. (2002) *Them and Us? The Public, Offenders and the Criminal Justice System*, Institute for Public Policy Research, London

White, P. (1998) *The Prison Population in 1997: A Statistical Review: Research Findings No. 76*, Home Office, London

Young, J. (1997) 'Charles Murray and the American prison experiment: the dilemmas of a libertarian' in Murray, C. (ed.) *Does Prison Work?*, Institute of Economic Affairs, London

Health policy

8 Hugh Bochel

Issues in Focus

For many people the National Health Service has epitomised the post-war welfare state. The idea of universal healthcare, available free at the point of use and funded from general taxation, has become generally accepted within the United Kingdom. Yet there remain very important debates over the direction and shape of health policy, some of which have been highlighted in media and political debates in recent years, while others, arguably also of great significance, have received much less attention. This chapter provides an overview of health policy, drawing on past and current developments through:

- a consideration of the creation and development of the National Health Service over the first 30 years of its existence

- examination of attempts to reform the pattern of provision by the Conservative governments from 1979 to 1997

- attention to New Labour's initiatives including increased funding for the NHS, a more central role for primary care and health promotion.

Healthcare has long been seen as one of the main functions of the welfare state. The first real state involvement came with the **Public Health Acts** of the mid-19th centuries, which began to introduce improvements in areas such as sanitation and planning, which, in turn, had a significant impact in reducing deaths from infectious diseases. During the second half of the 20th century health issues became largely focused on treatment, and the NHS in particular, although recent years have seen an increased concern with inequalities in health, including those associated with economic and social factors.

Growth of state involvement in health

During the 19th century the state became involved in health services primarily through the introduction of public health legislation designed to reduce the threat of infectious diseases such as cholera and typhoid. The Public Health Act 1848 is often associated with the work of Edwin Chadwick, Secretary to the Poor Law Commission, and his supporters. The Act provided the basis for the provision of adequate water supplies and sewerage systems, but while some local authorities were enthusiastic about such provision, others were less positive and chose to take less action. In 1872 the Public Health Act created sanitary authorities, which had a responsibility to provide public health services. Three years later the Public Health Act 1875 brought together existing legislation and established a framework for the development of public health for the next 50 years (Baggott 2000).

Another perspective was brought to government involvement in health with the National Insurance Act 1911. Introduced despite opposition from large parts of the medical profession, who feared both state control of their work and negative financial consequences for themselves, this Act provided income during sickness and unemployment and free care from GPs for some groups of workers earning under £160 per annum. To make the Act palatable to doctors the Liberal government agreed that payment should be based on the number of people on a doctor's list – the capitation system – rather than as a salary, thus preserving GPs' independence. In addition, it was agreed that the system should be administered by panels, including the insurance companies and friendly societies that had previously played a significant role in providing cover against ill health, rather than by local authorities. Over the next 30 years this provision grew and by the mid-1940s about half of the British population was covered by insurance under the Act while around two-thirds of GPs were involved (Ham 1999). However, it was only the insured workers who were covered, not their families, and it was only GP services, and not hospital care, that were provided by the scheme.

Public hospital provision in the UK developed out of the workhouses provided under the Poor Law, while there were parallel developments in the voluntary hospital system that grew out of provision by religious organisations and, later, charitable giving by the rich. However, during the 19th century, with the growth of medicine as a science, voluntary hospitals became more selective, giving greater attention to the needs of people with acute illnesses at the expense of those who had chronic illnesses or infectious diseases. As a result, the workhouses often provided for those whom the voluntary hospitals would not accept. However, the Metropolitan Poor Act 1867 and the Poor Law Amendment Act 1868 allowed for the provision of infirmaries separate from workhouses and provided a recognition that the state had a responsibility to provide hospital care for poor people. The Local Government Act 1929 arguably moved a step closer to allowing for a national health service, transferring workhouses and infirmaries to local authorities, with the intention that this provision could develop into a local authority hospital service. In addition, since 1845, local authorities had been required to develop hospitals (asylums) for people with mental health problems or people with learning difficulties. By the outbreak of the Second World War local authorities were therefore responsible for a range of hospitals, and these were brought together with the voluntary hospitals as part of the Emergency Medical Service during the war.

Between the First and Second World Wars a number of reports had highlighted problems with existing provision, including over the need for greater planning and coordination and made suggestions for change. The publication of the Beveridge Report on Social Insurance and Allied Services in 1942 made the case for the reform of the social security system together with a national health service and provided added momentum for change. In 1944 the coalition government published a White Paper proposing a national health service and the election of a Labour government in 1945 made the establishment of a national health service almost certain. The necessary legislation was passed in the National Health Service Act 1946. In the creation of the NHS local authorities lost control of their hospitals, which, with the voluntary hospitals, were placed under one system of administration.

Health policy, 1948–1979

As is now widely known, the National Health Service came into being on 5 July 1948 with the aim of providing comprehensive health services to all, free at the point of use and financed through general taxation. These principles have remained largely unchallenged in the period since then, while the NHS has also remained popular with the public.

However, the first decades of existence were not unproblematic for the NHS. There had been a general assumption at the time of its creation that it would reduce the overall level of ill health and that, as a result, expenditure would level off and even decline. Yet this was not the pattern and within years of coming into being the NHS was requiring additional expenditure. Prescription charges and a fee for dental treatment were introduced in 1952. The 1950s was also a period that saw consolidation and rationalisation, particularly of hospital services, although in contrast expenditure on capital was limited, amounting to only £100 million in the entire decade (Ham 1999). However, the 1962 Hospital Plan provided for a major increase in capital expenditure, based on district general hospitals serving populations of around 125,000. The 1960s also saw the first significant steps towards **community care**, rather than care in large institutions, following the Mental Health Act 1959 (see Chapter 6).

There were suggestions in the 1960s that some of the problems that had emerged in the NHS could be tackled through structural change and the Labour government of the late 1960s produced two Green Papers considering this. The Conservative government that followed took these ideas a step further in the National Health Service Act 1973, producing a new structure that came into operation in 1974 that was intended to achieve three main aims (Ham 1999): to unify health services by bringing them together under one authority (although GPs remained as independent contractors); to improve coordination between health authorities and local government services including through the introduction of matching boundaries; and to introduce better management. However, the new structure (consisting in England of 14 regional health authorities and 90 area health authorities) came under almost immediate criticism and one recommendation of the Royal Commission on the Health Service, which was established in 1976 and reported in 1979, was that the number of tiers of authority should be reduced.

Health policy, 1979–1997

However, while the Royal Commission had been established by a Labour government it was a Conservative government headed by Margaret Thatcher that was to act on the report. In the early 1980s the NHS was therefore reorganised again to create 192 district health authorities in England, which in most cases were no longer coterminous with local government. As with the 1974 changes, general practitioners remained outside the mainstream health authority structure, with family practitioner committees overseeing these services. Changes were also made in Northern Ireland, Scotland and Wales.

However, ideological pressures within the Conservative government were mounting for change that would go beyond concerns with effective structures. As with other elements of the welfare state (and indeed the wider public sector) some on the New Right were seeking more radical reforms, including some calls for the replacement of the NHS with private health insurance. However, even after the Conservatives won the 1983 general election their concerns continued to focus on the management of the health service and, in particular, on attempts to make it more efficient and businesslike, including through learning from the private sector. A report in 1983 by Roy Griffiths (then managing director of the Sainsburys supermarket chain) recommended the introduction of general managers at all levels of the NHS, both to improve the quality of management and to take greater control from hospital doctors.

This was a significant change as until this point doctors had arguably exercised considerable control over the service, yet now they were increasingly drawn into management of resources. In a further change recommended by Griffiths, the government created an NHS management board and a health services supervisory board to strengthen central NHS management.

NHS funding and internal markets

While not adopting the approach supported by some on the New Right in seeking to replace the NHS with private health insurance, the Conservatives did try to encourage market forces within the health service. Alan Enthoven, an American academic, had suggested that forms of markets could be created within health services by encouraging those providing services to compete for patients and had argued that this would drive up standards and increase accountability (Enthoven 1985). At the same time, there was evidence of significant funding problems for the NHS, with authoritative reports by the Kings Fund (1988) and the Social Services Select Committee (1986, 1988) highlighting the problems. In the winter of 1987 it became apparent that many health authorities were finding it difficult to keep expenditure within limits, wards were being closed to save money and parts of the medical profession, including the presidents of three royal colleges, were claiming that the NHS was in need of additional finances. In the short term the government provided an additional £100 million of funding, but the Prime Minister, Margaret Thatcher, also established a small committee, chaired by herself, to review the future of the NHS. Although the review was conducted in private and organisations such as the British Medical Association were not called to give evidence and in spite of speculation that the government would seek to use the review to introduce far-reaching changes to the NHS, in reality there was little appetite for truly radical reform. Instead the idea of introducing internal markets emerged as a major strand of the White Paper, *Working for Patients* (Department of Health 1989).

The White Paper stated the government's intention to preserve the basic principles on which the NHS had been founded and within it the emphasis lay heavily on means of improving the delivery of health services through a separation of purchaser and provider responsibilities, the creation of **NHS trusts** and **GP fundholders** and a series of internal markets where purchasers would be able to buy services from different providers. However, the White Paper did announce additional changes: the concern with management remained significant with the creation of the NHS management executive and a policy board to replace the NHS management board and the supervisory board, with attempts to strengthen the managerial role of health authorities and the new family health services authorities (which replaced the family practitioner committees); in an attempt to make doctors more accountable for their performance, general managers were to be given a greater role in the management of clinical activity, while audit was to become a routine part of clinical work in hospitals and general practice.

Also in 1989 the government published a White Paper, *Caring for People*, which built on a second report by Sir Roy Griffiths, this time on the future of community care. Although having a very different emphasis from *Working for Patients*, this White Paper required local authorities to play the lead role in community care, but in collaboration with the NHS and other voluntary and private sector bodies (see also Chapter 6).

These changes were introduced in the NHS and Community Care Act 1990 and the internal market began to develop from 1991 as the number of NHS trusts and GP fundholders began to increase. However, the success of the reforms was questionable, with supporters and opponents being able to interpret the available evidence in different ways. Conservative ministers argued that waiting times were being reduced and that the number of patients being treated was increasing and that these showed that the NHS was becoming more efficient and responsive; however, others suggested that these changes derived at least in part from the increased funding that the NHS was receiving. Similarly, the conclusions of academics and others were mixed, with Le Grand and his colleagues, for example, concluding that the reforms had made little change, either positive or negative (Le Grand, Mays and Mulligan 1998).

Public health measures

Where public health and health improvement were concerned, in 1980 the Conservative government found itself confronted by the Black Report on *Inequalities in Health* (Black Report 1980), which examined inequalities in health and produced a number of recommendations to reduce class inequalities in health, including increasing child benefits and improving housing conditions. However, the government did not find the analysis or recommendations to its liking and little action was taken.

The 1980s also saw the spread of HIV/AIDS and the consequent development of policies that sought to combat this. The principal method used was to seek to encourage people to change their behaviour and lifestyle. This approach also underpinned much of the other preventive work of the time, including campaigns aimed at reducing smoking and alcohol misuse.

By the 1990s the government had progressed to the production of a White Paper, *The Health of the Nation* (Department of Health 1992), which set targets for health improvement in five key areas: coronary heart disease and stroke; cancer; mental health; HIV/AIDS and sexual health; and accidents. While many welcomed the strategy it was also widely criticised, including over the worth of the targets (variously seen as too ambitious or unlikely to be met on the continuation of current trends), a perceived unwillingness to tackle the tobacco and alcohol industries and a failure to take social inequalities and deprivation into account (see Baggott 2000).

The Conservative governments also sought to involve GPs and dentists more in preventive work, including through the introduction of new contracts in 1990. Those for GPs included requirements for health checks for new patients and those aged 75 or over, while targets were introduced for vaccinations, immunisations and screening for cervical cancer and encouragement was given for additional health promotion work. Similarly, the new contracts for dentists also sought to stress the requirement for preventive work as well as restorative treatments.

Private health provision

Since 1948 the National Health Service has been the dominant provider of healthcare in the UK, but private provision has continued to play a significant role, accounting for around 15 per cent of health expenditure (Ham 1999). For many, private healthcare can be extremely expensive and for that reason much treatment is paid for by private health insurance, for which there are a number of providers, including specialists such as BUPA and general insurers such as Norwich Union. From the 1970s the number of people covered by private health insurance has almost tripled, reaching nearly seven million in 2000 (Office of National Statistics 2002), although the bulk of this rise took place during the 1970s and 1980s and the 1990s saw little change.

However, private health insurers are also affected by the cost of paying for healthcare and as a result face pressure to keep costs down. For this reason, the range of services provided is frequently limited while providers seek to reduce their potential exposure to those who might be likely to make the heaviest financial demands, such as people with long-term chronic health problems.

"I'm afraid it's bad news Mr. Hooper, I've just got the report on your finances."

Source: www.CartoonStock.com

Health policy since 1997

On coming to power Labour faced a number of challenges in relation to health policy. Many of these have been outlined earlier in this chapter, but they included: the perpetual dilemma of how adequately to fund the National Health Service; what to do about the internal market introduced by the Conservatives; how to make best use of primary health services, provided by general practitioners; and evidence of growing social class inequalities in morbidity and mortality. By December 1997 the government had produced a White Paper, *The New NHS. Modern. Dependable* (Department of Health 1997) (see Policy eye 8.1), which reflected the government's desire for modernisation but at the same time took a pragmatic approach to what was already in place.

NHS funding

While the funding of the NHS has been a problem for almost all governments since 1948, by the 1990s issues such as waiting lists, winter bed shortages in hospitals and rationing of services were bringing this to the fore again. Labour's commitment, prior to the 1997 general election, to abide by the Conservatives' plans for public expenditure for two years, made it impossible for the government to make radical changes to funding the NHS. However,

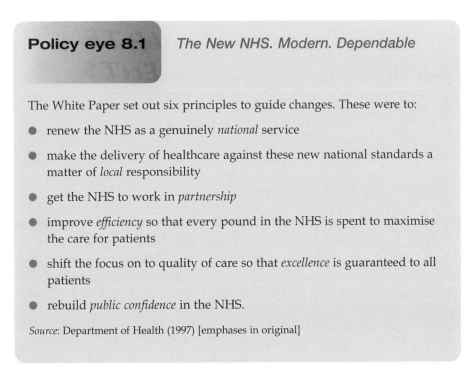

Policy eye 8.1   *The New NHS. Modern. Dependable*

The White Paper set out six principles to guide changes. These were to:

- renew the NHS as a genuinely *national* service

- make the delivery of healthcare against these new national standards a matter of *local* responsibility

- get the NHS to work in *partnership*

- improve *efficiency* so that every pound in the NHS is spent to maximise the care for patients

- shift the focus on to quality of care so that *excellence* is guaranteed to all patients

- rebuild *public confidence* in the NHS.

Source: Department of Health (1997) [emphases in original]

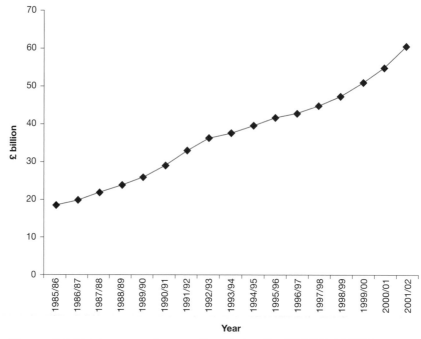

Figure 8.1 Total managed expenditure in health, 1985/86–2001/02

Source: Based on HM Treasury (2003) Table 3.2

following the **Comprehensive Spending Review**, in 1999 the government undertook to increase spending on the NHS by £21 billion over the next three years, an annual increase of 4.7 per cent in real terms (Figure 8.1). Despite this increase, NHS funding remained an issue, including at the 2001 general election, and in the 2002 Budget the Chancellor, Gordon Brown, announced a further rise in NHS spending of an average of 7.4 per cent a year in real terms for five years, with the total amount going on the health service to increase from £72.1 billion in 2002/3 to £105.6 billion in 2007/8. This would, over the period, bring the proportion of GDP spent on the NHS to more than the average EU expenditure on healthcare (Table 8.1 shows expenditure on health in selected states). However, even a report commissioned by the Treasury, published in 2002, suggested that there remain a number of factors, including public expectations, developments in medical technology and demographic change, which will continue to put pressure on healthcare resources and expenditure, meaning that there will be a need for further increases in expenditure over the next 20 years (Wanless 2002).

One of the controversial aspects of Labour's approach to the financing of the NHS has been the use of the **private finance initiative** (PFI) to fund a programme of new hospital building (see Policy eye 8.2). Given Labour's traditional hostility to privatisation, and particularly the long-standing commitment to a health service free at the point of use and funded from general taxation, the PFI was viewed suspiciously by many of the party's MPs and supporters, while others were sceptical about the value for money offered,

Table 8.1 Total expenditure on health as a % of GDP, 2001

Australia	9.2
Canada	9.7
Denmark	8.6
France	9.5
Germany	10.7
Ireland	6.5
Italy	8.4
Japan	8.0
Spain	7.5
Sweden	8.7
Switzerland	11.1
United Kingdom	7.6
United States	13.9

Source: OECD (2003)

particularly over the long term. Nevertheless, the government saw this as central to its plans for the NHS and pushed ahead with it.

Reforming primary care

As with many other areas of policy, Labour placed great emphasis on some of its key ideas, including the notions of 'modernisation' and using 'what works', reflecting debates of the time around the 'Third Way'. Given

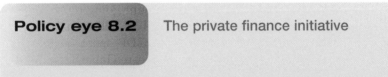

Policy eye 8.2   The private finance initiative

The Private Finance Initiative was introduced by the Conservative Chancellor, Norman Lamont, in 1992. The form of PFI that has been most relevant to the NHS is where a private contractor designs, finances, builds and, potentially, even operates a facility such as a hospital. A public sector body may then pay the private contractor agreed payments for the use of the facility over the contract period. When the contract comes to an end the facility may revert to either the private contractor or the public sector, depending on the agreement.

By September 2001 the Department of Health had signed 105 PFI deals worth more than £2.5 billion.

Source: Allen (2001)

Labour's opposition to the internal market prior to 1997 it had been anticipated that it would reverse the policy. In practice, the new government accepted many of the reforms, although it did abolish the GP fundholding scheme. However, even in this area it sought to establish some of the principles of fundholding through the creation of primary care groups (Ham 1999) that included all of the GPs in an area, covering populations of up to around 250,000 people. The intention of this change was that PCGs would be responsible to district health authorities, which in turn would take a strategic approach to identifying health needs and the planning of appropriate provision. These were to be set out in health improvement programmes, to be produced by each health authority but taking into account local interests. However, the new process went further, allowing some PCGs to make a transition to primary care trusts (PCTs), which are independent of health authorities and which are able to provide a full range of community services and to commission hospital services. The emphasis on primary care created by the growth in the number of PCTs was further encouraged in *The NHS Plan* (Department of Health 2000), which made PCTs (there were over 300 in England by early 2004) the main bodies responsible for the planning and delivery of primary care. The implications of these changes are significant, with PCTs expected to be responsible for around 75 per cent of the NHS budget by 2004, compared with the 15 per cent that had been held by GP fundholders during the 1990s. The steady shift towards a health service led by primary care that had begun under the Conservatives was therefore continued under Labour.

PCGs were also clearly seen by the government as a means of integrating provision, with GPs, community nurses and other professionals working together to reduce the fragmentation and gaps in services that had existed under previous organisational models.

Structural change

Foundation hospitals

One of the politically most controversial elements of Labour's approach to the NHS was the creation of foundation hospital trusts. This development differed from previous reorganisations of the health service through the establishment in England of 'foundation hospitals'. In the first phase, hospital trusts that had achieved three-star performance ratings were invited to apply for foundation hospital trust status, a form of 'earned autonomy', with freedom from central control and the ability to borrow money from private sources. Foundation hospitals were to be locally controlled, intended to provide greater accountability to local people, with public and staff forming a membership that would elect representatives to the board. Members will collectively own the trust, roughly along the lines of a cooperative society, although if a trust were to fail control would pass back to the Department of Health. The government's stated intention was that foundation hospitals should be free to choose the services that best suit their local community without pressure from the NHS or Whitehall bureaucracies. However, opponents expressed concerns over a number of issues, including the danger of a 'two-tier' health service, for while the intention was that by 2008 all hospital trusts should have the opportunity to gain foundation status, the first foundation hospitals would be able to provide better services and take the best staff, while lower status hospitals might not have the chance to recover. Others feared the danger of a return to the internal markets of the 1990s, a lack of genuine democracy and creeping privatisation. Nevertheless, the government achieved a narrow majority for its legislation in a vote in the House of Commons in 2003 and 25 NHS trusts applied to be in the first wave of foundation trusts.

Other reforms

As with preceding governments, Labour found the level of demand for healthcare a major challenge. One response was the apparently straightforward means of increasing funding as discussed later, although it is clear that such increases frequently take years to have an impact in terms of any significant improvement in the availability of services to patients. A second, more targeted response emerged from the 1997 manifesto commitments to reduce waiting lists, with the 1997 to 2001 government establishing a waiting list initiative including setting targets for a reduction in the number of people on waiting lists. However, in 2001 the waiting list initiative was ended, at least in part as a result of the pressure on NHS staff and concerns that simple non-urgent operations were being prioritised to reduce waiting lists rather than more urgent but more time-consuming treatments. Instead, the government announced that it was to seek to reduce waiting times for operations to six months by 2005. The development of NHS Direct, a 24-hour telephone-based service, was another attempt to channel demand in the first instance, encouraging the public to move away from the traditional reliance on a visit to a doctor.

Labour also sought to move towards a more even 'national' level of provision in some respects, including creating the National Institute for Clinical Excellence (NICE) and the Commission for Health Improvement (CHI). NICE was established in 1999 to provide patients, health professionals and the public with authoritative, robust and reliable guidance on 'best practice' across health technologies (including medicines, medical devices, diagnostic techniques and procedures) and the clinical management of specific conditions. Among its responsibilities is to make recommendations to the government on the cost effectiveness and affordability of treatments. The Commission for Health Improvement is the independent inspection body for the NHS in England and Wales, including both NHS trusts and PCTs. It has a number of roles including: routine inspections (clinical governance reviews); investigating serious service failures; reporting on key issues, such as coronary heart disease; publishing performance ratings; and undertaking joint inspections with other bodies. CHI is also responsible for monitoring and reviewing the implementation of standards set out in National Service Frameworks in England and Wales. These National Service Frameworks set out national standards, or benchmarks, for particular services or care groups (such as coronary heart disease or older people), involve strategies for achieving these targets and set out milestones against which progress can be measured. The introduction of these new bodies and their activities has impacted on health professionals by identifying NHS organisations and professionals as responsible for both the quality and the consistency of clinical decisions.

In 2001 Labour created yet another new body, the NHS Modernisation Agency (Figure 8.2), to encourage 'modernisation' across a range of areas. During the Agency's first two years it concentrated on the issues of improving access, increasing local support, raising standards of care, and capturing and sharing knowledge widely. However, reflecting the modernisation agenda it had some underlying themes including leadership and workforce development.

Inequalities in health

The perceived failure of the preceding Conservative government to accept and seek to tackle structural causes of ill health meant that the New Labour

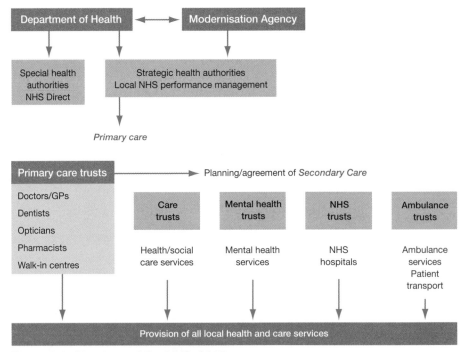

Figure 8.2 Structure of the NHS, 2003

*Source: R*edrawn from http://www.nhs.uk/england/aboutTheNHS/default. cmsx, 2 September 2004 © NHS Information Authority

government faced demands to produce a new approach to promoting public health. The publication of the Acheson Report (Acheson 1998) further added to the focus on this, noting that in some areas health inequalities had actually widened since the Black Report. The government's approach to health improvement was set out with the publication of the Green Paper for England, *Our Healthier Nation* (Department of Health 1998a), which placed greater emphasis on economic, environmental and social causes of ill health than had *The Health of the Nation*. The new document set out four key areas and targets for 2010: for cancer, to reduce the death rate among people under 75 by at least one-fifth; for coronary heart disease and stroke, to reduce the death rate in people under 75 by at least two-fifths; to reduce the death rate from accidents by at least one-fifth and serious injury from accidents by at least one-tenth; and for mental illness, to reduce the death rate from suicide and undetermined injury by at least one-fifth. While the Green Paper was generally welcomed, some noted that there was an emphasis on reducing mortality, rather than morbidity; others were concerned with the failure to set national targets for reducing health inequalities.

The government also prioritised smoking and drug use as areas for action. In 1998 the government published *Smoking Kills. A White Paper on Tobacco* (Department of Health 1998b) which set out its intentions to reduce smoking among children and young people, to help adults, particularly the most disadvantaged, to give up smoking, and to offer especial support to pregnant women. By 2003 the government had introduced a variety of measures designed to help achieve its aims, although some critics believed that further actions, such as banning smoking in public places or curtailing the availability of tobacco, were necessary. Where drugs were concerned, in 1998 the government appointed Keith Hellawell as National Anti-Drugs Unit Coordinator (or 'drugs tsar') to coordinate action across government as a whole to reduce drug misuse. He was responsible for the production of a ten-year strategy designed to achieve this but resigned in 2002 on the same day that the government announced its intention to downgrade cannabis from a Class B to a Class C drug.

It is apparent that under Labour the emphasis on individuals' improving their own health remains, as during the Conservatives' years in government, through changing lifestyles and making choices about healthy and unhealthy behaviours. But, at the same time, there has come an awareness that there are health problems associated with factors such as low educational standards, poor housing conditions, poverty and unemployment and that there are links between social inequality and inequalities in health.

Labour also sought to give health authorities a leading role in their attempts to reduce health inequalities, requiring them to assess the health needs of their local populations and to develop strategies for meeting those needs, working with PCGs/PCTs, local authorities and other local interests. This emphasis on collaboration and partnership across organisations is reflected in another strand of Labour policy designed to help tackle health inequalities. A number of health action zones were established in 1998 and 1999 to identify and meet health needs in certain deprived areas. As with education action zones (see Chapter 5) they received additional funding for a number of years and were expected both to involve a wide range of local stakeholders and to take innovative approaches to achieving their objectives.

However, the measurement of health inequalities remains a complex and often contentious task and while there is increasing acknowledgement of the relationships between economic and social status and health, the pattern of these links is not always clear and the determination of cause and effect is even less so. This, in turn, means that determining appropriate responses to health inequalities remains problematic.

Private health provision

Private health provision scarcely emerged as an issue during Labour's first six years in office. Nevertheless, after a period of stability during the 1990s the number of people with private health insurance rose by 5 per cent between 1999 and 2000, although this was due to cover paid for by companies, as the number of individual subscribers actually fell at the same time (Office of National Statistics 2002). It is also worth noting that despite the growth in private health since the 1980s, the proportion of expenditure on healthcare that comes from the public purse in the UK (82.2 per cent in 2001) remains significantly higher than in many other countries (for example, France 76.0 per cent, Germany 74.9 per cent, Italy 75.3 per cent) and is only slightly lower than it was in 1960 (85.2 per cent) (OECD 2003).

Devolution

The future development of health policy was also affected by Labour's delivery of its commitment to devolution for Scotland and Wales and the creation of the Northern Ireland Assembly. As with some other aspects of social policy, health policy and the organisation of the NHS have always differed between the component parts of the United Kingdom, but the devolved administrations in Scotland and Wales were each given powers over the NHS in their countries. In Scotland, the Executive has its own Health Department, which oversees the work of 15 area health boards and 24 NHS trusts. In an attempt to encourage integration of service delivery, it is also responsible for some other aspects of social policy and in particular for community care. Similarly, the Welsh Cabinet has a member responsible for health and social services, including the NHS in Wales, with local health boards having been created with boundaries that are coterminous with local authorities. In Northern Ireland, health and social care have long been overseen by integrated health and social services boards. The result of this, as has been noted elsewhere in this book, is that devolution has brought with it the potential for much greater diversity of approaches in the coming years.

Briefing 8.1   NHS facts and figures

In a typical week:

- 1.4 million people will receive help in their home from the NHS
- more than 800,000 people will be treated in NHS hospital outpatient clinics
- 700,000 will visit a NHS dentist for a check-up
- NHS district nurses will make more than 700,000 visits
- over 10,000 babies will be delivered by the NHS
- NHS chiropodists will inspect over 150,000 pairs of feet
- NHS ambulances will make over 50,000 emergency journeys
- NHS Direct nurses will receive around 25,000 calls from people seeking medical advice
- pharmacists will dispense approximately 8.5 million items on NHS prescriptions
- NHS surgeons will perform around 1,200 hip operations, 3,000 heart operations and 1,050 kidney operations.

Source: The NHS Explained, www.nhs.uk/thenhsexplained/what_is_nhs.asp, 30 January 2004

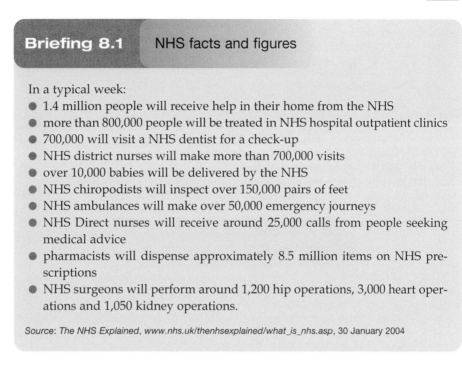

Summary

This chapter has outlined the development of health policy in Britain and has examined some of the major issues around healthcare and health promotion including:

- continued significant reforms of the NHS throughout its existence, and particularly from the 1970s onwards, with governments seeking to improve efficiency, management, accountability and responsiveness, as well as to control expenditure

- the perennial problem of meeting demand for healthcare (Briefing 8.1) and, in particular, the level of funding for the National Health Service, with governments having sought to tackle this in a variety of ways, with New Labour having made significant financial commitments from 1999 onwards to bring spending to more than the EU average

- although the NHS dominates health expenditure in the UK there remains a significant private sector, accounting for more than 15 per cent of expenditure and with around seven million people covered by private health insurance

- the role of primary care, with successive governments seeking to shift the emphasis of healthcare away from hospital-based provision to primary care, initially under the Conservatives through new contracts for GPs and dentists and the creation of GP fundholders, and then under Labour through primary care groups and primary care trusts

- evidence of the persistence, and even widening, of health inequalities, including those grounded in economic, environmental and social factors. The White Paper, *Our Healthier Nation*, saw shifts towards some recognition of the importance of these factors and established targets for the reduction of the death rate in four key areas. However, critics continued to question the government's emphasis on reducing mortality rather than morbidity, its commitment to reducing health inequalities and its willingness to tackle producer interests such as the alcohol and tobacco industries.

Discussion and review topics

1 How true is it that the National Health Service is really a 'national treatment service'?

2 How successful is Labour's planned increase in expenditure on the NHS likely to be in improving the quality of provision?

3 What are the strengths and weaknesses of the arguments for and against the use of private investment in the National Health Service?

4 Are Labour's policies likely to result in a reduction in inequalities in health?

Further reading

Baggott, R. (2000) *Public Health: Policy and Politics*, Palgrave, Basingstoke – this book gives a good overview of the development of public health and many of the issues around its role

Baggott, R. (2002) *Health and Health Care in Britain*, Palgrave, Basingstoke – a good and wide-ranging introduction to healthcare

Ham, C. (1999) *Health Policy in Britain*, Palgrave, Basingstoke – the fourth edition of this useful work which provides a thorough coverage of many aspects of health policy

Klein, R. (2001) *The New Politics of the NHS*, Prentice Hall, Hemel Hempstead – this book examines the ways in which governments have sought to tackle the problems and challenges facing the NHS

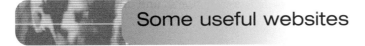

Some useful websites

www.doh.gov.uk – provides information on the work of the Department of Health, policies, publications and a wide range of statistics

www.hsj.co.uk – the website of the *Health Service Journal* includes up-to-date articles on a variety of health policy and health management topics

www.kingsfund.org.uk – the King's Fund website not only provides access to information and publications on the Fund's own work, but also has links to a large number of other organisations

www.nhs.uk – this is the official gateway to the websites of NHS organisations in England (see also www.n-i.nhs.uk, www.show.scot.nhs.uk and www.wales.nhs.uk)

References

Acheson, D. (1998) *Independent Inquiry into Inequalities of Health: Report*, The Stationery Office, London

Allen, G. (2001) *House of Commons Library Research Paper 01/117: The Private Finance Initiative*, House of Commons, London

Baggott, R. (2000) *Public Health: Policy and Politics*, Palgrave, Basingstoke

Black Report (1980) *Inequalities in Health*, Department of Health and Social Security, London

Department of Health (1989) *Working for Patients*, HMSO, London

Department of Health (1992) *The Health of the Nation*, The Stationery Office, London

Department of Health (1997) *The New NHS. Modern, Dependable*, The Stationery Office, London

Department of Health (1998a) *Our Healthier Nation*, The Stationery Office, London

Department of Health (1998b) *Smoking Kills. A White Paper on Tobacco*, The Stationery Office, London

Department of Health (2000) *The NHS Plan*, The Stationery Office, London

Enthoven, A. (1985) *Reflections on the Management of the NHS*, Nuffield Provincial Hospitals Trust, London

Ham, C. (1999) *Health Policy in Britain*, Macmillan, Basingstoke

HM Treasury (2003) *Public Expenditure Statistical Analyses, 2003–2004*, HM Treasury, London

King's Fund Institute (1988) *Health Finance: Assessing the Option*, King's Fund Institute, London

Le Grand, J., Mays, N. and Mulligan, J. (eds) (1998) *Learning from the NHS Internal Market*, King's Fund, London

OECD (2003) *OECD Health Data 2003*, OECD, Paris

Office of National Statistics (2002) *Social Trends 32*, The Stationery Office, London

Social Services Select Committee (1986) *Public Expenditure on the Social Services*, HMSO, London

Social Services Select Committee (1988) *Resourcing the National Health Service*, HMSO, London

Wanless, D. (2002) *Securing our Future Health: Taking a Long-Term View*, HM Treasury, London

Housing policy

9

Brian Lund

Issues in Focus

In contrast to education and healthcare, ability to pay has always been the main criterion for the distribution of housing. Nonetheless, during the 20th century, the recognition that many people could not afford 'adequate' accommodation helped to stimulate a variety of forms of state intervention in the housing market. This involvement reached its zenith in the mid-1970s but, since the early 1980s, state action has been concentrated on mitigating the extreme consequences of the operations of a free market in housing. This chapter:

- examines the reasons for the development of state intervention in the housing market

- considers the 'rolling back' of the state from housing provision in the 1980s and 1990s

- explores the tenure structure of the United Kingdom

- examines the relationships between housing policy, homelessness and social exclusion

- considers the links between housing and community care.

In the 19th century, the ideas of 'classical' economists such as Adam Smith influenced thinking about 'the housing issue'. They believed that housing was a **commodity** and the free market should determine its supply and distribution. '**Laissez-faire**' was revived in the 1960s by 'neo-classical' economists who asserted that state intervention in the housing market during the 20th century had generated far more problems than it had solved (Hayek 1960; Pennance 1969). 'Neo-classical' economists are prepared to allow only two exceptions to the general maxim that the state should 'leave to be'. These are to sanction action to remedy '**externalities**' such as the diseases spreading from unsanitary dwellings and the eyesores of dilapidated houses and to permit an income subsidy to the poor to enable them to afford a minimum level of housing supplied by the private sector.

Other economists claim that housing has special characteristics that, taken together, indicate that a free housing market would operate inefficiently and produce hardship. They maintain that housing supply is **inelastic** relative to demand because land is an absolute scarce resource, the existing housing stock is immobile and there is a long production time in constructing new dwellings (Le Grand, Popper and Robinson 1984). Moreover, houses are expensive relative to average incomes so, in a free market, those on low incomes would be unable to afford the good-quality homes necessary for full participation in the civic life of the community (Hills 1998).

State intervention in the housing market

Regulation and 'nuisance' removal

In the 19th century, as part of its developing role in promoting public health by eliminating 'externalities', local government acquired powers to regulate building standards and remove the 'nuisances' of individual unfit dwellings and 'slum' areas. However, the role of local government in the *provision* of new homes was strictly limited. It was not until the Housing of the Working Classes Act 1890 that local authorities obtained a clear general power to build homes and then it was only on the condition they did not make a loss on any scheme (Morton 1991). Subsidised housing was regarded as the domain of the voluntary, housing association sector, the 'subsidy' being donations from wealthy benefactors or a 'philanthropic' agreement to limit the return on investment to 5 per cent.

Subsidised council housing

A specific housing issue, distinct from concerns about the social threat of the 'slum' and the impact of inadequate water supply and poor sanitation on public health, started to emerge at the end of the 19th century (see Briefing 9.1).

Briefing 9.1   The housing question: circa 1900

A range of solutions to 'the housing question' were put forward at the turn of the century. Subsidised local authority housing had some supporters but many 'New' Liberals and trade unionists regarded subsidies as a 'dole', unsuited to the 'independent' working man. The land issue was at the heart of the most radical proposals. In *Garden Cities of Tomorrow* (1902) Ebenezer Howard argued that cheap land in rural areas could be used to build garden cities where citizens could enjoy the benefits of both town and country. The 'New Liberalism' and the Labour Movement concentrated on land taxation, asserting that taxing land at its site value would prevent land hoarding and, by depressing the price of land, make houses cheaper. Advocates of new towns thought that council housing was a way of achieving some of their objectives. However, new towns and land taxation had little impact on the solution to the 'housing problem' adopted at the end of the First World War.

The developing labour movement and the 'New' Liberalism questioned whether market capitalism was capable of supplying the dwellings necessary to overcome the housing shortage. How could free enterprise meet the housing requirements of the working class when the rent of a new, two up two down terraced house, was about 25 per cent of the average earnings of manual workers (Holmans 1987)?

The First World War was the watershed in British housing policy. With house building terminated until the war was over, even the most ardent free market economist could not argue that supply would meet demand. Rents increases in Clydeside prompted rent strikes and, in 1915, the government responded by freezing rents and giving tenants **security of tenure**.

Subsidised state housing was an outcome of **rent control**. If rents were to be controlled at below market level how could the private sector supply sufficient homes when it had failed even under free market conditions? The Housing and Town Planning Act 1919 introduced a central state subsidy to local authorities to encourage them to build houses. Such subsidies remained a central pillar of housing policy for 60 years. Central government used subsidy variations to direct local authorities to build either for 'general needs' to increase the overall housing stock or for the 'specific' needs arising from slum clearance (see Figure 9.1).

Dwellings designed for 'general needs' were usually of good quality but those erected for former slum dwellers were often flats built at high densities and with poor community facilities.

Other forms of state intervention in the housing market

Subsidised council housing and rent control were the main mechanisms of housing policy up to 1979 but the state also intervened in the housing market

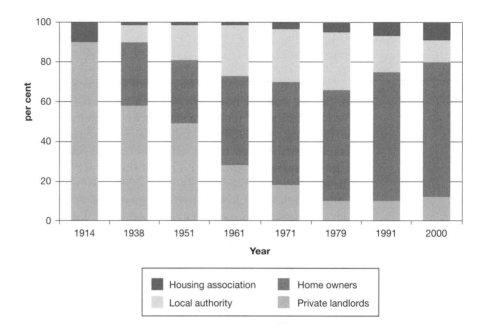

Figure 9.1 Housing tenure, 1914–2000 (United Kingdom)
Source: Based on Holmans (2000) Table 14.12 and Wilcox (2002) Table 17a

in other ways. The Town and Country Planning Act 1947 protected 'green belts' around the conurbations from development. Mandatory improvement grants for basic amenities and tax concessions, especially tax relief on mortgage interest, stimulated home ownership. The idea of improvement areas, first used by local authorities under the Housing Act 1930, was revived in the 1970s. The purpose of this neighbourhood-based housing action was to encourage owners of property to invest in improvement in the knowledge that their neighbours would also invest. Such simultaneous action would boost the image of the entire area and thereby stimulate further investment.

Conservative housing policy, 1979–1997: state to market: market to state

Between 1915 and 1979 state intervention in the housing market helped to transform the United Kingdom tenure structure. Until the middle 1970s, the Conservative Party adopted a pragmatic approach to council housing. It was prepared to assist local authorities to build homes for 'general' needs in times of extreme housing shortages. In addition, as part of a policy to contain the working class in urban areas, it was willing to subsidise housing within the conurbations for those displaced by slum clearance. In contrast, Margaret Thatcher, who had absorbed the New Right critique of state housing, regarded council housing as the embodiment of all that was wrong with the welfare state (see Briefing 9.2).

The right to buy was the flagship of Conservative housing policy (Figure 9.2). Selling council houses was not a new idea but the Housing Act 1980 gave local authority tenants a statutory right to buy at a substantial discount. The Housing Act 1988 and the Local Government and Housing Act 1989 marked a further step in the eclipse of council housing. This legislation gave the government the power to control the rents set by individual local authorities. It also allowed council tenants to choose to transfer their dwellings to another landlord and permitted the government to establish housing action trusts. These trusts would take ownership of a council estate from a specified local authority, renovate the dwellings and then sell them to 'alternative' landlords. However, tenants showed little interest in choosing an 'alternative' landlord and housing action trusts gained modest momentum only when the government allowed tenants to return to their local authority when their estate had been improved. Unexpectedly, the main mechanism by which the council housing stock was reduced, other than the right to buy, was *voluntary* transfer. Some local authorities transferred their dwellings to housing associations, often ones specially created for the purpose of stock transfer. By 1997 the percentage of dwellings rented from a local authority had declined to 17 per cent. Moreover, the sector was becoming increasingly 'residualised' with higher proportions of tenants without work and living on a low income (Bingley and Walker 2001).

Briefing 9.2   The New Right and council housing

The 'neo-classical', sometimes called the 'New Right', critique of council housing includes the following points:

- a local authority monopoly of rented accommodation for families produces inefficient management

- subsidies create a 'featherbedded', 'dependent' tenant

- the very existence of subsidised council housing prevents the development of a flourishing private landlord sector

- subsidised housing allows low-income groups to live in expensive areas and thereby creates an unlimited demand for council housing (Hayek 1960).

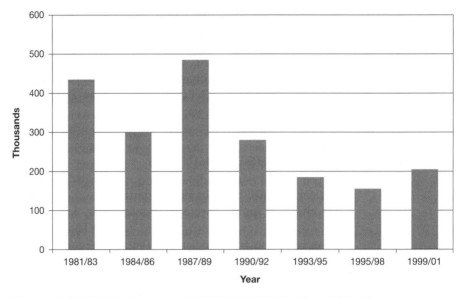

Figure 9.2 Right to buy sales, 1981/83–1999/2001 (Great Britain)

Source: After Wilcox (2002)

Policy eye 9.1   Consumer and producer subsidies

Historically, the state has subsidised housing by giving grants to producers (local authorities and, since 1974, housing associations). These organisations usually used their subsidies to reduce the general level of rents charged to tenants. Consumer subsidies go directly to tenants. Housing Benefit is now the major form of consumer subsidy. Between 1979 and 1996 producer subsidies were reduced and the savings directed towards Housing Benefit.

Changes made to the Housing Benefit system in 1986 were related to the Housing Act 1988 and the Local Government and Housing Act 1989. Nicholas Ridley, the minister responsible for housing at the time, explained the reform:

I was determined to weaken the almost incestuous relationship between some councils and their tenants. Absurdly low rents and a monopoly position in providing rented housing allowed some councils to make their tenants entirely dependent upon them ... I saw the solution as being to provide housing benefit on a sufficiently generous scale to enable all tenants to be in a position to pay their rents, and at the same time to bring rents up towards market levels. This would put all classes of landlords – councils, housing associations and private landlords – into the same competitive position.

Ridley (1992: 87–8)

Private landlords

The 1988 Housing Act also contained clauses aimed at transforming the private landlord sector. All tenancies commencing after the end of January 1989 were decontrolled. Tenants would have to pay the market rent for a property and landlords could let their dwellings as 'assured shortholds' with very limited security of tenure for tenants.

Housing associations

In the early 1980s, Mrs Thatcher regarded **housing associations** as part of the 'unproductive' public sector because their loans and grants added to the **Public Sector Borrowing Requirement**. The Housing Act 1988 changed the nature of housing associations. Renamed 'registered social landlords', they were to have more in common with private landlords than local authorities. Their properties were to be let within the same legal framework as private landlords, they would borrow a larger share of their capital from the financial markets and a higher proportion of their revenue would come from market rents supported by Housing Benefit. Suitably transformed, the registered social landlord sector expanded rapidly in the 1990s, and, by 1997, registered social landlords owned 5 per cent of the housing stock.

Housing Benefit

Historically state support for rented accommodation consisted of 'producer' subsidies to local government (Policy eye 9.1). Local authorities usually used these subsidies to reduce the general level of rents rather than to charge 'differential' or 'rebated' rents according to the incomes of their tenants. The Conservatives Housing Finance Act 1972 made provision for council house rents to increase to match the 'fair' rents in the private landlord sector. It also introduced a national system of means-tested rent rebates and allowances, known, after 1982, as Housing Benefit. Housing Benefit was reformed in 1986. If a tenant's income were below a set threshold it became possible for *all* the rent, up to a maximum determined by rent officers, to be paid through Housing Benefit. However, Housing Benefit became more selective. The 'taper' (the rate Housing Benefit is reduced for each pound of income above the threshold) was increased from 29 per cent on gross income to 65 per cent on net income (Hills 1992) with the result that Housing Benefit now makes a major contribution to the 'poverty trap'.

Home ownership

Margaret Thatcher's admiration of market economics was matched by her commitment to home ownership. The Conservatives promoted owner occupation by discounts on the market value of dwellings sold under the right to buy, the continuance of tax relief on mortgage interest and direct subsidies to housing associations to promote low-cost home ownership schemes. However, the early 1990s were difficult years for homeowners. House prices increased rapidly in the mid-1980s but subsequent increases in interest rates and a recession meant that more people were unable to meet their mortgage commitments. House prices fell leaving many homeowners with 'negative equity' – a debt greater than the current value of their dwelling.

New Labour and housing policy

'Social' housing

Traditionally, the Labour Party has been the champion of council housing but New Labour's 1997 manifesto promised only to invest the capital receipts from the sale of council houses to promote 'a three-way partnership between the public, private and housing association sectors to promote good **social housing**' (Labour Party 1997: 26).

New Labour released capital receipts as promised but 1997 to 2001 were lean years for investment in council housing because the government adopted the Conservatives plans for mainstream spending. The poor investment outlook prompted more local authorities to opt for voluntary stock transfer. Despite opposition from tenants in many areas, large-scale stock transfer from local government to registered social landlords increased from 22,248 dwellings in 1996/7 to 132,360 in 2000/1 (Wilcox 2002: 157).

New Labour's Housing Statement *Quality and Choice: A Decent Home for All: The Way Forward for Housing* promised 'to bring all social housing up to a decent standard by 2010' (Department of Environment, Transport and the Regions/Department of Social Security 2000b: 8). The Treasury supported this

---

Policy eye 9.2   Arm's-length management organisations

To establish an arm's-length management organisation (ALMO) councils create a council-owned company that manages their housing stock. The houses remain in the council's ownership and the tenants keep the same tenancy arrangements, but the board set up to run the company takes the key decisions. Tenants form part of the board with councillors and independent community representatives. Unlike stock transfer, there is no requirement to hold a tenant ballot to set up an ALMO.

objective with a cash injection but there is an estimated £19 billion repair backlog in the local authority sector (DETR/DSS 2000a: 1). Thus, the use of private finance, via outright stock transfer or the Private Finance Initiative and the development of arm's-length management organisations will be necessary to meet the 2010 target (see Policy eye 9.2).

The registered social landlord sector (mainly housing associations) expanded from 1,133,000 dwellings in 1996 to 1,602,000 in 2000 (Wilcox 2002: 90). Stock transfer from local government was the main source of this increase with New Labour setting a target of 200,000 transfers a year. Resources for new build were limited between 1997 and 2001 and this, combined with cost increases, meant that new building starts declined from 29,399 in 1996 to 16,763 in 2001 (Wilcox 2002: 96).

The private landlord sector

New Labour's contentment with the operations of the private landlord sector was reflected in its limited proposals for change. Its 1997 manifesto promised only 'protection where it is most needed for tenants in houses in multiple-occupation' by 'a proper system of licensing by local authorities which will benefit tenants and responsible landlords alike' (Labour Party 1997: 26). This promise was not redeemed in England and Wales but *Quality and Choice: A Decent Home For All: The Way Forward for Housing* stated that the government remained 'committed to introducing a compulsory licensing system for Houses in Multiple Occupation' (DETR/DSS 2000a: 28). It added that the government would also consider the selective licensing of private landlords operating in low-demand areas.

Home ownership

House prices started to increase in 1994 and a decline in interest rates allowed the Conservatives to withdraw some of the tax relief on mortgage interest to reduce the Public Sector Borrowing Requirement. Under New Labour house prices increased rapidly from an average of £60,754 in 1997 to £113,665 in 2002 (Nationwide Building Society 2002). This house price boom contributed to a public sector recruitment problem in certain areas. In response, the government introduced the Starter Home Initiative to assist key workers, particularly nurses, teachers and the police to buy where high prices would otherwise prevent their living in or near to the communities they serve.

Devolution

Under the 1998 Scotland Act housing policy, but not Housing Benefit policy, became the responsibility of a Scottish Executive accountable to the Scottish parliament. Despite this devolution of power, the Housing (Scotland) Act 2001 followed the direction of English policy. It made provision for a new form of tenancy – the Scottish Secure Tenancy Agreement – to be applied to both local authority and housing association tenants. This change was designed to facilitate stock transfer, as was the placing of both housing associations and local government under the supervision of Communities Scotland, an arm of the Scottish Executive. The Government of Wales Act 1998 gave the Welsh Assembly more limited powers than the Scottish parliament. As Williams has noted:

> Although there have been no dramatic new policies introduced, a gradual programme of change is evident. Some of this parallels developments in England but typically there is detailed tailoring to Welsh circumstances or a different approach has been adopted altogether.
>
> Williams (2002:23)

The most significant departure from English policy has been the development of a community housing mutual model for stock transfer. This model, which puts tenants at the centre of the organisations set up to receive local authority dwellings, was developed to counter Welsh resistance to established forms of stock transfer.

Housing Benefit

Lower unemployment and the eligibility restrictions introduced by the Conservatives restrained the cost of Housing Benefit but expenditure remained over £11 billion in 2001. The Green Paper *Quality and Choice: A Decent Home for All* (DETR/DSS 2000b) included a number of proposals for reform but, at first, the government concentrated on improving the administration of the existing scheme. In 2002, the Department for Work and Pensions announced that a flat-rate standard local housing allowance would be introduced in the deregulated private rented sector. This reform would give 'a new deal for tenants' because:

> [T]enants who rent a property at below the standard allowance or who move to a cheaper property in their local area, or who negotiate to keep the rent below the standard allowance, will be able to keep the difference – putting the decision in their hands.
>
> Department for Work and Pensions (2002:4)

However, although existing tenants will be protected, new tenants who cannot find a cheap property will lose out and the 'radical' reform does little to alleviate the contribution of Housing Benefit to the 'poverty trap'.

Housing and social exclusion

The Social Exclusion Unit, directly accountable to the Prime Minister, was established in 1998. It defined social exclusion as 'a shorthand term for what can happen when people or areas suffer from a combination of linked problems such as unemployment, poor skills, low incomes, poor housing, high crime environments, bad health and family breakdown' (Social Exclusion Unit 2002). Two of its first three reports focused on housing.

Unpopular housing

The government first recognised the problem of unpopular local authority housing in the late 1970s. It attributed the cause of this 'difficult to let' problem to poor housing management (Power 1987) and identified local estate management, plus greater tenant participation, as the solutions. A 'Priority Estates Project' was set up aimed at encouraging local authorities to adopt decentralised and participatory management systems.

In contrast to the 'poor housing management' explanation of 'problem estates', Coleman (1985) blamed bad design. She claimed to have discovered high correlations between indicators of 'social malaise' (litter, graffiti, excrement, vandalism and children in care) and design features such as dwellings per entrance, dwellings per block and overhead walkways. Coleman's 'architectural determinism' was combined with the 'priority estates' approach in the Estates Action Initiative. Launched in 1986, this initiative allocated significant resources to selected local authorities that produced acceptable plans involving decentralised, participatory housing management, physical improvements, economic regeneration and tenure diversification. Housing action trusts, the single regeneration budget, City Challenge and the Estates Renewal Challenge Fund provided additional resources for estate renewal.

New Deal for Communities

The Social Exclusion Unit's report *Bringing Britain Together: A National Strategy for Neighbourhood Renewal* (1998b) concentrated on 'deprived neighbourhoods' rather than 'problem estates'. It underlined the poor local authority housing management and the poor design explanations of 'problem estates' in stating:

> Poor neighbourhoods are not a pure housing problem. They are not all the same kind of design, they don't all consist of rented or council housing, and they are not all in towns and cities. They aren't all 'estates', or 'worst', nor do the people who live there want them described that way.
>
> Social Exclusion Unit (1998b: para. 1.2)

'Several thousand' poor neighbourhoods in England were identified, characterised by multiple problems coexisting in the same area. The Social Exclusion Unit attributed the overall failure of earlier programmes to a lack of 'joined-up' thinking and action, too many initiatives, a dearth of resident participation and a concentration on 'bricks and mortar' rather than 'social' capital. Oddly, given that 'initiative-itis' was one of the reasons given for the failure of previous attempts, a new programme was announced to add to the growing list of New Labour area-based initiatives. The *New Deal for Communities* promised long-term funding for 39 'pathfinder' authorities to tackle high levels of crime; educational underachievement; poor health; and housing and the physical environment in an intensive and coordinated way. It was supplemented by other measures announced when the 18 policy action teams (PATs), set up to coordinate policy at central level, had completed their 'thematic' policy reviews. The Unpopular Housing Policy Action Team identified 377,000 local authority dwellings, 89,500 registered social landlord dwellings and 461,000 private sector dwellings as unpopular and in areas of low demand (DETR 2001).

Neighbourhood renewal

The conclusions of the policy action teams were brought together in *A New Commitment to Neighbourhood Renewal: National Strategy Action Plan* (Social Exclusion Unit 2001). This report emphasised the coordination of mainstream services at the local level and the salience of resident participation in developing and implementing improvement schemes.

> Departments have worked at cross purposes on problems that required a joined-up response. Too much reliance was put on short-term regeneration initiatives in a handful of areas and too little was done about the failure of mainstream public services in hundreds of neighbourhoods ... Government failed to harness the knowledge and energy of local people, or empower them to develop their own solutions.
>
> Social Exclusion Unit (2001: para. 6)

The importance of **local strategic partnerships**, bringing together local authorities, other public services, residents and private, voluntary and community sector organisations, was stressed as was the idea of a manager to coordinate mainstream services at a neighbourhood level. The government announced the creation of a new Neighbourhood Renewal Fund to facilitate joint action at neighbourhood level. This fund would be available to the most deprived local authorities to help them to prepare and implement neighbourhood renewal schemes involving the appointment of neighbourhood managers and the coordination of mainstream services.

Rough sleeping

In the late 1980s far more people, especially young people, were seen sleeping on the streets of London and other large cities across the UK. A new term – 'rough sleepers' – entered the discourse on housing policy. The 'roughness' of the rough sleepers was seen as a threat to law and order. As Margaret Thatcher explained: 'Crowds of drunken, dirty, often abusive and sometimes violent men must not be allowed to turn central areas of the capital into no-go zones for ordinary citizens' (Thatcher 1995: 603).

Initially the government's response to the increased visibility of single homelessness was to cut Housing Benefit so that it did not 'add to the already too evident lure of the big city for young people' (Thatcher 1995: 603). However, the number of rough sleepers continued to increase and, in 1990, a Rough Sleepers Initiative was introduced aimed at contacting people sleeping rough in London, offering an emergency hostel place and then a 'move on' to permanent accommodation. This initiative reduced the number of people sleeping rough but street homelessness remained a visible problem throughout the 1990s.

New Labour's 1997 manifesto declared 'there is no more powerful symbol of Tory neglect in our society today than young people without homes living rough on the streets' (Labour Party 1997: 26). A report by the Social Exclusion Unit estimated that, in June 1998, 1,850 people were sleeping rough in England. It stressed the 'personal troubles' of rough sleepers, pointing out, for example, that 25 per cent of young rough sleepers had a stepparent, compared to the national average of 4 per cent and that 50 per cent of older rough sleepers had a 'disturbed childhood'. There was a high incidence of mental illness, alcohol problems and drug misuse among older rough sleepers. Many had experienced 'institutional' life with 50 per cent having been in prison, between 25 and 33 per cent in local authority care and 20 per cent in the armed forces (Social Exclusion Unit 1998a).

New Labour set a target to reduce the number of rough sleepers by two-thirds by 2002. It allocated £143 million to a programme similar to the Conservative's Rough Sleepers Initiative but extended to selected towns and cities outside London. The programme's objective was to encourage rough sleepers to 'come in out of the cold'. Once in centres and free from the street homelessness culture they would be helped to find homes and jobs and over-come any drug or alcohol dependency. A Rough Sleeping Unit was set up to promote 'joined-up thinking'. The Ministry of Defence was asked to review its discharge policies for members of the armed forces and the Home Office was required to examine how ex-prisoners are helped to find accommodation.

In late 2001 the government announced that it had reduced the number of rough sleepers in England to 532 – a notable achievement despite the doubts expressed about the accuracy of the count (Homeless Link 2001; White 2001). However, this reduction in rough sleeping may be difficult to sustain given the constant flow of people moving to London in search of work and the estimated 106,000 'hidden' single homeless people living in bed and breakfast accommodation, hostels and squats or sleeping on friends' floors (Crisis 2002).

Statutory homelessness

The National Assistance Act 1948 placed a duty on local authorities to provide 'temporary accommodation for persons in urgent need thereof, being need arising in circumstances that could not reasonably have been foreseen'. The duty to supply temporary accommodation fell on local authority welfare departments (the forerunners of social services departments) *not* housing departments.

As was revealed in the television drama/documentary *Cathy Come Home*, first broadcast in 1966, most welfare departments interpreted their duties in a restricted way. They offered very poor accommodation for a restricted period, separated partners and sometimes took the children of the homeless parents into local authority care (Lund 1996: 85). The Housing (Homeless Persons) Act 1977 was an attempt to ameliorate the circumstances of homeless families. The Act defined homelessness in terms of having no legal right to occupy accommodation. If a person accepted as homeless was in priority need, not intentionally homeless and had a local connection then the local *housing* authority had a duty to provide temporary accommodation while the local authority arranged secure permanent accommodation.

Despite restrictions on the obligations imposed on local authorities – people without children, for example, were not in 'priority need' unless 'vulnerable because of age, mental illness, handicap or physical disability' – recorded

"Good news, Harry. According to new council rules, we are now classed as detached home owners."

Source: www.CartoonStock.com

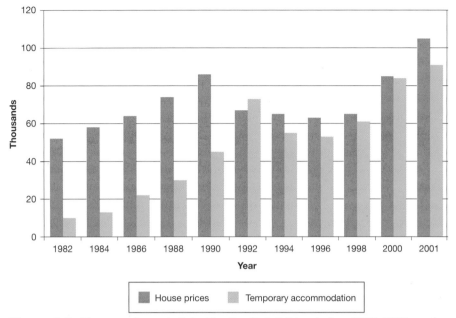

Figure 9.3 House prices deflated by the Retail Price Index, 1982–2001, and households in temporary accommodation

Source: Based on Nationwide Building Society (2003) and Wilcox (2002) Table 17a

homelessness soared in the 1980s. The Conservative government attributed the increase to the 'perverse incentives' inherent in the Housing (Homeless Persons) Act 1977. It asserted that, because legislation placed duties on local authorities to house the homeless families, then 'inevitably this makes the homelessness route seem a more attractive way into subsidised housing for those wishing be re-housed' (Department of the Environment 1994: 3). Thus, under theHousing Act 1996, local authorities became obliged to provide temporary accommodation only when satisfied that other suitable accommodation was not available. Moreover, the allocation of local authority dwellings was divorced from the duty to provide accommodation for homeless people. Local authorities had to offer dwellings only in accordance with guidelines incorporated in the Act. Homelessness was not included as a category of need for which 'reasonable preference' was to be given in allocating 'social housing' although homeless people might receive priority under other categories.

In opposition, New Labour condemned the Housing Act 1996. Its 1997 manifesto promised to 'place a new duty on local authorities to protect those who are homeless through no fault of their own and are in priority need' (Labour Party 1997: 23). This pledge was partially redeemed in 1997 when 'households who are being accommodated by the main homelessness duty' was added to the list of categories of need that local authorities were required to give reasonable preference to in allocating dwellings. However, significant change to the Housing Act 1996 had to wait until New Labour's second term. The Homelessness Act 2002 imposed a duty on local authorities to develop a homelessness strategy, abolished the two-year limit on the provision of temporary housing and extended the definition of priority groups. It also made it unlawful for local authorities to discharge their duties simply by offering an applicant an assured shorthold tenancy in the private rented sector.

Statutory homeless, having declined between 1992 and 1996, started to rise in 1997, following the rise in house prices (see Figure 9.3). New Labour's response to this increase was to set up a Bed and Breakfast Unit charged with spreading good practice and allocating additional resources to the authorities with the most pressing problems. Its target was to ensure no homeless family with children would have to live in a bed and breakfast hotel except in an emergency and then for not more than six weeks.

Housing and community care

The term 'community care' is subject to a variety of interpretations (see also Chapter 6) but, since the late 1950s, community care policy has been directed to delivering care and support to the person's own home rather than in the 'institutional' settings of hospitals, residential care homes, nursing homes and hostels. Given this objective the quality of the accommodation available to people with care and support requirements is an important dimension of community care.

Purpose-built accommodation and support

Good 'social landlords' can provide considerable help to people with special requirements through their everyday housing management activities. Nonetheless, some people may require additional assistance and, in the past, such aid was provided in 'supported housing'. Help was linked to 'bricks and mortar' provision, in the belief that clustering of people with support needs would lead to more effective and efficient support.

In the 1980s and 1990s supported housing schemes developed in a haphazard manner. Social services departments, health authorities, the probation service and housing associations used a variety of funding streams to meet the growing need for 'accommodation with support' arising from the closure of larger institutions. The creative use of funding packages from a variety of sources – the Audit Commission (1998: 93) identified 25 funding mechanisms – helped to promote a form of 'community care'. However, concern was expressed at the possible motives underlying some of the projects (the shunting of long-term costs to other authorities and onto Housing Benefit) and whether the pattern of provision was in line with need. The government's immediate response to these issues was to urge health, social services and housing to cooperate in assessment and in commissioning supported housing based on studies of existing provision and the extent of need. In addition 'floating support' (help unconnected with a specific 'special needs' housing scheme) was promoted. In 1999, following the publication of the consultation paper *Supporting People – A New Policy and Funding Framework for Support Services* (Department of Social Security 1998), the government announced that fiscal incentives would be introduced to promote planning and cooperation. By the end of 2003 funding streams for housing-linked support was to be united in a single pot distributed by local government (see Policy eye 9.3).

Adapted properties

Grants are available to help frail elderly people and people with a physical or sensory impairment to live in their own homes. Homeowners, private sector tenants and the tenants of registered social landlords can apply for a mandatory, means-tested, Disabled Facilities Grant. For council tenants the work is usually funded by the housing department. Social services departments also have powers to fund adaptations but their contribution is usually limited to less costly work.

The Audit Commission has identified lengthy delays in the process of adapting property with some applicants waiting as long as two years for routine adaptations (Audit Commission 1998: 29). It attributed these delays to a dearth of financial resources, inefficient processes (linked to the number of agencies involved) and the shortage of occupational therapists. Heywood (2001) demonstrated the success of home adaptations in improving the health, safety and independence of disabled people but noted how, in some cases, the attempt to save money had produced unsuccessful major adaptations. A study of local authority performance in delivering adaptations identified significant variations in the performance of local authorities in organising adaptations. Less than 25 per cent had a joint housing and social service team to deal with

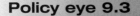

Policy eye 9.3   Sheltered housing

In terms of dwellings provided, sheltered housing for elderly people is by far the largest form of purpose-built accommodation with support. However, as the Audit Commission has commented: 'Sheltered housing was the 1970/1980s public service response to the issue of caring for older people. It predates care in the community as we now know it' (Audit Commission 1998: 27). Today, the emphasis of community care policy is on the delivery of support to the person's own home rather than moving the person to the source of support. Accordingly, the demand for sheltered housing with low levels of support is likely to decline and existing schemes will need to respond to the requirements of very frail elderly people.

adaptations and more than 35 per cent had no target times for processing applications (Age Concern and Radar 1999).

Lifetime homes

The idea of 'lifetime homes', developed by the Joseph Rowntree Foundation, is that all dwellings should be built to design standards to make them convenient and accessible for all sections of the population. This will then make it easier for people with disabilities to live in and to visit ordinary houses in ordinary streets and has the potential to save money on future adaptations. In 1999 some of the lifetime homes design features were incorporated into the Building Regulations and the Housing Corporation demands standards close to lifetime homes norms as a condition for assisting registered social landlords to develop new homes.

General housing and community care

Given that the aim of community care is to deliver care and support in the person's own home, the general availability of good-quality, affordable dwellings is vital to the success of the policy. In the past, mandatory grants have been available to assist householders to improve their dwellings to a standard above the statutory definition of unfitness. Such mandatory grants are now discretionary, a move that threatens the current level of expenditure on the improvement of the private sector housing stock. In addition, the availability of low-cost accommodation has declined in many parts of the country. The right to buy has deprived local authorities of dwellings since 1980 and, even in areas where there is an ample supply of 'social housing', much of it is in run-down neighbourhoods totally unsuitable for people with support needs.

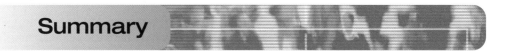

Summary

This chapter has suggested that housing, never 'decommodified' to the same extent as education and healthcare, was thoroughly 'recommodified' in the 1980s and 1990s. By 1997 the 'marketed' sector – home ownership and private landlordism – accounted for 80 per cent of the housing stock:

- New Labour has not changed the bearing of housing policy as set by the Conservatives but, although it has accepted the dominance of market forces, it has demonstrated a commitment to intervene, when necessary, to secure minimum standards. Initiatives such as the licensing landlords in 'stress' areas, the 'decent' homes programme and the remits of the Bed and Breakfast and Rough Sleeping Units indicates a focus on supplementary and particular interventions to secure minimum standards. However, the overall dominance of market forces appears to be intensifying housing problems; the incidence of statutory homelessness, for example, has followed the rise in house prices.

• In its attempts to maintain minimum standards, New Labour has been pushed towards more active intervention in the housing market, for example, in order to tackle the housing shortage in London and the wider southeast the government designated four growth areas where new 'sustainable communities' would be created by development agencies supported by public funds.

• As with other areas of social policy, at least one part of Labour's response to housing problems has been to seek to encourage 'partnership' and 'joined-up' policymaking, although it remains arguable how successful such initiatives have been in improving the provision of appropriate housing.

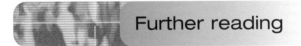

Discussion and review topics

1 How important are changing tenure patterns in housing?

2 What should the role of registered social landlords be in the provision of housing?

3 In what ways can a consideration of housing contribute to tackling social exclusion?

4 What are the main arguments for and against subsidies for rented housing?

Further reading

Balchin, P. and Rhoden, M. (2002) *Housing Policy*, Routledge, London – a good general introduction to housing policy

Hamnett, C. (1999) *Winners and Losers: Home Ownership in Modern Britain*, Routledge, London – looks at the key issues and inequalities that are associated with home ownership including income, class, gender and 'race'

Murie, A. and Malpass, P. (1999) *Housing Policy and Practice*, Macmillan, London – a thorough and accessible introduction to the topic

Some useful websites

www.crisis.org.uk – Crisis is a charity for solitary homeless people. Its website provides a range of facts and publications

www.lga.gov.uk – the Local Government Association provides information and briefings on a range of housing-related issues from the perspective of local government

www.odpm.gov.uk – the Office of the Deputy Prime Minister's website provides information on the government's policies on housing, homelessness and related subjects

www.shelter.org.uk – a charity that campaigns on homelessness, Shelter gives access to facts and publications, as well as to www.homelessnessact.org.uk, which gives information on the Homelessness Act and related topics

References

Age Concern/Radar (1999) *Disabled Facilities Grants – Is the System Working?*, Radar, London

Audit Commission (1998) *Home Alone: The Role of Housing in Community Care*, Audit Commission, London

Bingley, P. and Walker, I. (2001) 'Housing subsidies and work incentives in Great Britain', *The Economic Journal*, 111, 86–103

Coleman, A. (1985) *Utopia on Trial*, Hilary Shipman, London

Crisis (2002) *Hidden Homeless Campaign*, http://www.crisis.org.uk/about/crisis_hidden_homeless.php

Department for Work and Pensions (2002) *Building Choice and Responsibility: a Radical Agenda for Housing Benefit*, The Stationery Office, London

Department of the Environment (1994) *Access to Local Authority and Housing Association Tenancies: A Consultation Paper*, Department of the Environment, London

Department of the Environment, Transport and the Regions/Department of Social Security (2000a) *Quality and Choice: A Decent Home for All, The Housing Green Paper*, The Stationery Office, London

Department of the Environment, Transport and the Regions (2000b) *Quality and Choice: A Decent Home for All: The Way Forward for Housing*, The Stationery Office, London

Department of the Environment, Transport and the Regions (2001) *Unpopular Housing: A Report of the Policy Action Team 7*, The Stationery Office, London

Department of Social Security (1998) *Supporting People – A New Policy and Funding Framework for Support Services*, Department of Social Security, London

Halsey, A. H. and Webb, J. (2000) *Twentieth-Century British Social Trends*, Palgrave, London

Hayek, F. A. (1960) *The Constitution of Liberty*, Routledge, London

Heywood, F. (2001) *Money Well Spent: The Effectiveness and Value of Housing Adaptations*, Policy Press, Bristol

Hills, J. (1992) *Unravelling Housing Finance: Subsidies, Benefits, Taxation*, Clarendon Press, Oxford

Hills, J. (1998) 'Housing: a decent home within the reach of every family' in Glennerster, H. and Hills, J. (eds) *The State of Welfare: The Economics of Social Spending*, Oxford University Press, Oxford

Holmans, A. (2000) 'Housing' in Halsey, A. H. and Webb, J. *Twentieth-Century British Social Trends*, Palgravve, London

Holmans, A. E. (1987) *Housing Policy in Britain: A History*, Croom Helm, Beckenham

Howard, E. (1902) *Garden Cities of Tomorrow*, Faber, London

Homeless Link (2001) *Street Homelessness: The Way Forward*, http://www.homeless.org.uk/db/20010815112525

Labour Party (1997) *New Labour because Britain Deserves Better*, Labour Party, London

Le Grand, J., Popper, C. and Robinson, R. (1984) *The Economics of Social Problems*, Macmillan, Basingstoke

Lund, B. (1996) *Housing Problems and Housing Policy*, Longman, London

Nationwide Building Society (2003) *UK House Prices since 1952* http://www.nationwide.co.uk/hpi/downloads/UK%20house%20price%20since%2019 52.xls

Morton, J. (1991) *Cheaper Than Peabody*, Joseph Rowntree Foundation, York

Pennance, F. G. (1969) *Housing Market Analysis and Policy*, Hobart Paper No. 48, Institute of Economic Affairs, London

Power, A. (1987) *Property Before People*, Allen & Unwin, London

Ridley, N. (1992) *'My Style of Government': The Thatcher Years*, Fontana, London

Social Exclusion Unit (1998a) *Rough Sleeping*, The Stationery Office, London

Social Exclusion Unit (1998b) *Bringing Britain Together: A National Strategy for Neighbourhood Renewal*, The Stationery Office, London

Social Exclusion Unit (2001) *A New Commitment to Neighbourhood Renewal: National Strategy Action Plan*, The Stationery Office, London

Social Exclusion Unit (2002) http://www.socialexclusionunit.gov.uk

Thatcher, M. (1995) *The Downing Street Years*, HarperCollins, London

White, G. (2001) 'Charity questions rough sleepers cut'. *Housing Today*, 6 December

Wilcox, S. (2002) *UK Housing Review 2002/2003*, Chartered Institute of Housing/Council of Mortgage Lenders in association with Joseph Rowntree Foundation, York

Williams, P. (2002) 'Stand and deliver! Tackling the housing challenges in post-devolution Wales', in Wilcox, S., *UK Housing Review 2002/2003*, Joseph Rowntree Foundation, York

Ethics, risk and social policy

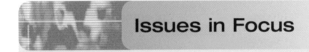

10 Hugh Bochel

Issues in Focus

While ethical considerations have always been a part of social policy, they have not always received overt consideration within the subject. Yet increasingly they can be seen to impinge on people's lives, both as recipients and providers of services. This is perhaps most apparent with regard to the rationing and targeting of services, but includes the behaviour of professionals and has also spread into new areas including reproductive technologies, ranging from topics such as in vitro fertilisation to cloning.

Ethical concerns can be wide ranging in their relationship with social policy, from issues such as abortion, adoption and euthanasia to topics such as charging and rationing. In addition, increasingly attention has also been paid to the idea of 'risk' and some of the implications this has for social policy, whether in relation to fears about food safety, choices in health care, or the balance between public and private provision.

Seeking to outline some of the key considerations in relation to these matters, this chapter examines:

- different approaches to ethical theory

- the implications of these for our understanding of issues

- the application of ethics to practical issues

- why 'risk' has become more important in social policy.

Ethical issues in social policy can be examined from a number of perspectives. They can be grounded in some of the traditional key concepts of social policy, such as social needs and social problems, related to notions of rights, equality, social justice and choice, linked with concepts such as efficiency and effectiveness or related to notions of altruism and reciprocity. They also emerge strongly from **applied philosophy**, for example with regard to the practitioner–patient relationship in healthcare.

'Being ethical' might be seen as always conforming to a particular view of what is right and what is wrong, so that two people with conflicting views over what is right and wrong would make different choices about what actions to take. This can easily be seen in debates over abortion, where one doctor might believe that it is wrong to destroy a group of cells that could become a human being, while another might believe that a pregnant woman has the right to make choices about her body. Here the entire idea of morality seems to be difficult, as it appears to be subject to interpretation, contestation and conflict. However, many moral philosophers argue that this is not the case and that some decisions and actions can be seen as being of a higher moral calibre than others.

However, debates about ethics can be even more complicated than they may at first appear. To take the example of euthanasia, where there has been considerable debate about the rights and wrongs of such action, including varying moral and ethical perspectives, some disabled people have argued that because disabled people's lives are sometimes perceived as less worthwhile (and more 'tragic' and burdensome) there is a greater danger that additional pressures might be brought to bear on them. This draws in part upon the view that the legalisation of 'assisted dying' (or assisted suicide) may bring further pressures to bear on some groups, including not only disabled people, but also older people who fear becoming a burden; however, it also draws on debates about whether all lives have equal value; and it raises questions about whether individuals' 'informed choice' might be the same if support and resources were provided to enable people to live in a dignified manner.

In seeking to look in more detail at these issues, it is, loosely speaking, possible to draw a rough divide between ethical theory and applied ethics, although the latter clearly draws on the former for guidance while the former frequently seeks to anticipate the challenges of the latter. The next sections of this chapter seek to develop the consideration of ethics and social policy within this context.

Ethical theory

Ethical theory inevitably has a philosophical bent. It draws heavily on concepts of morality and explanations of how our behaviour affects others. While some moral 'choices' may appear relatively easy to make, such as whether a health or social care professional should report a case of child sexual abuse, in many cases it is not possible to reach a straightforward decision about whether an action is right or wrong or good or bad (Briefing 10.1 provides one thinker's view of what ethics is). Making difficult decisions is further complicated by the awareness that our own moral outlook and thinking is inevitably shaped and affected by others, including family, friends, community and society. Yet if individuals are to make their own decisions it is generally seen as desirable that they do so independently and that they do not simply reflect the views of others. While it may be possible, and sometimes appropriate, to learn from the views and experiences of others, it is equally the case that collective wisdom is not necessarily correct, as can be evidenced from examples such as slavery, genocide or denying women the right to vote.

One way in which we can seek to analyse and evaluate our views more critically is through a more abstract consideration of issues. LaFollette (1997) suggests that we can make three principal mistakes in ethical deliberations:

- We can apply ethical principles inconsistently – for us to defend our moral views successfully it is essential that they are *consistent*; conversely, inconsistency is frequently seen as a weakness in the arguments of others. This is true whether the debate is over abortion, rationing of healthcare or freedom of speech. Inconsistency can therefore often be a compelling reason to reject someone's moral position.

Briefing 10.1   Ethics (one view)

What ethics is not	What ethics is
• Prohibitions particularly concerned with sex – moral issues around sex that are not unique.	• Living according to ethical standards so long as people believe it is right do as they are doing.
• An ideal system that does not work in practice – different perspectives on ethics can successfully argue that in ethics the failure of short, simple rules is not a failure of ethics as a whole.	• Takes a universal point of view – ethics requires a view that goes beyond the 'I' or 'you'.
• Something intelligible only in the context of religion – ethical behaviour does not require a religious underpinning.	• Can draw on a variety of approaches, including utilitarianism/consequentialism and deontology.
• Relative or subjective – ethical reasoning is possible.	

Source: Adapted from Singer (1993)

- We can use inappropriate moral standards – not only is it important to be consistent; we must also base our arguments on appropriate guidelines or standards (*correct principles*) and theorising about ethics is a good way of identifying the best standards or guidelines.

- We can apply moral standards inappropriately – even if we have identified what is morally relevant and seek to act consistently based on that, we can still make moral mistakes, for example if we try to protect someone's feelings or to protect ourselves or through lacking the personal and verbal skills to be honest in a way which will not harm others. *Correct application* of moral standards is therefore important.

Are moral judgements matters of opinion?

It is sometimes argued that moral judgements are simply 'matters of opinion'. However, an implication of this would be that if moral judgements are *just* opinions, all opinions may be equally good (or bad) and it would not therefore be possible morally to scrutinise the judgements of ourselves or others. This is likely to be an undesirable situation and it is generally accepted that not all moral opinions are in reality equally reliable. For instance, an opinion that is clearly based on misinformation, lack of perception or on bizarre or outrageous principles would be viewed by most people as inferior to one that is based on full information, shrewd perception and moral principles that have been subject to and withstood the careful scrutiny of others. In addition, in some circumstances we are required to make an informed decision that will profoundly affect others, and that will require appropriate moral choices.

Importantly, abiding by ethical principles should not be viewed as being the same as following the law. The law may be, and often is, informed by ethics, but at times it may oppose ethical principles, with one of the most commonly used examples of this being laws that existed in Nazi Germany. Individuals have frequently rebelled against laws on ethical grounds. It is also apparent that laws change over time, as has been the case with abortion.

Role of theory

Even in cases where people agree that an issue should be evaluated, at least in part, by criteria based on **morality**, there is often disagreement about how this should be done. This is clear with regard to absolute and relative definitions of poverty or whether long-term social care for older people should be free or paid for, as well as arguments such as those for and against abortion and capital punishment. However, people do not normally simply make moral judgements and are usually prepared to explain and give reasons for their views. For example, anti-abortionists may claim that abortion is not justified as the foetus has the same right to life as other people, while pro-abortionists may argue that a woman has the right to decide what happens to and in her body. In such debates, the protagonists are usually putting forward some feature of their view that is supposed to underpin their evaluation. Such arguments can be developed. To take the case of capital punishment, it may not be sufficient simply to argue over whether capital punishment deters crime, but it may be necessary to discover exactly how important the deterrent is. Ethical theories are therefore concerned to undertake systematic discussions of theoretical questions; they seek to identify the relevant moral criteria, to gauge the weight or significance of those criteria and to provide a sense of how we can determine whether an action or decision satisfies those criteria. However, as is explored later in the chapter, ethical theories do not and cannot tell us how we should act in all situations. Rather, what they do is to offer different criteria of moral relevance and to direct our attention to specific features of action.

Broadly speaking, there can be said to be two main classes of ethical theory: consequentialist and deontological. While there are other moral theories it is these that shall be considered here. The consequentialist approach is that we should choose the available action with the best overall consequences, while deontological theory suggests that we should act in ways that are circumscribed by moral rules or rights that are defined, at least in part, independently of consequences.

Consequentialism

Consequentialists argue that we should act in ways that produce the best consequences. In making a decision we would therefore seek to identify the available options, trace the likely moral consequences of each and then select the option with the best outcome for all concerned. Yet, while this approach appears to have considerable appeal, for it is hard to argue against achieving the best outcome, it may be difficult to determine which consequences should be considered and how much weight should be given to each, for without that information it is not possible to know how to act. The best-known form of consequentialism is *utilitarianism*, often summarised as being about choosing 'the greatest happiness for the greatest number'. Again however, this is not as simple as it may first appear and, for example, there are differences between *act utilitarians*, who claim that we should determine the morality of each action by deciding which action is more likely to promote the greatest happiness of the greatest number, and *rule utilitarians* who argue that the concern should not be whether one *particular* action is likely to promote the greatest happiness of the greatest number, but whether one particular *type* of action would, if done by most people, promote the greatest happiness of the greatest number. An act utilitarian might therefore conclude that in a particular instance a lie would be justified as it maximises the happiness of all those concerned, while a rule utilitarian might argue that since the result of everyone lying would be a reduction in happiness it would be best to have a rule against lying, even if in a particular case lying would appear to give the greatest happiness to the greatest number (Briefing 10.2). Teichman (1996) identifies a number of problems with consequentialism:

- It cannot be put into practice as short-term consequences cannot be predicted with certainty and long-term consequences cannot be predicted at all.

- It is not possible to weigh one person's happiness or pleasure against that of another, neither can a person's present happiness be weighed against their future potential happiness.

- Consequentialism in practice would be likely to damage the rights of individuals and minority groups in favour of the happiness of majorities.

- There would be risks of politicians deciding what sort of results were the most important, potentially leading them to make decisions in the interests of themselves and their supporters at the expense of others.

- Consequentialism would mean that justice could be overruled where an act of injustice might be thought likely to produce better results.

There are also other problems with utilitarianism, including that not all utilitarian philosophers accept that happiness should be the measure of the greatest good, with possible alternative principal values including friendship, health, knowledge or personal autonomy.

Deontological theory

In contrast to consequentialists, deontologists argue that our moral choices can be seen, to some extent, as independent of consequences. For deontologists

---

Briefing 10.2   An ethical dilemma

On whether to tell a client that his wife is sleeping with another woman in order to have the school fees for her son paid. Mma Ramotswe:
  'It is unethical for a detective to lie to the client. You can't do it.'
  'I can understand that,' said Mma Makutsi. 'But there are times, surely, when a lie is a good thing. What if a murderer came to your house and asked you where a certain person was? And what if you knew where that person was, would it be wrong to say: "I do not know anything about that person. I do not know where he is." Would that not be a lie?'
  'Yes. But then you have no duty to tell the truth to that murderer. So you can lie to him. But you do have a duty to tell the truth to your client, or to your spouse, or to the police. That is all different.'
  'Why? Surely if it is wrong to lie, then it is always wrong to lie. If people could lie when they thought it was the right thing to do, then we could never tell when they meant it.' Mma Makutsi, stopped, and pondered for a few moments before continuing. 'One person's idea of what is right may be quite different from another's. If each person can make up his own rule ...' She shrugged, leaving the consequences unspoken.

Source: Alexander McCall Smith (2003) *Tears of the Giraffe*, Abacus, London, pp. 170–71.

acts and decisions must not only be in accordance with, but also for the sake of duty or obligation. For example, obligations such as not to kill or steal, are not justified simply on the grounds that following such rules will always produce the best consequences, but because they are underpinned by some other judgement, whether this emerges from abstract reasoning, intuition or some other form of principles. While consequentialist approaches may be attractive for their apparent rationality, deontological ideas are appealing as they suggest that we can discover that some ways of acting are right while others are wrong.

From a deontological perspective decisions should therefore be made by referring to considered principles, rather than on the basis of expedient calculation, and what is most important is not the outcome, but whether a person acts according to a perceived obligation, and intends that some good come about. If telling the truth is a moral duty, then telling the truth is the right way to act even if the result is to cause more misery than happiness. For deontologists it is wrong to ignore these principles as to do so allows us to choose decisions that are made on the basis of contingency and, even more problematically, while breaking faith with principles may appear to be beneficial in the short term, in the longer term the consequences will not be better. Rule deontology in theory therefore gives predictability, with rules being recognised and respected. However, in the case of almost any rule there will be times when a judgement might be made that the outcome may be better if the rule is broken. There will also be times, perhaps even more awkwardly, particularly for many areas of social policy, when different rules come into conflict and it is necessary to choose between them. And in such situations, even if it is possible to choose one rule over another, the position that it may sometimes be better if a rule is broken would still be likely to apply.

Act deontology is a form of deontology that on the face of it is almost self-contradictory. Rather than following rules, act-deontologists assume that each situation is different and that each individual must make their own judgement. The moral obligation for act deontologists is to be true to themselves. While arguably being difficult or impossible to put into practice, act deontology does direct us towards a different consideration of moral rules and, in particular, to recognise that simply because a rule has worked successfully in the past it may not do so in each subsequent situation, as each circumstance will have its own unique features. It also highlights the argument that a person should be true to themselves in each situation and should not operate differently in their 'professional' and 'ordinary' lives, a line of reasoning often of great relevance to many professionals involved with areas of social policy.

Justice

The concept of 'justice' is widely used in social and political theory. It is also important in ethics. While it is used in many different ways these can perhaps be subdivided into two principal categories: concerns over 'fairness' and 'appropriate punishment for wrongdoing'. While the latter is clearly of importance to society, it is the former category that is of concern here. However, even 'justice as fairness' is not a straightforward concept, as, for example, it could be interpreted as 'to each according to her/his need', 'to each according to what s/he deserves', or 'to each according to her/his rights'.

One approach that is frequently used in considering justice is that of the philosopher John Rawls (1973), through which he argues that unequal possession and distribution of qualities such as power, wealth and income are unacceptable in a society unless they actually work to benefit the worst off members of society. Although this is a complex argument a simplified version is given here. Rawls uses the hypothetical situation of people as free, logical and disinterested beings, about to enter into a social contract with everyone else in order to form a just society; yet a key feature of this is that no one knows what or where they will be in the society, so that the social contract is to be made behind a 'veil of ignorance' – no one would know in advance whether they would be rich or poor, male or female, young or old, ill or healthy, employer or employee. He then asks us, as potential social contractors, to consider which principles should be adopted by the society in order to be just? Rawls' own answer is that there should be two main principles of justice, with the first taking precedence in the event of any conflict between them:

1   Each person should have an equal right to the maximum amount of liberty consistent with a similar liberty for others, so that each person has the same right to freedom as any other, unless that freedom works against the freedom of others. The basic liberties, for Rawls, are political liberty, the right to property, freedom from arbitrary arrest and being within a system of law that deals impartially with those who fall under its remit.

2   Any social and economic inequalities should be arranged to ensure that they work to everyone's advantage, including the worst off in society. Inequalities may be inevitable, but if these work only to benefit those who are already privileged they should not be allowed. For Rawls, a justifiable inequality would be a surgeon who is well off, but only because her skills contribute to the well-being of all, so that a society without the services of the rich surgeon would be worse off.

Of course, Rawls' argument can be criticised, for example over whether equality should come after liberty, as the social contractors might feasibly conclude that the equal distribution of resources is the best way of ensuring justice within society. However, whatever the rights and wrongs or the nuances of the arguments, it is clear that Rawls' theory highlights the strong connection between morality and politics and, in particular, suggests that if social structures do not allow all people the opportunity to achieve their potentials then morality is not being created to the greatest degree possible. Since most work related to social policy is arguably moral in nature and often sits on basic principles of justice and fairness, then it is of moral concern because it itself can be directly responsible for increasing or decreasing the level of morality achieved.

Feminist ethics

It is possible to identify feminist critiques of traditional ethical approaches. While these reflect the diversity of feminist approaches (see also Chapter 14), Porter (1999) suggests that there are three interrelated features of feminist ethics (personal experience; context, with an emphasis on the idea that context is important in informing morally appropriate choices; and nurturant relationships, with care, nurture and relationships being central to the consideration of ethics) which, while also important for other ethical perspectives, provide a distinctiveness for feminist ethics through being located in women's experiences, challenging gendered dualisms and enabling the development of alternatives.

These arguments can have an impact on the way that we understand ethics. Many feminists would, for example, challenge Rawls' liberal justice perspective, arguing that people are not rational, disembodied individuals and that, instead, it is important to recognise that identity is constituted and affected by a variety of ties, links with communities and social structures. Similarly, feminists may argue that it is necessary to recognise the existence of gendered moral perspectives, for example over the extent to which men and women display care, and that it may be appropriate to examine power relationships rather than simply suggesting that men and women have different moral perspectives.

Applied ethics

Applied, or practical, ethics is clearly concerned with the application of ethics or morality to practical issues. Part of the reason that ethics and morality are so important to social policy is that many actions will involve intervention in the lives of others, whether this is in terms of healthcare, social care, housing or other areas of policy. It is possible, as many writers do, to discuss ethics with regard to most aspects of life.

There are a number of areas where ethical debates are immediately apparent and can have an direct effect on policy, such as those around abortion, conception and euthanasia. In areas such as these there is considerable material available from groups campaigning for and against different positions and from others with interests in those debates. For example, Singer, in *Practical Ethics* (1993) examines a variety of topics, some of which have a clear social policy dimension, including notions of equality, abortion, euthanasia and divisions between rich and poor countries. Although not seeking to provide a comprehensive consideration of the relevance of applied ethics to social policy, this section briefly considers three very different areas of concern where ethical debates have clear relevance to the development and implementation of policy: rationing, human genetics and professional ethics.

Rationing

Rationing and targeting of resources has long been a significant feature in the discussion and delivery of public services. Arksey (2002) has pointed out that in healthcare, in particular, media coverage has at times been intense, while there has also been periodic concern over rationing in other fields, such as the provision of social care or social housing. It is arguable that in areas such as these, decisions are increasingly being driven according to what is available, rather than what individuals need. Indeed, rationing is inevitably a major dilemma for social policy as resources are not limitless and problems can rarely be solved simply through an ever greater input of resources. It is therefore necessary to devise strategies for rationing, whether the provision is of education, healthcare or social security benefits (Briefing 10.3). Arksey argues that rationing is of itself not necessarily bad or undesirable, as, if based on the principle of 'equity based on need', people with equal need could receive equal treatment and those with the greatest needs would receive top priority, although, of course, issues over the level of resourcing of each service would remain.

If the example of healthcare is followed here, one approach to rationing that

Briefing 10.3   Forms of rationing

- *Rationing by denial* – turning people away on the grounds that they are not suitable or their needs are not urgent enough; the threshold of eligibility for a service is raised and lowered to match supply and demand.
- *Rationing by selection* – the converse of rationing by denial; providers of services select clients who are most likely to benefit from intervention, who are seen as deserving cases, or who are least likely to cause problems.
- *Rationing by deflection* – potential recipients are diverted towards another service, for example a social services problem being redefined as a health or housing problem.
- *Rationing by deterrence* – discouraging entry into the system, through barriers such as receptionists, lack of provision of information, queues or costs.
- *Rationing by delay* – demand can be discouraged by delay, with appointments weeks or months ahead, or through waiting lists.
- *Rationing by dilution* – rather than reducing services the scale and depth of them is reduced so that users are not excluded, but everyone receives less, for example through cutting appointment periods for doctors or raising class sizes in schools.
- *Rationing by termination* – in some cases delivery of a service may be ended, with doctors discharging patients or social workers closing cases.

Source: Adapted from Klein, Day and Redmayne (1996) pp. 11–12

received considerable attention during the 1980s and 1990s was suggestions for measures to allow the calculation of priorities through criteria such as the relief of symptoms, quality of life and likely survival time. Quality-adjusted life years (QALYs) were one such method proposed in the United Kingdom, while in the United States the state of Oregon devised and implemented a form of rationing based on a set of costs and benefits. In terms of the arguments outlined earlier in this chapter, initiatives such as these can arguably be seen as representing a shift from a deontological approach to consequentialism, with the emphasis being on the assessment of the consequences of human actions. They can also be criticised in a similar way as they tend to an approach whereby as long as there is more 'good' (cost-effective life) than 'bad' (expensive life) then particular actions can be said to be justified.

However, one of the strongest arguments for the adoption of measures such as QALYs is that they expose the often hidden rationing that already takes place and the injustice of some of the decisions that have existed within the NHS and suggests that these might have been avoided had the structure and funding of the NHS been different. Supporters of QALYs produced a variety of arguments for their use including that they provide a way of making priorities explicit, to compare the costs and effectiveness of different treatments and therefore to make the most cost-effective use of resources. Even some critics accept that they have a use in helping to remind us that decisions about rationing may not always be because overall resources are lacking, but because decisions are made to use resources for other purposes.

While QALYs have not been formally accepted as part of UK healthcare, the NHS does provide another example of the ways in which rationing has become more explicit. With the creation by the Labour government of the National Institute for Clinical Excellence (NICE) in 1999, for the first time there was a national body responsible for advising professionals, patients and the public in England and Wales about the use of health technologies (medicines, medical devices, diagnostic techniques and procedures and the clinical management of specific conditions). NICE was also intended to help ensure that provision of drugs and services should become more even across different parts of England and Wales. While NICE has a wide range of responsibilities, perhaps the most obvious to the public has been its decisions about which drugs and treatments should be available through the NHS. For example, in early 2002 NICE decided that access to the drug irinotecan, used for treating bowel cancer, should be heavily restricted, although it had become standard treatment for the condition in the United States and much of Europe.

Critics have also argued that the denial of drugs on prescription, following decisions made by NICE, effectively leads to a two-tier service, with those who can afford to pay for treatment doing better than NHS patients, effectively failing to end the 'postcode prescribing' that NICE was established to prevent. Rationing has therefore been shifted even further in the direction of class and ability to pay, so that it is only those patients who can afford private treatment who have access to some treatments.

It is clear from this brief consideration of rationing within the NHS that ethical analysis can have significant implications and that the application of ideas based on interpretations of consequentialist or deontological approaches, as well as notions of justice, could be used to explore many of the existing practices on which rationing is based. A consequentialist, and particularly a utilitarian view, would emphasise an approach which produced collective benefit. Consequentialists might also favour decision making based on the use of more 'objective' measures rather than on considered moral principles that might arise from a deontological perspective. Given this, even from the short discussion thus far, it is perhaps possible to suggest that the provision of healthcare has been moving towards a more consequentialist position than was previously the case.

Science, human genetics and reproduction

Scientific advances in recent years have brought a series of major questions to the fore around **human genetics** and reproduction (as well as those around agriculture and food). In the context of this chapter it is possible only to outline some of these challenges and examples of the dilemmas that they are introducing. However, it is safe to say that they are both wide ranging and profound and that many may have significant long-term implications for both individuals and societies. Some of those that have been most apparent have been around human fertilisation, with for example, concerns over cloning, 'designer babies' and the use of embryos in researching the understanding and treatment of disease having been widely raised in the media in recent years. The wider issues related to human genetics have also come more to the attention of the public, with the possible implications of genetic testing and genetic manipulation raising the prospect of further difficult ethical decisions in the future.

In the United Kingdom the response of governments to the emergence of these new challenges has largely involved the introduction of new regulatory and advisory bodies, such as the Human Fertilisation and Embryology Authority and the Human Genetics Commission.

The Human Fertilisation and Embryology Authority was created following the Human Fertilisation and Embryology Act 1990 to regulate and advise on infertility treatment and embryology research. Perhaps inevitably, in an area where there are major ethical dimensions and disagreements, and where laws made even a decade before are challenged by rapid scientific advances, there has been extensive use of the courts. The HFEA has been involved in a number of high-profile cases, including its attempts in the 1990s to prevent the widowed Diane Blood from using her dead husband's sperm to conceive children in the absence of his written consent, a battle she ultimately won through using EU law to travel to Brussels for treatment, and that of Zain Hashmi (see Policy eye 10.1). It is apparent here that there are a number of complex and interrelated issues. However, from one perspective a key ethical dimension could be seen as Zain's parents' intention being to use their unborn child to help their existing son. The second child would come to no harm, apart from taking blood and its birth would help Zain. But were they right to propose to

Policy eye 10.1   Zain Hashmi – ethics and the legal system

Zain Hashmi was born with a genetic blood disorder, beta thalassaemia, leaving him needing frequent blood transfusions and threatening his life. Having failed to find a donor with matching tissue, in December 2001 his parents, Raj and Shahana Hashmi were given permission by the Human Fertilisation and Embryology Authority to attempt to create a new sibling whose umbilical cord blood could be used to cure Zain. The proposal was that embryos would be screened and if one were to match Zain's tissue type and was also free of beta thalassaemia, it would be implanted in Shahana Hashmi's womb. This went one step beyond the HFEA's previous decisions, which had been limited to licensing pre-implementation genetic diagnoses, allowing parents at risk of having a child with genetic disorder to have their embryos screened and only those that were unaffected implanted. This was the first time that the HFEA had allowed such a move and although the Authority insisted that this was a one-off decision it was seen by others as setting an ethical precedent for the parents of other children who suffer from life-threatening disorders that can be cured only by bone marrow transplants and for whom no suitable donor can be found. A legal challenge to this was launched by Josephine Quintavalle of the group Comment on Reproductive Ethics (CORE), which believed that IVF techniques should be used only for the benefit of the baby concerned, not to help a sibling. CORE argued that the HFEA had no power to license the new process and the High Court ruled in CORE's favour. However, in April 2003 the Court of Appeal overturned this decision allowing the Hashmis the possibility of proceeding with treatment.

The entire affair was made more complicated by the existence of the Human Rights Act, as the HFEA had earlier been concerned that, had it not given the Hashmis permission to go ahead, they might have challenged such a decision legally as violating Zain's right to life.

use their new child as a means to an end? Clearly this is not an easy question to answer.

Where human genetics is concerned, the government created the Human Genetics Commission in 1999 to review the likely benefits and risks of advances and to address the ethical, legal and social implications arising from these advances. It sees a key element of its work as consulting with and informing the public and other stakeholders. One of the first areas to be affected by awareness of the potential implications of these advances in genetics has been the world of insurance, particularly over genetic screening and testing and their implications. In April 1997 the Council of Europe adopted a convention that stated that there should be no discrimination against a person on the grounds of their genetic heritage. While the UK has not ratified that convention it does serve to indicate the levels of concern about the uses of genetic tests and the ways in which they may create new or reinforce existing inequalities. In the UK in 2001 the Human Genetics Commission made a number of recommendations, including a three-year moratorium on the use of genetic test results by employers and from October 2001 the insurance industry and the government agreed a five-year moratorium on the use of **predictive genetic tests** for most policies, with only those for large sums of money being excluded. Daykin et al. (2003) have identified a number of philosophical considerations around this issue, each of which relates to traditional social policy concerns:

- *solidarity and mutuality* – with insurance schemes operating on principles of solidarity and equality, there has been confusion between solidarity and mutuality

- *moral hazard* – where individuals may change their behaviour patterns because they have taken out insurance, perhaps exercising less caution because they are protected against particular risks, with insurers fearing that advances in genetic testing may increase the likelihood of moral hazard

- *concepts of fairness in insurance* – these change over time with, for example, distinctions between smokers and non-smokers now taken into account in risk categories in a way that would not have been seen as acceptable previously. It could be argued, for instance, that it is unfair to penalise people who inherit genetic 'conditions' as they can do nothing to affect that situation.

- *adverse selection* – the situation where those seeking cover have more information about their true level of risk than does the insurer, which they can use to their advantage when buying insurance.

However, for some people the ethical concerns go much further, sometimes reflecting past concerns over **eugenics**. For example, Kerr (2003) notes that while there are significant differences, emphases such as those on personal responsibility and public education are similar. There have also been fears that because for the great majority of genetically identified conditions there are no new therapies, pre-natal screening can often lead to abortion of a foetus and that this, in turn, may be seen as 'an attempt to get rid of disabled people' (BCODP 2000). However, others seek to differentiate the two issues and argue that a women's right to choose should not be used to imply a particular view of a condition that might lead to a disability.

Again, many of the arguments around genetics can be examined from either a consequentialist or a deontological perspective. For consequentialists, it would obviously be the consequences that arise from any use of human genetics that would be important, rather than a pre-existing idea of the right or wrong of an action. A deontological perspective, contrariwise, would argue that in addition to the consequences the right or wrong of the type of action to be taken would be important, whether or not the outcome was to be good.

Professional ethics

For social policy, additional obvious links with ethics come in relation to professional practice and in the arenas of health and social care in particular, where social, political and technological changes have seen the development of ethical codes or guidelines for many professions. Many professions now have codes written for them, including doctors, nurses and psychologists. Used in this sense 'profession' tends to mean a self-regulating organisation that controls entry into particular occupations through recognition of the achievement of the necessary knowledge and skills. Ethical codes for such groups tend to form part of the statement about the profession and its standards so that 'professional standards' are seen as distinct from those standards that may be imposed by other bodies, such as governments, even though there may be overlap between them. However, while such codes can provide valuable guidance they can be criticised for implying that a professional who meets the requirement of the code is fulfilling all their moral obligations. Similarly, the extent to which such codes are comprehensive and coherent can be debated and frequently there is a need for further clarification and guidance.

Seedhouse (1988) raises two important questions, arising out of the debate about ethical theory as discussed earlier in this chapter, which although he applies them to healthcare, are more generally applicable:

● How can we be ethical when we do not know for certain what it is to be ethical?

Source: www.CartoonStock.com

● How can we be ethical when we do not agree among ourselves what it is to be ethical?

He then seeks to help answer his own questions and to enable a more practical use of moral reasoning through the introduction of an 'ethical grid' (Figure 10.1) which he intended to be a instrument to help health workers reason morally, but which he argues could be used by others in society. His approach draws on a social aspect to moral reasoning rather than some of the alternatives, such as that of Beauchamp and Childress (1994), discussed later, which is founded more in the medical model. The grid consists of four layers: blue, which lies at the centre and provides the core rationale, consisting of boxes that 'present a rich and fruitful theory of health' (p. 129); red, which focuses on duties and motives, corresponding largely with deontological theories, with boxes that 'are intimately related to the richest sense of health' (p. 135); green, drawing on consequentialist approaches to 'focus attention on the necessity

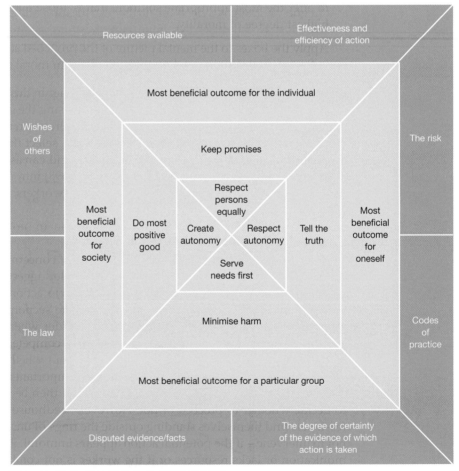

Figure 10.1 Seedhouse's 'ethical grid'

Source: After Seedhouse (1988)

always to consider the consequences of any proposed intervention' (p. 137); and black, involving external considerations such as the law, professional codes of practice or the wishes of others. Seedhouse and those who favour the idea of the ethical grid argue that its use can clarify processes and complex situations and promote confidence in moral reasoning.

Seedhouse suggests that the ethical grid can be utilised in a variety of situations, ranging from reading of moral issues in newspapers or when watching television, through to use in practice by professionals. He suggests four steps in the use of the grid:

1   Consider the issue intuitively, without referring to the grid and attempt to consider the ramifications of possible actions, including the basic positives and negatives of the various options, to develop an initial position.

2   Consider the grid and a first layer (often the blue layer because of its centrality to the rationale of health work).

3   Consider all the other aspects of the grid and select those boxes that appear to offer the most appropriate solution, that is, those that appear to offer the highest degree of morality.

4   Apply the boxes to the mental picture of the proposed action. This will give both a course of action and a justification of it in moral terms.

It is important to note here, that as outlined earlier in this chapter, there may be no 'correct' answers and that two individuals using the grid to examine one situation may come up with different actions. It therefore remains the responsibility of individuals to justify their decisions and select that which produces the highest degree of morality; it is this that the grid can assist with.

In the second edition of his book, Seedhouse (1998) introduces an additional device designed to help, in this instance, health workers, which he calls the 'rings of uncertainty' (Figure 10.2). Ring A might be no or very little uncertainty, Ring B, some uncertainty, C, considerable uncertainty and D, total uncertainty.

With the rings Seedhouse also notes a variety of concerns: technical competence, resources, law, communication and ethics. He suggests that the rings can be used to help with the consideration of possible actions, so that a health worker could subdivide the rings into appropriate sections. A doctor considering undertaking a minor operation might consider where in the rings their situation lies with regard to resources, technical competence, ethics and the law. Similarly, if a professional was concerned about whether child abuse had occurred, Ring C might suggest that it would be important to seek the involvement of others in making a decision. They would then be in a better position to decide whether to proceed or not. However, Seedhouse is clear that if professionals find themselves standing outside the rings of uncertainty they ought not to intervene – if the potential action appears immoral, illegal, beyond communication or lacks resources or if the worker is not competent to undertake the action, then it should not be done. However, he also notes that there can be exceptional circumstances when action is still justified, so that just because an

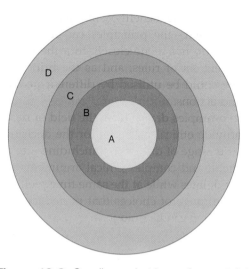

Figure 10.2 Seedhouse's 'rings of uncertainty'

Source: After Seedhouse (1998)

action is illegal does not necessarily mean that it should always not be taken, perhaps particularly where there is a strong ethical case for doing so. For some people the position regarding euthanasia would be an example of this, as was abortion before its legalisation.

A rather different and in many respects a more traditional approach to establishing professional guidance has been taken by Beauchamp and Childress (1994) who set out four principles for medical ethics:

1 *respect for autonomy* – the obligation to respect the decision-making capacities of autonomous persons – actions that enhance autonomy are seen as desirable while those that diminish autonomy are seen as undesirable

2 *non-maleficence* – the obligation to avoid causing harm

3 *beneficence* – the obligation to provide benefits and balance benefits against risks

4 *justice* – obligations of fairness in the distribution of benefits and risks in terms of the consequences of an action.

They argue that these four clusters of principles are central to biomedical ethics, although they note that while non-maleficence and beneficence have long been central to medical ethics the concepts of respect for autonomy and justice have only more recently been recognised as of importance.

Beauchamp and Childress recognise that different moral principles can and do conflict, and that in some instances there may be no clear 'correct' decision, but argue that by using these principles, either on their own or in combination, medical professionals should be able to reason about what should be done and, generally, but not on every occasion, be able to resolve the moral questions that they meet in their work.

While this approach has the benefit of simplicity, it is equally possible to criticise it for the same reason – the 'principles' can be interpreted as a checklist of desirable values and do not relate closely to a theory that justifies their use together as a coherent set of rules; and as the principles can be accused of lacking detail, they could be utilised by different people to justify very different positions and actions.

From these two examples drawn from the field of healthcare, it is apparent that seeking to provide ethical guidance for the decisions of professionals is not easy. There are a range of difficulties, including attempting to encapsulate what may be difficult and complex ethical arguments into fairly simple and straightforward guidelines while at the same time seeking to ensure that these are applicable to the range of choices that professionals can face and recognising that each situation can be unique.

Risk

In recent years the concept of 'risk' and its implications have come more to the fore in society and there is now very considerable discussion of different aspects of 'risk' in many areas of social policy. It is possible to conceptualise 'risk' in many different ways, ranging from approaches that seek to provide 'objective' measures of probability and harm to those that see risks as entirely social or cultural constructions (Ball and Boehmer-Christiansen 2002; Kemshall 2002). These include:

- *The rational actor* – this has arguably been the approach that has dominated traditional, number-based methods of assessing risk, with both individuals and institutions seen as rational entities that seek to balance risks with benefits. While it has historically formed the basis of risk assessments, it has come under increasing criticism, particularly for what critics see as its inappropriateness in the consideration of many social phenomena.

- *Reflexive modernity* – a view that recognises that expert-based and numerical risk assessment are no longer as widely accepted as they once were and that science and technology alone do not provide sufficient justification for decisions. From this perspective traditional risk assessment can be criticised for shifting risk elsewhere (to others, to nature or to the future) and instead it can be argued that there is a need to recognise and take account of different views and positions, rather than attempting to set rules for behaviour. As a result there will be a need for organisations to become reflexive entities that are able to respond to the changes and complexities of contemporary society.

- *Cultural theory* – emphasising the relationship between values and beliefs and perceptions of risks, this approach examines how risks are selected as being of concern and how they become legitimated for public attention. Risks can therefore be seen as being chosen for their usefulness to the social system, contributing to social cohesion and creating distinctions between insiders and outsiders.

● *Social constructivism* – a perspective that again rejects the traditional rational actor approach and tends to see risks and risk assessments as socially constructed and therefore amenable to criticism and deconstruction. Similarly, social processes are seen as contributing to the formulation of concerns and the way in which risks are perceived. Disputes over the levels or acceptability of risk can be seen as disputes over values and meaning.

Some of the major areas of debate in recent years have arisen as a result of scientific advances, and perhaps particularly in plant, animal and human genetics, such as genetic manipulation and cloning and have been grounded in risk as uncertainty. For example, the introduction of genetically modified foods has generally been portrayed by government and by industry as matters of science, with clearly calculated probabilities that can be established through scientific trials, along the lines of the rational actor model outlined earlier. However, media, pressure group and public concern has tended to reflect the alternative perspectives, focusing on the problems in calculating risks in such fields, the difficulty in being aware of the potential consequences until it is too late and a lack of trust in the 'experts'. This suggests that it is necessary to be aware that 'risk' and the acceptability of risk go beyond simple scientific calculation and are grounded in views that have their own logic and rationale to those making their own decisions.

For social policy these debates over risk have a number of implications. In particular, the development of social theories of risk, combined with a growing scepticism among members of the public, has raised questions about the creation of many policies. For example, in many policy areas, ranging from food safety through health and social care to the presence of paedophiles in the community, while governments may seek to develop actuarial approaches that govern access to services on a statistical calculation of risk, this may conflict with the range of perceptions of risk and the meanings that risk has in society.

In addition, changes to the welfare state, including the greater use of the market in the provision of welfare, arguments about the rationale for state welfare and perceived new threats, such as those from globalisation, further complicate the relationship between risk and social policy. The concept of a 'risk society', where traditional certainties can no longer be taken for granted and where the risks of anticipated events influence decision making (see Beck 1992; Giddens 1990, 1991), has potentially significant implications for social policy and for the welfare state, including such questions as whether state welfare can transform society and whether traditional forms of welfare are able to respond to challenges such as exclusion, oppression, increasing costs and moral hazard. At the level of individuals, social policy has, over the past two decades, moved to a position where individuals are responsible for their own risk management, both by shifting the burden of provision away from the state and through emphasising personal choice. To a considerable extent this has resulted in a move away from the state taking responsibility for risk and towards individuals being responsible for risk or, in cases of last resort, professionals of social welfare agencies. Some writers therefore argue that social policy is no longer principally about meeting the needs of individuals or the pursuit of the collective good, but is now primarily concerned with the prevention of risk and the displacement of risk-management responsibilities onto individuals.

At the practical level the idea of 'risk' has been taken on board in relation to many welfare services. For example, in the personal social services some user groups have advocated the need for risk to challenge the practices of professionals that they have seen as serving to limit individuals' choices and maintain professional power. However, at the same time risks have often been viewed negatively so that many services have worked towards risk avoidance, with the result that in areas such as mental health there has been an increased emphasis on compulsory treatment for some mentally ill people living in the community. In child protection, Munro (1999) has argued that the emphasis on risk has meant that professionals may overestimate risk of abuse, as the dangers to children and to themselves of making a mistake can be so great.

It is apparent, therefore, that while the idea of 'risk' has become a more central part of social policy than in the past, there is as yet little agreement on its implications, either at the individual or societal level. Nevertheless, an understanding of risk and its differing interpretations and meanings can add substantially to our understanding of social policy.

Summary

This chapter has introduced a general consideration of ethics and risk as they can relate to social policy. These are complex and almost constantly changing areas. Nevertheless the chapter has sought to:

● Provide an introduction to ethical theory and, in particular, to consequentialist and deontological approaches and the differing implications and interpretations of decisions that these can lead us to. Both of these have appeals, consequentialism in its apparent direction towards decisions that will create the greatest happiness and deontologicalism in its suggestion that we can base decisions on considered principles and obligation.

● Illustrate the application of ethics to practical issues and to demonstrate that historical social policy debates, such as rationing, and new issues, such as human genetics, can be examined using ethical theory and that the use of ethical ideas does not provide us with a 'correct' answer to difficult decisions although they can encourage ethical reflection and reasoned and defensible explanations for particular choices.

● Consider different approaches to professional ethics and guidance to professionals in the social policy arena, noting again the emphasis on helping resolve moral questions rather than necessarily reaching a 'right' decision.

● Examine the emergence of 'risk' as a significant factor in social policy debates, at both individual and collective level, and the possible implications of this for the development of ideas of responsibility and forms of welfare provision whether by individuals or by the state.

Discussion and review topics

1 Compare the strengths and weaknesses of QALYs in ethical terms compared with existing forms of rationing of healthcare.

2 What ethical and moral concerns might apply to a person who knows that they have a 50% chance of carrying a disease that might lead to long-term chronic illness? Would these change if they decide to have a child who might inherit that disease?

3 What might Seedhouse's ethical grid and rings of uncertainty and Beauchamp and Childress' four principles suggest to a medical professional faced with a patient refusing, on religious grounds, a blood transfusion that might save her life?

4 Why have changing views of risk encouraged a shift from state to individual responsibility for welfare?

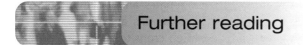

Further reading

Beauchamp, T. and Childress, J. (2001) *Principles of Biomedical Ethics*, Oxford University Press, New York – the four principles discussed within this book have been one of the most widely used frameworks for medical ethics

Hugman, R. and Smith, D. (1995) *Ethical Issues in Social Work*, Routledge, London – provides a fairly broad coverage of ethical issues related to social work, including considerations of confidentiality, managerialism, and empowerment, providing some counterbalance to the general dominance of discussions of healthcare within much of the available literature

Klein, R., Day, P. and Redmayne, S. (1996) *Managing Scarcity: Priority Setting and Rationing in the National Health Service*, Open University Press, Buckingham – a thorough consideration of the rationing of healthcare in the UK. Although now somewhat dated it continues to provide a good discussion of the topic

Seedhouse, D. (1998) *Ethics: The Heart of Health Care*, John Wiley & Sons, Chichester – the second edition of this book expands considerably on the first and introduces new 'tools' for decision making; Seedhouse provides a perspective on ethics that is markedly different from the more traditional approach of Beauchamp and Childress

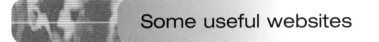

Some useful websites

www.basw.co.uk – the British Association of Social Workers' site provides one example of a professional code of ethics

www.bbc.co.uk/religion/ethics – a limited number of ethical issues are considered in some depth on the BBC's web pages

www.ethics-network.org.uk – the UK Clinical Ethics Network provides case studies, guidance and other information primarily on healthcare ethics

www.hgc.gov.uk – the website of the Human Genetics Commission provides information on the regulatory and advisory framework for human genetics in the United Kingdom including links to a number of other relevant organisations

www.nice.org.uk – established under the Labour government in 1999 the National Institute for Clinical Excellence aims to provide guidance on health technologies and the management of specific conditions. This site provides access to much of the Institute's work

www.nuffieldbioethics.org – the Nuffield Council on Bioethics is a non-governmental body that aims to contribute to debates and policymaking in bioethics. It demonstrates the range of work in this area from research involving animals through genetically modified crops to genetic screening and stem cell research

References

Arksey, H. (2002) 'Rationed care: assessing the support needs of informal carers in English social services authorities', *Journal of Social Policy*, 31, 81–101

Ball, D. J. and Boehmer-Christiansen, S. (2002) *Understanding and Responding to Societal Concerns*, Health and Safety Executive Research Report 34, Health and Safety Executive, London

Beauchamp, T. and Childress, J. (1994) *Principles of Biomedical Ethics*, Oxford University Press, New York

Beck, U. (1992) *Risk society: Towards a New Modernity*, Sage, London

British Council of Disabled People (2000) 'The new genetics and disabled people', BCODP, Derby

Daykin, C. D., Akers, D. A., Macdonald, A. S., McGleenan, T., Paul, S. and Turvey, P. J. (2003) 'Genetics and insurance – some social policy issues', presented to the Institute of Actuaries, 24 February 2003

Giddens, A. (1990) *The Consequences of Modernity*, Polity, Cambridge

Giddens, A. (1991) *Modernity and Self-identity*, Polity, Cambridge

Kemshall, H. (2002) *Risk, Social Policy and Welfare*, Open University Press, Buckingham

Kerr, A. (2003) 'Rights and responsibilities in the new genetics era', *Critical Social Policy*, 23, 208–26

Klein, R., Day, P. and Redmayne, S. (1996) *Managing Scarcity: Priority Setting and Rationing in the National Health Service*, Open University Press, Buckingham

LaFollette, H. (1997) 'Theorizing about ethics', in LaFollette, H. (ed.) *Ethics in Practice*, Blackwell, Cambridge, Ma

Munro, E. (1999) 'Protecting children in an anxious society', *Health, Risk and Society*, 1, 117–27

Porter, E. (1999) *Feminist Perspectives on Ethics*, Longman, London

Rawls, J. (1973) *A Theory of Justice*, Oxford University Press, Oxford

Seedhouse, D. (1988) *Ethics: The Heart of Health Care*, John Wiley & Sons, Chichester

Seedhouse, D. (1998) *Ethics: The Heart of Health Care*, 2nd edn, John Wiley and Sons, Chichester

Singer, P. (1993) *Practical Ethics*, Cambridge University Press, Cambridge

Teichman, J. (1996) *Social Ethics: A Student's Guide*, Blackwell, Oxford

Exploring the boundaries of social policy

11

Catherine Bochel

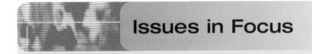

Issues in Focus

Over the last 20 years it has become increasingly apparent that social policy analyses have a much wider relevance than had previously been generally recognised. This chapter will consider why it is that issues that were not previously regarded as being within the domain of social policy are now seen as having relevance to social policy issues and concerns.

Traditionally, social policy has primarily been concerned with areas such as health, housing, education and the personal social services, as covered elsewhere in this book (see also Chapter 1), but with the continued development of the subject of social policy, combined with changes in society, it is now possible to argue that the scope of analysis of social policy can appropriately and usefully be broadened. Authors such as Cahill (1994 and 2002), Fitzpatrick (2002) and Huby (2001) have highlighted the relationship between 'new' and 'traditional' social policy concerns, and the resonance that studying these can have. This chapter therefore:

- examines the development of the subject and the extension of social policy analyses to areas other than the traditional concerns

- focuses on issues of food, the environment and sustainability, transport and travel and ICT, to illustrate links with key social policy ideas

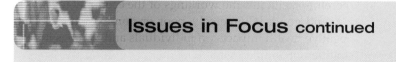

Issues in Focus continued

● considers the implications of these for social policy and society.

While, at one stage, it was possible crudely to characterise the study of social policy as largely concerned with five main areas of service delivery – education, health, housing, the personal social services and social security – the contents of the remainder of this book makes clear that the subject has developed significantly. This chapter demonstrates that the application of social policy to new areas continues to develop.

New and traditional social policy concerns

Briefing 11.1 sets out some of the new and old social policy concerns in order to illustrate the scope and permeability of the boundaries of social policy. It is important to recognise that these areas of interest are effectively a web of interconnecting policy concerns, impacting not only on one another, but also on issues such as social exclusion, lifestyle and quality of life, which in turn can be linked to topics such as the role of big business, globalisation and the world economy (see Chapter 16).

To illustrate the complexity of this we can consider the role of transport. Good public transport can be important to people without private transport, such as those on low incomes, people in isolated rural communities and to people in congested cities, in enabling access to work and facilities. Transport

Briefing 11.1	Developing social policy concerns
Late 20th and 21st-century concerns	**Traditional concerns**
Food	Health
Environment and sustainability	Housing
Transport and travel	Education
ICT	Personal social services
Work and new forms of money	Social security
Leisure	Employment

therefore facilitates the workings of the economy in transporting people, services and goods. Conversely, poor or non-existent public transport may have negative health impacts on individuals and families in respect of limiting possibilities of employment and hence affecting the level of income (in turn, restricting possibilities for consuming food and other goods), reduced possibilities for socialising and poorer access to facilities such as GP surgeries, dental provision or crèches and is likely to be detrimental for the economy, reducing government income from taxes and therefore their ability to provide services.

Clearly, social policy analysts also have to recognise that there is a possibility (or even a likelihood) that inequalities in these areas may replicate and/or reinforce existing social divisions. There may also be some role for government in monitoring or seeking solutions to such problems. Therefore, alongside a consideration of the effects of these issues on individuals and families, we also need to examine the wider policy context and consider how governments are responding to these issues. The role of other bodies such as the media and pressure groups may also be worthy of consideration.

Setting the context: the changing nature of social policy

As outlined in Chapter 1, the subject of social policy has not always existed as we know it today, and has developed in a number of different ways over the years. However, it is possible to argue that for a considerable period the study of social policy and administration was based on the traditional welfare state and tended to focus around subjects such as health, housing, poverty, education, the personal social services, employment and social security. Much of this was set in the context of the post-war consensus, over a period stretching from 1945 to the 1970s, when the major political parties were in broad agreement over many aspects of the welfare state, such as the maintenance of full employment, funding of the NHS and a basic standard of social security provision, despite differences in political ideology.

This consensus came to an end in the mid- to late 1970s and rapid change began to take place. A new language of politics and social policy emerged centred around 'Thatcherism'. Emphasis, which had previously been on collective provision, now shifted towards the individual, underpinned by New Right ideology with its desire for reduced state intervention and greater individual responsibility, which in New Right terms justified a cutback in collective provision to tackle concerns around inequality and social exclusion. During this period much emphasis was placed on the restructuring of the welfare state. New terminology and 'buzz words' appeared – choice, participation, cost, efficiency and effectiveness all became a major part of the language of government. Those who had previously been seen as 'service users' were now viewed as 'consumers' who were to have a say in the

operation and delivery of services. This period saw the introduction of privatisation, internal markets such as those in the NHS and education, the use of
performance measures and standards, a centralisation of power and the reform
and residualisation of local government.

Change continued after 1997 under the Labour government. The 'Third
Way' was adopted by some as an argument for a mix of market and state provision in welfare, albeit in a very different sense from that of the post-war
consensus and there was arguably a greater recognition of the structural causes
of poverty, inequality and social exclusion, but at the same time individuals
were expected to recognise that they had duties and responsibilities to society
in return for social rights and services. These issues are all dealt with in greater
depth elsewhere in this book.

Alongside these developments changes have been taking place in the global
economy. Food policy, one of the areas with which this chapter is concerned, is
no longer simply about local or national policy, increasingly it is about
European and global policy. It concerns powerful lobbies, such as the food
industry that use its contacts in government to help shape policy and steer
regulations in the direction that food retailers and manufacturers find most
beneficial. On the other side, however, are the interests of the consumers, who
are usually much less powerful. Multinational and transnational companies
and the ways in which they operate, impact on transport, the environment,
work and many of the issues that can be associated with a broader interpretation of social policy.

Inequalities have become accentuated between those at the top, who are
highly paid, and those at the bottom, who are not. Inequalities are further
heightened by the consumerist nature of society today. Through the media we
are constantly bombarded with products and images that we are encouraged
to believe we 'need'. Local services and facilities such as shops, health centres
and various welfare services are declining in preference to centralised facilities.
These tend to require travel, costing money, causing environmental damage
and increasing the risk that those who are poor or who do not have access to a
car or good local transport facilities may be excluded. A further consequence
of the consumer society we live in is the massive amount of waste we produce
through our consumption.

These areas impact on social policy concerns and therefore need to be taken
seriously by governments and consideration given to policies and approaches
that might help to minimise any new inequalities that might arise from them.
The remainder of this chapter considers a range of very different concerns that
reflect the broader boundaries of social policy and that have been explored by
social policy analysts: food, the environment, transport and travel, and information and communication technology. Given the potentially huge debates
around these issues the discussion here is inevitably limited and focuses on
particular aspects of these debates.

Food

Food is regularly headline news on the television and in the newspapers, be it over concerns with GM foods, intensive farming methods, the use of fertilisers and pesticides, antibiotics and growth promoting agents or scares over problems such as BSE, listeria and salmonella. The role of the media has helped to create a climate of public awareness and concern, which, in turn, has helped keep food on the agenda. In recent years, one of the reasons that food has been in the public eye has been because of concern over the growing number of people who are obese (Briefing 11.2). In early 2004 the Royal College of Physicians, the Royal College of Paediatrics and Child Health, and the Faculty of Public Health published a report, *Storing up Problems: The Medical Case for a Slimmer Nation*, which suggested that more than half of the UK population is either overweight or obese and that, if current trends were to continue, at least one-third of adults, one-fifth of boys and one-third of girls would be obese by 2020. In 2001 the National Audit Office found that obesity was costing the NHS at least £500 million a year and the economy £2 billion. So here food can be seen to impact on health, and poor health, in turn, impacts on the economy. This also raises implications for education in tackling the link between poor health and diet.

Briefing 11.2   Key facts about obesity in England

- 1 in 5 adults is obese.
- The number has nearly trebled over the last 20 years.
- Nearly two-thirds of men and over half of women are overweight or obese.

The four most common problems linked to obesity:	Estimated human cost:	Estimated financial cost:
• Heart disease	• 18 million sick days a year	• £½ billion a year in treatment costs to the NHS
• Type 2 diabetes	• 30,000 deaths a year resulting in 40,000 lost years of working life	• Possibly £2 billion a year impact on the economy
• High blood pressure	• Deaths linked to obesity shorten life by 9 years on average	
• Osteoarthritis		

Source: After National Audit Office (2001) p. 1

There are other concerns over diet and nutrition. Fewer people now cook their own meals, either using the numerous fast food outlets or relying on the rapidly growing market for ready meals. This means that we have less control over the nutritional content of our food. Ready meals and food from fast food outlets are often high in fats, salt and sugar. Furthermore, everyday foodstuffs often contain large amounts of additives and flavourings. This leads some to argue that there should be a role for government in regulating food manufacturers and retailers to ensure that the food we eat is safe. For example, in May 2004 the Health Select Committee of the House of Commons produced a report recommending that the Food Standards Agency draw up a traffic light system of food and drink labels, with red for high-energy foods, amber for medium, and green for low, and that these be backed by legislation (Health Committee 2004). At the same time, the government was being encouraged by some groups to consider whether to restrict the marketing of foods to children. However, others argue that diet and related issues should remain a matter for individual choice and that governments should not interfere.

These issues are compounded by the dominance of the large supermarket chains and major food producers in the supply of food to the consumer and this has a whole range of social policy impacts. In general, smaller local stores are unable to compete on price or the range of goods available in supermarkets and risk being forced out of the market. The supermarket then becomes the main supplier of food to consumers in the area. By relying on a small number of producers, they are able to influence the choices available to the consumer, but the supermarkets' primary concerns might be about the shelflife or appearance of food, rather than with its taste or quality. In addition, pricing policies within supermarkets often mean that fresh, 'healthy' food is more expensive than less healthy options. People on low incomes may find supermarkets expensive and, without a car or without access to good public transport, perhaps in outlying rural areas, may find that it is difficult to get to them. Thus, income affects choice of food and this in turn impacts on diet and health. The dominance of a few large food producers and retailers may therefore create hardship for groups such as low-income families, older people, disabled people and homeless people. In these ways, food moves on to the social policy agenda alongside some of the more traditional concerns of the subject.

Food interests

In the UK there are powerful bodies that represent the interests of food manufacturers and retailers, notably the British Retail Consortium and the Food and Drink Federation, that act as pressure groups (see Chapter 2) and that are skilled in lobbying government and shaping the food agenda to promote the interests of the food industry. As governments have sought to improve food safety and related health issues, lobbying has become intense, as was the case in 2004 when the Labour government was considering whether to work with the food industry and produce voluntary guidelines to tackle obesity or whether to press ahead with legislation.

In the past there have been concerns that the interests of consumers have been neglected by policymakers because of the dominance of producer interests and, in part as a result of these anxieties, in 2000 the government established the Food Standards Agency to act as a watchdog for consumer interests and public health in relation to food.

Pressures do not operate solely at national level, but are occurring in Europe and globally, with one example of the latter being the accusation in early 2004 that the United States was trying to sabotage the World Health Organisation's guidelines designed to curb rising obesity and disease, which could be damaging to its food and drink corporations. However, the big corporations are not always successful in getting their way. For example, the multinational company Monsanto had to abandon its worldwide **genetically modified** (GM) wheat project following pressure from US and Canadian farmers who feared the introduction of GM wheat would lead to the collapse of their markets in Europe and Japan, where consumers had shown much greater resistance to GM food. Within the European Union, the Common Agricultural Policy has also been a major factor affecting food production and policy, providing subsidies to producers (which generally benefit larger farms and encourage more intensive methods of agriculture), rather than encouraging measures that are good for the environment.

It is important to recognise that there are a number of different interests at work in relation to food production, distribution and safety. On the one hand, there are the food and drink corporations, which are often able to influence the agenda of governments through effective lobbying; and, on the other, there are consumers and health organisations. However, the reality is that, as is the case in many areas of social policy, these groups have differing levels of power and ability to influence the agenda and political decisions and that at present manufacturers and retailers can often have more influence than consumers.

Government policy

Following the Second World War, British governments generally sought to increase the amount of food being produced and to keep the costs of food down for consumers. As noted already, within the European Union, the Common Agricultural Policy also encouraged intensive farming, although its emphasis on subsidising farmers inevitably meant that consumers paid more for some products. For much of the post-war period therefore, food safety policy was concerned with ensuring that health legislation and regulations were enforced, rather than with a broader view of the consumer interest or public health. However, following a number of food safety crises, including BSE, the Labour government established a new Department of the Environment, Food and Rural Affairs and a Foods Standards Agency, in an attempt to shift some of the emphasis back to wider food safety issues and to give a greater voice to consumers.

However, food is also important at a more micro level. Until 1992, when the White Paper, *Health of the Nation*, was published, Conservative governments had largely pursued an individualistic approach to food policy in which the individual consumer was responsible for their own health and diet through their food choices. This publication marked an important change in government policy so that, as Lang notes, there was 'a shift in policy from the denial of food poverty to an exploration of coping strategies' (Lang 1997: 223). Now the relationship between diet and income was recognised, hailing a shift towards a more structural approach in terms of government policy and a nutritional taskforce was established to consider issues such as catering education and school meals.

From 1997 the Labour governments aimed to build on this structural approach and to strike 'a new balance – a third way – linking individual and wider action' (DOH 1999: para. 1.27). The White Paper *Saving Lives: Our Healthier Nation* recognised the importance of a combination of physical activity and a balanced healthy diet. The Department of Health therefore sought to focus on matters such as the links between cancer, heart disease and diet and the health benefits of eating five portions of fruit and vegetables a day. This involved a variety of 'healthy eating' initiatives, such as the National Fruit Scheme aimed at schoolchildren, which sought to provide a free piece of fruit a day for every child under the age of six from 2004. The government also initiated a Healthy Schools Programme where health information was provided to teachers, education and health professionals, as well as to young people and others, that related to the National Curriculum and to the National Healthy School Standard.

While the government might claim to be taking some actions, critics have noted that in many respects this has been insufficient. For example, as noted earlier, the Food Standards Agency was established in 2000 following the **BSE crisis** to protect the public interest in food. However, its accounts for 2002 showed that only 10 per cent of its budget was spent on diet quality and nutrition issues. There have also been accusations that the individualist perspective remains largely dominant, as the attitude appears to be that if consumers are provided with information (for example, through correct labelling of food), they are in a position to make an informed choice. Similarly, at European level there is a European Food Safety Authority, but its priorities are hygiene, labelling, safety and new technologies, rather than more general consumer interests.

Food is clearly an important social policy issue. It has impacts on diet and on health. Government and the food industry have a responsibility in enabling individuals to make healthier choices. In particular, government can intervene to regulate food manufacturing and retailing in order to help reduce inequalities in this area. In the past governments have pursued a policy of leaving food decisions to the free market and have been unwilling to challenge the dominance of the food producers and retailers. This has suited big business, which has a major influence in food policy. More recently government has started to pursue a more structural approach, but the extent to which governments are willing to challenge the major food interests and to force change remains to be seen.

The environment and sustainability

The Brundtland Commission, established in 1987 by the United Nations Commission on Environment and Development, developed a definition of sustainability that is about 'meeting the needs of the present without compromising the ability of future generations to meet their own needs' (Brundtland Commission 1987: 43). This concern with sustainability has gathered pace in recent years as governments have begun to take on board the importance of 'green' issues and as attention has been paid to their implications for social policy. Neglect of such issues in the past has led to damage to the natural environment, pollution and land being stripped of its natural resources.

Britain annually generates around 30 million tonnes of rubbish, most of which is buried or burned. Much of this comes from the unnecessary packaging of consumer goods. Because producers do not have to take into account the cost of disposal of packing when they set the price of the finished goods, there is no incentive for them to cut down on unnecessary packaging. This is an example of what economists call 'market failure', where prices fail to reflect full social costs. To add to this the UK has one of the lowest recycling rates in Europe, recycling only around 12 per cent of its waste. The Labour government has set a target for this to rise to 25 per cent by 2005/6 but it seems unlikely that this will be met.

These are issues of concern for social policy. They affect our quality of life in a variety of ways, including pollution of the environment, the quality of the food we eat, our health, and our very existence. But, as with the issue of food, there are a range of different interests at play. The United States, a major polluter, refused to endorse the 1997 **Kyoto Protocol** on greenhouse gas emissions and has taken the stance that big business has no responsibility for tackling climate change. In the United Kingdom the government has taken a different position, demonstrating at least some commitment to sustainability issues and appearing likely to meet, or at least get close to, its internationally agreed target under the Kyoto Protocol for reducing greenhouse gases. At the same time however, there are concerns from some business leaders in the UK that the cost of implementing these new responsibilities are too high for businesses. As with the issue of food, there are push and pull factors at play. Different bodies have different agendas and it is likely to be the least powerful that lose out. Huby puts this well when she says that 'it is useful to recognise that the people benefiting most from environmentally damaging activities are not usually the people who would benefit most from policies to alleviate them. The latter tend to be people living on low incomes and those for whom age, disability, gender or race means that they lack the means, resources or power to avoid or ameliorate the effects of living in a degraded environment' (2001: 298).

Government policy

It was recognition of some of these issues and concerns by national governments that led to an **Earth Summit** in Rio in 1992. One of the main developments to emerge from this was Agenda 21. This aimed to promote environmental and sustainable development through a 'global action programme' across all participating countries. Local Agenda 21 in turn emerged from this, based on the idea, that because of their range of responsibilities, local authorities were best placed to incorporate environmental issues into their policies and practice. Cahill notes that: 'Undoubtedly, the most active and enthusiastic response to Rio in the UK came from those local authorities who adopted Agenda 21. UK local authorities have been among the pace-setters in the drive towards local sustainability' (2002: 22). Tony Blair used the 1997 Earth Summit in New York as an opportunity to broaden Local Agenda 21, announcing that he wanted all local authorities to adopt such strategies by 2000. The most recent world summit on sustainable development took place in Johannesburg in 2002 and again the UK government saw this as an opportunity to build on Local Agenda 21. As a result, while there has been a requirement for local authorities to establish recycling plans and encourage schemes in their areas, some have done this not only for household waste but also for garden waste. In addition, from 2006 local authorities will be forced to ensure that all electrical and electronic waste is separated from all other household rubbish.

The environment and sustainability are important issues that the government is now beginning to address, although not to the satisfaction of all. While this is to be welcomed, it is important that the relatively new emphasis on 'green issues' is not seen in isolation but is integrated into all areas of policy-making at both local and national level, including areas such as transport (see next section), food, education and health.

Transport and travel

Transport has consequences for many areas of relevance to social policy including the economy, the environment, food and social life. These in turn impact on issues such as quality of life, inclusion and exclusion. Good transport systems for passengers and freight are vital for the workings of the economy. Road, rail, water and air transport are key to transporting goods not only from one part of the country to another but also from destinations around the globe. Globalisation has created new opportunities for business in opening up worldwide markets (see Chapter 16). For example, supermarkets source their produce from around the globe, enabling the consumer to purchase many types of fruit and vegetables all year round, regardless of the season. For individuals, travel to distant destinations provides the opportunity to experience other cultures and broaden their knowledge of the world. This has been aided by the growth in ICT (discussed later in this chapter), which has enabled communication between people on opposite sides of the world to take place at the touch of a button, reducing distances of both time and space.

However, while opportunities may have been created, there are also downsides to the revolution in transportation and travel. The volume of traffic on our roads has increased, causing pollution, road damage, traffic congestion, noise, increasing the chances of accidents and having consequent effects on the health of people who live on or near to busy traffic routes. Many of these are clearly issues of concern to social policy analysts. If we have access to good transport systems then this has the potential to benefit our work and social lives. However, this is frequently skewed. For example, in 2001 one in four households in Great Britain did not have access to a car and this varied significantly across social groups: more than two-thirds of one person pensioner households and just under half of lone parent households with children did not have access to a car; in contrast, fewer than one in ten couple family households did not have access to a car (Central Statistical Office 2004: Table 12.10). Not surprisingly, not having access to a car increases reliance on public transport and certain groups, including people living in the most deprived areas of the country, are forced to rely on bus services.

For people who do not own a car, or who do not have access to good public transport, the effects can be damaging. Access to jobs and facilities may be restricted, with consequent effects on people's economic and social life. Research for the Social Exclusion Unit has suggested that both the lack of transport and the cost of transport can be barriers to getting a job and has been linked to young people dropping out of college (SEU 2003). The research also found that people who are reliant on public transport often experience problems attending their local hospital and that access to local supermarkets can be difficult. These issues have consequences for the range of facilities available in communities and for those who live there. If there are few shops, those that do exist may be more expensive and offer less choice, little by way of library facilities may discourage learning and difficulties in accessing leisure facilities may make it hard to encourage participation in sport, with consequent negative impacts on health and well-being and opportunities for social life. The research also highlighted the disproportionate effects of transport policy on different groups in society. For example, traffic pollution may put children, pregnant women and those with respiratory illnesses at risk. In poor neighbourhoods this is more likely to trigger asthma attacks and exacerbate existing medical conditions. The health impacts of traffic pollution are further compounded by the likelihood of accidents. Grayling et al. show that 'children in the ten per cent most deprived wards were more than three times as likely to be pedestrian casualties as their counterparts in the ten per cent least deprived wards' (2002: 6), highlighting the link between poverty and child deaths on the road.

So transport is not merely about travelling; it is clearly much more than this. Poor transport is a contributor to social exclusion, 'it restricts access to activities that enhance people's life chances, such as learning, health care, work, and food shopping' (SEU 2002: i) and 'deprived communities also suffer the worst effects of road traffic through pollution and pedestrian accidents' (SEU 2003: 13). These are all reasons why transport is of concern to social policy analysts in the 21st century and why it is an issue for government.

Transport/travel interests

Car manufacturers, road haulage firms and fuel companies all have a major interest in a transport policy that favours road users. Big businesses, super-market chains and others also seek to influence policy in a way that will benefit them. There are also a variety of other pressure groups, such as those that seek to represent pedestrians and campaign on environmental concerns and other issues such as health. As with the issues of food and the environment discussed earlier, these interest groups have different agendas and varied abilities to lobby government, which is affected by factors such as the amount of power they each wield, public opinion and the role of the media.

Government policy

Transport policy is multi-faceted, serving economic, social and environmental goals. It has the potential to affect social exclusion and inclusion and to impact on the quality of life in communities. The 1998 White Paper *A New Deal for Transport* (DETR 1998) recognised much of this in setting out a framework to promote healthy lifestyles by encouraging walking and cycling and in acknowledging the threat to health through accidents, traffic noise, vibration and pollution. *Transport 2010: The 10 Year Plan* (DETR 2000), built on the White Paper, setting targets in relation to road safety to reduce the number of people killed or seriously injured in road accidents. It also discussed measures to contribute towards meeting the target from the Kyoto Protocol to reduce greenhouse gas emissions. From this perspective we can see at least an element

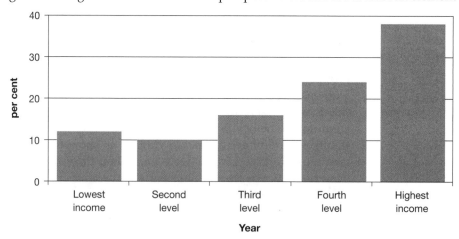

Figure 11.1 Who benefits from transport spending?

Source: Redrawn from *The Guardian* 21.5.02. Copyright © The Guardian

of 'joined-up' government in the linking of environmental, transport and health issues.

The government aimed to implement the plans set out in the ten-year plan through a partnership with the private sector and local government and investment of £180 billion. However, Figure 11.1 illustrates that public spending on transport benefits the rich more than it does the poor. Just under 40 per cent of benefits go to the richest 20 per cent of households, while only 12 per cent of benefits go to the bottom one-fifth of households. Much of the investment is going into roads and railways with less money for footpaths and bus services and this benefits richer people because they tend to make longer journeys, mainly by car and rail. Poorer people lose out because they tend to make fewer journeys, mostly on foot and by bus.

Perhaps one of the biggest question marks over Labour's transport policies has been its attitude to the car. In the early years of the government it emphasised an integrated transport policy, but it later, perhaps fearing being seen as 'anti-car', played down measures such as road pricing by shifting much of the onus for these onto local authorities (although the Mayor of London, Ken Livingstone, did introduce such a charging scheme and a number of other cities are considering the idea) and in 2000 scrapped the fuel-price escalator which had been introduced under the Conservatives in 1993 to increase taxation on petrol fuel faster than inflation in an attempt both to increase government income and to discourage car use.

Information and communication technology

The growth of new technology has impacted enormously on areas such as work, money, leisure, travel, communication, consumption and the environment. This has led to a blurring of the boundaries between our public and private lives as the development of mobile phones, digital technology, the internet and wireless networks is transforming the ways in which we work and use our leisure time.

Access to a huge range of information is available at the press of a button. Through the internet we can download documents, search for specific information, access market information on customers and market products to a worldwide audience. As consumers we can search for products and select the supplier that offers the product at the cheapest price, often below the price in shops. With the growth of cable networks and satellite broadcasters numerous TV channels can be brought into our homes, increasing the choice available to the consumer. We can now select from dedicated channels for films, cartoons, sport, cookery, shopping, chat shows and so on. Technology can also bring social policy issues into people's lives. We can sit at home and watch debates on homelessness, poverty and sometimes participate by phoning in or interactively. We can see debates on programmes such as *Newsnight* on current issues with professionals, politicians and others. Soap operas dramatise social policy issues such as teenage pregnancy, drug and alcohol addiction and so on. These can help raise consciousness around social policy issues and people can learn about what is going on in the world and how the actions of others impact on people's lives.

Modern methods of communication such as mobile phones and email have reduced both real time and space. We can be in almost constant contact for work or leisure. We can work from home and on the train and can bring the world into our personal space. We can communicate with customers, family and friends from across the other side of the world via technology that enables us to see one another while we speak. Communication has become faster and the divide between the public and private worlds of the individual has become blurred. In the welfare state sector technology has the potential to make life easier for both professionals and consumers of services. Recent years have seen major attempts by government to provide services online, with initiatives ranging from those such as NHSdirect to online payment of council bills. It has also been suggested that the appropriate use of ICTs could help reduce social exclusion, for example in raising skills levels for employment, developing, individual's self-esteem and providing networks to bring communities together (Policy Action Team 15, 2000)

There are, however, a range of negative impacts of this revolution in ICT. For example, one of the main contributors to exclusion from this ICT revolution is cost. To take advantage of much of this choice we have to pay. If you can afford a computer and to pay for access to the internet and for the running costs of mobile phones, then you can be part of this growth in new technology and the opportunities it brings. However, those who cannot afford to pay may be disadvantaged and excluded from access to knowledge. The Policy Action Team 15 (2000) report noted, for example, that those in deprived neighbourhoods and in lower socio-economic groups have lower use of PCs and the internet than was the case for the UK as a whole. Similarly, research by Pilling, Barrett and Floyd (2004) showed that many disabled users required assistive devices (aids, equipment, adaptations) to access a computer or the internet and that the

Source: www.CartoonStock.com

cost of such devices was also a problem for some respondents. There is therefore a danger that existing social divisions may be replicated or reinforced through new developments in ICT.

The growth in new technology has also raised other issues. For example, one challenge is associated with the regulation of information – there are issues around balance of coverage, access for independent producers, content and appropriateness. One element of these developments has also raised new health concerns, with mobile phones and masts having been linked by some to concerns over cancer. And there are concerns over data protection, privacy and civil liberties, with some expressing fears over the amount of data that is collected by the state and other organisations and the uses to which this may be put.

Government policy

In November 1996 the Green Paper *government.direct* (Cabinet Office 1996) was published, providing a prospectus for the electronic delivery of government services. It envisaged the introduction of direct, electronic one-stop access to public services, to be available 24 hours a day, 7 days a week, in the manner of 'direct' banking or insurance services. This was embraced by the incoming Labour government and the White Paper *Modernising Government* (Cabinet Office 1999) confirmed the central place of electronic government in the government's plans and promised that all government services would be available electronically by 2005, although this target was later revised to 2008.

The government's electronic strategy has the potential to create positive outcomes for many. But a key issue that remains for social policy is that of access for individuals and groups to this ICT revolution, particularly those on low incomes.

Summary

This chapter has sought to examine and explain the relevance of social policy beyond the traditional boundaries and concerns of the subject. However, it is worth noting that there are many different ways in which 'old' and 'new' concerns can be linked. One final example is Pahl's (1999) work on the use of new forms of money, such as credit cards, smart cards and internet banking. She noted: 'There are clear patterns of exclusion from the electronic economy, which reflect education, income, employment status, gender and age. Those who are "credit rich" tend also to be "information rich" and "work rich"; those who are "credit poor" tend also to be "information poor" and "work poor" (p. viii). 'Those who are poor, unemployed or elderly are less likely to use credit cards than those who are in employment; and, except when they are in full-time employment, women are less likely to use credit cards than men' (p. 69). Research such as this has a range of implications for social policy and illustrates how new and old concerns come together.

In this chapter a number of issues have been highlighted:

● the constantly changing and permeable barriers of the subject of social policy, with economic, social, political and technological developments combining to produce both new areas of study for social policy analysts and new impacts on existing areas of social policy concerns

● that social policy ideas and analyses continue to be relevant to new economic and social developments, so that each of the topics examined in this chapter – food, the environment, transport and ICT – is amenable to social policy analysis and to considerations of issues such as inequality, equity, exclusion and inclusion, as well as to other social policy concerns such as the appropriate roles of public and private sectors and the means of policy formulation, implementation and evaluation

● there is a danger that existing social inequalities and divisions will be replicated and reinforced – the chapter has illustrated that in relation to each of the areas studied there is evidence that groups that have traditionally been the focus of social policy are in danger of losing out and being further excluded by recent developments, and there is a need for analysts and policymakers to be aware of this and that action, including potentially government intervention, may be necessary to ensure that greater social exclusion does not result.

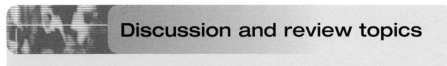

Discussion and review topics

1 Why is food important for social policy?

2 To what extent are 'green issues' compatible with traditional social policy concerns?

3 What might a transport system that emphasised accessibility and inclusion look like?

4 Will the government's emphasis on the use of ICT to deliver services reduce or exacerbate social inequalities?

Further reading

Cahill, M. (2002) *The Environment and Social Policy*, Routledge, London – this book explores the relationship between environmental concerns (including housing and urban development, food and work) and social policy and the role of governments with regard to these

Grayling, T., Hallam, K., Graham, D., Anderson, R. and Glaister, S. (2002) *Streets Ahead: Safe and Liveable Streets for Children*, IPPR, London – dealing with child pedestrian accidents, this booklet highlights the links between deprivation and high casualty rates

Pahl, J. (1999) *Invisible Money – Family Finances in the Electronic Economy*, Policy Press, Bristol – a report on a study that examines the ways in which men and women use new forms of money and that highlights the potential for greater polarisation and inequality

Policy Action Team 15 (2000) *Closing the Digital Divide: Information and Communication Technologies in Deprived Areas*, Social Exclusion Unit, London – this report (also available through the Social Exclusion Unit's website, listed in the following section) examines the importance and potential role of ICTs in relation to helping people who live in deprived neighbourhoods

Some useful websites

www.dft.gov.uk – the Department of Transport's website gives access to government policy and other documents in transport and related issues

www.foodstandards.gov.uk – the site of the Food Standards Agency, which provides advice and information to government and consumers about food safety, including nutrition and diet

www.jrf.org.uk – the Joseph Rowntree Foundation funds a wide variety of research and publishes the results on a range of social policy issues. Its website gives access to some of the results and recommendations as well as providing links to other organisations

www.nacab.org.uk – the National Association of Citizens Advice Bureaux provides a variety of publications including on research, policy issues and advice to consumers on this site

www.socialexclusionunit.gov.uk – the Social Exclusion Unit has produced a number of publications that deal with some of the issues covered in this chapter together with many others

References

Brundtland Commission (1987) *Our Common Future*, Oxford University Press, Oxford

Cabinet Office (1996) *government.direct*, The Stationery Office, London

Cabinet Office (1999) *Modernising Government*, The Stationery Office, London

Cahill, M. (1994) *The New Social Policy*, Blackwell, Oxford

Cahill, M. (2002) *The Environment and Social Policy*, Routledge, London

Central Statistical Office (2004) *Social Trends 34*, The Stationery Office, London

Department of Health (1999) *Saving Lives: Our Healthier Nation*, The Stationery Office, London

Department of the Environment, Transport and the Regions (1998) *A New Deal for Transport: Better for Everyone: The Government's White Paper on the Future of Transport*, The Stationery Office, London

Department of the Environment, Transport and the Regions (2000) *Transport 2010: The 10 Year Plan*, The Stationery Office, London

Fitzpatrick, T. (2002) *Environmental Issues and Social Welfare*, Blackwell, Oxford

Grayling, T., Hallam, K., Graham, D., Anderson, R. and Glaister, S. (2002) *Streets Ahead: Safe and Liveable Streets for Children*, IPPR, London

Health Committee (2004) *Obesity*, third report of session 2003/4, House of Commons, London

Huby, M. (2001) 'Food and the environment', in May, M., Brunsdon, E. and Page, R. (eds) *Understanding Social Problems: Issues in Social Policy*, Blackwell, Oxford

Lang, T. (1997) 'Dividing up the cake: food as social exclusion', in Walker, A. and Walker, C. (eds) *Britain Divided: The Growth of Social Exclusion in the 1980s and 1990s*, Child Poverty Action Group, London

National Audit Office (2001) *Tackling Obesity in England*, NAO, London

Pahl, J. (1999) *Invisible Money – Family Finances in the Electronic Economy*, Policy Press, Bristol

Pilling, D., Barrett, P. and Floyd, M. (2004) *Disabled People and the Internet: Experiences, Barriers and Opportunities*, Joseph Rowntree Foundation, York

Policy Action Team 15 (2000) *Closing the Digital Divide: Information and Communication Technologies in Deprived Areas*, Social Exclusion Unit, London

Royal College of Physicians, Royal College of Paediatrics and Child Health and Faculty of Public Health (2004) *Storing up Problems: The Medical Case for a Slimmer Nation*, Royal College of Physicians, London

Social Exclusion Unit (2002) *Making the Connections: Transport and Social Exclusion – Interim Findings from the Social Exclusion Unit*, Social Exclusion Unit, London

Social Exclusion Unit (2003) *Making the Connections: Final Report on Transport and Social Exclusion*, Social Exclusion Unit, London

Part III

Theorising social policy

The New Right: neo-liberalism and neo-conservatism

12

Robert Page

Issues in Focus

This chapter will explore what has come to be known as the 'New Right' approach to welfare. This tradition has two largely complementary components – neo-liberalism and neo-conservatism. As Barry (1999) points out: 'The label New Right tends to describe those conservatives who have adapted market economics to the traditionalist political value structure; although their reverence for the conventional moral code marks them off from the economists on some important issues' (p. 56). The chapter will:

- address the distinctive features of both of these perspectives

- examine how insights from both these traditions have been 'combined' to form the New Right approach to the welfare state

- consider the development of the New Right welfare agenda in Britain in relation to the Thatcher (1979–1990) and Major (1990–1997) governments.

The New Right ideas that have been so influential over the past three decades are rooted in both neo-liberalism and neo-conservatism. While these traditions have much in common, it is useful to highlight the distinctive features of each perspective.

Neo-liberalism

Neo-liberalism represents an attempt to revive the ideas of classical liberalism that came to the fore in the late 18th and early 19th centuries, not least as a result of the work of two influential political economists – Adam Smith and David Ricardo. Four aspects of neo-liberal thought are of particular importance:

● freedom

● individualism

● the free market

● the role of government.

Freedom

Freedom or liberty is accorded central importance in neo-liberal thought. Individuals are deemed to have a fundamental right to exercise their own choices in life unrestrained by the views or actions of others. As Heywood (2003) notes: 'Freedom consists in each person being left alone, free from interference and able to act in whatever way they may choose. This conception of liberty is "negative" in that it is based upon the absence of external restrictions or constraints upon the individual' (2003: 31). It is acknowledged, however, that this commitment to freedom should not be interpreted as support for 'licence'. Following Mill (1859), it was accepted that free individuals are not entitled to inflict harm on others. In short, all individuals should be able to maximise their freedom but not at the expense of the liberty of others.

Importantly, neo-liberals reject the so-called 'positive' version of liberty under which an individual is seen as having a right to 'realise his or her potential, attain skills and knowledge and achieve fulfilment' (Heywood 2003: 39). Broader freedom of this kind, they would argue, can lead to unjustifiable constraints on more prosperous citizens in the form of, for example, high taxation to ensure that the life plans of others are fulfilled. While it is seen as appropriate to formulate rules relating to mutual non-interference, attempts to provide resources for the purpose of self-fulfilment are believed to give rise to arbitrary and unjust procedures that undermine personal freedom.

Individualism

Neo-liberals place great emphasis on individualism. As Leach (2002) states: 'Individual human beings, rather than nations, races or classes are the starting point for any theorizing about society, politics or economics' (2002: 25).

According to the neo-liberals, individuals are the best judges of their own well-being. Moreover, they are seen as self-interested rather than selfless with a capacity for self-reliance. Indeed, those most committed to this individualism contend that there is no such entity as society or indeed a separate 'public' interest. Instead, there is merely an unstructured collectivity of self-reliant individuals pursuing their own interests. Such individuals have no obligations to society neither should they expect to receive any benefits from society. This does not, however, preclude individuals from entering into voluntary agreements or arrangements with others to meet their mutual needs.

The free market

Neo-liberals are staunch advocates of the free market, judging this to be the best way to meet the diverse and complex needs of individuals in an efficient and equitable way. As May (2002) explains: 'A market is a way of allocating resources, formed when individuals voluntarily engage in the exchange of goods or services at openly advertised prices which adjust over time to balance supply and demand' (2002: 140–41). By means of open competition, those who are able to produce goods of a requisite quality at the lowest possible price are likely to prosper. Adams (1998) notes that 'A good quality product of low price will always outsell an expensive poor quality product. Makers of the latter will have to improve quality and cut costs and price to compete. Thus, competition ensures the best quality at the lowest prices and maximum efficiency amongst firms who must satisfy their customers or go out of business' (1998: 85). Moreover, given that the price mechanism brings demand and supply into equilibrium over the longer term, external regulation of markets is seen as unnecessary.

According to the neo-liberals, the free market satisfies the principle of **equity** by virtue of the fact that all exchanges are voluntary. The fact that market activity may benefit the fortunate as much as the talented or the industrious is not seen as problematic by leading neo-liberal thinkers such as Hayek. As Tomlinson (1995) points out: 'Hayek does *not* argue that the reward pattern generated in a market economy is just. He is consistent in not applying that word to any set of outcomes: justice is a purely procedural term' (1995: 22). In short there should be no barriers to market entry and no outside interference in the pattern of market rewards.

Role of government

Neo-liberal enthusiasm for the market is matched by a less than positive attitude towards government activity. While it is accepted that government has a role to play in areas such as rule making, arbitrating in the case of disputes and in the provision of a limited range of public goods that cannot be provided by the market such as defence, more extensive forms of intervention are rejected. Neo-liberals have expressed particular concern about the growth of economic interventionism in the latter half of the 20th century. Attempts to 'adjust the spontaneous order generated by market transactions' (Pierson 1996: 82) are rejected on the grounds that no government will ever be able to amass or analyse the necessary information to make effective decisions. In consequence, economic outcomes will always prove less satisfactory than those that would have been achieved through free market activity.

The neo-liberals are particularly vexed by the tendency of social democratic governments to intervene in the economy on the grounds of social justice (Hayek 1967). The pursuit of this goal leads, they contend, to the confiscation of wealth from the successful, prolonged periods of dependency for the needy, and the curtailment of personal freedom (see Pierson 1996: 83). Moreover, neo-liberals contend that the expansion of non-market provision has encouraged economically irresponsible behaviour on the part of self-interested governments and voters. As Pierson (1996: 83) explains, both these groups 'are able to avoid or at least to deflect the consequences of spending decisions and thus to seek benefits without taking due account of costs'.

Neo-conservatism

Neo-conservatism attempts to revive some of the social principles associated with 19th-century conservatism. Heywood (2003) has identified three principal concerns of neo-conservatism:

● law and order

● public morality

● national identity.

Law and order

Neo-conservatives hold a rather pessimistic view of human nature, believing that it is possible only to constrain, but not to alter, self-seeking behaviour. They reject the notion that crime can be explained by reference to structural inequalities. Instead, they identify the 'base' instincts of individuals as the prime cause of criminality. They contend that 'people can only be persuaded to behave in a civilised fashion if they are deterred from expressing their violent and antisocial impulses' (Heywood 2003: 75). In consequence, neo-conservatives believe that more consistent forms of discipline within the home and in schools, as well as tougher law and order measures, are necessary to counter the contemporary growth in crime and anti-social behaviour.

Public morality

The neo-conservatives have expressed unease about the challenge to traditional values and morals that emerged in the 1960s, not least among those who were young and increasingly affluent. The greater social acceptability of more diverse lifestyles and attitudes is viewed as a serious threat to social stability. As Willetts (1994) states: 'Many people fear that our values are under threat. The evidence ranges from the petty incivilities of everyday life through to the rise in violent crime. Above all, what we seem to suffer from is a preoccupation with me and now. The capacity to defer gratification, essential to civil society and economic progress, seems to be under threat' (1994: 17). Neo-conservatives believe that it is necessary to challenge the growth of 'alternative' lifestyles by a much more vigorous defence of 'conventional' morality and support for the nuclear family, which they believe is essential for the preservation of social cohesion.

National identity

In contrast to neo-liberals, neo-conservatives also display a strong attachment to the notion of a nation state. If citizens are encouraged to understand and value their common heritage and culture, this will strengthen social bonds and promote unity within society. Not surprisingly, therefore, neo-conservatives maintain that the growing acceptance of **multiculturalism** will undermine national identity and threaten social stability. This has led them to advocate tighter controls on immigration and asylum seekers and to support measures that foster integration and assimilation rather than promote cultural diversity. The circumscribed nature of such integration is reflected in neo-conservative resistance to deeper forms of integration at the European or supranational level.

Neo-liberalism and neo-conservatism: two sides of the same coin?

As Briefing 12.1 illustrates, there are some underlying tensions between the neo-liberal and neo-conservative approaches. For example, neo-conservatives are concerned about the threat posed to social stability by the economic doctrines of neo-liberals. Once rampant individualism has been unleashed in the market, neo-conservatives fear that it will quickly spread to civil society thereby undermining self-restraint, obligation and a sense of community. Gray (1998) observes that neo-liberalism has undermined 'the virtues that it once relied upon. These virtues – saving, civic pride, respectability, "family values"

Briefing 12.1   Tensions within conservatism

Liberal New Right	Conservative New Right
Classical liberalism	Traditional conservatism
Atomism	Organicism
Radicalism	Traditionalism
Libertarianism	Authoritarianism
Economic dynamism	Social order
Self-interest/enterprise	Traditional values
Equality of opportunity	Natural hierarchy
Minimal state	Strong state
Internationalism	Insular nationalism
Pro-globalisation	Anti-globalisation

Source: Heywood (2003: 101)

– are now profitless museum pieces' (1998: 38). It is not surprising therefore that neo-conservatives are so unwilling to embrace **globalisation**, fearing that it will unleash forces that undermine the unifying propensities of the nation state.

However, the differences between neo-liberals and neo-conservatives should not be exaggerated. Indeed, the emergence of the New Right perspective serves to confirm the underlying compatibility of these two traditions (see Gamble 1988). As Heywood (2003) points out: 'Neoliberal and neoconservative views usually do coincide, and it is this attempt to fuse economic liberalism with social conservatism that gives the New Right its distinctive character' (2003: 100–101). Even those who would perceive themselves as firmly on one side of this divide often hold views that include elements of the opposing tradition. For example, Tomlinson (1995) suggests that Hayek's neo-liberal persona can be questioned:

His liberal credentials are evident in the primacy accorded to liberty in his scale of political goals, the emphasis on individuals as the best judges of their own interests, and the desire for tight constitutional limits on distrusted parliamentary democracies. On the other hand, the veneration of tradition, the belief in evolutionary progress, and the distrust of reason as the basis for government action appear much more typical of conservative thought.

Tomlinson (1995: 21)

The New Right and the welfare state

Given its neo-conservative and neo-liberal roots, it is not surprising to find that those who subscribe to the tenets of the New Right have objected to the welfare state on grounds of principle and practice. These objections can be broadly categorised as philosophical, economic and social.

Philosophical objections

The New Right has objected to the construction of a welfare state on philosophical grounds. First, as was noted previously, the collective action required to establish and administer a welfare state is seen as ill advised given the impossibility of obtaining the requisite information to design such a system to meet the complex needs of citizens. Second, the New Right object to the fact that unlike the impartiality of spontaneous market transactions, welfare state activity has been underpinned by wholly inappropriate notions of social justice in which the distribution of scarce resources is 'decided by some all-encompassing merit table' (Tomlinson 1990: 41). Third, the New Right believes that the welfare state poses an unacceptable threat to personal freedom. To compel citizens to pay for collectively organised services, which they may be ineligible or unwilling to use, ultimately by threat of criminal sanction, is seen as undermining individual liberty. For those without the requisite post-tax income to opt for non-state provision, the denial of choice is seen as a serious erosion of personal freedom and yet another step on the road to serfdom (Hayek 1944).

Economic objections

New Right commentators have voiced a number of concerns about state welfare activity. Non-market provision of this kind is seen as having a number of inherent flaws. It is argued that the absence of a market mechanism makes it extremely difficult to decide what services should be supplied at what cost at a particular point in time. As was noted earlier: 'The virtue of the market ... is that it acts as the central nervous system of the economy, reconciling the supply of goods and services with the demand for them. It allocates resources to their most profitable use and thereby ensures that consumer needs are satisfied' (Heywood 2003: 94). Faced with this informational deficit, politicians and civil servants have to estimate the level of various forms of need and attempt to provide sufficient resources to meet this 'demand' mindful of the fact that taxpayers may prove unwilling to support the requisite level of funding. As Seldon (1981) comments, the 'only judgement that can be safely made' about the level of NHS expenditure 'is that it is the *politically* ideal proportion. It is decided by politicians actuated by short-term motivations of election or re-election. It has only an uncertain and remote link with the *medically* ideal expenditure, as doctors would like, and even more remote with the *economically* ideal expenditure as the public would wish' (Seldon 1981: 22–3). Another economic criticism of state welfare activity concerns the lack of consumer choice. Given that most citizens cannot afford to purchase private forms of welfare, they have little choice but to use public provision. If such services fall short of their expectations they are thus unable to employ the 'exit' strategy (withholding their custom) that can be pursued in commercial transactions. Instead, they can only resort to complaining about current service (a strategy often termed as 'voice') in the hope that this might lead to improved provision in the future. A further deficiency raised by the New Right concerns the way in which the welfare state serves the interests of providers rather than users. They reject the notion that public sector workers are more likely to be committed to the efficient provision of high-quality services because of an enhanced sense of selflessness or duty allegedly lacking among their private sector counterparts (see, however, Le Grand 2003). Public choice theorists such as Tullock (1965) and Buchanan (1986) highlight the way in which these supposedly selfless public servants show more interest in their terms and conditions, staffing levels and budget allocations rather than the needs of users. In their view the absence of market disciplines means that the providers of public services have few incentives to contain costs, improve efficiency, keep abreast of new developments or respond swiftly to consumer preferences. As one leading New Right exponent concludes:

> The *monopolistic position* of the welfare services prevents them from learning from competition and from experience, or from attending other than trivially and inadequately to their clients' needs and concerns. Their *bureaucratic structure* consistently prevents them from operating with the adaptable flexibility and attention to changing circumstances that we take for granted from service-providers in the private sector. Their *colossal scale* inhibits innovation and encourages depersonalized routinization. The commitment of their managers at all levels to *centralized planning* stands in the way of local and individual initiative and enterprise, and precludes genuine concern with the reactions of clients and consumers.
>
> Marsland (1996: 107)

The growth of the welfare state is also seen as having a negative effect on the economy more generally. For example, in an influential assessment of the postwar economy published in the mid-1970s, Bacon and Eltis (1976) argued that the large increase in welfare spending since 1945 had served to undermine Britain's economic performance, by transferring scarce resources from the 'productive' private sector into the 'non-productive' public sphere. Furthermore, New Right commentators argue that the rising level of taxation required to finance welfare expansion has created work disincentives. The imposition of higher tax rates is seen as creating inflationary pressures in the economy as workers seek to protect their living standards through higher pay demands. High tax rates can also lead to increased levels of tax avoidance and evasion as citizens seek to resist what they regard as unjust levies.

Social objections

According to the New Right the operation of the welfare state has also given rise to a number of undesirable social effects. First, the rationing procedures that have been introduced in order to restrict demand for 'free' need-based provision have been criticised on the grounds that certain groups are much better able to access such services because they possess the necessary skills or attributes to 'work' the system. As Harris and Seldon (1977) contend: 'The market pays attention only to how people will pay. It is not interested in their accents, family origins, occupations, social connections, colour ... [or] political influence' (1977: 117).

It is argued, second, that the granting of rights to various welfare services has encouraged citizens to neglect their responsibilities for meeting their own needs and those of their dependants. It is contended that one of the fundamental problems with state welfare is the lack of any explicit demands or expectations on those who receive help. As Marsland (1996) notes: 'Rights-based welfare provides continuing, explicit, almost irresistible encouragement to clients to demand more and more by way of fulfilment of the state's irresponsible promises, while giving nothing in return' (1996: 177).

Third, instead of ameliorating particular social problems, it is contended that state welfare measures can actually cause more harm than good. Murray (1990) has argued that the growth of single motherhood can be linked to more generous forms of state support that has served to lift 'a large portion of low-income young women above the threshold where having and keeping a baby became economically feasible' (1990: 30). Inflexible welfare regulations can also discourage honesty on the part of claimants. For example, recipients of means-tested social security benefits have little incentive to provide accurate assessments of their financial assets or to declare some meagre earnings if it leads to a marked decrease in their benefit 'entitlements' (see Field 1995: 35–7).

Fourth, the more libertarian New Right thinkers are concerned that state welfare can act as an oppressive form of social control. Increasing levels of monitoring and surveillance are seen as posing an unwarranted threat to individual freedom.

A fifth charge levelled at the welfare state is the way in which it has led to the creation of a so-called 'dependency culture'. As Glennerster (2000) explains: 'The argument is that the Welfare State has displaced the role of the family as the main provider of welfare; children no longer look after their elderly parents, parents cannot control their children, fathers abandon their families; without a role model of a nuclear family teenage boys become "yobs" and teenage girls become unmarried mothers' (2000: 196). For commentators such as Charles Murray (1990), this counter-culture tends to become concentrated in particular neighbourhoods that become increasingly divorced from, and threatening to, 'mainstream' society.

The sixth social objection is that state welfare has 'crowded out' alternative welfare providers. It is argued that increasingly diverse and responsive forms of familial, voluntary and private welfare would have evolved had they not been deliberately suppressed by an overbearing state sector (Green 1996).

Seldon (1981) contends, for example, that if the voluntary sector had been able to evolve in an organic way it would have 'far outshone the standardised, unresponsive, conservative, costly, politically-distorted institutions of the welfare state' (1981: 16).

Reforming the welfare state

New Right commentators have put forward various policy proposals that are intended to counter the adverse effects of the welfare state. Those on the neo-liberal wing have argued for a significant reduction in state welfare activity, particularly in the provision of services such as education, health and housing. Those who are genuinely unable to afford non-state provision due to inadequate resources would then be provided with assistance, often in the form of vouchers, to obtain the necessary service. Importantly, neo-liberal commentators such as Seldon (1981) believe that all such benefits including cash transfers should be subject to stringent eligibility criteria such as needs and means tests.

While both Hayek and Friedman acknowledge that there is a place for residual state welfare provision, Charles Murray is more sceptical. The ineffectiveness of federal welfare initiatives in the USA has led him to advocate greater local experimentation in service delivery. For instance, he has argued that 'a state with a relatively small caseload and a history of effective non-governmental social welfare' should be given the opportunity 'to cut off all benefits for girls under the age of 21' (Murray 2001: 160). He contends that a measure of this kind could reduce 'the amount of damage that continues to be caused by high-density nonmarital births' (2001: 160).

While the 'neo-conservatives' are also keen to see a reduction in unnecessary state welfare activity, they are less sceptical than their 'neo-liberal' counterparts about the possibility of securing effective welfare reform. Lawrence Mead (1986), for example, is a firm advocate of a more paternalistic form of state welfare (see Deacon 2002: 49–62). In discussing recent US reforms, he contends that 'in the past, welfare satisfied virtually nobody, on the left or right. It provided needy families only meagre support while fomenting, or at least condoning, social problems among the poor, particularly unwed pregnancy and nonwork. Recent reforms – by enforcing work, restraining dependency, and making work pay – have made welfare more legitimate and improved its capacity to support families' (Mead 2001: 201–202).

Neo-conservatives are particularly keen to encourage the expansion of the voluntary welfare sector, which they believe can often better meet the welfare needs of citizens as well as be an important source of service innovation. Voluntary welfare activity is also seen as having a key role to play in binding a community together. As Willetts (1992) contends: 'It is the paradox of the welfare state that whilst on the one hand it embodies our sense of solidarity with others, it can also alienate us from others. The person sitting in his cosy living room during a cold snap, wondering why the social services do not check the old lady next door epitomizes the price that we can pay for the welfare state' (1992: 148).

The New Right and British social policy since 1945

Although New Right ideas came to the fore in debates on British social policy from the mid-1970s onwards, it is important to recognise that these ideas were promoted in the immediate post-war period, not least in Hayek's influential book *The Road to Serfdom* (1944). Indeed, the fact that this volume provided intellectual ballast to counter the growing influence of Labour's collectivist message at the time of the 1945 general election led the then Conservative Party chairman to forgo '1.5 tons of its precious paper assignment for the general election campaign' (paper was one of a number of items which were rationed at this time) so that Routledge 'could publish an abridged version of the book before the end of the campaign' (Cockett 1995: 93).

While Hayek's objections to economic interventionism continued to resonate in Conservative circles following their defeat in the 1945 general election, a more positive attitude towards state welfare activity began to emerge. Although the Conservatives opposed some of Attlee's welfare initiatives, most notably Bevan's health reforms, their approach was broadly supportive. This is reflected in R. A. Butler's speech during the second reading of the National Insurance Bill in 1946: 'The whole philosophy behind these measures, in which, I make it plain, we have played our part and shall play our part, is that the good things of life shall be more widely shared; we look forward to a society in which the more unfortunate members are free from the direst dread of penury and want' (quoted in Raison 1990: 16).

Although Conservative support for the welfare state remained contingent rather than unconditional, there was a clear desire to ensure that the post-war Conservative Party should be perceived as supporters, rather than opponents, of the welfare state, particularly as they were keen to shed their 'uncaring' reputation acquired during the 1920s and 1930s. Indeed, they were often dismayed to find that they were given so little credit for the part they had played in the 'creation' of the modern welfare state during the period of the wartime coalition government.

One distinctive Conservative approach to social policy was set out in a famous pamphlet published in 1950 entitled *One Nation: A Tory Approach to Social Problems* (Macleod and Maude 1950). This publication reaffirmed Conservative support for the maintenance of full employment and support for the NHS. It also called for an increase in public sector house building and for improvements in technical schools and colleges. However, it also identified some weaknesses in Labour's strategy. The egalitarian aims of Labour's welfare policy were regarded as misconceived and the shift towards universalism was deemed to be jeopardising the position of those in greatest need. Concern was also expressed about the ways in which Labour's approach was stifling initiative and undermining voluntarism.

Although there were periodic questions about the costs of the welfare state throughout the 13 years of Conservative government from 1951 to 1964, it proved difficult for 'New Right' ideas to take hold in this or any other sphere of government policy. Nevertheless, the case for a more neo-liberal economic and social policy continued to be advanced in some quarters and this eventually bore fruit in the late 1960s and early 1970s.

New Right resistance

In an attempt to counter what was seen as the pejorative influence of collectivist ideas in society, the Institute of Economic Affairs was founded in 1955. Under the direction of Ralph Harris and Arthur Seldon, the IEA published a number of pamphlets and research papers outlining the case for neo-liberal economic and social ideals. In terms of social policy pamphlets were published on the inequities of state pensions (Seldon 1957), the need for greater choice in healthcare (Lees 1961) and housing (Pennace and Gray 1968).

At first the IEA made limited headway in promoting its neo-liberal ideas, not least among Conservative MPs. However, following the party's electoral defeat in the 1964 general election, the possibility of reshaping Conservative policy along neo-liberal lines was being taken more seriously by influential politicians such as Enoch Powell, Geoffrey Howe and Keith Joseph. Howe's (1965) ideas concerning privately funded second pensions, outlined in a pamphlet entitled *In Place of Beveridge*, were subsequently incorporated into the party's 1966 manifesto.

Further electoral defeat in 1966 served only to strengthen the influence of neo-liberal ideas. By the time of the 1970 general election the Conservative Party had embraced many neo-liberal ideas. According to Willetts (1992) the party's programme was 'more Thatcherite than the 1983 manifesto – and probably even the manifesto of 1979' (1992: 42). This change of direction came to public prominence following a pre-election conference held at the Selsdon Park Hotel in the early part of 1970. A host of free market policies were put forward for consideration including tax cuts, curbs on trade union powers, reduced government support for failing industries and the ending of prices and incomes policies. In terms of welfare policy, the need for greater targeting of resources was suggested, as was the imposition of charges for the board and lodging component of inpatient NHS stays. This embrace of neo-liberal ideas led the Labour leader Harold Wilson to coin the phrase 'Selsdon man' in an effort to portray the Conservatives as the hard-hearted enemies of full employment, the welfare state and economic interventionism. According to Raison (1990), although this epithet could be justified in terms of changes in Conservative *economic* policy, it was an inaccurate caricature of the party's *social* policy, so that: 'Nobody could say that the social policy discussed at Selsdon Park and then endorsed in the 1970 manifesto, *A Better Tomorrow*, represented a radical change of direction' (1990: 69).

At first it appeared that the government of Edward Heath (1970–1974) would pursue 'Selsdon'-style policies. The new Minister of Trade and Industry, John Davies, wasted no time in declaring that taxpayers' money should no longer be spent on bailing out so-called 'lame-duck' industries. An Industrial Relations Bill was introduced under which an industrial relations court was to be established to enforce strike ballots and cooling-off periods in an effort to curb trade union power. However, the non-interventionist stance of the new government unravelled in the light of rising inflation (which had been fuelled in part by Barber's expansionist budget in 1971), unemployment and the threat of bankruptcy at both Rolls-Royce and the Upper Clyde shipbuilders. According to Morgan (1990) therefore: 'By mid-1971, Selsdon man had been decently interred and the government's policy went into rapid reverse' (1990: 322).

The return to interventionism did not, however, provide an effective solution to the underlying economic problems facing the Heath government. It did, however, have some positive effects in the social policy field, most notably in education. During Margaret Thatcher's period as Education Secretary, the minimum school leaving age was finally raised to 16 and plans for the establishment of the Open University were allowed to proceed despite treasury objections. A subsequent White Paper, *A Framework for Expansion* (1972) envisaged substantial growth in education spending (under which 90 per cent of 4 year olds would be eligible for a free, part-time nursery place by 1981), an expansion in teacher numbers (a 40 per cent increase by 1981) and further growth in the higher education sector.

Heath's failure to combat the severe economic difficulties that beset his government during the early 1970s by interventionist means, served to strengthen the hand of the neo-liberals. The party's defeat at the 1974 election, which Heath had called 'ostensibly on the issue of the respective powers, responsibilities and rights of governments and trade unions' (Deakin 1994: 51) led to the development of a New Right economic and social strategy.

One key figure in this process was Keith Joseph who had hitherto been regarded as a '**One Nation**' Heath loyalist (Denham and Garnett 2001). Persuaded by the monetarist critiques of commentators such as Milton Friedman, Alfred Sherman and Alan Walters, Joseph now took the view that the interventionist strategy pursued by the Heath government (of which he had been a high-spending minister at the DHSS) was misconceived and had fuelled both inflation and political discord.

The establishment of the Centre for Policy Studies in 1974, which Joseph chaired with Margaret Thatcher as his vice-chair, provided the institutional base for a concerted challenge to 'One Nation' Conservatism. In a series of well-publicised speeches, Joseph argued that the inflationary increase in the money supply during the Heath administration should have been tackled by monetarist means even though this would have increased unemployment. He also shifted his position on the relationship between welfare benefits and behaviour. In a contribution to a 'One Nation Group' pamphlet in 1959 entitled *The Responsible Society*, he had argued that there was no causal link between welfare benefits and dependency. But now he acknowledged that 'a generous welfare system could produce a harmful form of dependency after all' (Denham and Garnett 2001: 101).

When Heath decided to seek re-election as leader of the Conservative Party in 1975, Joseph was expected to stand against him on a New Right platform. However, after a controversial speech in Edgbaston, in which he appeared to condone the compulsory sterilisation of impoverished working-class mothers, (in addition to having personal reservations) (Denham and Garnett 2001), Joseph decided not to oppose Heath, leaving the way clear for his 'acolyte' Margaret Thatcher. Although initially regarded as too inexperienced and unpopular to stand for senior office (one *Sunday Express* columnist described her as being 'totally out of touch with anybody but carefully corseted, middle-class, middle-aged ladies' (quoted in Campbell 2000: 287)), Thatcher rose to the challenge. She gave a series of impressive performances both in parliament, in her role as shadow Deputy Treasury spokesperson, and in constituency associations, where she promoted the ideas of freedom, choice and private ownership. After defeating Heath in the first leadership ballot, Thatcher saw off challenges from Whitelaw and Howe in the second round to become leader of the party.

By the time of the 1979 general election, the framework of a New Right economic and social agenda had begun to take shape. The party's manifesto stressed the importance of controlling inflation, trade union reform, cutting income tax, better targeted welfare spending and a greater commitment to self-help on the part of both individuals and communities (Conservative Party 1979). Although the Conservatives' lead in the opinion polls fell away steadily during the election campaign, they achieved an overall majority of 43 seats with 43.9 per cent of the vote thanks in no small part to the support of so-called C2 voters (skilled workers), who had traditionally voted Labour.

The Thatcher years, 1979–1990

During the first Thatcher term (1979–1983), the key priority of the government was economic rather than social reform. Accordingly, emphasis was given to the control of inflation, reducing the role of the state, curbing the powers of trade unions and the creation of an entrepreneurial climate through such means as tax cuts and other incentives. At first the Thatcher government found it difficult to control inflation as a result of some of its own initiatives as well as external shocks, such as the steep rise in oil prices in 1979. The impact of income tax cuts (the standard rate was reduced from 33 per cent to 30 per cent and the top rate from 83 per cent to 60 per cent), higher VAT (a new unified rate of 15 per cent was introduced) and the decision to honour the Clegg Committee's recommendations on public sector pay saw inflation increase to 18 per cent in 1980. High interest rates also led to a slowdown in economic activity as firms found it difficult to compete in overseas markets. Output fell sharply and by the autumn of 1981 unemployment topped 2.8 million (twice the level of May 1979) and exceeded 3 million by 1982/3. Such adverse indicators led many commentators to predict that the Thatcher government would have to make an economic 'U-turn'. However, Thatcher and her Chancellor, Geoffrey Howe, remained resolute. The tight economic policy was maintained and inflation was brought down to 4.5 per cent in 1983, albeit at the cost of a high level of unemployment.

In terms of trade union reform, the Conservatives adopted an incremental approach. The Employment Act of 1980 outlawed so-called secondary

picketing (at firms not directly involved in a dispute) and made it more difficult for unions to operate closed shops (compulsory union membership for all
employees). Further legislation in 1982 outlawed the closed shop, restricted the
scope of industrial action and made unions liable for any infringements. As
Clarke (1996) notes, these incremental measures succeeded in 'tying down the
trade unions with a thousand silken cords' (1996: 369).

Although no precise strategy for welfare reform was put in place during the
first term of the Thatcher government, there were indications of the direction
in which they were moving. For example, social security spending was tightened by linking benefit increases to the rise in prices rather than earnings – a
policy that led to a steady decline in the real value of the basic pension and
other entitlements. In addition, payments to strikers were cut, earnings-related
additions to unemployment and sickness benefits were withdrawn and some
of the costs of the sick pay scheme were transferred from government to
employers. In education, expenditure on both schools and universities was
substantially reduced, the push for comprehensivisation was halted, the statutory requirement to provide school meals and milk was withdrawn and an
assisted places scheme introduced. Under this last measure, subsidised places
in independent secondary schools were to be offered to able children from
poorer backgrounds, as a means of resurrecting the direct grant system, which
had been abolished by Labour in 1976. Housing bore the brunt of Conservative
spending cuts. Expenditure was cut from £5.5 billion in 1979 to £3.7 billion by
1984. This was due in part to what proved to be one of the Conservatives' most
popular policies, the sale of council houses. Between 1979 and 1983 nearly half
a million homes were sold off at discounted prices.

The second term

Following further electoral success in 1983, in which the Conservatives gained
an overall majority of 144 seats (albeit on a lower share of the total vote), a
more concerted 'New Right' attack on the welfare state was anticipated.
Although this amounted to less than a full-frontal assault, further steps were
taken to rein in welfare expenditure, in order to deliver promised cuts in personal taxation and to improve the level of efficiency and effectiveness of public
services. In the case of social security, a wide-ranging review was undertaken
in four key areas – pensions, housing benefit, supplementary benefits and benefits for children and young people. Although this led to a number of policy
recommendations, including the abolition of the state earnings related pension
scheme (which was not implemented), the introduction of Family Credit (to
replace Family Income Supplement) and the Social Fund (which aimed to
reduce the cost of discretionary payments by the greater use of loans rather
than grants), the impact on overall spending levels was negligible.

The drive for greater efficiency in the NHS led to the introduction of a more
tightly managed system so that Treasury spending targets could be achieved.
Cleaning, catering and laundry services were put out to tender, staffing levels
were reviewed, clinical autonomy was diluted by managerial dictats on prescribing and treatment costs. Importantly, during their tenures as Health

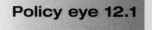

Policy eye 12.1   Examples of New Right-influenced legislation

1980 Housing Act – introduced a statutory right of tenants to buy their own council houses, at market prices less a discount

1980 Social Security Act – broke the link between the inflation uprating of some benefits (including the state pension) and earnings

1986 Social Security Act – phased out the state earnings-related pensions scheme, encouraged private provision of pensions, simplified the benefits system, replaced Family Income Supplement with Family Credit and replaced supplementary benefit single payments with discretionary lump-sum loans

1988 Education Reform Act – introduced parental choice of schools, the National Curriculum and local financial management of schools

1988 Housing Act – sought to encourage the transfer of local authority housing stock to new landlords following ballots of tenants

1989 Local Government and Housing Act – outlawed local authorities subsidising council house rents from other areas of activity

1990 NHS and Community Care Act – introduced NHS Trusts and GP fundholders with internal markets in the NHS and laid down a new framework for community care with a vision of local authorities as *enablers* rather than providers of services

Secretary, both Norman Fowler (1981–1983) and Kenneth Clarke (1984–1987) were prepared to be confrontational with those members of the medical profession and their representatives who were opposed to change.

In contrast, a more cautious approach was adopted by Keith Joseph at the Department of Education (1981–1986). Indeed, in response to public disquiet he decided to abandon plans for education vouchers in schools and tuition fees in higher education.

The third term

A number of commentators have argued that a distinctive New Right approach to welfare only really gathered pace during the third term of the Thatcher government (Policy eye 12.1). Certainly, greater emphasis was given to welfare reform in the party's manifesto *The Next Moves Forward* (Conservative Party 1987). The party committed itself to raising standards in education, providing better housing for all, improving the health service and reforming 'the tangled web of income-related benefits' (Conservative Party 1987: 54).

Education

New education reforms had been unveiled at the end of the Conservatives' second term (see also Chapter 5). These included the introduction of a national curriculum, formal testing of children at the ages of 7, 11 and 14 and the establishment of around 20 city technology colleges. Within six weeks of their third election victory in June 1987, Education Secretary Kenneth Baker had released four consultation papers that elicited some 20,000 replies 'from an educational world stunned at the scale of what was contemplated' (Timmins 2001: 436). Despite the numerous objections and criticisms the Education Reform Act came into effect in 1988. This Act introduced a National Curriculum for all state schools and set out the levels of knowledge, skills and understanding (attainment targets) that all pupils would be expected to achieve by the ages of 7, 11, 14 and 16. National testing was to be introduced so that standards could be monitored and disseminated. The Act paved the way for the creation of grant-maintained schools, which could opt out of local authority control and receive funding directly from the Department of Education. The Act provided opportunities for the local management of schools (LMS), whereby head teachers and governing bodies were given greater autonomy over the running of their schools. Specialist city technology colleges (funded from both public and private sources) were to be established to act as centres of excellence in local communities. In the tertiary sector a new funding body – the Universities Funding Council (UFC) – was established to exercise more direct control over university spending while the polytechnics were to be 'freed' from local authority control paving the way for their rebranding as 'new' universities.

Housing

The Conservatives attempted to consolidate their highly successful council house sales policy by further measures aimed at reducing the role of local authorities in the building, ownership, management and regulation of housing (see Chapter 9). Under the Housing Act 1988, tenants were provided with an opportunity to vote for a new landlord under a policy known as 'tenants choice'. Housing action trusts were seen as the solution for the most run-down estates. This involved the control of an estate passing from the local authority to a new independent landlord, who would be expected to improve the housing stock. These initiatives did not prove particularly successful. By 1994, only five housing action trusts had been established and these deviated in intent from the Conservatives' initial proposals. Although there were some transfers to non-council landlords, these tended to be initiated by local authorities that were keen to dispose of their housing stock. 'By mid-1994, thirty local authorities – nearly all small, nearly all Conservative and nearly all in the south – had transferred half a million tenants in 150,000 homes to housing associations, raising £1.2 billion in the process' (Timmins 2001: 433–4). Significantly, some 3.7 million houses in England remained under municipal control in 1994, compared to a figure of 4.2 million in 1988.

Health

Although the 1987 manifesto referred to the need to improve the health service there was no mention of fundamental changes. However, by 1990, the government had embarked on what Glennerster (2000: 189) terms 'the biggest change in the structure and logic of the service since the 1946 Act' (see Chapter 8). The decision to opt for major reform was taken after it became clear that the previous squeeze on NHS spending had become unsustainable. Cash-strapped health authorities were forced to close hospital beds and cancel operations. Industrial action was becoming more frequent and doctors were calling on the government to save the NHS. As the crisis deepened Mrs Thatcher announced, much to the surprise of her fellow ministers and civil servants, that there would be a thoroughgoing review of the NHS. A small review team headed by Thatcher herself was established. It included the Minister of Health, John Moore, his deputy Tony Newton, Nigel Lawson and John Major from the Treasury and Roy Griffiths, the Prime Minister's personal adviser. After reviewing several policy options, it was decided to maintain a tax-funded service, but to aim to increase the efficiency and effectiveness of that service by means of internal markets. The new Health Secretary, Kenneth Clarke, published a White Paper entitled *Working for Patients* in 1989. Its central idea was to create a split between the *purchasers* of healthcare, which would be undertaken by health authorities and GP budget holders, and *providers* (private and public hospitals). Despite opposition from both the Labour Party and the British Medical Association, the National Health Service and Community Care Act received Royal Assent in 1990. As the title of the Act indicates reforms to the system of community care were also implemented (see also Chapters 6 and 8). The government had been concerned about the growing social security bill for residential care costs that had risen from £10 million in 1979 to some £2 billion by 1991 as result of greater use being made of this form of public funding. The decision was taken to transfer the responsibility for the care of elderly people from the social security system to local authorities. However, local authorities were not permitted to spend this new revenue stream on 'in-house' services. The Act stipulated that the key task of local authorities was to assess the needs of elderly people and prepare community care plans leaving the provision of services to private and voluntary organisations. As Glennerster (2000) points out: 'The reform of community care thus fitted into what was now emerging as the common pattern of social policy reforms in the Thatcher period – continued state funding but a variety of forms of private and public providers' (2000: 191).

Social security

Although there were some significant developments in the delivery of social security during the Conservatives' third term, it proved difficult to dismantle the core structure established by the post-war Labour government (see Chapter 3). As Deakin (1994) points out: 'The contributory system remained in place, albeit in attenuated form. Means-tested benefits were increased in scope as an essential ingredient in the Government's programme to increase the scope of targeting, but some universal benefits continued in operation, notably child benefit' (1994: 177).

The pronouncements of John Moore, who had been appointed as Secretary of State at the Department of Health and Social Security in 1987, certainly conveyed sympathy for New Right ideas. He attacked the growth of the 'dependency culture' and fully supported those initiatives that attempted to tackle this problem such as the decision to compel 16 and 17 year olds to undertake youth training rather than subsist on Income Support. His preference for targeting was reflected in his decision to freeze the level of Child Benefit (a universal benefit) for three successive years (1988–91) and to 'pump some of the saving into means-tested family credit' (Timmins 2001: 446). Moore also directed his fire at the 'poverty lobby' suggesting that they were exaggerating the extent of real deprivation by equating poverty with legitimate forms of inequality. Moore's attack might have had greater resonance had it not been made at a time in which income inequality was rising. While Lawson's tax-cutting budget of 1988 improved the living standard of 'top executives on £70,000 a year' by £150 per week (Timmins 2001: 448), many claimants found their incomes reduced as a result of the implementation of earlier social security cuts which had been initiated by Moore's predecessor, Norman Fowler. The position of the most vulnerable was further undermined by the introduction of the Social Fund, which replaced non-repayable hardship grants by loans.

Moore's successor, Tony Newton, adopted a less strident tone, although his decision to press on with the introduction of the Child Support Agency, which attempted to ensure that absent parents provided greater financial support for their children, proved ill fated.

Undoubtedly, the most dramatic event of the Conservatives' third term was the abrupt end to Margaret Thatcher's premiership in 1990. At this time the economic outlook was uncertain as the short economic boom following the 1987 general election had given way to a recession in 1989. The replacement of the household rating system by a Community Charge, or, as it became better known,

Source: www.CartoonStock.com

the Poll Tax (levied on each adult in a household), proved highly unpopular. The charges were vastly higher than the government had predicted and the only gainers appeared to be the wealthy. Many people refused to pay the new tax and an anti-Poll Tax rally at Trafalgar Square in 1990 was the occasion of serious public disorder. The Prime Minister's position was most seriously threatened, however, by a succession of ministerial resignations – Heseltine, Ridley, Lawson and Howe – linked wholly or partly to European issues. Although Thatcher won the first round of a subsequent leadership contest by 204 votes to 152, she failed to secure a sufficient majority to prevent a second ballot. Faced with dwindling support from both within her cabinet and in the parliamentary party she decided to step down. The situation that greeted her successor, John Major, was far from positive. The economic outlook was decidedly gloomy with inflation, unemployment and the balance of payments deficit all on an upward curve. Although the inflation rate fell in 1991, a recession had taken hold and the effects of this were particularly acute for many homeowners who were faced with higher interest rates and declining house prices. The Poll Tax proved to be an enduring problem until Michael Heseltine introduced a new Council Tax scheme in 1991. On the European front, Major was able to placate the Eurosceptic wing of his party by securing the right for Britain to opt out of the Social Chapter, minimum wage regulation and the Exchange Rate Mechanism. Although there was a strong feeling in many quarters that Labour would win the April 1992 general election, Major defied the pundits, gaining an overall majority of 21 seats.

The Major years, 1992–1997

The Party's 1992 election manifesto provided a clear indication that the Major administration would continue with the New Right economic agenda of the Thatcher years. Emphasis was given to lower taxation, 'the right to own', privatisation and deregulation. In terms of social policy, a less doctrinaire approach was adopted. For example, assurances were given about the party's continued commitment to the NHS, the basic state retirement pension and Child Benefit. Certainly Major did not appear to share Thatcher's antipathy towards the welfare state. As he states in his autobiography:

> When I was young my family had depended on public services. I have never forgotten – and never will – what the National Health Service meant to my parents or the security it gave despite all the harsh blows that life dealt them ... These personal experiences left me with little tolerance for the lofty views of well-cosseted politicians, the metropolitan media or Whitehall bureaucrats, who made little use of the public services in their own lives, and had no concept of their importance to others.
>
> Major (2000: 246–7)

However, he accepted the New Right view that services were often 'run carelessly, wastefully, arrogantly and ... more for the convenience of the providers than the users, whether they were parents, pupils or patients' (Major 2000:

245). Accordingly, he fully supported the drive for public sector reform. His decision to introduce the Citizen's Charter in July 1991 was intended to empower service users by providing improved information about the quality and performance of services, greater powers of redress and compensation and increased opportunities to use alternative services if existing provision proved unsatisfactory. By 1997, some 42 individual charters had been published. In addition, some 650 charter marks had been awarded to organisations that had met stipulated service standards (1996).

In the key areas of social policy, the Major government did not seek to introduce a raft of new reforms. Instead, it sought to ensure that the welfare reforms of the third Thatcher term took root.

Health

In terms of healthcare, the main task facing the Major government was the implementation of the key measures outlined in the National Health Service and Community Care Act of 1990. This was a sizeable task not least because new administrative arrangements such as self-governing hospital trusts and GP fundholders were introduced without lengthy consultation or preparation (see Chapter 8). The introduction of the internal market in healthcare proved administratively expensive. For example, the number of senior managers employed in the NHS rose from 16,000 in 1991 to 26,000 by 1995 (Webster 2002: 203). Crucially, the new system did little to ease the financial problems that continued to beset the NHS. As Timmins (2001) notes: 'NHS growth dropped from a real terms increase of almost 6 per cent in 1992–3 to a tenth of that a year later. Bottomley [the then Health Secretary] got it up to 3.78 per cent the following year, but it then slid away to barely 1.5 per cent in 1995–96 and 0.6 per cent in the run up to the 1997 election' (Timmins 2001: 516).

Towards the end of the Major government, public concern about the negative impact of the Conservatives' market-based reforms led the new Health Secretary, Stephen Dorrell, to reaffirm his party's commitment to the NHS. In a White Paper entitled *A Service with Ambition*, Dorrell emphasised that the intention of the government's reforms had merely been to improve the NHS not undermine it (Webster 2002: 205–206).

Education

The Major government was faced with the task of overseeing the implementation of the major legislative change, namely the Education Reform Act of 1988. This Act had given rise to 'a dual process of change, with moves towards both decentralisation and centralisation' (Ball 1998: 146–7). In terms of the former, schools were encouraged to become 'more innovative, risk-taking and entrepreneurial than their LEA counterparts' (Ball 1998: 147) by opting for grant-maintained status. Those that decided to remain under local education authority control were also given greater budgetary discretion under the Local Management of Schools (LMS) initiative. The most significant centralising measures were the introduction of a National Curriculum, the systematic testing of pupils, league tables of performance and increased inspection.

During his tenure as Education Secretary, John Patten experienced considerable difficulties in persuading teachers of the merits of either the National Curriculum or the new testing regime. In order to meet these concerns, he appointed Sir Ron Dearing to head a new School Curriculum and Assessment Authority, which subsequently pared back the National Curriculum and restricted national testing to just three subjects. These measures served to placate the teachers, although their wrath was subsequently transferred to the Office for Standards in Education (OFSTED), whose head, Chris Woodhead, appeared to revel in highlighting the inadequacies of contemporary teaching.

Although the Major government introduced some modifications to the Thatcher education reforms, it saw no reason to change direction. Indeed, by the time of the 1997 general election manifesto, the need to enhance educational standards by monitoring the performance of schools and teachers and assessing the progress of children from the age of five was once again emphasised. Parents were to be provided with a nursery education voucher to enable them to select the most appropriate form of pre-schooling for their children. The assisted places scheme was to be extended and efforts were to be made to expand the number of selective grant-maintained schools.

Social security

New Right ideas also underpinned the social security policies of the Major government to a significant extent. During his period as Social Security Secretary, Peter Lilley (1992–1997) introduced a number of reforms that were intended to bring spending under control. In a further attempt to rein in the social security budget, the eligibility criteria for a number of benefits were tightened or changed. For example, a new Incapacity Benefit was introduced in 1993. It included a more stringent 'work test', which it was hoped would secure a 7 per cent reduction in claimant numbers. Tougher benefit rules were introduced for asylum seekers and a less generous Housing Benefit scheme was developed. The value of the state earnings related pension scheme was further reduced while plans were put into effect to raise the pension age for women to 65 with effect from 2010. Lone parent benefit rates were also frozen in 1996.

Arguably, the most significant change made by Lilley was the introduction of the Jobseekers Allowance in 1996, which cut the period of entitlement to non-means-tested benefit from 12 months to 6 and merged it with Income Support for unemployed people. In order to stress the importance of making a rapid return to the job market, those seeking this form of assistance were required to demonstrate that they were actively seeking work.

New Right ideas were also evident in Major's ill-fated 'Back to Basics' campaign, in which he called for a return to traditional teaching methods, greater respect for the family and a concerted attack on crime. It was hoped that this campaign would lead to a fundamental reappraisal of the 'modernist' agendas, which had taken hold in areas such as education, healthcare and social work. However, the campaign quickly became associated, at least with certain sections of the media, with a puritanical moral crusade. Following media revelations about the private lives of both ministers and backbenchers, which led to the resignation of one junior minister, the campaign came to an abrupt halt.

It would be inaccurate to suggest that welfare issues were of paramount importance to the Major government. As with previous administrations, Major was faced with serious economic problems. The decision to withdraw from the Exchange Rate Mechanism on what came to be known as 'Black Wednesday' in September 1992 undermined the government's reputation for economic competence. In addition, Major faced serious divisions within his party divisions over Europe that eventually led him to seek re-election as leader of the party in 1999. Although Major easily defeated his opponent John Redwood, he accurately forecast that there would be 'many storms ahead' (Major 2000: 645). Despite presiding over a fast improving economy, it was clear that the period of Conservative rule was coming to a close. As Lowe (1999) concludes: 'The government was deeply split over membership of the European Union, besmirched with "sleaze" and beset by a relentless series of crisis from fat cats to mad cows' (Lowe 1999: 313). In such circumstances, few were surprised when a resurgent Labour Party under the vibrant leadership of Tony Blair returned to power at the 1997 general election.

The New Right legacy

While it is clear that New Right thinking informed the social policies of both the Thatcher and Major governments, there are differences of opinion over the extent to which they managed to change the fundamental character of the welfare state.

A number of New Right commentators have expressed their disappointment over the timidity of Conservative reforms in areas such as healthcare and education, believing that a more ambitious programme of reform should have been pursued (see Denham and Garnett 1998; Green and Lucas 1992; Ridley 1991).

Others have highlighted the 'resilience' of the welfare state in the face of an ideologically inspired onslaught. Although there were significant shifts in terms of expenditure patterns on particular services, welfare spending as a percentage of GDP remained remarkably constant over the Thatcher and Major years. The strength of the welfare state during this period has been attributed to the fact that the public appears to remain deeply attached to collectivism in areas such as health and education.

Public opinion surveys, however, have also revealed the fluid nature of support for the welfare state. For example, there is evidence that a number of New Right ideas have grown in popularity. For example, less than 40 per cent of those interviewed in the *British Social Attitudes* survey in the period from 1998 to 2000 felt that it was the task of government to redistribute income from rich to poor, compared to around 50 per cent in 1989 and 1991 see Table 12.1

Overall, it could be argued that the greatest achievement of the New Right has been at a 'cultural' or attitudinal level. Those who continue to question the need for welfare reform, who advocate the merits of administered rather than managed services, who prefer the terms patients or tenants rather than customers or users, who contend that citizens have altruistic as well as self-interested characteristics, are likely to be regarded as outmoded or worse. The success of this cultural onslaught is reflected in New Labour's acceptance of a number of New Right themes. As Ferguson, Lavalette and Mooney (2002: 165) conclude, the Thatcher and Major governments 'did succeed to a significant extent in securing legitimation for the role of the market in the delivery of heartland social and welfare services, and in the role of management in securing cost effectiveness. More significantly perhaps, they also created a new culture around welfare that New Labour were quick to embrace'. This theme will be returned to in Chapter 13.

Table 12.1 Redistribution and welfare spending, 1987–2000

	1987	1989	1991	1993	1994	1996	1998	1999	2000
Government should redistribute income to the less well off	%	%	%	%	%	%	%	%	%
Agree	45	50	49	45	51	44	39	36	39
Neither	20	20	20	21	23	26	28	27	24
Disagree	33	29	29	33	25	28	31	35	36
Government should spend more money on welfare benefits for the poor	%	%	%	%	%	%	%	%	%
Agree	55	61	58	53	50	43	43	40	38
Neither	23	23	23	25	25	29	29	30	31
Disagree	22	15	18	20	23	26	26	28	30

Source: Hills (2001: 15) Table 1.10

Summary

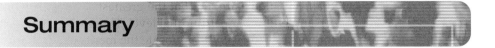

This chapter has examined the development and influence of New Right ideas and, in particular, their impact on the Conservative governments from 1979 to 1997. From this analysis it is possible to draw a number of conclusions:

- While there are a number of tensions between the neo-liberal and neo-conservative strands of thought these should not be overstated and, indeed, it is arguable that it was the fusion of these two traditions that gave the New Right its distinctive character, combining economic liberalism and social conservatism.

- The New Right developed a significant critique of the welfare state, grounded in philosophical, economic and social objections.

- Strategies of reform emerging from the New Right have included proposals for significant reductions in the level of state welfare activity, often suggesting the maintenance only of a safety net for those genuinely unable to provide for themselves, together with an expansion of provision by the private and voluntary sectors.

- New Right influence over social policy arguably reached its peak during the third Thatcher term of government, with major reforms in education, housing, health and social security, although it is also possible to argue that the New Labour governments of 1997 and 2001 continued to accept the strength of New Right arguments in a number of areas.

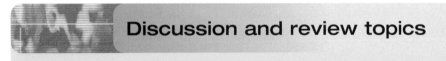

Discussion and review topics

1 Why did New Right ideas emerge so strongly in the Conservative Party in the late 1970s and early 1980s?

2 To what extent were different realms of social policy under the Conservative governments of 1979–1997 influenced by New Right ideas?

3 What were the main arguments put forward by the New Right for the introduction of markets into state welfare during the 1980s?

4 How convincing are New Right critiques of the welfare state?

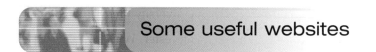

Further reading

George, V. and Page, R. (eds) (1995) *Modern Thinkers on Welfare*, Prentice Hall/Harvester Wheatsheaf, Hemel Hempstead – the chapters on Hayek and Friedman provide short introductions to the ideas of these writers

Hayek, F. A. (1944) *The Road to Serfdom*, Routledge & Kegan Paul, London – for those who wish to go back to one of the original sources and the inspiration for many New Right ideas

Marsland, D. (1996) *Welfare or Welfare State?*, Macmillan, Basingstoke – contains a critique of the welfare state and proposals for reform, emphasising self-reliance and the market

Pierson, C. and Castles, F. G. (2000) *The Welfare State Reader*, Polity, Cambridge – the section on 'responses from the right' contains reading from Hayek, Mead and Murray

Some useful websites

www.adamsmith.org.uk – the Adam Smith Institute is an organisation that campaigns for free market policies. This website contains information on its work and publications

www.cps.org.uk – a right of centre think tank founded by Keith Joseph and Margaret Thatcher

www.iea.org.uk – the site of the Institute of Economic Affairs provides information on news, events and publications from this free market think tank; it also provides links to a good range of other relevant organisations

There are also a number of other organisations of interest, such as the Institute for the Study of Civil Society (www.civitas.org.uk), Politeia (www.politeia.co.uk) and the Social Affairs Unit (www.socialaffairs unit.org.uk).

References

Adams, I. (1998) *Ideology and Politics in Britain Today*, Manchester University Press, Manchester

Bacon, R. and Eltis, W. (1976) *Britain's Economic Problem: Too Few Producers*, Macmillan, London

Ball, S. J. (1998) 'Education policy', in Ellison, N. and Pierson, C. (eds) *Developments in British Social Policy*, Macmillan, Basingstoke

Barry, N. (1999), 'Neo-classicism, the New Right and British social welfare', in Page, R. M. and Silburn, R. (eds) *British Social Welfare in the Twentieth Century*, Palgrave, Basingstoke

Buchanan, J. (1986) *Liberty, Market and the State*, Harvester Wheatsheaf, Hemel Hempstead

Campbell, J. (2000) *Margaret Thatcher, Volume One: The Grocer's Daughter*, Jonathan Cape, London

Clarke, P. (1996) *Hope and Glory*, Allen Lane, London.

Cockett, R. (1995) *Thinking The Unthinkable*, Fontana, London

Conservative Party (1979) *The Conservative Manifesto 1979*, Conservative Central Office, London

Conservative Party (1987) *The Next Moves Forward: The Conservative Manifesto 1987*, Conservative Central Office, London

Deacon, A. (2002) *Perspectives on Welfare*, Open University Press, Buckingham

Deakin, N. (1994) *The Politics of Welfare*, Harvester Wheatsheaf, Hemel Hempstead

Denham. A. and Garnett, M. (1998) *British Think-Tanks and the Climate of Opinion*, UCL Press, London

Denham, A. and Garnett, M. (2001) 'From "guru" to "godfather": Keith Joseph, "New" Labour and the British Conservative tradition', *The Political Quarterly*, 72, 97–106

Ferguson, I., Lavalette, M. and Mooney, G. (2002) *Rethinking Welfare: A Critical Perspective*, Sage, London

Field, F. (1995) *Making Welfare Work: Reconstructing Welfare for the Millennium*, Institute of Community Studies, London

Gamble, A. (1988) *The Free Economy and the Strong State*, Macmillan, London

Glennerster, H. (2000) *British Social Policy Since 1945*, Blackwell, Oxford

Gray, J. (1998) *False Dawn*, Granta, London

Green, D. G. (1996) *Community Without Politics*, IEA Health and Welfare Unit, London

Green, D. G. and Lucas, D. (1992) 'Private welfare in the 1980s', in Manning, N. and Page, R. (eds) *Social Policy Review 4*, Social Policy Association, Canterbury

Harris, R. and Seldon, A. (1977) *Not From Benevolence . . . 20 Years of Economic Dissent*, Institute of Economic Affairs, London

Hayek, F. A. (1944) *The Road to Serfdom*, Routledge & Kegan Paul, London

Hayek, F. A. (1967) *Studies in Philosophy, Politics and Economics*, Routledge & Kegan Paul, London

Heywood, A. (2003) *Political Ideologies: An Introduction*, Palgrave Macmillan, Basingstoke

Hills, J. (2001) 'Poverty and social security: What rights? Whose responsibilities?', in Park, A., Curtice, J., Thomson, K., Jarvis, L. and Bromley, C. (eds) *British Social Attitudes: The 18th Report*, Sage, London

Howe, G. (1965) *In Place of Beveridge*, Conservative Political Centre, London

Le Grand, J. (2003) *Motivation, Agency and Public Policy*, Oxford University Press, Oxford

Leach, R. (2002) *Political Ideology in Britain*, Palgrave, Basingstoke

Lees, D. S. (1961) *Health Through Choice*, IEA, London

Lowe, R. (1999) *The Welfare State in Britain Since 1945*, Macmillan, Basingstoke

Macleod, I. and Maude, A. (eds) (1950) *One Nation: A Tory Approach to Social Problems*, Conservative Political Centre, London

Major, J. (2000) *John Major: The Autobiography*, HarperCollins, London

Marsland, D. (1996) *Welfare or Welfare State?*, Macmillan, Basingstoke

May, M. (2002) 'Markets in welfare', in Alcock, P., Erskine, A. and May, M. (eds) *The Blackwell Dictionary of Social Policy*, Blackwell, Oxford

Mead, L. M. (1986) *Beyond Entitlement*, Free Press, New York

Mead, L. M. (2001) 'The politics of conservative welfare reform', in Blank, R. and Haskins, R. (eds) *The New World of Welfare*, Brookings Institution Press, Washington, DC

Mill, J. S. (1859) *On Liberty*, Dent, London

Morgan, K. O. (1990) *The People's Peace*, Oxford University Press, Oxford

Murray, C. (1990) *The Emerging British Underclass*, IEA Health and Welfare Unit, London

Murray, C. (2001) 'Family formation reform', in Blank, R. and Haskins, R. (eds) *The New World of Welfare*, Brookings Institution Press, Washington, DC

Park, A., Curtice, J., Thomson, K., Jarvis, L. and Bromley, C. (eds) (2001) *British Social Attitudes: The 18th Report*, Sage, London

Pennance, F. G. and Gray, H. (1968) *Choice in Housing*, IEA, London

Pierson, C. (1996) *The Modern State*, Routledge, London

Raison, T. (1990) *Tories and the Welfare State*, Macmillan, London

Ridley, N. (1991) *My Style of Government*, Hutchinson, London

Seldon, A. (1957) *Pensions in a Free Society*, Institute of Economic Affairs, London

Seldon, A. (1981) *Wither the Welfare State*, IEA Occasional Paper No. 60, Institute of Economic Affairs, London

Timmins, N. (2001) *The Five Giants*, HarperCollins, London

Tomlinson, J. (1990) *Hayek and the Market*, Pluto, London

Tomlinson, J. (1995) 'Hayek' in George, V. and Page, R. (eds) *Modern Thinkers on Welfare*, Prentice Hall/Harvester Wheatsheaf, London

Tullock, G. (1965) *The Politics of Bureaucracy*, Public Affairs Press, Washington, DC

Webster, C. (2002) *The National Health Service*, Oxford University Press, Oxford

Willetts, D. (1992) *Modern Conservatism*, Penguin, Harmondsworth

Willetts, D. (1994) *The Family*, W. H. Smith Contemporary Papers No. 14, W. H. Smith, London

From democratic socialism to New Labour

13 Robert Page

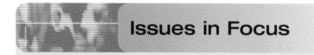

Issues in Focus

This chapter will examine the development of the Labour Party's approach to social policy in the period from the end of the Second World War. During this period the party first pursued a democratic socialist welfare strategy (1945–1951) before adopting a more overtly social democratic approach during their periods in government in the 1960s and 1970s. After general election defeats in 1979 and 1983, Neil Kinnock (1983–1992), and John Smith (1992–1994) made significant attempts to change the Party's policies, image and organisation, although the Conservatives remained in power, winning both the 1987 and 1992 elections. Following Smith's death in 1994, Tony Blair became leader and took Labour to substantial election victories in 1997 and 2001. This chapter examines some of the features of Labour's changing approach to social policy and the experiences of previous Labour governments, focusing on:

● the democratic socialist phase in the immediate post-war period, with social policies grounded in a universalistic approach

● the shift towards a social democratic approach and the Labour governments of the 1960s and 1970s

● New Labour's 'Third Way' approach to social policy from the mid-1990s.

The democratic socialist phase, 1945–1951

The Labour government of 1945–1951 subscribed to what can broadly be described as a democratic socialist approach to both economic and social policy. As Francis (1996) contends, the programme of the Attlee government was 'intended to serve as the first instalment in the transition to a future socialist society, albeit one which was compatible with, and indeed celebratory of, the British political tradition' (1996: 54).

Labour's democratic socialist strategy in this post-war period had an economic and a social dimension and it is useful to look at each of these in turn.

Economic policy

Labour stressed the importance of both public ownership and planning in its economic policy.

Public ownership

The emphasis given to public ownership in the Labour Party constitution of 1918 was intended to demonstrate its commitment to a socialist rather than liberal reformist political strategy. The transformation, rather than the amelioration of capitalism, was seen as vital if a socialist commonwealth were to be created. Public ownership was to play a major role in this process. However, as Francis (1997) has argued, the practicalities of nationalisation were not spelt out in any detail, so that 'Nationalisation ... remained a vague, almost utopian aspiration rather than a coherent, well-defined component of a socialist programme for a future Labour government' (1997: 69).

Although the Labour Party was still strongly committed to nationalisation at the end of the Second World War, there was a growing diversity of opinion concerning the precise purpose of this measure. On the one hand, nationalisation continued to be seen by many as an essential means for countering the unstable and exploitative nature of capitalism. It was viewed as a powerful vehicle in preventing 'concentrations of private economic power' as well as in redistributing property and promoting 'industrial democracy' (Francis 1997: 68). Others, such as Douglas Jay (1937), focused on the part that nationalisation could play in tackling inefficiency and poor industrial relations. Labour's adoption of the so-called Morrisonian form of nationalisation in 1937 (under which autonomous, profit-seeking public boards made up predominantly of ex-private sector managers were entrusted to run the newly nationalised industries, rather than workers or civil servants) suggests that Jay's more pragmatic approach to nationalisation was becoming increasingly influential.

Following its landslide election victory in 1945, the new Labour government pressed ahead with its manifesto commitments on public ownership. As Thorpe (2001) points out: 'The Bank of England and civil aviation were nationalized in

1946; coal, rail, road haulage, and cable and wireless in 1947; and electricity and gas in 1948' (2001: 108). By the end of the 1940s some 20 per cent of the British economy was in public hands. The nationalisation of the steel industry proved more problematic. The 'pragmatists' objected to this measure on the grounds that the industry was operating efficiently under private control and that the steelworkers' unions were not clamouring for a change of ownership. Although it was decided to press ahead with this measure, cabinet divisions resulted in implementation being delayed until after the 1950 general election.

At the end of its first term in office the Labour government reviewed its approach to public ownership. Two contrasting views emerged. 'Fundamentalists' such as Bevan (1952) believed that it was important to press on with further nationalisations in order to ensure that the relationship between 'public and private property' was 'drastically altered' (Bevan 1952: 118–19). In contrast, 'consolidators' such as Morrison advocated a more cautious approach, arguing that the impact of the first wave of nationalisations should be carefully evaluated before further initiatives were considered. The reservations of the consolidators were based in part on the recognition that public support for nationalisation was waning. As Brooke (1995) notes: 'The public corporation model of public ownership, designed for efficiency and impartiality, did not spark much interest, excitement, or loyalty' (1995: 20).

In terms of official party policy the consolidators' perspective gained the upper hand. The nationalisation plans put forward in Labour's election manifesto of 1950 were far more modest than in 1945, 'listing as it did merely water supply, cement, meat, sugar refining and industrial insurance' (Francis 1997: 66). In its subsequent election manifesto of 1951 even this nationalisation 'shopping list' was dropped and replaced by a vague pledge to take over 'concerns which fail the nation' (Thorpe 2001: 123).

Planning

Labour also believed that government needed to be more actively involved in planning the economy. However, as Thompson (1996) reminds us: 'There was no generally accepted conception of what economic planning was and how it should be implemented' (1996: 168). G. D. H. Cole (1950) and other contributors to the influential collection *Keep Left* (Crossman, Foot and Mikardo 1947) favoured what was known as 'direct' planning, using physical controls such as production quotas, the direction of labour and rationing. Such measures were deemed necessary to ensure that scarce resources were allocated on the basis of need or efficiency rather than misdirected 'by the irrational and anti-social forces of the market' (Francis 1997: 41). Others believed that socialist objectives could be achieved through 'indirect' forms of planning such as monetary or fiscal measures. From this perspective **Keynesian techniques** such as demand management could be used for socialist ends.

Although the post-war Labour government displayed a willingness to use both direct and indirect forms of planning, the latter assumed greater importance from the late 1940s onwards, not least because of a growing acceptance of the advantages of 'free' market activity.

Social policy

In terms of social policy Labour's main goal during this period was to achieve greater levels of security and inclusivity.

Security

Taking its lead from Beveridge's highly influential wartime *Report on Social Insurance and Allied Services* (1942), the post-1945 Labour government was determined to ensure that citizens were afforded greater protection against the vicissitudes of life such as unemployment, sickness, disability, widowhood and old age. Importantly, this objective was not to be achieved solely through social policy. The maintenance of **full employment** was seen as a vital factor in promoting financial security. The government intervened in the economy in highly effective ways to achieve this objective. As Brooke (1995: 16) points out: 'Between 1945 and 1951, unemployment averaged 310,000 a year, compared to 1,716,000 for the period 1935–9. Only once, during the fuel crisis of 1947, did unemployment briefly approach the levels of the interwar period'.

The Labour government also introduced a raft of social reforms to increase citizens' economic security. In particular, the government wanted to alleviate the fear of poverty. To this end it introduced a social insurance scheme that provided protection against unemployment, sickness, injury and old age. A **means-tested** national assistance scheme was also put in place in an effort to ensure a minimum living standard for all citizens. Although Labour's reforms in this sphere drew heavily on the Beveridge Report there were some notable departures. For example, Beveridge's recommendations concerning open-ended entitlement to unemployment insurance benefits and the phasing in of retirement pensions were rejected. In addition, Labour's decision to set insurance benefits at a relatively low rate coupled with regional variations in rent levels meant that increasing numbers of 'insured' citizens had to claim additional means-tested benefits in order to obtain a subsistence income.

Labour also sought to enhance citizens' well-being by introducing free healthcare for all. Prior to the establishment of the National Health Service in 1948, access to healthcare was restricted to the better off and to those members of the working class who were covered by the National Insurance scheme (which afforded little in the way of protection for dependants) or by virtue of trade union or friendly society membership. As Jones and Lowe (2002: 82) point out, the creation of the NHS 'removed from ordinary people one of their greatest historic fears: that they or a member of their family would suffer ill-health, or die, because they could not afford proper medical care'.

Inclusivity

The second key element of Labour's social strategy was inclusivity. In an effort to combat the sharp social divisions that characterised pre-war Britain, Labour sought to develop state services that would cover the vast majority of citizens (**universalism**) rather than for those with inadequate incomes (**selectivity**). Under the National Insurance scheme of 1946, workers were required to make weekly contributions in exchange for defined benefits in times of need. Given that this scheme was designed to accord with Beveridge's notion of a social minimum rather than a more generous standard, the solidaristic underpinning of this measure was limited. Indeed, those with higher disposable incomes were encouraged to make voluntary arrangements if they required enhanced forms of protection.

In contrast, the NHS was designed in a way that increased the possibility of greater social solidarity. As Jones and Lowe (2002) explain: 'By guaranteeing to everyone in times of need *free* and equal access to *optimum* care, it represented the idealism of the welfare state – far more so, for example, than social security where only *minimum* benefits were provided in return for insurance contributions' (2002: 82). Although the continued availability of private healthcare and the persistence of regional variations of care within the fledgling service worked against the grain of solidarism, the NHS did, in the view of a number of influential commentators, serve to erode class barriers in British society.

In other areas of social policy inclusivity proved more difficult to implement. Bevan had hoped that high-quality local authority housing would appeal equally to working-class and middle-class households. However, he was forced to acknowledge that housing had a class dimension and accordingly, agreed to the provision of 'special categories of better housing stock to minister to the needs of middle-class managers' (Morgan 2002: 89).

In terms of education, Labour's adherence to the 1944 Act limited the prospects for increased inclusivity. While the guarantee of free education for all children between the ages of 11 and 15 (Labour raised the school-leaving age to 15 in 1947) improved working-class access to secondary education, it had limited effect on the class composition within the various types of schools. As Smith (1996: 24) points out: 'Middle-class children continued to attend grammar schools while the majority of working-class children were placed in the secondary modern schools'. The class divide in education was also accentuated by the growth of private schooling during this period.

The limited success of Labour's policy of inclusion can be explained in part by the fact that it had not entirely resolved the dilemma of whether welfare services should be provided on the basis of citizenship, contribution or merit.

Two other features of the Labour government's democratic socialist strategy during this period should also be noted. First, there was a clear determination to use the tax system to create a more egalitarian society. Both Dalton (who was Chancellor of the Exchequer from 1945–1947) and his successor Cripps (1947–1950) built on the progressive tax system that had been introduced during the war. By the end of Labour's first post-war government, a surtax had been introduced on all incomes over £2,500 per annum, which 'effectively imposed a ceiling on post-tax incomes of little more than £6,000' (Francis 1996: 48). Death duties on larger estates were also increased in an effort to counter the large disparities in wealth holdings.

Second, Labour was keen to do more than merely improve the material well-being of the disadvantaged. It also wanted to ensure that citizens had greater opportunities to serve their communities and lead more fulfilling lives. To this end, citizens were encouraged to become more actively involved in civic regeneration and to participate in more creative pastimes such as classical music, the theatre and the visual arts rather than 'escapist' entertainments such as the cinema, which were thought to promote attitudes that were not appropriate to a 'responsible society'.

Crucially, however, Labour's expectation that 'the citizenry would yield morally and spiritually "towards socialism in everyday life"' (Black 2003: 13) failed to materialise. Their attempt to build a socialist commonwealth did not appear to resonate with the public at large. In a sense Labour appeared to be moving too far ahead of public opinion. While there was solid support for full employment and the welfare state, a public appetite for 'deep' socialism was hard to detect. Indeed, following Labour's defeat in the 1951 general election there was a growing demand for a more 'realistic' social democratic strategy.

Towards social democracy, 1951 and beyond

While it would be inaccurate to suggest that Labour's general election defeat of 1951 led to the adoption of a social democratic rather than democratic socialist political strategy, there was a clear shift towards the former. While Bevan and others on the left of the party continued to regard more extensive forms of public ownership as essential for the creation of a socialist society, consolidators such as Morrison and Gaitskell believed that it was now necessary to 'look beyond the old gospel of more and more nationalisation, "workers' control" or class appeals to "soak the rich"' (editorial in *Socialist Commentary* 1951, quoted in Fielding 1997: 32), not least because of the need to appeal to floating middle-class voters.

What were the distinguishing features of this revisionist social democratic approach? As was noted earlier, the revisionists rejected the idea that public ownership was essential to counter the undesirable aspects of capitalism. It was now thought possible to harness the positive virtues of the market by the application of Keynesian forms of economic management. As Shaw (1996) points out:

> Keynesianism had rendered the economic case for public ownership obsolete. Using Keynesian fiscal and monetary policies, a government could now fix the level of demand at a level sufficient to maintain steady growth, full employment and rising living standards. By managing the level of demand it could counter the sharp swings of the business cycle and thereby avoid depressions and mass unemployment.
>
> Shaw (1996: 52)

Moreover, according to revisionists, the redistributive gains of public ownership were likely to be small particularly if private owners were to be offered compensation. As Shaw (1996) continues, nationalisation was seen as 'a far less effective method for promoting equality than fiscal methods, such as a steeply progressive income tax, the taxation of wealth and unearned income and the expansion of the social services' (1996: 52).

In addition, the revisionists believed that equality should be regarded as the guiding principle of modern socialism, rather than the gradual socialisation of industry. Equality could be achieved through high levels of welfare spending, which would be financed through higher levels of economic growth and a moderately redistributive tax system. While the government was seen as having a key role in removing unjust inequalities, it should not attempt to create a uniform egalitarianism. Accordingly, material inequalities that served the public interest were seen as perfectly legitimate by the revisionists. However, inequalities of respect based on outmoded class attitudes were not. As Shaw (1996) makes clear:

> Revisionism ... signalled a rapprochement between the egalitarian and welfare aspirations of socialism and the capitalist mixed economy. Henceforth Labour defined its mission in terms of the fairer distribution of income, wealth and power within the framework of the managed market economy. The prime areas for pursuing its goals lay in the sphere of social policy.
>
> Shaw (1996: 55)

Crosland's highly influential text *The Future of Socialism* (1956) did much to enhance the revisionist case. According to Crosland, the characteristics of post-war capitalism differed markedly from those of the 1930s. It was now more stable and responsive to various forms of government intervention. Full employment had greatly increased the relative power of the trade unions at the expense of owners. The power of the latter had also been weakened as a result of the emergence of a more autonomous socially responsive managerial class. 'In short, business no longer had the capacity to frustrate a Labour government and the Party could safely continue its pursuit of equality and social justice within the framework of a mainly private-owned, market economy' (Shaw 1996: 53). The revisionist case had also been strengthened by Gaitskell's accession to the leadership following the retirement of Attlee in 1955.

Following Labour's third consecutive post-war electoral defeat in 1959, Gaitskell attempted to ensure that revisionism was embedded within the party by campaigning, albeit unsuccessfully, for the abandonment of Labour's formal commitment to public ownership (Clause 4) and by his resolute opposition to a unilateralist defence policy.

The success of revisionism resulted in social policy taking centre stage in the pursuit of a more equal and just society. However the success of this 'social' strategy was inextricably linked to the performance of the economy and the economic turbulence that Labour encountered during its subsequent periods in office (1964–1970 and 1974–1979) hindered its ability to introduce effective egalitarian social policies.

Social democracy in practice, 1964–1979

1964–1970

Following Gaitskell's sudden death in 1963, Harold Wilson became leader of the party. He developed a modernised economic and social agenda, which united the party and proved electorally successful. On returning to government in 1964, Labour aimed to boost the economy by means of a more scientific and technologically informed industrial policy, overseen by a new Ministry of Technology. Importantly, as far as traditionalists were concerned, the need for government intervention and planning were deemed essential if the nation were to benefit from these advances in science and technology. A Department of Economic Affairs was established with the aim of devising a plan for increased growth. When the national plan was finally published in the autumn of 1965, an ambitious target for GDP growth (25 per cent) over the period from 1964 to 1970 was set, the achievement of which would require an annual growth rate of nearly 4 per cent. In addition, an Industrial Reorganisation Corporation was established, which was 'designed to direct state investment into corporate enterprises, to gain greater governmental control over the private sector, and to change the structure of private industry' (Jones 1996: 78–9). Measures of this kind reflected Labour's determination to ensure that classless meritocrats, rather than aristocratic amateurs, would run industry in the future.

Labour's social policy programme was equally ambitious. They proposed to build 500,000 homes each year, raise pensions and other social security benefits, increase NHS expenditure, abolish prescription charges, raise the school leaving age to 16 and expand higher education. More generally, they sought to reduce inequalities in income and wealth and create a more tolerant society.

Labour's social agenda proved difficult to implement, not least because of the adverse economic conditions that it had to contend with for much of its time in office. The first major difficulty was a serious balance of payments deficit caused by the previous Conservative Chancellor of the Exchequer, Maudling's, pre-election spending boom. Labour's understandable reluctance to counter this problem by means of a devaluation of sterling, given previous negative experiences during Cripps' Chancellorship, proved, with the benefit of hindsight, to be a misjudgement.

Although Labour set a prudent 'fiscally neutral' budget in November 1964, it was 'poorly received by the City and world financial opinion' (Shaw 1996: 70). As a result there was a run on the pound that could only temporarily be stemmed 'by a combination of overseas borrowings from the main central banks, especially the US Federal Reserve, standby credits from the IMF and higher interest rates' (Shaw 1996: 70–71).

By the time Wilson called a general election in 1966, the government had succeeded in gaining a sufficient degree of economic control to achieve re-election, although this had required an array of deflationary measures including a stringent prices and incomes policy, which was only reluctantly accepted by the unions. It was not long, however, before the new administration was facing a damaging seamen's strike and another sterling crisis. Again, the path of devaluation was eschewed. Protecting the value of the pound in order to 'preserve Britain's role as a world banker and to keep sterling as a major reserve currency' (Morgan 1992: 269) was given priority over the maintenance of high employment levels, growth and social expenditure. Accordingly, public expenditure cuts amounting to some £500 million were introduced as well as a wage and price freeze. Although these measures provided some short-term economic respite, the pound came under renewed pressure. Unwilling to contemplate a further range of deflationary measures, the government finally opted for devaluation in November 1967. Even a drastic measure of this kind failed to placate the financial markets. In consequence, further fiscal and monetary restraint was required to shore up the 'devalued' pound. It took a further two years of tough government actions before the new Chancellor, Roy Jenkins, could justifiably claim to have restored the fortunes of the economy, at least in terms of currency stability and the balance of payments.

Labour found it difficult to meet some of its welfare objectives because of these economic difficulties. For example, NHS prescription charges, which had been abolished in 1964 in fulfilment of a manifesto commitment, were restored in 1968 as part of a round of expenditure cuts. The decision to delay the raising of the school-leaving age from 15 to 16 and the failure to publish details of a national superannuation scheme until 1969 can also be linked to the need to constrain public expenditure. In addition, although some 2 million new homes were built under Labour's housing drive (1965–1970), the quality (system built) and design (high rise) of these dwellings were criticised.

Labour also failed to integrate private schools into the state system. The Public Schools Commission, which had been set up in 1965, merely sought to remove the tax advantages of those private boarding schools that refused to offer places to state school pupils and to abolish direct government grants for private grammar schools.

Achievements

Given the economic problems that the Labour government faced during this period we should, Thorpe (2001) contends: 'Be more surprised at what the government was able to do, than condemnatory of what it failed to achieve in social policy' (2001: 154). Certainly, Labour did make progress in a number of areas. Although Labour's commitment to provide pensioners with a non-means-tested income guarantee proved difficult to implement, efforts were made to ensure that the incomes of the elderly poor were improved. Structural reform (the creation of the Supplementary Benefits Commission), more sensitive benefit procedures (a less stigmatised 'rights-based' service) and a more generous and flexible payment system led to real improvements in the living standards of many poorer pensioners. The government also introduced earnings-related unemployment and sickness benefits, increased National Insurance benefit levels and abolished the earnings rule for widows. Other initiatives included the introduction of a means-tested rate and rent rebate system and a redundancy pay scheme.

Progress was also made in the area of state education (see also Chapter 5). Under arguably the most famous and effective advisory circular in the history of social policy (10/65), local authorities were requested to submit plans to the Department of Education for the development of non-selective secondary schooling. As Timmins (2001: 242) notes: 'By 1970 the proportion of pupils in schools that at least in name were comprehensive had risen from 10 to 32 per cent, and by the time Labour left office only eight authorities were actively refusing to submit plans'. Labour also built on previous Conservative attempts to increase the number of places available in higher education. This was achieved by allowing colleges of advanced technology to become universities and by the expansion of separate, although nominally equal, local authority- controlled polytechnics, which would specialise in more vocationally oriented programmes that better met the needs of industry. The needs of non-traditional students such as those who were already in work or who were at home providing care for children were to be met by the introduction of the Open University's distance-learning courses.

Although Labour's record on both public spending and redistribution (of income if not wealth) was creditable during its period of office, it failed to inspire either its own supporters or the general public in the way that the Attlee government had managed. The level of scepticism was such that it even had to counter the claim made by the Child Poverty Action Group in the general election campaign of 1970 that the poor were actually becoming poorer under Labour. As Ellison (2000) sums up, 'the abiding image' of the 1964–1970 Labour government was 'of a party beset by criticism from within and without, in many ways doing its best to maintain the welfare state that it had created but, owing to constant economic difficulties, failing to live up to the egalitarian hopes of its supporters' (Ellison 2000: 435).

1970–1979

Labour's defeat in the 1970 general election led to renewed questioning about the revisionist social democratic approach that the party had been pursuing. Crucially, concerns were raised about the ability of government to exercise economic control in the era of the multinational corporation. It was contended that 'the private sector of the economy was no longer responsive to persuasion and incentives offered by government, and that a major extension of public ownership into the private manufacturing sector was required if a reforming government was to deliver its economic policy objectives' (Tomlinson 2000: 63). The establishment of a National Enterprise Board, which would take a stake in some leading companies in order to promote improved levels of performance, was seen as a key way of overcoming this difficulty. It was also recognised that a new concordat with the trade unions was required. A Social Contract was proposed which would commit the trade unions to wage restraint in exchange for government commitments to pursue full employment policies, high levels of public spending and repeal of Conservative industrial relations legislation.

Although Labour's 1974 manifesto was 'appreciably more left-wing than in 1964' (Timmins 2001: 314) including as it did a promise to 'bring about a fundamental and irreversible shift in the balance of power and wealth in favour of working people and their families' (Labour Party 1974: 15), this did not signify the jettisoning of a broadly social democratic approach. Those hoping for more significant progress in the sphere of public ownership quickly realised that key members of Wilson's new government did not share their enthusiasms. Indeed those ministers, such as Benn (the new Industry Secretary) and his deputy Heffer, who favoured increased nationalisation, were systematically frustrated by their cabinet colleagues.

Like its predecessors, the Labour government of 1974–1979 also encountered severe economic difficulties during its period of office. The expectation that high levels of public expenditure could be met by enhanced growth failed to materialise. This disappointment was compounded by the inability of the trade unions to constrain inflationary wage demands as insisted on under the Social Contract. As a result, by the spring of 1975, the Chancellor, Dennis Healey, sought to gain cabinet approval for public expenditure cuts. Initially this proved difficult, but pressure on sterling in the summer of 1975 enabled Healey to secure agreement. In addition, the trade unions agreed to a proposal to limit all pay awards to a maximum of £6 a week. These measures brought some temporary relief for the government in the shape of output growth and falling inflation. However, by 1976, the government was once more forced on to the defensive as a result of growing international unease, reflected in a continuing fall in the value of sterling despite high interest rate levels, about the underlying state of the British economy. In order to ease this pressure the Callaghan government sought a substantial loan from the International Monetary Fund that necessitated further cuts in public expenditure. These measures proved to be something of a turning point. Growing North Sea oil revenues and an upturn in international trade bolstered the British economy to such an extent that the possibility of winning a further term in office was beginning to take hold by 1978. Such optimism proved short lived as the latest phase of Labour's pay policy unravelled. As Tomlinson (2000: 67) notes, the decision to 'enforce a five per cent pay norm when inflation was several points higher was too much for workers and unions'. Although the impact of the 'winter of discontent' that followed was not as extreme as has often been asserted, it undoubtedly contributed to Labour's electoral defeat in 1979.

Although the economic challenges faced by the 1974–1979 Labour government restricted its room for manoeuvre in the area of social policy, a number of initiatives were pursued. For example, in an attempt to limit public funding of private welfare it was decided to abolish direct grant schools in October 1975 and phase out pay beds in the NHS. The impact of both these measures proved disappointing for many egalitarians as they merely led to an expansion of private provision. The vast majority of direct grant schools opted to rejoin the private sector rather than accept comprehensive status, while the lengthy phasing-out period for pay beds did little damage to the long-term prospects of private medicine. As Timmins (2001) notes: 'Just as abolishing direct grant schools had expanded the private education sector, so phasing out pay beds ... helped the private medical sector to grow. By an awful irony, Barbara Castle had become the patron saint of private medicine' (2001: 338).

Achievements

In the case of social security, the government fulfilled its manifesto commitment by substantially increasing the level of pensions and uprating the value of this and other long-term benefits (except those for the unemployed) according to the annual growth in prices or earnings (whichever was the higher). This latter measure ensured that pensioners would be able to share in any growing prosperity. The government also introduced a state earnings relation pension scheme in 1975, based on an individual's best 20 years of earnings, which was of particular benefit to those whose earnings peaked at the beginning of their career, female carers and those with interrupted work records. A number of other benefits were also introduced including Child Benefit (albeit after protracted debate), mobility allowance, invalid care allowance and a non-contributory invalidity pension.

Although there was less progress in the area of housing, Labour did freeze council rents on its return to office and introduced a Housing (Homeless Persons) Act in 1977 that underlined the importance of improving the housing rights of vulnerable groups such as lone parents and victims of domestic violence.

A renewed challenge to social democracy, 1979–1983

Despite positive measures of this kind, Labour's departure from office in 1979 once again led to a focus on its shortcomings rather than its achievements. Crucially, doubts were increasingly aired about the viability of a social democratic welfare strategy. On the economic front the limitations of Keynesian demand management were readily acknowledged. Indeed from 1975 there was a decided shift towards a more monetarist economic policy. As Timmins (2001) explains: 'The magic prescription of growth, public expenditure and full employment, paid for by higher taxation and perhaps slightly higher inflation, had ceased to work. Labour was discovering ... that you could have the inflation and taxation, but without the growth and full employment' (Timmins 2001: 313–314). Moreover, the downward pressure on welfare spending from 1975 led to increased scepticism about the possibilities of a redistributive welfare strategy. Although Labour did not experience any dramatic loss of support in the 1979 general election (securing as it did 36.9 per cent of the vote compared to 39.2 per cent in October 1974) its defeat heralded intense debate within the party about the way ahead.

At first there was a concerted attempt to take the party in a democratic socialist direction. A range of internal party reforms ensured that the parliamentary party and the leadership were no longer able to thwart the more radical policy agenda emerging from the party conference and from activists. This leftward shift led a number of revisionists such as Jenkins, Owen, Williams and Rodgers to leave Labour's ranks to form the Social Democratic Party in 1981. The ascendancy of the left within the Labour Party was reflected in the 1983 manifesto. Among the party's commitments were large-scale public ownership, protectionism, unilateral nuclear disarmament and withdrawal from the European Community. However, this move to the left proved short lived. Labour's catastrophic performance in the 1983 general election, in which their share of the popular vote fell to just 27.6 per cent led to what Jones (1996) has termed the rebirth of revisionism. Under the leadership of Neil Kinnock (1983–1992) and subsequently John Smith (1992–1994) the party made a concerted attempt to change the organisation, image and policies of the party in order to improve its electoral prospects. Although these changes led to a steady improvement in Labour's electoral performance (30.8 per cent in 1987 and 34.4 per cent in 1992), the extent of Labour support proved insufficient to challenge Conservative dominance. It was only with the emergence of New Labour that an electoral breakthrough was finally achieved.

New Labour and the Third Way

While it is difficult to pinpoint the precise moment when New Labour 'emerged', the election of Tony Blair as Labour leader in 1994, following the sudden death of John Smith, was certainly a pivotal moment. Blair was keen to make a decisive break with the past. The concept of the Third Way, which had been developed by the sociologist Anthony Giddens (1998), was subsequently adopted to describe this new approach.

Given that the term Third Way had previously been used in the context of both Italian fascism and Swedish social democracy, the need for definitional precision was paramount (see Blair 1998; Giddens 1998, 2000, 2002). According to Giddens, the Third Way represents an attempt 'to transcend both old-style social democracy and neoliberalism' (1998: 26). Crucially, however, both Blair and Giddens have been keen to stress that the Third Way should be regarded as a modern variant of social democracy. As Giddens explains:

> The new social democracy seeks to preserve the basic values of the left – a belief in a solidary and inclusive society, a commitment to combating inequality and protecting the vulnerable. It asserts that active government, coupled with strong public institutions and a developed welfare state, has an indispensable role to play in furthering these objectives. But it holds that many traditional leftist perspectives or policies either no longer do so, or have become directly counterproductive.
>
> Giddens (2002: 15)

Not surprisingly, perhaps, others have come to different conclusions concerning New Labour's Third Way. Some have detected much greater continuity with the Old Labour tradition; some contend that the Third Way has much in common with neo-liberalism; some have considered it to be a variant of Christian Democracy. Others highlight the ways in which US and Australian policy initiatives have informed Third Way thinking (for example, Deacon 2002; King and Wickham-Jones 1999).

In terms of the current discussion the key issue is whether New Labour's Third Way can be said to represent a continuation of social democracy or whether it signals a decisive break with the past. In order to explore this issue it is useful to examine the key elements of New Labour's approach to both economic and social policy.

New Labour and economic policy

In its approach to the economy, New Labour has sought to distance itself firmly from both democratic socialist and 'traditional' social democratic ideas. At the outset New Labour moved swiftly to disassociate itself from what it regarded as outdated 'fundamentalist' policies such as public ownership, economic planning and the redistribution of income and wealth. The decision to replace Clause 4 of the Party's constitution in 1995 (which had formally committed the party to common ownership of the means of production) (Briefing 13.1) with a broader statement of aims including support for the market and the rigour of competition, signalled New Labour's determination to adopt the more 'flexible, innovative and forward-looking policies' which Blair (1998: 1) and others regarded as vital for electoral success.

Briefing 13.1   Clause 4 of the Labour Party constitution

Up to 1995 Clause 4 of the Party's constitution was:
To secure for the workers by hand or by brain the full fruits of their industry and the most equitable distribution thereof that might be possible on the basis of the common ownership of the means of production, distribution and exchange, and the best obtainable system of popular administration and control of each industry or service.

Following the 1995 revision it reads:
The Labour Party is a democratic socialist party.
We believe that by the strength of our common endeavour we achieve more than we achieve alone, so as to create for each of us the means to realize our true potential and for all of us a community in which power, wealth and opportunity are in the hands of the many, not the few.

Importantly, New Labour also wanted to distance itself from the revisionist economic agenda associated with Crosland (1956). For Blair a 'statist social democratic' model of this kind might have been appropriate in an era when there was a significant level of job security, low unemployment and relatively closed national economies. However, Blair argued that changes in the global economic environment, the deregulation of financial markets and the shift from manufacturing to service sector employment, necessitated the development of a more modern approach to economic policy. Demands to promote full employment by means of deficit financing were rejected and calls for a return to corporatist policy agreements were brushed aside. For New Labour there was a clear need to respond positively to current economic developments rather than attempt to reshape the world to fit into the more comfortable frameworks of the past.

To demonstrate this shift in emphasis New Labour has become avowedly pro-market rather than merely market tolerant. As New Labour's Chancellor Gordon Brown (2003) contended:

> Instead of being suspicious of enterprise and entrepreneurs, we should celebrate an entrepreneurial climate – encouraging, incentivising and rewarding the dynamic and enthusing more people from all backgrounds and all areas to start up businesses – enabling markets to work better and strengthening the private economy.

New Labour's enthusiasm for the market is such that it has no objection to greater private involvement in 'areas where previously the public interest was seen to be equated with public ownership' (Brown 2003).

Source: www.CartoonStock.com

Embracing the market has led New Labour to acknowledge 'that substantial personal incentives and rewards are necessary in order to encourage risk-taking and entrepreneurialism' (Mandelson and Liddle 1996: 22). Indeed, one of the defining characteristics of New Labour has been its desire to legitimise rather than penalise economic success. For example, in an interview with Jeremy Paxman on BBC's *Newsnight* programme shortly before the 2001 general election, Tony Blair was adamant that he had no desire to increase the personal taxes paid by leading sports stars in order to narrow the gap between rich and poor. Moreover, New Labour is reluctant to intervene in cases where the distribution of market rewards is '*not* a true reflection of personal responsibility and effort' (Vandenbroucke 2001: 170), provided that there is fair and open competition for such rewards. As Adonis (1997: 23) concludes: 'While New Labour wants to help the poor as a matter of principle, it refuses to hit the rich as a matter of principle. It is this which separates Old Left from New Left'.

New Labour has taken a number of practical steps in order to demonstrate its pro-market credentials and its commitment to fiscal and monetary stability. Shortly after coming to power in 1997, the Bank of England was given autonomy in the setting of interest rates, the stringent spending plans of the previous government were adhered to, the standard or higher rates of income tax were not to be increased and Corporation Tax was lowered.

New Labour has, however, been keen to refute the idea that they have embraced a neo-liberal economic agenda, citing in their defence the introduction of the National Minimum Wage and enhanced trade union rights. The limitations of the market are clearly recognised. As Giddens (2000: 36) makes clear: 'Excessive dependence on market mechanisms has to be avoided for clear reasons. Markets respond to the desires of consumers, but as they do so can compromise other wants or needs. Markets can breed a commercialism that threatens other life values'. For New Labour 'there is a sphere of relationships – which encompasses family, faith and civic society' (Brown 2003), in which commercialism has no place. Market involvement in areas such as health is seen as requiring a tight regulatory structure in order to promote both efficiency and equity.

New Labour and social policy

New Labour is firmly committed to welfare reform. While it is accepted that post-1945 welfare initiatives played a key role in combating the giant evils identified by Beveridge (want, squalor, idleness, ignorance and disease), New Labour believes that more innovative welfare arrangements are now required to meet the challenges of labour market change, diverse family formations and increased consumerism. Reform is also deemed necessary to rectify some of the original design flaws of the classic welfare state. According to Giddens (2000: 33): 'Even in its most developed forms, the welfare state was never an unalloyed good. All welfare states create problems of dependency, moral hazard, bureaucracy, interest-group formation and fraud'. In addition, it is readily accepted that Crosland's optimistic assumptions about the egalitarian potential of state welfare have failed to materialise.

Policy eye 13.1   Five key features of New Labour's approach to welfare

1   An emphasis on an active, rather than passive welfare state. As the Commission on Social Justice famously remarked, 'the welfare state must offer a hand-up rather than a handout' (1994: 223–4). In practice, this means that those benefit recipients who are capable of undertaking paid work should be encouraged to return to the labour market as quickly as possible in order to avoid the debilitating effects of long-term dependency. New Labour has introduced a wide range of measures to encourage labour market participation including various New Deal schemes to aid employability and financial support in the shape of the minimum wage and tax credits in order to ensure that there is a financial incentive to return to work.

2   A conviction that clearer distinction should be drawn between public services and the public interest and that the latter is not always best served by the former. For example, Giddens (2002) contends that the public interest may be advanced by the increased involvement of 'mutuals, social enterprises, not-for-profit trusts and public benefit corporations' (2000: 65) in service delivery. Similarly, Brown (2003) has also defended increased private sector involvement in both the financing and delivery of public services on public interest grounds. In the case of the Private Finance Initiative he has argued that there should be no principled objection against PFI expanding into new areas in which the public sector is able to procure a defined product adequately and at no risk to its integrity and where the private sector has a core skill that the public sector can benefit and learn from.

3   A belief that a modern welfare state should better reflect the consumerist ethos of the age. Services should be centred on the needs of users rather than providers. According to Blair (2003), the public 'want education and health free at the point of use – but they don't want services uniform and undifferentiated at the point of use, unable to respond to their individual needs and aspirations'. In an effort to extend choice within the public sector New Labour has encouraged secondary schools to apply for 'specialist' status by virtue of expertise, including in science, languages and sport. In addition encouragement has been given to new independent providers to assume responsibility for the delivery of publicly funded education in a number of inner city areas under the city academy scheme.

4   A contention that a modernised welfare strategy must be based on a redefinition of the relationship between individuals, the community

Policy eye 13.1 continued

and the state. While the state is still seen as having an important role in the funding and, in many cases, the provision of services, individuals are now expected to take on more responsibility for their own welfare and for the well-being of their neighbourhood. To this end, citizens are being encouraged to adopt a more reciprocal mindset in which state support is seen less as an unconditional right but rather as a tied 'gift' which should be repaid by a willingness to undertake education, training and job seeking. In addition, individuals are to be encouraged to take a more active role in their local communities on the grounds that they are not only better equipped to identify problems but also to devise solutions that will work and provide sustainable benefits.

5   A belief that those delivering local services should be 'freed from red tape and empowered to innovate to meet local demands' (Blair 2002: 23). While it is acknowledged that localism of this kind might prove difficult to reconcile with New Labour's desire to establish 'a national framework of standards and accountability with floor targets beneath which no public service should fall' (Blair 2002: 21), no fundamental incompatibility is perceived, not least because increased autonomy will only be granted to those deemed to be performing effectively.

In devising its welfare strategy (Policy eye 13.1) New Labour has attempted to reflect rather than lead 'public' opinion. Given the public's apparently limited appetite for 'altruistic' forms of redistribution, New Labour has attempted to devise more overtly self-interested measures. This has led to efforts to improve the range and quality of those services that are most highly valued by the middle classes such as education and health. It is envisaged that improvements in these areas will prevent 'better off patients and parents' (Blair 2003) from opting out of the public sphere.

The continued willingness of the middle classes to fund services that are used predominantly by poorer groups is also deemed to necessitate the introduction of proactive welfare policies, such as the New Deal, which encourage early reconnection with the labour market.

Equality and opportunity

New Labour's desire to maximise its electoral support among aspirational citizens who live in areas that are 'neither privileged nor deprived' (Gould 1998: 46) has also necessitated a revised approach towards the notion of equality. While it is still strongly committed to equality of respect and equality of opportunity, the pursuit of equality of outcome has now been abandoned. Equality of respect or worth has been identified as a central New Labour value. According to Blair (1998: 3) all individuals are entitled to equality of respect 'whatever their background, capability, creed or race'. The government is seen as having a vital role to play in responding to the needs of those who lack basic rights, not least by tackling all forms of 'discrimination and prejudice'.

New Labour also remains committed to the principle of equality of opportunity:

> The government believes that everyone should have the opportunity to achieve their potential. But too many people are denied that opportunity. It is wrong and economically inefficient to waste the talents of even one single person.
>
> Department of Social Security (1999: 1)

Purposeful government action is seen as essential in order to ensure that no child is prevented from fulfilling its potential by virtue of poverty (which Labour has pledged to eradicate within a generation), substandard education or training or some other form of social exclusion. Many of Labour's initiatives, such as SureStart, under which additional support is provided for families with young children living in deprived neighbourhoods, are designed to equalise opportunities. It is envisaged that measures such as these will enable children to acquire the necessary education, skills and training to compete in a changing and uncertain labour market.

In contrast, the pursuit of equality of outcome is rejected. As Brown (1999) explains:

> We reject equality of outcome not because it is too radical, but because it is neither desirable or feasible ... predetermined results imposed, as they would have to be, by a central authority and decided irrespective of work, effort or contribution to the community, is not a socialist dream but other people's nightmare of socialism.
>
> It denies humanity rather than liberates it. It is to make people something they are not, rather than helping them to make the most of what they can be. What people resent about Britain today is not that some people who have worked hard have done well. What angers people is that millions are denied the opportunity to realise their potential and are powerless to do so. It is this inequality that must be addressed.
>
> Brown (1999: 42)

A social democratic Third Way?

New Labour's revised approach to equality coupled with its desire to reform the welfare state has led some commentators to question whether this signals a departure not only from the tenets of democratic socialism but also from social democracy. As Gamble and Wright (1999: 4) point out: 'Some of the strongest criticism has come from self-professed guardians of the social democratic tradition, who believe that certain core ideas such as redistribution, universalist welfare and economic regulation, as well as the link between

Labour and the trade unions, cannot be abandoned without abandoning social democracy itself'. However, given that social democracy 'is not a particular historical programme or regime or political party or interest group, or even an unchanging set of values' (1994: 2), it is possible to argue that the Third Way does represent 'social democracy renewed' (Blair 2001: 10).

It could equally well be argued, however, that New Labour's attempt to create a tolerant, inclusive entrepreneurial society that offers opportunities for all, as opposed to the more overtly egalitarian vision associated with Crosland, lies outside the boundaries of social democracy. It might be more appropriate to describe New Labour's approach as mildly progressive rather than social democratic. Certainly, the term 'progressive' might be a better descriptor of New Labour's desire to 'combine values traditionally associated with Europe – fairness, solidarity – with the economic dynamism traditionally associated with the US' (Blair 2001: 11). Of course, it remains to be seen whether a broad term of this kind will prove sufficient to enable New Labour to distinguish itself from both democratic socialism and contemporary conservatism.

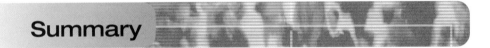

Summary

This chapter has explored the shift from Old Labour to New Labour since 1945. The shift from the democratic socialist approach of the Attlee government (1945–1951) to the more overtly social democratic strategy of the Wilson and Callaghan administrations in the 1960s and 1970s has been charted. From this we can suggest that:

- Social policy needs to be examined in the context of the wider economic situation and that the social policies of Labour governments have frequently been affected by the perceived needs of the economy.

- It can be argued that the post-war period has seen a series of shifts in Labour's approach to both economic and social policy, with democratic socialist and social democratic influences resulting in different policy approaches.

- While it may be possible to argue that 'equality' has been a consistent part of the aims of Labour governments, the meaning of this and the methods used in attempts to achieve it have varied significantly.

- It remains a matter of lively debate as to whether New Labour's Third Way should be regarded as a decisive break with traditional Labour values and practices or whether it will come to be regarded as the latest stage in the history of social democracy.

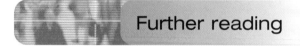

Discussion and review topics

1 How true is it that the Labour government of 1945–1950 sought to use economic and social policy to achieve equality?

2 Why did Labour's 'revisionists' argue in the 1950s and 1960s for a shift towards social democratic policies?

3 How successful have post-war Labour governments been in achieving their social policy goals?

4 Is Blair's Third Way simply a reworking of traditional social democracy?

Further reading

Crosland, C. A. R. (1956) *The Future of Socialism*, Jonathan Cape, London – one of the classic works arguing for revisionist social democracy

Fielding, S. (2002) *The Labour Party: Continuity and Change in the Making of New Labour*, Palgrave Macmillan, Basingstoke – this book examines the emergence of New Labour and argues that there is substantial continuity between 'old' and 'new' Labour

Giddens, A. (2000) *The Third Way and its Critics*, Polity, Cambridge – in this book Giddens seeks to respond to some of the criticisms of his earlier book *The Third Way*

Powell, M. (ed.) (2002) *Evaluating New Labour's Welfare Reforms*, Policy Press, Bristol – provides an assessment of the achievements of New Labour's initial welfare reforms

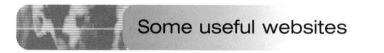

Some useful websites

www.fabian-society.org.uk – the website of the Fabian Society, a think tank that was involved with the creation of the Labour Party and which has maintained those ties

www.ippr.org.uk – the Institute for Public Policy Research, a left-leaning think tank that has been influential during the New Labour years

www.labour.org.uk – the Labour Party's own website provides a variety of information about the Party, its policies and activities

References

Adonis, A. (1997) 'New Labour, new plutocracy, old poor', *The Observer*, 7 August

Bevan, A. (1952) *In Place of Fear*, Heinemann, London

Beveridge, W. (1942) *Report on Social Insurance and Allied Services*, HMSO, London

Black, L. (2003) *The Political Culture of the Left in Affluent Britain, 1951–64*, Palgrave Macmillan, Basingstoke

Blair, T. (1998) *The Third Way: New Politics for the New Century*, Fabian Pamphlet No. 588, Fabian Society, London

Blair, T. (2001) 'Third way, phase two', *Prospect*, March, 10–13

Blair, T. (2002) *The Courage of Our Convictions*, Fabian Ideas No. 603, Fabian Society, London

Blair, T. (2003) 'Progress and justice in the 21st century', Inaugural Fabian Society Annual Lecture, London, 17 June

Brooke, S. (1995) *Reform and Reconstruction*, Manchester University Press, Manchester

Brown, G. (1999) 'Equality – then and now' in Leonard, D. (ed.) *Crosland and New Labour*, Macmillan, Basingstoke

Brown. G. (2003) 'A modern agenda for prosperity and social reform', speech given to the Social Market Foundation, Cass Business School, London, 3 February

Cole, G. D. H. (1950) *Socialist Economics*, Gollancz, London

Commission on Social Justice (1994) *Social Justice*, Vintage, London

Crosland, C. A. R. (1956) *The Future of Socialism*, Jonathan Cape, London

Crossman, R., Foot, M. and Mikardo, I. (eds) (1947) *Keep Left*, New Statesman, London

Deacon, A. (2002) *Perspectives on Welfare*, Open University Press, Buckingham

Department of Social Security (1999) *Opportunity For All: Tackling Poverty and Social Exclusion*, The Stationery Office, London

Ellison, N. (2000) 'Labour and welfare politics', in Brivati, B. and Heffernan, R. (eds) *The Labour Party: A Centenary History*, Macmillan, Basingstoke

Fielding, S. (1997) *The Labour Party: 'Socialism' and Society Since 1951*, Manchester University Press, Manchester

Francis, M. (1996) 'Not reformed capitalism, but . . . democratic socialism: the ideology of the Labour leadership, 1945–1951', in Jones, H. and Kandiah, M. (eds) *The Myth of Consensus*, Macmillan, Basingstoke

Francis, M. (1997) *Ideas and Policies Under Labour 1945–1951*, Manchester University Press, Manchester

Gamble, A. and Wright, T. (1999) 'Introduction: the new social democracy', in Gamble, A. and Wright, T. (eds) *The New Social Democracy*, Blackwell, Oxford

Giddens, A. (1998) *The Third Way*, Polity, Cambridge

Giddens, A (2000) *The Third Way and its Critics*, Polity, Cambridge

Giddens, A. (2002) *Where Now for New Labour?*, Polity, Cambridge

Gould, P. (1998) 'A roar from the suburbs', *Prospect*, December, 46–9

Jay, D. (1937) *The Socialist Case*, Faber, London

Jones, M. and Lowe, R. (eds) (2002) *From Beveridge to Blair*, Manchester University Press, Manchester

Jones, T. (1996) *Remaking the Labour Party: From Gaitskell to Blair*, Routledge, London

King, A. D. and Wickham-Jones, M. (1999) 'Bridging the Atlantic: the democratic (party) origins of welfare to work', in Powell, M. (ed.) *New Labour, New welfare State*, Policy Press, Bristol

Labour Party (1974) *The Labour Party Manifesto: Let Us Work Together – Labour's Way Out of the Crisis*, Labour Party, London

Mandelson, P. and Liddle, R. (1996) *The Blair Revolution*, Faber, London

Morgan, K. O. (1992) *The People's Peace: British History 1945–1990*, Oxford University Press, Oxford

Morgan, K. O. (2002) 'Aneurin Bevan', in Jefferys, K. (ed.) *Labour Forces: From Ernest Bevin to Gordon Brown*, I. B. Tauris, London

Shaw, E. (1996) *The Labour Party Since 1945*, Blackwell, Oxford

Smith, H. L. (1996) *Britain in the Second World War*, Manchester University Press, Manchester

Thompson, N. (1996) *Political Economy and the Labour Party*, UCL Press, London

Thorpe, A. (2001) *A History of the British Labour Party*, Palgrave, Basingstoke

Timmins, N. (2001) *The Five Giants*, HarperCollins, London

Tomlinson, J. (2000) 'Labour and the economy', in Tanner, D., Thane, P. and Tiratsoo, N. (eds) *Labour's First Century*, Cambridge University Press, Cambridge

Vandenbroucke, F. (2001) 'European social democracy and the third way: convergence, divisions, and shared questions', in White, S. (ed.) *New Labour: The Progressive Future?*, Palgrave Macmillan, Basingstoke

Alternative approaches to social policy

14   Tony Fitzpatrick

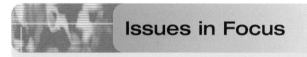

Issues in Focus

Since the 1970s state welfare has been subject to repeated critique and, indeed, sometimes attack by a series of thinkers, social movements and political parties. Views about the nature of social policy have evolved as a consequence. In the academy there are many who have sought to defend the basic principles of state welfare while attempting to broaden the application and understanding of those principles. In this chapter we review some of the key ideas that have been influential in this respect:

● feminism

● ethnicity and anti-racism

● disability

● theoretical implications that arise from a consideration of these.

The welfare state's record with respect to certain social groups has been one of ambivalence. These groups are characterised by 'social divisions' such as gender, ethnicity, age, dis/ability and sexuality. In this chapter we focus, for reasons of space, on women, ethnic minorities and disabled people. In many respects, the welfare state has benefited these groups immeasurably, providing a degree of opportunity, aid and support that would otherwise be lacking. Yet, in other respects, the welfare state has let these groups down by either not addressing important sources of disadvantage and discrimination, by addressing them inadequately and half-heartedly or even by compounding the injustices that many women, ethnic minorities and disabled people often experience. The intention of this chapter is to review the dimensions of this ambivalence. In the next three sections we examine each group in turn before bringing the various threads together in order to reflect on some contemporary theoretical debates regarding social policy.

Feminism

For women the ambivalence noted earlier seems to derive from prevailing conceptions of work and citizenship (see, for example, Lister 2003; Pascall 1997). It could be argued that the post-Second World War welfare state was based on the satisfaction of two conditions: first, high levels of employment and wages so that there would be lots of earners paying tax and fewer people claiming benefits; and, second, lots of unpaid work being performed in the home, including many services that might otherwise have to be financed by the public sector or charged for in the market. These conditions were treated as ideal since, once they are in place, the government will receive a healthy amount of tax while having fewer demands to meet through social expenditure. Unfortunately, what this 'breadwinner' model appears to generate is a certain bias against forms of activity that do not fit the ideal. It means that wage earning is valued above care giving since, to orthodox notions of economic productivity, the former is a much more visible (and measurable) source of social contribution than the latter. And it therefore follows that independence within the labour market is valued above domestic labour as a superior form of citizenship. While the two conditions just specified are rarely present in anything like an ideal form, nevertheless, the bias in favour of 'wage-earning citizenship' is evident in all welfare states (see Briefing 14.1).

There is nothing in the principle of state welfare that says that breadwinners have to be men and caregivers have to be women. Close your eyes and it is (just) possible to imagine a society in which most women go out to work and most men stay at home to nurse the baby, make the beds and so on. Gender inequalities were not born with the creation of state welfare. However, given that gender inequalities have prevailed within societies across recorded history it would have been miraculous had the assumptions underpinning them not found their way into the institutions and services of the welfare state. In other words, the bias in favour of wage-earning citizenship manifests itself as a bias against the work (of care and domestic maintenance) that is still largely performed by women.

One common example used to illustrate this point is that of the Beveridge Report. Buried in the dry prose of *Social Insurance and Allied Services* is the claim that women have 'other duties' (Beveridge 1942: 53) than those associated with earning, that is, being a wife and mother. Beveridge, therefore, inspired the

Briefing 14.1   Feminism

While having its roots in the 18th and 19th centuries, feminism became an important political, economic and social movement in the 20th century. After the Second World War the so-called 'second wave' feminism emerged and challenged the fundamentals of what it saw as a patriarchal society in which women are oppressed and effectively silenced. In one respect this has involved criticising social institutions, relations and practices as inherently masculinist, that is, as embodying male-centred ways of thinking and acting. More radical versions of feminism have therefore developed socio-cultural critiques that aim to encourage alternative ways of thinking and interacting. At the turn of the 21st century some regard feminism as old fashioned, given the advances made by many women in recent decades; others, however, argue that the feminist revolution had still only barely begun.

creation of a benefits system where women earned their entitlements through the insurance contributions of their husbands or were even encouraged to opt out of paying contributions altogether – a provision that was ended in the late 1970s but that continues to inflict hardship on many thousands of elderly women today. Another example is that of Eleanor Rathbone who was campaigning as early as the 1920s for a family allowance to be paid directly to the mother. This was resisted for many years by, among others, trade unions, which feared that it would undermine their campaigns for a decent, 'family wage' and as a result something similar to Rathbone's proposal (Child Benefit) was not introduced for another 50 years.

The welfare state therefore attracts the kind of critiques that feminists and women's groups have long directed towards the broader patriarchies of modern society. There are two key aspects to patriarchy. The first and most obvious dimension is the economic. Income and wealth continue to be concentrated on the wallet rather than the purse, in the form of wages for instance. In the UK women's average hourly earnings are about 80 per cent that of men's, although this does compare favourably to 64 per cent in 1970 (Curtis 2002). Women are more likely than men to be in part-time rather than full-time employment, in low-paid service occupations, at the bottom rung of the promotional ladder and in jobs that are still identified as 'women's work' (clerical and secretarial, for instance). These economic inequalities both feed into and out of the welfare state. On the one hand, they leave women more vulnerable to poverty and so more dependent either on benefits (usually means tested) or on a male breadwinner; on the other, affordable childcare facilities are often scarce and so do not allow many women to escape from the least attractive parts of the labour market. Some groups are particularly vulnerable to this vicious circle: 61 per cent of lone mothers are in poverty, for example (Howard et al. 2001).

The second aspect of patriarchy is more cultural and symbolic and concerns the way in which women are often identified with their 'nature', the capacity to bear children, and so are easily regarded as the natural caregivers, whereas men are represented as being able to rise above nature as the primary architects of culture and civilisation. In short, patriarchy is also a form of mis-recognition in which women are reduced to their supposed biological destinies of marriage, pregnancy and child rearing. The feminine is therefore constructed in such a way that it occupies a subordinate position to the masculine: female identity is the 'otherness' of masculinity, that which men are not. The welfare state fails to challenge this kind of symbolic injustice to any great extent. The 'male breadwinner' model continues to be the norm. Where gender equality is promoted this model assumes that women must do what men do, compete for advantage within the labour market; where it is not promoted then a women's place is still assumed to be in the home. Quite often, however, social policies embody both of these aspirations with many women now experiencing a double burden of breadwinning *and* care giving.

The feminist critique of social policy is, then, ultimately a critique of the 'sexual division of labour', the division which prods men out into the public spheres of wage-earning citizenship and which tethers many women to the private sphere of the home, even though as many women as men now earn some kind of wage. None of which is to pretend that the picture is all negative for state welfare. There are few women and even fewer feminists who have, over the years, added their voices to those calling for the welfare state's abolition or retrenchment. On the contrary, their preference has usually been for more and better welfare rather than less. For all of its faults, then, state welfare is widely regarded as an enabling institution whose loss would be incalculable, even if its potential for gender equality still remains underdeveloped. So, far from demonstrating hostility to the principles of welfare, women have been

"That's a very good suggestion,
Miss Wilson - perhaps one of the
men would like to make it?"

Source: www.CartoonStock.com

influencing policy making and welfare reform for many years across a variety of political parties, organisations and campaigns. We might say that women exist both within the political mainstream and outside it: working for practical change but without relinquishing the demand for more radical reforms.

We might follow Fraser (1997) in identifying three models of welfare reform to which feminists aspire (Briefing 14.2). The first model is that of the 'universal breadwinner' where equality with men is held to require an equality of wages and opportunities within the job market. In many respects, this is the model that has been most readily accepted by politicians and policymakers since it corresponds most closely with the breadwinner ideal sketched earlier and yet appeals to widely held intuitions about the unfairness of any gender bias within employment. This is not to claim that the rise in female employment over recent decades was motivated by a pursuit of this model, but the model does seem to describe an attractive version of equality. The problem with it is that it easily leaves the sexual division of labour intact; it places all of the emphasis on women's rights to enter the labour market but none on the obligations that male partners have to perform carework in the home.

The second model outlined by Fraser is one she terms 'caregiver parity'. This is where women continue to identify with the sphere of domestic labour but far greater recognition to it is accorded by social policies. This might involve a system of 'wages for housework', an idea that was popularised by many women's groups in the 1970s. The problem with this approach is that it does not correspond with the wishes of many (although not all) women to participate in employment and it risks essentialising female identity along the lines suggested earlier, by characterising women in terms of their biologies. In addition, although governments often pay lip service to the value of the work performed in the home this rarely translates into comprehensive systems of support.

The third model – one that Fraser herself advocates – is that of the 'universal caregiver'. There is a sense in which this synthesises the previous models. On the one hand, it celebrates the greater participation of women in employment but, on the other, it treats wage earning as one of a number of important sources of social value. Indeed, it shifts the focus towards care as an activity on which so much else – including a healthy labour market – depends and suggests that men have as many care-giving responsibilities as women. The

Briefing 14.2   Fraser's three models of feminist welfare

- **Universal breadwinner** – women are emancipated by earning and owning as much as men.
- **Caregiver parity** – women should do most of the caregiving but this should be valued as highly as wage earning.
- **Universal caregiving** – caregiving should be valued as highly as wage earning; men and women should share both activities equally.

universal caregiver model therefore demands that men and women can exit and enter the workplace and the home freely and on equal terms; it would demand not only considerable institutional reform, but also a 'culture shift' whereby more men than at present recognise the value of caring as well as earning.

As already indicated, welfare states have looked most favourably on the universal breadwinner model but success has been modest even here. Feminist researchers have long maintained that it is the male breadwinner model that prevails (Lewis 1992), although subtle and important differences between countries are discernible (Daly 1999; Lewis 2001; Sainsbury 1999). By and large it is countries where **social democracy** has wielded a large amount of influence that attract the most praise, since social democrats tend to be more egalitarian than those of other political persuasions and this commitment obviously implies support for equality between men and women. So the Scandinavian nations are singled out as examples for others to follow, since it is here that female participation in employment is highest, where women's wages are more comparable to men's and where goods such as childcare and parental leave are most heavily supported or provided by the state.

However, even in the social democracies the emphasis has been placed more on the job market than on the domestic sphere. Men have made room for women in the former but have been generally reluctant to spend more time in the latter. What this has created, then, is a 'dual breadwinner' model of one-and-a-half-earner households: the primary earner is still usually the male partner with the women still expected to perform the carework and the work of sustaining the home. So, one of the next big tasks for social democrats concerns the need to consolidate the gains made by women by reorganising patterns of working time and emphasising the importance of unwaged work.

The attraction of Fraser's universal caregiver model is therefore apparent. Gender equality demands an equality between the public and private and the genuine freedom of movement of men and women between them without the cultural and structural barriers that currently prevail. So the challenge is not only for social democrats but for all those who are determined to resolve the ambivalence we discussed earlier and ensure that the women-friendly features of state welfare are brought much more to the foreground.

Ethnicity and anti-racism

Similar kinds of ambivalence affect ethnic minorities, only here we have a radically different set of background assumptions to understand.

National identity would seem to depend on forms of exclusion as well as inclusion: who is outside the national walls can be as important as who is inside. And with nation states having dominated the world stage for the last two centuries the assumption that 'nation' should correspond with that of

Briefing 14.3   Ethnicity

The term 'race' has become a discredited one within the humanities and social sciences since it refers to biological and genetic essences that most academics now deny exist. The preferred alternative is that of 'ethnicity', since this allows differences to be acknowledged while locating the source of those differences in cultural and historical contexts rather than according to physical categories, such as skin colour. The concept, therefore, has a much wider application than that of race, one that permits analysis of oppressive and exploitative social structures.

'race' has been widely held – even if the reality has been somewhat more complex (Gilroy 1987). Indeed, 'race' is itself a socially constructed (and loaded) term without much biological or genetic credibility (see Briefing 14.3). Nevertheless, the cultural overlap of nation with race has been very strong and so national identity has often been held to depend on the exclusion of 'other races'.

In the UK the association has always been particularly sharp due to the country's imperial past where its status as the world's greatest power in the 19th century owed much to its cultural domination, its military reach and its access to overseas markets and resources. Commentators from Rudyard Kipling to George Orwell, both of whom had experience of 'the colonies', fell into the easy assumption of British (and usually English) superiority where national strength depended on keeping the 'lesser breeds' under control. Even in his influential report, the 'other duties' to women by Beveridge, involved not simply childbirth, but also rearing the next generation of Empire makers in a post-war world that he must have imagined would largely resemble the pre-war one:

> In the next thirty years housewives as mothers have vital work to do in ensuring the adequate continuance of the British race and of British ideals in the world.
>
> Beveridge (1942: 53)

With the termination of the Empire, Britain's relations with its former colonies underwent a swift and traumatic change, the effects of which are still being felt. Post-war immigration became a source of moral panic, although usually, of course, when the immigrants were black. Consequently, the politics of the last half-century has often been a debate, even when it did not appear as such, about Britishness and ethnic identity (Parekh 2001). 'We used to be over there', many people must have thought to themselves, 'and now *they* are coming over *here*'. In other words, although racism has a diversity of social and psychological origins, in the UK it has often been articulated as a proxy for regret about the country's apparent decline as a world power, what might be called the 'Alf Garnett syndrome'. The effects of this have been varied. Immigration policies became more and more restrictive from very early on, 'race relations' became part of the political vocabulary, many urban local authorities became the champions of equal opportunities and, more recently, we have witnessed a series of panics about asylum seekers.

Despite the innovative work on combating racism and discrimination that has emerged wherever black communities and local government were most willing to talk to one another, policy making and, it has to be said, policy research were slow to recognise the significance of ethnic diversity (Lewis 1998; 2000). Racial issues have therefore occupied the blind spot of British social policy and it is rare to find any significant reference to it in social policy books or government documents prior to the 1980s. 'Race relations' was certainly an important topic, but one that was for a long time thought to be somehow separate from issues surrounding the welfare state. Britain's colonial past may have bred the assumption that no great evolution in the nation's culture and institutions was necessary: 'If they do have to migrate here then the least they can do is to become like us.' In other words, the welfare state was assumed to be colour blind and so already an engine of racial equality. These tenets have been challenged only gradually. This has involved not simply an exposure of the welfare state's failings but also a repudiation of the view that colour blindness is a desirable ideal after all (as if the history of discrimination and domination can suddenly be wiped away) and so of the idea that equality is separable from an appreciation of ethnic difference and diversity.

Consequently, not only do welfare systems generate many discriminatory and prejudicial effects, whether directly or indirectly, but the subject is still struggling for a full recognition of their nature and implications (Modood et al. 1997). In recent years – especially following the Macpherson Report into the murder of Stephen Lawrence – this confusion has revolved around the notion of 'institutional racism'. The term refers to racism which is less the property of individuals, and so manifest in particular actions, and more a general characteristic of systems, collective practices and relations that have not yet become sensitised to ethnic pluralism. It is the claim that institutional racism cannot simply be reduced to *this* action or *that* belief that makes it so controversial since the implications are considerable. First, it discards the crude individualism that has underpinned British political debate for many years now. Second, it suggests that even those who genuinely reject racism may transmit it in some form or another, depending on the institutional context. Finally, it implies that because racism is inscribed within institutions then more radical actions than most people seem willing to contemplate are required to address it. For social policy, the controversy involves asking not only whether organisations such as schools and hospitals carry the traces of institutional racism, but also whether the discipline itself is implicated. Does institutional racism lie not only in *what* we see but in the *ways* in which we see? It is issues such as these with which the subject is only slowly coming to grips.

Researchers have therefore been far more adept at identifying racial inequalities than they have been at asking some of the deeper questions. Examination of the labour market constantly throws up examples of such inequalities. For example, the unemployment figures demonstrate that men and women from

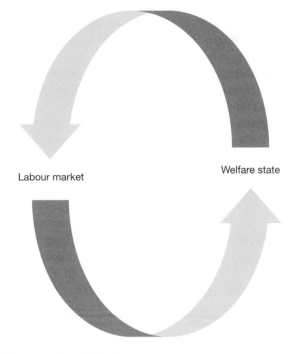

Figure 14.1 Vicious circle of disadvantage

ethnic minorities are twice as likely to be unemployed as their white counterparts, regardless of whether the economy is growing or receding. There are, however, some important variations, with black African, black Caribbean, Pakistani and Bangladeshi groups being particularly disadvantaged, whereas employers seem less likely to discriminate against Asian and Chinese groups. Ethnic migrants tended to have been employed either in the public sector or in the low-waged, low-skilled parts of the private sector and so have suffered disproportionately from the economic restructuring of the last 20 years. Those who find themselves in the 'secondary' labour market are often trapped there over the long term and those who do penetrate the 'core' of well-paid, highly skilled, desirable and secure jobs still tend to occupy the lower rungs of the occupational ladder.

As with many women, disadvantage in the job market propels disadvantage in the welfare state which feeds back into the job market and so on, initiating a vicious circle from which it can be difficult to escape (Figure 14.1). The interaction of employment patterns with the benefits system is important in accounting for the fact that ethnic minority communities are three or four times more likely to be poor than the rest of the population (Craig 1999; Howard et al. 2001). Low-paid work makes people more likely to be shunted towards the least attractive parts of the welfare state. It makes black households more reliant on means-tested benefits and so less able, for instance, to accumulate substantial occupational or private pensions. It leaves black people more likely to be living in local authority housing, and often in the poorest estates, less likely to be owner-occupiers and four or five times more likely to be homeless.

And so it leaves black children more likely to be concentrated on schools in deprived areas that have to cope with all the social problems that deprivation brings.

Consequently, a lower proportion of black children go on to further and higher education.

What does a politics of anti-racism imply for the welfare state? If social policies should aim to fulfil the basic needs of all in order to facilitate social participation then where do race and ethnicity fit into the picture? We could follow the path advocated by Young (1990) when she calls for a system of group representation whereby disadvantaged groups are given a collective voice and the ability to veto anything that they perceive as furthering their disadvantage. The problem with this approach is that it risks fragmenting the social fabric and, in fact, there is evidence to suggest that the welfare state serves ethnic minorities most effectively when its foundations are universalistic (Brown 1999). Perhaps, then, we should stress the commonality of needs along the lines suggested by Doyal and Gough (1991), needs that could be said to conjoin all ethnic groups, while recognising that the measures that satisfy the needs of one group are not necessarily going to satisfy those of another. This is also to follow the approach of Sen (1992) when he argues that although people share the same ends (the desire for well-being, for example) they possess different capabilities and policies have to be shaped so as to reflect these differences.

If this approach – one of being sensitive to differences within a universalistic framework – is convincing then it seems to prescribe social policies which, while aimed at social justice and all this involves (such as reductions in income inequalities), are additionally sensitive to the 'satisfiers' and capabilities that currently characterise ethnic minorities. This could, among other things, mean addressing the forms of discrimination – institutional or otherwise – that continue to infect the labour market more effectively. Indeed it is curious that, in an age that has never stressed the virtues of employment more, this has not occupied the foreground of employment policy. On the contrary, New Labour's lurch towards workfare-style reforms – where benefit claimants are penalised for refusing to work or train – represents an individualised and pathologised set of assumptions that arguably go in the opposite direction. If black men and women are twice as likely to be unemployed at any one time then workfare is a means of entrenching discrimination rather than combating it.

But what are the alternatives? Equal opportunity policies certainly but, today, everyone speaks the language of **equal opportunities** yet few can imagine that this by itself is sufficient. Should we prefer quota systems where firms are required to discriminate positively in favour of ethnic minorities? There are potential drawbacks with this approach, however, in that it risks 'segregating' the abilities of black people (Fitzpatrick 2001). Or is there a happy medium where job creation policies are specifically targeted on ethnic minority communities? Whatever the solution it is clear that, since the health of the welfare state depends considerably on the health of the labour market, higher levels of employment for black men and women are necessary if the vicious circle of discrimination, that the welfare state helps to keep in motion is to be slowed down and eventually stopped.

Disability

The familiar pattern of ambivalence also reappears when we consider the case of disabled people. Here, too, the welfare state's record is mixed at best but we can only understand why when we explore the prevailing background assumptions (see Briefing 14.4).

A disability is easily regarded as a property of the person in question, for what could be clearer than the fact that a man with limited sight or a woman with limited mobility simply are disabled? Society may or may not do enough to help disabled people but it is obvious where the disability lies. Yet this 'common sense' view is precisely what disability advocates have been challenging for the last 20 years or so (Oliver 1989, 1996; Oliver and Barnes 1998), the first step being, as with so many challenges to orthodox viewpoints, to rename and recategorise. The 'common sense' view derives from a 'medical model' where disability is assumed to be a physiological or psychological possession of the individual in question, a condition that can be treated by medical experts of one form or another. The disability is therefore an impairment or handicap that can cause certain social disadvantages that are not experienced by the able-bodied. The medical model is therefore heavily paternalist but arguably patronising also in that it regards disabled people as subjects for treatment rather than as agents in their own right. The background assumption at work is that there is an ideal norm (able-bodiedness) from which disabled people can be said to deviate.

In contrast to this medicalisation of ability most disability advocates have preferred a 'social model' where we recognise handicaps as social constructions and acknowledge disability as a relation, less a property of individuals and more a feature of the social environment. If the environment is unable to accommodate the diversity of abilities that characterise people then a disability derives not from a lack of sight or mobility but from the discriminations and systemic disadvantages that are socially inscribed. 'Disablism' is the name given to these discriminations and disadvantages and, just as institutional racism directs attention towards systems and collective practices, so 'institutional disablism' focuses on structures and processes that cannot simply be explained according to the views and actions of particular individuals.

The social model therefore requires that disablism be challenged in all its forms and along a number of fronts. Of key importance is the recognition that dis-ability is itself a loaded term, implicitly denoting a relation of superiority and inferiority. The alternative is either to construct a new vocabulary, an approach that some see as politically correct, or to reconfigure the vocabulary that we have so that we can appreciate the diversity of abilities that span humanity. If we acknowledge that we are all disabled in one form or another then disability may come to signify 'difference' rather than 'inferiority'.

> ### Briefing 14.4 Disability
>
> Disability is frequently 'medicalised' in that it is identified with a physical handicap that impairs the mobility and social interaction of the person in question. However, disabled people have long campaigned for an alternative understanding in which disability results from the unwillingness of society to accommodate people of differing ability. This 'social model' directs attention away from the view that disabled people are inferior to the so-called 'able-bodied' and allows an analysis of the extent to which disabled people are discriminated against and socially excluded.

This cultural struggle accompanies other challenges where the disability movement has confronted discriminatory institutions and policies. Of central importance here is the welfare state. Whereas state welfare has at least acknowledged the demands made on it by the medical model, because the social model requires a more substantial reorganisation of society welfare reforms have made only modest steps in this direction. Yet even setting these ambitious objectives to one side, social policies do not usually meet the needs of disabled people. Barnes and Baldwin (1999) estimate that 45 per cent of disabled people live in poverty. The unemployment rate for disabled people is two to three times higher than that for the rest of the population. Some of this is no doubt due to direct discrimination on the part of employers, although much of it is also indirect and institutional. If a disabled applicant possesses fewer qualifications and less training than other applicants, due to disadvantages experienced at earlier parts of her life, then the employer is likely to reason that the risk of hiring that applicant is simply too high. And those disabled people who *are* in employment are twice as likely to be in the periphery of the labour market than their non-disabled counterparts, earning about three-quarters of the average weekly wage and half as likely to be found in professional and managerial positions. All in all, about two-thirds of households with a disabled person receive no income from employment and almost one-third of those households are totally dependent on benefits.

As in the previous two sections, then, we once again meet the vicious circle within which the welfare state is embedded: labour market disadvantage both creating and being created by the failures of welfare services.

Before moving on, it is worth pointing out that the social model has not gone unchallenged, especially by those who want to focus on the body and social modes of embodiment (Shakespeare et al. 1997). Western traditions of thought have too often abstracted the self from its corporeality and mortality, preferring to treat the mind (*res cogitans*) as the essential home of human identity. But recently the body has become of more importance to social studies, a site of intersection where the mental, the emotional, the social and the physical can be said to come together (Turner 1996; Twigg 2000). On this reading it is not enough always to invoke social discriminations. True, disablism is institutional but it is also the case that disability does create real changes in ability in ways that the social model risks ignoring. The basic point was made years ago in a short story by H. G. Wells. The traveller in the country of the blind agrees to surrender his sight for the women he loves and because he comes to recognise that his perceptions will gain in other ways, but the loss of sight will still involve some sort of loss and Wells ends the story on a note of irresolvable ambiguity. Perhaps neither the medical nor the social model is entirely adequate, therefore.

Nevertheless, the basic criticism remains: the welfare state has done much but not enough to help disabled people liberate themselves. As before, however, this failure usually leads to demands for more welfare provision rather than less. What, then, does a politics of anti-disablism imply for the welfare state? As with ethnicity we are required to think about whether the needs of disabled people are differential or whether we should continue to speak the language of common human needs while recognising that disabled people possess satisfiers and capabilities specific to themselves. Social policy seems to have been occupied with the second of these approaches if we interpret 'special needs' policies in these terms. This means that, on the one hand, disabled people need what everyone needs, including a decent income, housing, transport and such like, but that they possess additional special needs within this framework. The education system, to take one example, has long been organised to accommodate the special needs of disabled children. The problem is that such policies have often ghettoised disabled people, labelling them as 'special cases' rather than as social actors capable of participating in the policymaking process itself (Beresford 1997). In other words, the stereotype of passive dependency continues to prevail.

Therefore, challenging disablism seems to require more than the kind of labour market focus discussed at the end of the last section – as important as this is. It appears to require an emphasis on the right to agency, to participate in society on terms that are not set by the non-disabled, reflecting, more often than not, a narrow series of assumptions about what disabled people are and are not capable of. This implies an emphasis on inclusive citizenship rather than the exclusions which a special needs approach has all too frequently engendered. At one level, inclusiveness demands greater efforts in some familiar areas of policy: strong and comprehensive legislation on discrimination, pay, entitlements and the working conditions of disabled people, as well as increases in the relevant benefits. It also means making available resources for carers and for systems of 'independent living'. And it implies challenging the discourse through which disability is presently constructed: creating one that stresses agency and interdependency rather than passivity and dependency.

Theoretical implications

The ambivalence that was mentioned at the start of the chapter has now been reviewed in greater detail. For each of the groups examined the welfare state has undoubtedly provided welcome benefits, yet it could not be claimed that its influence has been entirely positive. To some extent state welfare has not gone far enough (in terms of equal opportunities legislation, for instance) and in other respects it has hindered movement towards greater social justice (as when it propagates institutional forms of discrimination). Yet there are few who demand that the welfare state be dismantled. Instead, campaigners for women's issues, ethnic minorities and disabled people usually call for *better* welfare and so, while tending to support the levels of social expenditure advocated by social democrats (see Chapter 13), they also add some distinctive ideas of their own.

In essence, what is being questioned here is the identity of the subject that has underpinned modern systems of welfare (see Briefing 14.5). During the era of the 'classic' welfare state in the UK (1945–1979, roughly speaking) the emphasis was very much on full employment, nationhood and a large degree of state centralisation. By full employment was meant continuous, full-time employment and so implied male rather than female work since the latter was defined in terms of domestic responsibilities. Nationhood was treated as given and static, with the debate over immigration being organised around a discourse of assimilation with little attention being made to the changing dynamics of Britishness. State centralisation was premised on the belief that the main principles of welfare had been solved so that the emphasis had to be on the effective delivery of services by government to the client. Among other things this inspired a paternalism towards 'dependants' – those not held to be capable of looking after themselves – and so to the construction of dependency around the norm of able-bodiedness. In short, the ideal subject for whom this welfare state was designed was male, white and able-bodied (Hughes and Lewis 1998).

Despite the demise of the classic era and despite the fact that movements representing these groups examined in this chapter have been influential for a number of years, this subject is still the norm. Changes in the labour market have placed an even greater emphasis on employment and although, with the shift towards a post-industrial service economy, the 'feminine' qualities of flexibility and multitasking are more highly valued, we are still a long way from balancing domestic needs against those of the workplace. **Multiculturalism** is on the agenda but panics in recent years about British citizenship and identity, asylum seekers, ethnic disturbances (in Bradford and Leeds) and the rise of the far right across Europe demonstrate the extent to which a one-dimensional nationalism still dominates. It is a paradox that as nationalism becomes more fervent so the nationality it has appointed itself to defend becomes more fragile: the higher the walls of Britishness are built then

Briefing 14.5 Theories of welfare

Social policy is often regarded as a highly empirical subject, but it can only be fully understood with reference to a long history of political, social, philosophical and economic theories. For instance, if social policies are the means by which people are helped to achieve a decent level of health, income and education then what should be the main principle of distribution? Should we distribute to everyone or to particular groups of people, for example, the very poor? Should we distribute according to need, desert or entitlement? Therefore, while thinking about concepts and ideas can seem quite abstract and far removed from everyday life, doing so is crucially important if we are to understand society fully and decide how to reform welfare systems.

the less able are the foundations to support the weight. Yet rather than reconfigure itself nationalism usually prefers to blame the resulting instability on the 'outsiders' and the 'minorities'. Finally, state centralisation has been replaced with a consumerist model of choice and autonomy within a market setting, yet this tends to hegemonise abilities that most disabled people are thought not to possess. The perfect consumer would have full access to information about market conditions, would be primarily concerned to satisfy their preferences through rational decision making and would be able to mobilise their resources quickly and efficiently. Yet not only does the perfect consumer not exist but, in a disablist society, disabled people are even further excluded from the prevailing norms. The consumerist model already assumes a degree of choice and autonomy that many disabled people do not possess and which ignores the discourse of social interdependency on which most in the movement prefer to draw.

If the norm of male, white and able-bodied subjects still prevails then what might the appropriate response be? Many have been driven in recent years towards postmodern and post-structuralist ideas since these theories offer a way of deconstructing norms and ideals since they underline the complexities, instabilities and contingencies at work in the social world (Leonard 1997). A key figure here is Foucault who sets out to reveal the discursive conditions through which knowledge and ideas are generated. He argued that:

> It is already one of the prime effects of power that certain bodies, certain gestures, certain discourses, certain desires come to be identified and constituted as individuals . . . The individual is an effect of power, and at the same time, or precisely to the extent to which it is that effect, it is the element of its articulation.
>
> Foucault (1986: 98)

Discourses are the practices by which power operates on and through society according to prevailing norms. For instance, modern ideas of mental health regard 'madness' as an individual tragedy deserving of medical treatment directed towards the self, but Foucault (2001) shows how and why these assumptions, while seeming perfectly normal to modern eyes, are in fact a result of 17th- and 18th-century conceptions of reason and rationality. Madness was constructed as the 'other' of reason. Postmodernism and post-structuralism have therefore offered feminists, anti-racists and disability theorists a means of deconstructing the welfare subject and understanding the extent to which women have been constructed as the other of men, black people as the other of white ones and disabled people as the other of non-disabled ones. In each case, the first term is marginalised to preserve the domination of the latter. Welfare institutions do not, then, necessarily represent the upward curve of modern progress but may embody forms of power out of which our subjectivities are assembled.

What this seems to imply for social policy is the need for a greater recognition of difference so that the multiplicities of our social identities are no longer suppressed by a unilinear model of the self. To put it another way, we do not necessarily all aspire for the employment and lifestyle patterns of the white, able-bodied male, that were inscribed within the post-Second World War welfare state and welfare reforms must come to acknowledge this. One consequence of such recognition – and we have already touched on this point – is that we must revisit what we mean by universalism. Universal provision has often been regarded as the sine qua non of the welfare state: a response to the fragmentary services of the 19th century that allows basic needs to be met. But according to some (Thompson and Hoggett 1998) universalism may be a means by which difference has been suppressed. As noted earlier, the solution is not necessarily to abandon either universalism or the notion of welfare services as public institutions, but it may imply that we have to work into any universal frame of reference a greater sensitivity to particular differences. Provision might therefore be based on a model whereby universalism and particularism are seen to loop back on one another, so that it makes little sense to refer to the one without also referring to the other.

However, as the critics of postmodernism and post-structuralism point out, the emphasis on difference is potentially dangerous. Should *all* differences be respected and be respected *equally*? That hardly seems logical since it might mean according a recognition to the racist equal to that of the victim of racism, for example. Surely it cannot be the case that all differences are valuable. Focusing on differential identities also risks occluding what it is we hold in common, the similarities that make us human. And the theoretical fashion for difference and particularism seems to represent a cultural shift away from notions of class, material exploitation and social justice. Surely poverty, for example, is something to be eliminated, not celebrated as a sign of difference.

A number of counter-responses to these criticisms have emerged in recent years, one of the most influential being that of Fraser. Fraser (2001a; 2001b; Fraser and Honneth 2003) insists that postmodernism is not simply a celebration of difference but of only those differences that a framework of justice reveals to be significant. In fact, questions of cultural difference are inseparable from questions of material distribution for reasons that both postmodernists/post-structuralists and their various critics have neglected.

The former have tended to downgrade issues of distribution as deriving from social theories of class that they no longer take to be relevant; the latter have placed issues of cultural injustice in second place to those of distribution, as if material resources can be separated from their cultural forms. Fraser therefore calls for a convergence of redistribution and recognition. Without distributive justice we cannot achieve a proper recognition of difference because social status is weakened unless the person or group in question has access to an equitable share of goods and resources. Without acknowledging the importance of cultural recognition we cannot achieve distributive justice since we will continue to possess partial ideas of how to distribute goods and resources and who to distribute them to. Fraser's is therefore a theory of social justice that solidly incorporates the material and the cultural, the (re)distributive and the recognitive – and the previous sections were written with this incorporation in mind. It therefore offers a means of distinguishing between differences that should be recognised and those that should not.

Summary

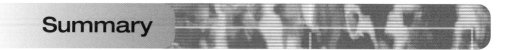

In this chapter we have seen why women, ethnic minorities and disabled people share an ambivalence towards state welfare, welcoming it in many respects while seeking to reconfigure it away from the welfare subject of the white, able-bodied male:

- In each case critics argue not against the basic principles of the welfare state but seek to broaden our appreciation of the social differences to which those principles have to apply. Postmodernist and post-structuralist ideas have been influential in this respect but throw up additional problems to do with preserving those aspects of the welfare state that deserve to be retained (universalism and distributive justice) while introducing into the picture those that social policy has tended to underemphasise (particularism and cultural recognition). Fraser's ongoing ideas concerning social justice offer a potential means of reconciliation.

- In short, the perspectives we have explored here could represent an important alternative to mainstream views concerning welfare reform. Here, too, the idea of moving away from the one-size-fits-all model has been popular but for conservatives this has suggested a greater role for markets while for social democrats (at least those who support the Third Way), this has impelled a series of public sector reforms. The problem with the conservative approach is that issues of distributive justice disappear almost entirely in the rush towards market efficiency. The problem with Third Way social democracy is that it introduces a surrogate market logic into the public sphere where economic criteria dominate through the imposition of league tables, performance-related pay, competitive tendering, perpetual auditing and assessment and an ethos of consumerism that may not be suitable for public goods.

● The shift away from state universalism implicit within both conservative and Third Way philosophies may compound the disadvantages experienced by women, ethnic minorities and disabled people by debilitating the welfare state's positive features (its ability to humanise capitalism) without addressing its negative ones.

● An alternative to this mainstream is suggested by those who stress the importance of user groups, civil associations, grassroots activism, communal provision and the democratisation of the welfare state. It suggests that overturning the disadvantages experienced by many women, black and disabled people requires a degree of material and cultural empowerment from the bottom up that we are still a long way from achieving. It also suggests that the story told in this chapter is a long way from being finished yet.

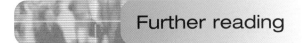

Discussion and review topics

1 How might state provision of welfare be reformed to take account of feminist critiques?

2 What does the concept of 'institutional racism' add to our understanding of social policy?

3 What might be the social policy implications of acceptance of the 'social model' of disability?

4 How far can arguments such as those put forward over gender, 'race' and disability be applied to other groups, such as gays and lesbians?

Further reading

Bagilhole, B. (1997) *Equal Opportunities and Social Policy*, Longman, London – this book considers the meaning of 'equal opportunities', outlines their development and considers the extent of equal opportunities for black people, disabled people and women within social policy

Lewis, G. (2000) *'Race', Gender, Social Welfare*, Polity, Cambridge – drawing on a range of perspectives, Lewis analyses the relationship between 'race', gender and social policy

Lister, R. (2003) *Citizenship: Feminist Perspectives*, Palgrave Macmillan, Basingstoke – grounded in the concept of citizenship, this book examines political and theoretical arguments and their implications for women

Oliver, M. and Barnes, C. (1998) *Disabled People and Social Policy*, Longman, London – provides a good overview of perspectives on disability and an examination of policies that could empower disabled people

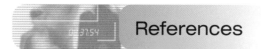

Some useful websites

www.eoc.org.uk – the Equal Opportunities Commission; www.drc-uk. org – the Disability Rights Commission; www.cre.gov.uk – the Commission for Racial Equality – the bodies responsible for tackling discrimination

www.homeoffice.gov.uk – the website of the Home Office provides official information on issues including immigration and nationality

www.womenandequalityunit.gov.uk – the government unit responsible for leading on gender equality and with a responsibility for sexual orientation

There are many other organisations with relevant websites including: the British Council of Disabled People (www.bcodp.org.uk); Citizenship 21 (www.c21project.org.uk/citizenship_21); Liberty (www.liberty-human-rights.org.uk); Outrage (www.outrage.co.uk); RADAR (www.radar.org.uk); Stonewall (www.stonewall.org.uk)

References

Barnes, H. and Baldwin, S. (1999) 'Social security, poverty and disability', in Ditch, J. (ed.) *Introduction to Social Security*, Routledge, London

Beresford, P. (1997) *It's Our Welfare*, National Institute for Social Work, London

Beveridge, W. (1942) *Social Insurance and Allied Services*, HMSO, London

Brown, M. (1999) *Race, Money and the American Welfare State*, Cornell University Press, Cornell

Craig, G. (1999) '"Race", social security and poverty', in Ditch, J. (ed.) *Introduction to Social Security*, Routledge, London

Curtis, P. (2002) 'Female graduates lose out on pay', *The Guardian*, 8 March

Daly, M. (1999) *The Gender Division of Welfare*, Cambridge University Press, Cambridge

Doyal, L. and Gough, I. (1991) *A Theory of Human Needs*, Macmillan, London

Fitzpatrick, T. (2001) *Welfare Theory: An Introduction*, Palgrave, Basingstoke

Foucault, M. (1986) *Power/Knowledge*, Longman, London

Foucault, M. (2001) *Madness and Civilisation*, Routledge, London

Fraser, N. (1997) *Justice Interruptus*, Routledge, London

Fraser, N. (2001a) *Adding Insult to Injury*, Verso, London

Fraser, N. (2001b) 'Recognition without ethics?', *Theory, Culture and Society*, 18, 21–42

Fraser, N. and Honneth, A. (2003) *Redistribution or Recognition*, Verso, London

Gilroy, P. (1987) *There Ain't No Black in the Union Jack*, Hutchison, London

Howard, M., Garnham, A., Fimister, G. and Veit-Wilson, J. (2001) *Poverty: The Facts*, CPAG, London

Hughes, G. and Lewis, G. (eds) (1998) *Unsettling Welfare*, Routledge, London

Leonard, P. (1997) *Postmodern Welfare*, Sage, London

Lewis, G. (2000) *'Race', Gender, Social Welfare*, Polity, Cambridge

Lewis, G. (ed.) (1998) *Forming Nation, Framing Welfare*, Routledge, London

Lewis, J. (1992) 'Gender and the development of welfare regimes', *Journal of European Social Policy*, 2, 159–73

Lewis, J. (2001) 'The decline of the male breadwinner model: implications for work and care', *Social Politics*, 8, 152–69

Lister, R. (2003) *Citizenship: Feminist Perspectives*, Palgrave Macmillan, Basingstoke

Macpherson, W. (1999) *The Stephen Lawrence Inquiry*, The Stationery Office, London

Modood, T., Berthoud, R., Lakey, J., Nazroo, J., Smith, P., Virdee, S. and Beishon, P. (1997) *Ethnic Minorities in Britain*, Policy Studies Institute, London

Oliver, M. (1989) *The Politics of Disablement*, Macmillan, Basingstoke

Oliver, M. (1996) *Understanding Disability*, Macmillan, Basingstoke

Oliver, M. and Barnes, C. (1998) *Disabled People and Social Policy*, Longman, London

Parekh, B. (2001) *The Future of Multi-Ethnic Britain*, Profile Books, London

Pascall, G. (1997) *Social Policy: A New Feminist Analysis*, Routledge, London

Sainsbury, D. (ed.) (1999) *Gender and Welfare State Regimes*, Oxford University Press, Oxford

Sen, A. (1992) *Inequality Re-examined*, Clarendon, Oxford

Shakespeare, T., Watson, N., Johnston, M. and Pinder, R. (1997) 'Defending the social model', *Disability and Society*, 12, 293–310

Thompson, S. and Hoggett, P. (1998) 'The delivery of welfare: the associationist vision', in Carter, J. (ed.) *Postmodernity and the Fragmentation of Welfare*, Routledge, London

Turner, B. S. (1996) *The Body and Society*, Sage, London

Twigg, J. (2000) *Bathing*, Routledge, London

Young, I. M. (1990) *Justice and the Politics of Difference*, Princeton University Press, Princeton, NJ

Part IV

European and international developments

European welfare states and European Union social policy

15   Rob Sykes

Issues in Focus

This chapter deals with the character and roles of the European Union's (EU) social policy in the context of the problems confronting European welfare states. Social policy is usually understood and analysed in terms of national boundaries and national policies. The EU, however, is a body linking together its member states in a variety of ways and affecting these states through a variety of policymaking and policy delivery processes including some, although not yet all, aspects of what is usually regarded as social policy. In order to explain how the EU may be affecting social policy in the member states, this chapter will review not only the development and current character of the EU's specifically social policy initiatives (and this in itself is complicated by the way in which social policy is regarded within the EU), but also set these initiatives in the context of the EU's main economic policies. Some analysts argue, indeed, that EU social policy is very much the 'poor relation' of the more developed and significant economic policies, such as the single market and the single currency (the euro). Others argue that although primacy may have been given by the EU to economic issues and policies in the past, EU social policy has now developed to become a (relatively) independent area of EU policymaking that increasingly affects the member states of the EU.

Different EU bodies, such as the Commission, the Council and the European Parliament, are involved in making EU policy alongside the governments of the member states. Does this then mean that EU policy,

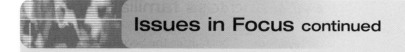

Issues in Focus continued

including EU social policy, is becoming 'transnational' – are we approaching a European welfare state? Having looked at the development and current character of EU social policy and how policy is made, the chapter will consider possible futures for EU social policy, including such important developments as the EU Declaration on Human Rights, the enlargement of EU membership in June 2004, and the proposed new Constitution for the EU.

In order to achieve these aims the chapter will explore:

● patterns of similarity and difference in European welfare states

● the development of the EU's social dimension – from Common Market to European Union

● social policymaking in the EU

● EU social policy now and in the future.

Patterns of similarity and difference in European welfare states

In this section we review some of the patterns of similarity and difference in the nature of social policy issues or problems confronted by different European Union welfare states. This will provide a background to understanding how and why the EU's social dimension has been developed and the ongoing issues for EU social policy. The best and most available source for statistical and other descriptive material about the comparative information referred to here is the European Union's own statistical service, Eurostat (see Briefing 15.1).

Briefing 15.1   Accessing EU information

The best and easiest way to find EU information is via its website, Europa. The main address for this website is http://europa.eu.int. Within this site the official, legal texts such as treaties and directives can be found, but also a whole range of other useful material on the EU's social and other policies, its institutions and so on. Statistical and allied materials can be found via the Eurostat site within Europa, most of it free. For further information on this and other sources on the EU refer to the further reading section at the end of this chapter.

A greying and less familial Europe?

As the 'baby-boomers' born after the Second World War reach retirement age there will be growing numbers of people in the elderly age groups. While at present people aged 65 and over represent about 16 per cent of the total population across the EU, those below 15 represent 17 per cent. However, by 2010 these ratios will become 18 per cent and 16 per cent respectively. The most dramatic increase will occur in the number of 'very old' people (those aged over 80), which will rise by almost 50 per cent over the next 15 years. Although the accession states that joined the EU in 2004 currently have a younger age structure than existing member states (those aged 65 and over are 13 per cent of the population, those under 15, 19 per cent), the overall effect on the age structure of the EU will be both small and temporary. In the medium to long term, acceding states will also tend to reinforce the population decline of the EU. Given low fertility levels, the proportion of children in the population is rapidly declining and by 2020 the share of older people in these states will approach the levels of the EU 15.

These rising old age-dependency rates are important for a number of reasons. First, there is the question of whether older people have adequate financial support, especially as they are now likely to live longer than in the past. The so-called 'pensions crisis' not only affects those who are currently approaching retirement age, however, but has serious implications for those now starting or into their work careers. All this is happening at a time when the proportions of people in work and paying taxes for welfare services are also declining. Put simply, a fundamental question confronting all EU member states is: 'Who will pay for pensions in the future?' Turning to less direct financial factors, clearly older people are likely to need health and other forms of care more than younger people. If services are not provided through state welfare systems, then there are two main alternatives for the care of older people: the market or the family. With regard to the latter, care of the elderly, and for that matter other 'welfare' provision through families, is being challenged by developments in family and household structures across the EU. Typically, there are fewer and later marriages, and also more marital breakdowns. In 2001 there were only five marriages per 1,000 inhabitants in the EU 15 compared with almost eight in 1970. The divorce rate for marriages in 1960 was 15 per cent, whereas for marriages entered into in 1980 the figure almost doubled to 28 per cent. The trend in the EU is towards smaller households, with more people living alone at all ages.

These are overall statistics; in some of the EU states these issues are more pressing since the age-dependency ratios, for example, are even higher than these averages. Table 15.1 indicates the old age-dependency ratios both for the EU overall and the 15 member states before the new accessions in 2004. As can be seen from these figures, the issues of old age-dependency are set to become particularly acute in Germany (D), Greece (EL) and Italy (I), while Ireland (IRL) will have the lowest ratio.

Table 15.1 EU age-dependency ratios

Key indicator	EU15	B	DK	D	EI	E	F	IRL	I	L	NL	A	P	FIN	S	UK

Old age-dependency ratio (population aged 65 and over as a percentage of the working age population (15–64) on 1 January)

	EU15	B	DK	D	EI	E	F	IRL	I	L	NL	A	P	FIN	S	UK
1990	21.6	22.1	23.2	21.6	20.4	20.2	21.1	18.6	21.5	19.3	18.6	22.1	20.0	19.8	27.7	24.0
1995	23.0	23.8	22.7	22.5	22.8	22.3	23.0	17.8	24.1	20.6	19.3	22.4	21.6	21.1	27.4	24.3
2000	24.3	25.5	22.2	23.9	25.6	24.6	24.6	16.8	26.6	21.4	20.0	22.9	23.8	22.2	26.9	23.9
2001	:	25.7	22.2	24.5	:	24.7	24.8	16.6	27.1	21.5	20.1	22.9	24.2	22.4	26.8	:
2010	27.3	26.7	24.6	30.3	29.2	26.8	25.5	17.3	31.3	23.6	22.3	26.3	24.5	24.9	28.1	24.2

Source: European Commission (2003), p.113

Unemployment

Unemployment is a continuing area of concern for the EU and all member states. In 2001 the total number of unemployed people in the EU stood at 12.8 million or 7.4 per cent of the labour force. This is the lowest rate since 1992. Looking at the trend in unemployment, in 1994 there was a peak rate of 10.5 per cent for the EU 15. The rates in Denmark, Spain, Portugal, Finland and the United Kingdom fell by more than 40 per cent during the period from 1994 to 2001 and in Ireland and the Netherlands, the 2001 rates are just one-third of the 1994 rates. The countries with the highest levels of unemployment continued to be Spain and Greece. Women are more likely than men to be unemployed in the EU and the female unemployment rate (8.7 per cent) was still more than two points higher than the male unemployment rate (6.4 per cent) in 2001. Table 15.2 illustrates the patterns of national variation.

Table 15.2 EU unemployment rates

Key indicator	EU 15	B	DK	D	EI	E	F	IRL	I	L	NL	A	P	FIN	S	UK

Unemployment rate (total unemployed individuals as a share of total active population; harmonised series)

	EU 15	B	DK	D	EI	E	F	IRL	I	L	NL	A	P	FIN	S	UK
2001 total	7.4	6.6	4.3	7.7	10.5	10.6	8.6	3.8	9.4	2.0	2.4	3.6	4.1	9.1	4.9	5.0
2001 men	6.4	6.0	3.8	7.7	7.0	7.5	7.0	3.9	7.3	1.7	1.9	3.0	3.2	8.6	5.2	5.5
2001 women	8.5	7.4	4.9	7.8	15.6	15.4	10.3	3.7	12.9	2.4	3.0	4.3	5.1	9.7	4.5	4.4
2000 total	7.8	6.9	4.4	7.8	11.1	11.3	9.3	4.2	10.4	2.3	2.8	3.7	4.1	9.8	5.8	5.4
1994 total	10.5	9.8	7.7	8.2	8.9	19.8	11.8	14.3	11.0	3.2	6.8	3.8	6.9	16.6	9.4	9.4
Unemployment 2001 (1,000)	12,861	286	123	3,073	457	1,892	2,221	68	2,248	4	198	137	212	238	225	1,485

Source: European Commission (2003), p.135

However, these national unemployment rates conceal significant regional differences within countries: for example, in Germany between the west (low) and east (high); in Italy between the north (low) and the south (high); and in the UK, between the north (high) and south (low). In 2000 in Germany, the unemployment rate ranged from less than half the national average of 7.9 per cent in Oberbayern (3.1 per cent) to 16.9 per cent in Dessau and Halle in Sachsen-Anhalt. Similarly, while many regions in the north of Italy were largely unaffected by unemployment, between 21 and 25 per cent of the workforce in the southern regions of Campania, Calabria and Sicily was unemployed. In the UK, Merseyside (13.2 per cent), in particular, had high unemployment compared with the southeast (2.2 per cent).

Regional differences in unemployment are even more pronounced among young people (those under 25 years of age). Dytiki Macedonia and Sterea Ellada in Greece and parts of Andalucia in Spain all recorded youth unemployment rates of 40 per cent or more in 2001 and several regions in southern Italy have rates of 50 per cent or more.

As if these rates of unemployment were not sufficiently problematic from an overall welfare viewpoint, what is even more worrying is the fact that a significant proportion of the unemployment in the EU is long term, that is, of 12 months or longer duration. In fact, just under half (44 per cent) of the unemployed in the EU have been out of work for this period or longer. Once again the rates of long-term unemployment vary across the EU: in Austria, Denmark and the Netherlands less than 1 per cent of the unemployed were affected, but in Greece, Italy and Spain the rates are around 5 per cent. Interestingly, the gender breakdown of long-term unemployment shows that while, in general, there is a greater likelihood of being in this category if you are a woman (3.9 per cent) than a man (2.8 per cent), in both the UK and Ireland the pattern is reversed, with men being almost twice as likely as women to be out of work for long periods. Once again, it is when we look at youth unemployment that the worst picture is revealed. The period of six months or more is used for measuring long-term unemployment among young people and, on this basis, although it had fallen from a level of 13.1 per cent in 1994, the level was still 6.9 per cent in 2001. Greek and Italian young people are particularly likely to be long-term unemployed (18 per cent and 20 per cent respectively).

Poverty and social exclusion

People living in households which are poor and/or where one or more adult is unemployed are also more likely to be suffering from some form of sickness or ill health, to be educated to a lower level and in general to suffer from exclusion form the full range of social, economic and cultural activities in their society. Two very simple measures of the pattern of relative wealth and poverty are the distribution of income by head and between different groups in a society. The usual indicator used in the EU to indicate a basic measure of wealth and poverty is the distribution of a country's **gross domestic product** (GDP) per head. Table 15.3 indicates the pattern of GDP per capita across the EU.

Table 15.3 GDP per head (index EU 15 = 100, in PPS*)

	EU 15	Euro 12	B	DK	D	EL	E	F	IRL	I	L	NL	A	P	FIN	S	UK
1995	100	101	113	118	110	66	78	104	94	104	172	110	111	70	97	103	97
2001	100	100	106	119	104	67	83	100	119	105	191	112	112	74	103	100	100

Source: Adapted from European Commission (2003), Annex II
*PPS stands for purchasing power standard or, as Eurostat explains it, purchasing power parities (PPP). These convert every national monetary unit into a common reference unit, the purchasing power standard (PPS), of which every unit can buy the same amount of consumer goods and services across the member states in a given year

What this simplistic measure shows is that in some countries, notably Greece, Portugal and Spain, the level of GDP per head is significantly below the EU average, and people in these countries may thus be regarded as 'poorer' than their counterparts in the rest of the EU. Although these measures are used as a basis for certain EU intervention programmes on a regional basis, notably the structural funds, it is obvious that not all citizens of a given country get an equal portion of the national GDP. Some groups, the 'rich', in each country get more than their proportional 'share' and some, the 'poor', much less. The distribution of income between different groups of the population varies in different EU countries. Using figures that refer to 1999, the top 20 per cent, or quintile, of the population received 4.6 times as much of the total income as the bottom 20 per cent of the population of the EU as a whole. This pattern of inequality is generally higher in the southern and non-continental countries: Portugal was the highest with the top quintile getting 6.4 times what the bottom quintile received, but Greece, Ireland, Italy, Spain and the UK were also above the EU average. Those countries with the least unequal distribution between top and bottom income quintiles were Denmark and Sweden (3.2), followed by Finland (3.4), Germany (3.6), and Austria and the Netherlands (3.7). In general, those member states with higher levels of inequality tend to have a lower level of average income (although the UK has both above-average income and above-average inequality).

It is also possible to analyse the likelihood of being in poverty against other factors such as patterns of employment and unemployment in a household, the age of household members or whether the household is headed by a lone parent. Certain household types display higher than average levels of being at risk of poverty: single parents with dependent children (38 per cent), young people living alone (32 per cent), old people living alone (24 per cent) and women living alone (24 per cent). Couples with three or more dependent children were also at high risk (25 per cent).

Again, the overall picture varies country by country. More than 50 per cent of single parents in Spain and the UK could be classified as having a 'low income' in 1999. Levels were also high (around 40 per cent) in Germany, Ireland, the Netherlands and Portugal. Over 30 per cent of households with more than three children in Italy, Luxembourg, Portugal, Spain and the UK had a 'low income'. Over 50 per cent of young people (those aged under 30) living alone had a 'low income' in Denmark and Finland. Levels were also above the EU average (32 per cent) in France, Germany, the Netherlands, Sweden and the United Kingdom. More than 60 per cent of old people (aged over 65) living alone had a 'low income' in Ireland. Rates were also high (over 50 per cent) in Denmark and Portugal compared with an EU average of 24 per cent. Women (compared with men) and children (compared with adults) are also more likely to be poor.

Summary

What do these patterns show and why are they of significance for social policy in the EU countries? The figures shown here serve to illustrate that the range of 'welfare problems' found in individual EU countries are broadly shared across all the member states. Thus, it is not surprising that as the European Community, as it was once known, and more recently the EU, as the body that links together the member states economically and politically, should consider providing some sort of social policy to deal with these problems. Even if, as we shall see in the next section, it has primarily developed alongside, and to a large extent as a corollary to, economic developments, it is nevertheless the case that a significant range of what could broadly be described as EU social policy has emerged. What is more, in the period since the establishment of the single European market, what the EU often refers to as its 'social dimension' has developed more rapidly. One of the reasons for this is that EU social policy has been seen to be a necessary support for developments such as the single market – put crudely, without schemes such as the structural funds, the effects of creating and extending the single market would have been likely to have consigned poorer countries to worsening conditions for many of their citizens and increasing affluence for others. These 'regional disparities', as they are known, have been increasingly regarded by leading figures within the European Commission and also by some, but not all, heads of government in the member states, as at best socially and ethically unfair, and at worst liable to create tensions that could challenge the achievement of a truly European single market. This approach to the development of EU social policy has sometimes been referred to as 'negative integration': in other words, social policy development across the EU that is primarily driven by the negative economic and political consequences if it did not occur.

What these patterns also clearly show is that there is a considerable amount of national and regional variation in the various welfare issues we have considered. While unemployment, for example, has been a continuing issue across all the EU member states, as we have seen, its level and other characteristics vary considerably both between EU countries and in the different parts of countries. What this suggests is that any EU intervention to deal with unemployment must not only seek to deal with it as a trans-EU problem, but also as a problem that affects some EU citizens more than others and in different ways. The same may be said about issues of old age-dependency, poverty and social exclusion and other areas we have not yet considered such as education, health policy, disability, housing and other urban issues. In short, the problems of social policy for the EU are not simply those of the member states multiplied by 15 or 25. Since the EU is now increasingly acting as a unified political and economic entity within a regional and global environment, then it is also increasingly being expected to intervene to help deal with the various social welfare problems that its citizens face. The EU might even be said to be causing some of its own welfare problems as, for example, it has sought to 'rationalise' (effectively, reduce the size of) certain industries such as coal and iron and steel. Whether it can or should intervene as some sort of 'European welfare state' over and above the national member states or whether it should do it alongside these member states in some sort of partnership is an ongoing debate to which we shall return. However, what is clear is that social welfare is now established as a key object of EU concern and intervention. What is more, as the EU enlarges these problems and the need for intervention are likely to increase, as we shall discuss at the end of this chapter.

Development of the EU's 'social dimension' – from Common Market to European Union

While this section is concerned with the development of EU social policy since the 1950s to date, it is by no means a comprehensive historical account of all the social policy related activities that occurred during this time. Rather, it simply attempts to indicate the key developments, focusing mainly on the most recent period from the 1990s, and to give an overall feel for the nature of EU social policy, as opposed to the social policy activities of the UK and other nation states. As will become apparent, there are definite characteristics and limits to what passes for social policy in the EU, although its role in this area is of increasing importance for both the member states and, arguably, the rest of Europe and even for non-European countries.

Article 2 of the Treaty on European Union states that the first objective of the EU is

> [T]o promote economic and social progress and a high level of employment and to achieve balanced and sustainable development, in particular through the creation of an area without internal frontiers, through the strengthening of economic and social cohesion and through the establishment of economic and monetary union.
>
> (Consolidated Version of the Treaty on European Union, 2002)

This rather vague statement usefully sets the context for any understanding of what EU social policy is and how it has developed since the start of the European Economic Community (EEC) in the 1950s, forerunner of the European Union, up to today. First, it clearly links economic and social policy;

second, it employs a key phrase 'economic and social cohesion', which recurs throughout the development of EU social policy; and third, it refers to economic and monetary union and the common market (this is what 'an area without internal frontiers' really refers to) as the context for social and economic policy interventions. We shall return to how we may characterise current EU social policy later, but first let us see how the so-called 'social dimension' has developed since the 1950s.

From Common Market to single market: 1950s to 1980s

In the Treaty of Rome (Article 2) that established the European Community of six member states (see Briefing 15.2) we find the first statement of its 'social dimension':

> [A] harmonious development of economic activities, a continuous and balanced expansion, an increase in stability, an accelerated raising of the standard of living and closer relations between the States belonging to it.

This statement set the tone for the EEC's social strategy for much of its early development. Thus in the period from 1958 to 1974 the EEC's approach to social policy was, essentially, to neglect it while focusing on economic and political matters. It was not until 1974 with the adoption of the first *Social Action Programme* (SAP) that what was increasingly referred to as the European Community (EC) was beginning to take a more active role in the promotion of a 'social dimension'. However, the 40 or so initiatives of the first SAP were still focused on labour market and employment-related issues. The three major objectives were:

● full and better employment

● improved living and working conditions

● worker participation.

Following the SAP's adoption, however, there was a significant surge of activity by the EC in the areas of education and training, health and safety at work, workers' and women's' rights and poverty.

It was in the 1980s that the idea of a 'social space' (*éspace social*) to complement the 'economic space' of the EC was first mooted as a central feature of the restructuring of the Community after its most recent enlargement and as it moved towards the establishment of a single market. The idea was taken up and promoted most vigorously by Jacques Delors, the European Commission's President from 1985 to 1995. Delors saw the idea of a social space as a necessary complement to the completion of the internal market. He also saw the development of a social space alongside the single European market (SEM) as a way of moving the EU forward from the deadlock that it

Briefing 15.2   Stages of EU enlargement

1952	The founding states: Belgium, France, Germany, Italy, Luxembourg, the Netherlands
1973	Denmark, Ireland, the United Kingdom
1981	Greece
1986	Portugal and Spain
1995	Austria, Finland, Sweden
2004	Cyprus, the Czech Republic, Estonia, Hungary, Latvia, Lithuania, Malta, Poland, the Slovak Republic and Slovenia

had reached over the social dimension. The most important piece of EC legislation for both economic and social policy to come out of this period was the *Single European Act* (SEA). The SEA linked various social policy 'flanking measures', as they were called, to the completion of the single market, and it thus represented a quite conscious attempt to complement EC economic policy with some form of EC social policy. The most important of these measures was what came from this point forward to be known as the structural funds (Policy eye 15.1).

The complementarity between EU economic and social policy becomes even more apparent when one considers the next significant development of the EC, the Social Charter. *The Community Charter of the Fundamental Social Rights of Workers*, adopted in 1989 by 11 of the 12 member states (with the UK as the exception), was accompanied by a second action programme of some 47 separate initiatives. It is important to note three important features of the Social Charter insofar as they consolidate certain key developments of previous EC social policy developments and also prefigure subsequent developments. The first feature is that the Charter is a charter of *workers'* rights. Although the term 'citizen' had originally been used in its drafting, a number of member states, not least the UK, objected to this form of words. This reflects both previous and subsequent foci of EC/EU social policy on labour market concerns rather than, as in the case of the *Council of Europe's Social Charter*, a broader concern with matters such as social and medical assistance as part of a broader perception of social rights and social policy. The second feature is that the Social Charter is not a binding document and leaves the relevant decisions and implementation to member states. The third feature is the non-involvement of the UK. Each of these characteristics has echoes in subsequent EC/EU social policy.

EU economic and social policies in the 1990s

The 1990s saw considerable political, economic and, to a lesser extent, social policy development. The signing in 1992 of the *Treaty on European Union* at

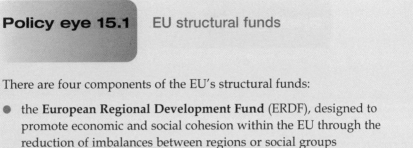

Policy eye 15.1   EU structural funds

There are four components of the EU's structural funds:

- the **European Regional Development Fund** (ERDF), designed to promote economic and social cohesion within the EU through the reduction of imbalances between regions or social groups

- the **European Social Fund** (ESF), designed to provide the main financial support for the EU's strategic employment policy objectives

- the **European Agricultural Guidance and Guarantee Fund** (EAGGF - guidance section), designed to help the structural reform of the agriculture sector and the development of rural areas

- the **Financial Instrument for Fisheries Guidance** (FIFG), designed to help the structural reform of the fisheries sector.

Maastricht in the Netherlands (usually referred to as the *Maastricht Treaty* for obvious reasons) was a major step forward for the member states in that it established a new form of organisation linking them together in a form unlike anything else, politically or economically, in the world. In legal terms the European Union became a combination of three elements or 'pillars' (Briefing 15.3).

The pillar with the major social policy remit continues to be the European Community, however, and this is why in extracts from treaties it is the 'Community', not 'the European Union', that is referred to.

The creation of the European Union brought with it significant development in social policy terms. The link between the proposals made on social policy as part of the *Treaty on European Union* and the preceding *Social Charter* is quite explicit. The principles of the Charter provide the basis for the *Agreement on Social Policy*, which was appended to the Maastricht Treaty and signed by all the member states except the UK. Thus the Agreement called for upward harmonisation of living and working conditions, improved health and safety at work, the promotion of 'social dialogue' between management and labour at the European level and equal pay for women and men. It also extended the EU's competence in the areas of education and vocational training.

Despite the at times heated debate that surrounded the discussions and final ratification of it in some of the member states, such as the UK and Denmark, the Agreement on Social Policy reached at Maastricht still represented more of a continuation of previous trends than a shift to a new level of social policy intervention by the EU. The significant difference between the Maastricht Agreement and earlier EC social policy provision is that the 11 signatories could take decisions that would be binding in some ways on the member states rather than being what were often referred to in EC jargon as 'solemn

Briefing 15.3   Pillars of the European Union

The First Pillar: the European Community – comprising the arrangements of the EC, ECSC and Euratom Treaties (the founding treaties), union citizenship, Community policies, Economic and Monetary Union, etc.

The Second Pillar – common foreign and security policy.

The Third Pillar – policing and judicial co-operation on criminal matters.

declarations'. Although it was never attempted, there was the possibility that the 11 signatories could have made social policy decisions under these arrangements that would have affected the UK as an EU member state, even though the UK had not signed up to the Agreement.

Following the creation of the European Union, in the mid-1990s two major White Papers set out its economic and social policy objectives for the longer term. They indicate the way in which the EU moved to a more strategic approach to both policy areas in response to continuing economic problems in the EU, such as high unemployment, to the prospect of a single currency, to the enlargement of the Union by the addition of new member states, and to the continuing issues of social and economic imbalances across the EU.

The central proposition of the White Paper on economic policy, *Growth, Competitiveness, Employment* (*GCE*), was that ways should be found of reducing unemployment and increasing employment opportunities through radical changes in the EU economy. However, what was needed above all was an economy characterised by solidarity – 'solidarity between those who have jobs and those who do not; solidarity between the generations; solidarity between the richer and poorer regions' and 'solidarity, lastly and most importantly, in the fight against social exclusion' (p. 15). This statement indicates the clear link drawn between the EU's economic and social policy objectives.

The major proposals in GCE were essentially a continuation of the supply-side initiatives of the type that characterised the structural funds. Thus, there were proposals for lifelong education and training provision with each country aiming towards universally accessible advanced vocational training. Government expenditure on the unemployed should be shifted to 'active measures' to promote employment.

The second White Paper, *European Social Policy: A Way Forward for the Union* (*ESP*), suggested that although levels of social solidarity in the EU had been higher than in either the USA or Japan in the past, 'such solidarity has been mainly passive. It is devoted to maintaining the incomes of large groups in society – by providing cash benefits through the redistribution of income, shouldered by an ever declining active population – without preparing them sufficiently to contribute to economic activity' (p. 11). It argued that there was a need to shift from the objective of assistance to the objective of employment generation and suggested that the key to both social and economic integration was employment: 'Continuing social progress can be built only on economic prosperity, and therefore on the competitiveness of the European economy' (p. 12).

Both the White Paper and the action programme that complemented it argued that, rather than more EU social policy legislation, there should be consolidation and encouragement of the various national systems to move towards the common goals identified in the White Paper. The structural funds, and, in particular, the European Social Fund, were identified as the main Union instrument for promoting cohesion.

The next major development in the 1990s was the preparation and signing of the new Treaty of the EU, the *Amsterdam Treaty*, which was designed to streamline the decision-making processes of the Union in preparation for enlargement and to allow EU policies to be developed without unnecessary delays caused by the individual member states. In both these regards the Amsterdam Treaty has been judged subsequently as a significant disappointment, if not a complete failure. Positive moves were made in some areas such as EU citizenship rights and the allowing of a greater role for the European Parliament in decision making. But the major questions of institutional reform were either fudged or simply postponed for later decision. Yet in the areas of social policy and the EU's broader socio-economic interventions it may be suggested that the Amsterdam Treaty was somewhat more successful. Following the return of a Labour government in 1997, the UK was finally

"I am sorry darling, but 454 grammes of flesh just sounds wrong to me."

Source: www.CartoonStock.com

brought back fully into the EU fold by agreeing to the incorporation of the Agreement on Social Policy signed by the other 11 member states at Maastricht. The agreement has now become an integral part (Title VIII) of the new Treaty. The new Article B at the very start of the new Treaty certainly appeared to commit the EU unequivocally to:

> [P]romote economic and social progress and a high level of employment and to achieve balanced and sustainable development . . . through the strengthening of economic and social cohesion.

There was also a new Community task (Article 2), which seemed to set social policy concerns right at the heart of the EU's project, albeit in economistic terms:

> [T]o promote throughout the Community a harmonious, balanced and sustainable development of economic activities, a high level of employment and of social protection, equality between men and women, sustainable and non-inflationary growth, a high degree of competitiveness and convergence of economic performance, a high level of protection and improvement of the quality of the environment, the raising of the standard of living and quality of life, and economic and social cohesion and solidarity among Member-states.

Yet perhaps the most significant part of the Treaty from a social policy perspective was the new chapter (3) on employment since, as we have already seen, employment policy has become the central focus of the EU's social dimension. Under this chapter the member states agreed to develop a coordinated strategy for employment and to regard promoting employment as a matter of common concern. Furthermore, the Community itself was committed to support the member states and, if necessary, complement their actions on employment.

Current issues and developments

So where does EU social policy stand at the start of the 21st century? All the treaties and other decisions that were reviewed earlier, alongside a whole raft of other measures, such as action programmes and observatories, mean that the social dimension of the EU has now become a much more developed and significant part of the overall activities of the EU. The range of interventions listed under the Directorate of Employment and Social Affairs now covers a very wide range of fields. These include: pensions and other forms of social protection; the European Social Fund; equal opportunities between women and men; anti-discrimination and fundamental social rights; health and safety; disability issues; social inclusion. These areas are in addition to a whole host of interventions focusing on the employment field. Beyond the Directorate of Employment and Social Affairs Directorate are a further range of social policy-related activities, which are the responsibility of the Directorate for Regional Policy, including the Regional Development Fund, the Cohesion Fund and the

Solidarity Fund. EU education and training policy falls within the remit of the Directorate General for Education and Culture. Although at present comparatively less developed than the other areas of EU social policy, there is also now a growing range of activities in the area of public health such as smoking and communicable diseases such as SARS and also food safety interventions. These areas fall within the remit of the Directorate General for Health and Consumer Protection. In short, the EU has come a long way from the very limited social policy activity of earlier years.

Social policymaking in the EU

In order to make sense of EU social policymaking and its impact on the member states it is necessary to have some idea of the key decision-making bodies of the EU. It is also important to understand how the basic processes of policymaking involve these bodies in different ways. This applies not only to policymaking, but also to policy delivery in the member states. In addition to the EU's own major policymaking bodies there are the different national governments and their sub-national administrative systems (such as regional and local government bodies), which together carry out the policies. A term which has frequently been used to describe the EU policymaking process, both for social policy and for other policy areas, is 'multilevel governance' (see also Chapter 2). This refers to the fact that social policymaking within the EU involves a variety of bodies: formal EU institutions and consultative bodies; national governments and sub-national organisations; politicians and full-time officials at both national and EU level; policy communities and so on. All these bodies may be involved in the policymaking process within the EU in different ways on different policies and at sub-national, national and transnational (European) levels. In this section we shall outline the key policymaking bodies for social policy, their roles, and what multilevel governance looks like in the social policy context.

Key EU social policymaking bodies

The key bodies in terms of EU social policymaking are:

- the European Commission
- the Council of the European Union and the European Council
- the European Parliament.

However, alongside these four bodies there are some other EU bodies that have a role in social policy development and delivery. Two of the most important are the European Economic and Social Committee and the Committee of the Regions.

European Commission

The European Commission represents the whole EU and has four main roles:

1 to propose legislation to Parliament and the Council

2 to manage and implement EU policies and the budget

3 to enforce European law (jointly with the Court of Justice)

4 to represent the European Union on the international stage, for example by negotiating agreements between the EU and other countries.

When the term 'Commission' is used it can refer to two different but related aspects of the overall institution. The first is as the 20 men and women commissioners appointed by the member states and the European Parliament who head up the different sections of the institution and take decisions. The second is as the institution itself and the permanent staff who work in its various offices and component agencies. Currently, the part of the Commission having the main responsibility for what most would recognise as social policy is called the Directorate General (DG) for Employment and Social Affairs. However, while a commissioner is responsible for the DG, day-to-day control rests with the person known as the Director General. However, the DG for Employment and Social Affairs is not the only one with some sort of social policy role. Policies relating to the structural funds, the Cohesion Fund and the Solidarity Fund are all managed through the DG for Regional Policy. There are also clear social policy links between the work of this DG and that for Employment and Social Affairs.

Council of the European Union and the European Council

These two bodies have been grouped together because, while they are separate entities, they are very much linked. What is more, and not least since the EU itself often refers to both bodies as 'the Council', it is very easy to get confused between them. To add to this difficulty there is another, non-EU, international organisation called the Council of Europe. Let us first look at the Council of the European Union (referred to here as 'the Council') then the European Council.

Formally, the Council is the EU's main decision-making body. It represents the member states and its meetings are attended by one minister from each of the EU's national governments. Which ministers attend depends on what subjects are on the agenda and there are nine different Council configurations depending on the policy areas. These include economic and financial affairs; education, youth and culture; justice and home affairs; agriculture and fisheries; and one that deals with employment, social policy, health and consumer affairs. Each minister acts on behalf of and commits his/her government to the decisions of the Council. Thus the Council has among its responsibilities the role of passing European laws: in many areas it makes policy and laws along with the European Parliament. Within this body decisions are made on the basis of what is known as qualified majority voting (QMV). This means that the countries with the larger populations, such as the UK, Germany and France get more votes than the less populous countries, such as Luxembourg and Ireland (Policy eye 15.2). The number of votes is not strictly proportional, however, since the smaller countries get more votes than population proportionality alone would justify. The idea behind this system of QMV is that individual countries cannot veto decision making in the policy areas where this system applies and also that the bigger countries alone cannot force through legislation against the wishes of the smaller countries. Under the new EU Constitution from 2004 the system of QMV was simplified and applied to more areas of policy. This is a highly contentious point, not least with regard to certain aspects of social and economic policy and the last section of this chapter will return to this.

The European Council is made up of the heads of state of the member states and its principal role is described in Article 4 of the Treaty on European Union as follows: 'The European Council shall provide the Union with the necessary impetus for its development and shall define the general political guidelines thereof.' What this means in practice is that although the European Council does not legally exist as an EU institution it is nevertheless a major decision-making body within it. Up to 2004 the Presidency of the Council rotated every

Policy eye 15.2   Qualified majority voting

Until 1 May 2004 countries each had the following votes:

Germany, France, Italy, the UK	10
Spain	8
Belgium, Greece, the Netherlands, Portugal	5
Austria, Sweden	4
Denmark, Ireland, Finland	3
Luxembourg	2

A majority of 62 of the 87 votes was required.

The system of QMV to be used after 1 May 2004 (when the ten new member states joined the EU) is based on 345 votes, with a qualified majority requiring 245 votes *and* a majority of member states *and* that the votes cast represent at least 62% of the EU's population. The votes per member state range from 29 (France, Germany, Italy and the UK) to 3 (Malta).

six months between the 15 member states so that each country could be said to be able to provide a particular lead or focus for the EU's work during that period; however, there were proposals to change this arrangement under the new Constitution. The meetings of the European Council provide the major 'set piece' events that punctuate the EU's yearly activities and it is often these events that receive the media coverage we see on our television and in newspapers. The probable reason for this is that these meetings provide crucial decision points when the EU as a whole agrees (or sometimes does not agree!) major policy developments.

European Parliament

The European Parliament (EP) is directly elected by the citizens of the EU member states. The members (MEPs) sit in broad party groupings, not in national blocs. As a whole the EP is thus supposed to make its decisions on an EU-wide not an inter-governmental basis.

The Parliament has three main roles:

1 It shares with the Council the power to make policies and laws.

2 It is expected to exercise democratic supervision over all EU institutions and, in particular, the Commission. It has the power to approve or reject the nomination of Commissioners and it has the right to censure the Commission as a whole.

3 It shares with the Council authority over the EU budget and can therefore influence EU spending. At the end of the procedure, it adopts or rejects the budget in its entirety.

The most common procedure for adopting (passing) EU legislation is 'co-decision'. This places the European Parliament and the Council on an equal footing and the laws passed using this procedure are joint acts of the Council and Parliament. It applies to legislation in a wide range of fields. On a range of other proposals Parliament need only be consulted. Parliament also provides impetus for new legislation by examining the Commission's annual work programme, considering what new laws would be appropriate and asking the Commission to put forward proposals. In this sense it could be argued that the EP has a policy-*formulation* role as well as a policymaking role. In practice, however, the European Council and the Commission are much more influential in the policy-formulation role.

So how do these bodies link together in terms of social policymaking? Although there are three main forms of decision making in the EU – co-decision, consultation and assent – the most common and increasingly used method is co-decision. In the co-decision procedure, Parliament and the Council share legislative power. The Commission sends its proposal to both institutions. They each read and discuss it twice in succession. If they cannot agree on it, it is put before a 'conciliation committee', composed of equal numbers of Council and Parliament representatives. Commission representatives also attend the committee meetings and contribute to the discussion. Once the committee has reached an agreement, the agreed text is then sent to Parliament and the Council for a third reading, so that they can finally adopt it as law.

The areas covered by the co-decision procedure include the major areas of social policy for the EU such as social security for migrant workers, social exclusion, equal opportunities and equal treatment, implementing decisions regarding the European Social Fund, education, vocational training, health and the European Regional Development Fund.

Despite this formal statement however, the analyst of policymaking in the EU needs to look at specific policies at particular times to see how different levels of the system operate together. It is almost impossible to provide a general statement about how this operates for all areas of policy, even when limited to a consideration of social policy. When discussing social policy, however, and in particular issues such as pensions, unemployment benefits and other forms of social protection it is quite clear that the member states have jealously guarded their right to make policy in these areas with only limited intervention from the EU. Both politically and financially, these areas of welfare provision are highly contentious and the EU now accepts that its role in these areas should be that of information collector, monitor and reporter of good practice that the different member states may choose to take account of in their own countries in their own ways. In this regard the EU and the member states are therefore applying two key principles of EU policymaking: *subsidiarity* and *proportionality*. The term 'subsidiarity' is used in the EU to refer to the principle that the EU should act as a body that complements rather than supersedes its member states' authority. Or, to put it in the EU's own terms: the Union does not take action (except on matters for which it alone is responsible) unless EU action is more effective than action taken at national, regional or local level. The idea of 'proportionality' complements subsidiarity and refers to the principle that EU action should only occur to the extent necessary to meet its treaty and other obligations. In practice, what this sometimes means is that social policy initiatives are developed 'indirectly' or via a previous EU decision or provision that may not seem, at first sight, to be completely relevant. An example of this is the way in which equal opportunities legislation affecting men and women has been progressed not through statements and policy proposals expressing the ethical, social or political case for equal opportunities, but rather about the need to provide a level playing field in employment and in more general economic terms across the EU. Thus some of the legislation about equal opportunities refers to the need for women workers to be treated equally across the EU to prevent certain countries or employers taking advantage of their competitors by employing cheaper female labour, while some draws on health and safety in the workplace provisions. The outcomes have, arguably, become significant for men and women beyond the workplace but they have had to be developed within the framework and principles of policymaking all the same.

EU social policy now and in the future

The EU now has a considerable range of social policy interventions that may be argued to affect not only the welfare states that are EU members, but also other welfare states in the rest of Europe. The reason why its social policy may be said to extend beyond the member states is that the model of social policy that is increasingly being developed within the EU has economic, as well as social and political implications for the other countries in Europe. Their governments and their citizens are part of an increasingly interlinked economic network within which welfare provisions are a crucial factor (see Chapter 16). Indeed, in the developing global economy the EU 'social model' might be said to have significance well beyond the boundaries of Europe. So what is the current character of this social model in the EU? How can we summarise the character and content of EU social policy at present and what can we say about its future possible development?

EU social policy summarised

As we argued earlier, the EU now has a range of social policy and social policy responsibilities as part of its activities. A useful summary of the overall picture can be found in the EU's Social Policy Agenda. This identifies the following main features:

- the European employment strategy
- improving working conditions and standards
- social inclusion and social protection
- equality of women and men.

Thus we might summarise the overall character of the EU's social policy as being predominantly focused on the labour market and work-related provisions, even where many of these provisions actually extend beyond the workplace in practice. To UK eyes this may seem unusual, but the link between social policy and employment has been a central feature of many of the other European welfare states almost since the inception of their modern welfare systems. To this extent, it may be the case that EU social policy is already encouraging a convergence around work and employment conditions as the focus for social policy provision in the future development of welfare provision across the EU. Three major studies of EU social policy by Geyer (2000), Hantrais (2000) and Kleinmann (2002) clearly indicate that social policy in the EU continues to have extremely strong links to the EU's economic project. Yet some have argued that this character may be changing somewhat, as a result of the spread of the EU's intervention beyond workplace issues – for example ethnic and racial discrimination, public health and human rights – and that it may possibly be developing the character of a more broadly based welfare system. Threlfall (2002), for example, has argued that the range of EU social policy intervention is now so broad that it is difficult to argue that the previous focus on labour market concerns can now be said to characterise its social policy interventions as a whole. What is more, she argues, the EU's Charter of Fundamental Rights already suggests a possible shift to a more citizen- (rather than worker-) based approach to welfare. Currently, the Charter is no more than a 'solemn proclamation', although each member state is a signatory to it. The Charter does not create any new power or task for the EU, but it does state that member states are expected to 'respect the rights, observe the principles and promote the application thereof' when implementing EU law (European Commission, undated). From a social policy perspective there are a number of very significant clauses in the Charter, which, were it to become something which was enforceable in law across the EU, would have some very significant impact. For example, Article 34 entitled 'Social security and social assistance' contains the following clauses:

1   the Union recognizes and respects the entitlement to social security benefits and social services providing protection in cases of maternity, illness, industrial accidents, dependency, or old age, and in the case of loss of employment

2   everyone residing and moving legally within the European Union is entitled to social security benefits and social advantages

3   in order to combat social exclusion and poverty, the Union recognizes and respects the right to social and housing assistance.

In Article 35 the Charter refers to the right to preventive healthcare and the right to medical treatment. Elsewhere in the Charter reference is made to a right to education (Article 14), the prohibition of discrimination on the grounds of race, sex, religion, birth, disability etc. (Article 21), that equality between men and women must be ensured in all areas, including employment and pay (Article 22) and to the right of children to have access to 'such protection and care as is necessary for their well-being' (Article 23). Were such provisions to become subject to legal enforcement as, for example human rights legislation now is in Britain, then one can imagine that this might lead further along the path towards a trans-EU welfare regime rather more integrated than the mix of different national welfare regimes that currently prevails. Some, who regard this prospect with alarm (for example the Conservative Party and other Eurosceptics in the UK), fear that the proposed move to an EU Constitution would have precisely this effect. The Constitution is associated with the enlargement of the EU by the addition of ten new member states on 1 May 2004 and to that we now turn.

The ten new member states are primarily from the ex-Soviet bloc – the Czech Republic, Estonia, Latvia, Lithuania, Poland, Hungary, Slovakia and Slovenia – plus two others from the south – Cyprus and Malta. Together, these countries added 74 million people to make a new EU total population of 455 million. However, the combined GDP of the ten new member states represents only 5 per cent of the total GDP of the EU 15 and, as Table 15.4 shows, the GDP of the new members is considerably below that of the EU average in almost all cases (see also Table 15.3).

So what are the implications of these facts for social policy in the EU following enlargement? In the first place, it is quite clear from the already stated policy of the European Commission that one of the first priorities in the period immediately after accession of these ten new countries is to bring their economies closer to the level of the rest of the EU. What this will mean in terms of direct EU intervention is that the structural funds that have previously been targeted at certain of the regions and countries within the EU 15 are now to be targeted on the new member states. Given that only a very small increase in the amount of these funds has been agreed by the member states, the clear outcome will be that some will get less in order that the new states may get more.

In order to join the EU the new member states were supposed to have achieved certain standards in terms of their welfare provision. Yet it is clear that the ex-Soviet bloc states have witnessed an almost total collapse of their social policy provisions at the same time that they have moved into the capitalist economic mainstream. What is more, as various studies indicate (see, for example, Ferge 2001) these countries have established economic and social policies that are much closer to the neo-liberal approach of the United States than to the mixed economies of welfare prevalent in the other EU states. This means that problems of unemployment, poverty and social exclusion as well as housing and social care provision, welfare provision for children and a whole host of other provisions are poorly catered for in some of the new member states. Some politicians in the western European member states fear that, as a result, significant numbers of people from eastern European countries will migrate to the west in search of work and a better standard of life, putting further pressure on the welfare systems of countries such as the Netherlands, the UK and others. Others argue that, given the ageing population and other factors discussed at the beginning of this chapter, the boost to the labour markets of the western EU economies offered by younger migrants and those with certain skills can only be beneficial to the receiving economies. There is clearly a political disagreement that will continue to develop in coming years as to which, if either, of these scenarios becomes reality. One

Table 15.4 Percentage GDP per head in the May 2004 accession states (index EU 15 = 100, in PPS)

	Cyprus	Czech Republic	Estonia	Hungary	Latvia	Lithuania	Malta	Poland	Slovak Republic	Slovenia
1995	83	62	34	46	25	32	53	34	46	63
2001	77	57	42	51	33	38	:	40	48	69

Source: Adapted from European Commission (2003), Annex IV

thing seems clear, however, and that is that the EU is set to change dramatically in the early years of the 21st century and EU social policy seems set to become one of the most contentious areas of development as both member states and the EU overall struggle to respond to these changes. It would certainly not be accurate to say that there is a 'European welfare state' within the EU at present. Social policy is still very much the preserve of the individual member states, albeit it within the context of an overall EU strategy that is very much focused on employment as the key to welfare. Yet a broad 'social model' could be said to exist that demarcates the EU from other welfare systems in other parts of the world. The future of this model could be seen to be under threat from a variety of pressures such as economic globalisation, demographic change and the simple problems of scale and differentiation between 455 million people. One analyst has, however, suggested that the enlargement process itself may prove to be one of the most damaging threats to this 'social model'. Vaughan-Whitehead (2003) argues that the move towards neo-liberal economic and social policies in the new states, a reduction of some social provisions in the existing member states and a similar 'modernisation' of the EU's social provisions, plus a move towards global markets and the seen imperative of making economies more flexible and competitive 'may well lead to a progressive collapse of social policy in an enlarged EU' (2003: 530). While this may prove to be too pessimistic a judgement, it does reinforce the view that change, rather than continuity, in EU social policy now seems the more likely prospect.

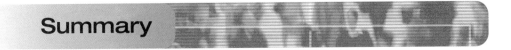

Summary

This chapter has explored the development of social policy within the EU, having reflected on the different patterns of need in the constituent member states. It suggests that:

- As we saw in the first section of this chapter, the EU 15 countries share a broad range of characteristics (associated with unemployment, poverty and an ageing population, for example) that generate social policy concerns both for the national governments and, arguably, for the EU itself.

- Although these social policy 'problems' may be broadly shared, their intensity and significance in some countries and regions are much greater than in others. Unemployment problems, for example, are generally much worse in the south than in the north of the EU, and since the May 2004 accession are even more problematic within most of the eastern European countries. This regional variation in social policy problems across the EU is a characteristic feature in the context of EU intervention.

● Economic targets and economic policy have been predominant in the EU, including in the development of social policy. Current policies have a distinctly 'economic' focus and refer largely to labour market and employment-related isuues. Thus, they do not have the full range that they may have in individual member states – they do not, for example, include policies on social care or housing. Nevertheless, the accumulated legislation and other forms of social policy intervention at the EU level are now extensive. There is no 'European welfare state' but there is now a significant body of EU social policy.

● Further change is likely. Two factors make this clear. First, the significance of the EU Charter of Fundamental Rights could mean that EU social policy changes character from an economic focus to one more linked to citizens' rights. Second, the accession of the central and eastern European states is likely to provide a significantly increased social policy 'burden' on the EU, which could mean that it has to undertake a fundamental restructuring of these policies for the whole EU.

Discussion and review topics

1 To what extent do the EU's member states face similar social problems?

2 Why has employment dominated the EU's social policy agenda?

3 Which bodies of the EU play the most important roles in formulating and implementing social policies?

4 What impact has the accession of ten new members states in 2004 had on the development of EU social policy?

Further reading

Geyer, R. (2000) *Exploring European Social Policy*, Polity, Cambridge – provides a comprehensive overview of the subject including development of EU social policy, its main areas and the role of the structural funds

Hantrais, L. (2000) *Social Policy in the European Union*, Palgrave Macmillan, Basingstoke – examines European social policy including as it relates to national policymaking and implementation

Kleinmann, M. (2002) *A European welfare state?*, Palgrave Macmillan, Basingstoke – this book covers the role of economic integration and its implications for the scope and aims of social policy

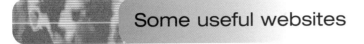

Some useful websites

The EU's websites provide a huge amount of information, much of it free to view and download. This is available from http://europa.eu.int

On EU social policy select 'Employment and social affairs' from among the various 'Activities' listed. This will provide most of the information on EU social policy, but useful information can also be found under 'Education, training and youth', 'Public health' and the 'Regional policy' activity links.

For information about the socio-economic situation in the various EU member states, the Eurostat web pages (http://europa.eu.int/comm/eurostat/) are a good source of information. For example, select the 'Themes' button and then the 'Population and social conditions' link.

References

European Commission (undated) Charter of Fundamental Rights Homepage. Published on the Web, http://europa.eu.int/comm/justice_home/unit/charte/index_en.html (04/05/2004)

European Commission (2003) *The Social Situation in the European Union 2003*, European Commission/Eurostat, Brussels

Ferge, Z. (2001) 'Welfare and "ill-fare" systems in Central-Eastern Europe', in Sykes, R., Palier, B. and Prior, P. M. (eds) *Globalization and European Welfare States: Challenges and Change*, Palgrave, Basingstoke

Geyer, R. (2000) *Exploring European Social Policy*, Polity, Cambridge

Hantrais, L. (2000) *Social Policy in the European Union*, Palgrave Macmillan, Basingstoke

Kleinmann, M. (2002) *A European welfare state?*, Palgrave Macmillan, Basingstoke

Threlfall, M. (2002) 'The European Union's social policy focus: from labour to welfare and constitutionalised rights?', in Sykes, R., Bochel, C. and Ellison, N. (eds) *Social Policy Review*, 14, The Policy Press, Bristol, 171–94

Vaughan-Whitehead, D. (2003) *EU Enlargement versus Social Europe? The Uncertain Future of the European Social Model*, Edward Elgar, Cheltenham

Globalisation, welfare and social policy: issues and developments

16

Rob Sykes

Issues in Focus

This chapter deals with one of the great controversies of current times: the development of globalisation in various forms throughout the world and its effects on our lives, socially, politically and economically.

The controversy is not simply about what globalisation *is*, however. It is also about whether globalisation is a 'good' or a 'bad' thing. The key issue that is contested is one that is central to our interest in welfare and social policy: does globalisation improve or worsen the welfare of the peoples of the world? As the chapter will explain, there are those who argue from either side, but can they both be right? The chapter examines some of the major questions around this debate:

- what is globalisation? contested ideas – contested reality?
- the variety of globalisation processes – social, political and economic;
- globalisation and welfare:
- globalisation and the future of welfare.

What is globalisation? Contested ideas – contested reality?

Although the term has become a part of our lives, 'globalisation' remains a fundamentally contested concept (see Briefing 16.1). For some, globalisation has already arrived in a variety of economic, social and political senses. Some of these, who are commonly termed 'anti-globalists', are critical of what is happening, suggesting that unfettered globalisation is detrimental to the economic, political and cultural interests of most ordinary people. This, essentially, is the position of those who demonstrate at meetings of the major governments, such as the G8 summits and European Union summits. Contrariwise, some 'globalists', such as the World Bank, the US government and other major governments in the west, accept that globalisation is a 'fact of life' in the contemporary world, but argue that, properly managed, it can and indeed does benefit people in both the richer and poorer countries of the world.

Then there are those who are sceptical of the claims that globalisation already exists, cannot be avoided and already conditions the lives of all in the contemporary world, whether for good or ill. For these, usually academic, writers, much of the discussion surrounding globalisation and many of the claims about its impact on our lives, are essentially hype and exaggeration and for this reason should be seen more as myth than reality.

In the context of this fundamental dispute both about whether globalisation even exists, as well as debates about the forms it takes and the impacts it may have, we clearly need to unravel the competing positions somewhat more before we can move on to consider globalisation's importance with regard to social policy.

The term 'globalisation' has been used to refer to a bewildering variety of phenomena: from the spread of worldwide financial linkages to the growing power of multinational corporations able effectively to control national and

Briefing 16.1   Definitions of globalisation

'Global capitalism, driven by the TNCs [transnational corporations], organized politically through the transnational capitalist class, and fuelled by the culture-ideology of consumerism, is the most potent force for change in the world today.' Sklair (2002)

'Global economic integration has supported poverty reduction and should not be reversed.' Collier and Dollar (2001)

'"Globalization" is a big idea resting on slim foundations.' Weiss (1998)

'Globalization, as conceived by the more extreme globalizers, is largely a myth.' Hirst and Thompson (1999)

international economic activities; from the spread of the 'Coca-Cola culture' and 'McDonaldisation' as both economic and social developments to the growth of worldwide television, telecommunications and the internet; from the growing influence of international organisations, such as the International Monetary Fund and the European Union, to the 'shrinking' of the world through air travel and mass tourism; from the growth of a high cost, consumer culture with recognised world brands such as Nike and Microsoft, to the increasing impoverishment of millions especially those living in the poorer countries of the world. We could extend this list almost endlessly – some see globalisation as evident in almost every aspect of our lives.

The central point here is that globalisation is both a contested concept and a contested reality. Not only are there disagreements about how globalisation should be understood, theorised and analysed, there are also disagreements about what actually constitutes globalisation in economic and/or social and/or political senses. What this means for anybody trying to make sense of globalisation is that they need to be constantly aware that both general discussions of globalisation, as well as accounts of the relationship between globalisation and other areas of social and economic life such as welfare policies of, say, the European Union, are intrinsically disputable. To provide a focal example of this sort of contestation, there are those (for example, the World Bank and most western governments) who argue that globalisation (ultimately) reduces world poverty and inequality, and those (such as the various groups of anti-global demonstrators and a number of governments in Africa, Asia and Latin America) who argue that it makes world poverty and inequality worse. This dispute is both about how globalisation does or does not increase poverty and inequality and about the evidence marshalled by each side to prove its point (the debate between Wade and Wolf (2002) is a good example of this).

Does this mean that arguments and conclusions about globalisation and its effects are simply a matter of choice? While it is true that the arguments about globalisation and the views that different people have about its role are certainly imbued with political and ethical preferences, in academic terms, at least, we can point to the way in which similarly disputed concepts have been dealt with to indicate how globalisation ought to be understood and analysed. The term 'democracy' has been subject to massive and continuing debate in both popular and academic realms. It is often used by politicians in various discourses about the alleged superiority of some forms of government and political processes over others; for example to denigrate the (alleged) failings of the politics of countries such as Iraq and North Korea as compared with the (alleged) strengths of countries such as the USA and the UK. George W. Bush continually used such discourse in general terms when talking of a *New World Order*, as well as a justification, in part, for the war on Iraq in 2003. Yet academics have deconstructed such essentially subjective and even emotional uses of the term democracy to illustrate that (a) political discourse about 'democracy' is essentially contestable – different people mean different things – and (b) it is possible to categorise in more or less objective terms what these different ideas of democracy and politics look like (see, for example, Held

1996). The debate about globalisation in recent years is gradually being subjected to similar academic deconstruction and analysis. While debates about globalisation – just like debates about democracy, political power, social class etc. – will continue to be characterised by conceptual and evidential dispute, it is already possible at least to separate out the different ways in which 'globalisation' is used and the different sorts of evidence which would be needed to test out these competing approaches. This is vital if we are to be clear about the possible links between globalisation and social policy. So let us unpack still further what has been suggested about the character of globalisation in terms of its social, political and economic forms (see cartoon on p346). Then we can see how these different elements are combined in arguments about globalisation and welfare and, indeed, suggest which of these approaches seem to provide the most useful framework for understanding what is happening in recent social policy developments.

The variety of globalisation processes – social, political and economic

As the previous paragraphs indicate, most arguments about the development of globalisation are either challenged or disputed by alternative readings. Borrowing from Held and McGrew (2002), we can recognise two broad groups: the 'globalisers' and the 'sceptics'. The first group is composed of those who argue that globalisation processes are already developed or are developing rapidly across the world. The second group are those who doubt that an overall system of globalisation has developed and suggest that many of the assertions made by the globalisers are either overstated and/or are less different from previous circumstances than the globalisers are prepared to admit. For reasons of space and emphasis, we shall not consider the arguments of the 'sceptics' in any detail in the following sections, focusing rather on the main assertions of the 'globalisers' so that we can then consider how far these assertions are borne out in the case of globalisation and social policy later. As will become apparent, however, many, if not most, of the assertions made by the globalisers are challengeable.

Social and cultural globalisation

It has been argued by a variety of sociologists and cultural analysts that communications systems now exist that are both instantaneous in their effect and global in their scope. Giddens (1990, 1991), Harvey (1989) and Robertson (1992) have each, in their different ways, suggested that not only are individuals, localities and nations now more effectively linked, but that the world now is (or appears to be) shrunk and compressed: we are living in a 'global village; there has been a shrinking of 'time–space distanciation'. Here the role of the internet, cable and satellite TV, cell phones and such like, are all cited as examples of the ways in which more and more people are able to experience life outside their own local and national contexts and even to partake of almost instantaneous communication with other people living thousands of miles away.

"Sorry lads.I'm closing this workshop down,and relocating in the far east."

Source: www.CartoonStock.com

Yet in the field of cultural studies and sociology it is not simply the role of information and communication technologies and other technologies that are considered: rather there is a concern with how social and cultural life has more generally been affected by and indeed affects globalisation processes. So it is both the consciousness of and responses to globalisation that such theorists concern themselves with. Some argue that a global awareness now exists for many people living around the world – we are all now, or so it is argued, 'global citizens'. This may mean that national, ethnic, class, gender and other distinctions are becoming less and less relevant. What is more, flows of migrant groups, tourists and refugees alongside the free flow of ideas, information, images and cultural products are all said to be contributing to forms of cultural globalisation. Indeed, for some, a 'global culture' already (incipiently) exists, even if its supposedly 'global' character has a very western/US form. Some then proceed to identify forms of cultural imperialism, a growth of cultural homogenisation and uniformity, while others see precisely the same processes facilitating and generating renewed forms of cultural identity and difference, such as ethno-nationalism and religious fundamentalism.

Political globalisation

In the field of politics and international relations much is made of the connection between economic changes and their consequences for national and international politics. For example, it is often argued that the very shifts in the world economy towards interlinkage and interconnectedness mean that the autonomy and authority of sovereign nation states is now challenged, if not superseded. Some go as far as to argue that globalisation theory is fundamentally about the role of the state as a political entity, while others argue that the demise of the (nation state) is a myth (see Weiss 1998).

Constraints imposed by international economic forces in a 'globalised' environment, and in particular by transnational corporations (TNCs, see Briefing 16.2) and **intergovernmental organisations** (IGOs) such as the World Bank and the World Trade Organisation, have, according to the former view, emasculated states as policymakers and as sovereign authorities within their national boundaries. There has also been a qualitative shift of power away from governments towards non-state actors such as businesses and industrial interests more generally, but also IGOs and **non-governmental organisations** (NGOs). The number of international organisations, all of whom may be said to affect, or even supersede the authority of nation states, is now quite large. As Figure 16.1 shows, these organisations operate in the fields of economic intervention, security, welfare and the environment.

Another dimension of the globalisation of politics is the way in which, it is argued, issues are increasingly perceived as global in character and thus requiring global solutions. In this sense political globalisation refers to the argument that social, economic, environmental issues are now essentially transnational and worldwide in both their significance and resolution.

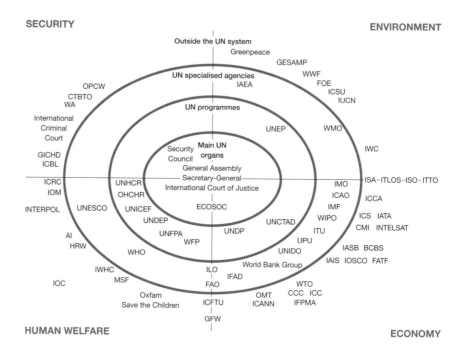

SECURITY

ENVIRONMENT

Outside the UN system
Greenpeace
GESAMP
WWF
UN specialised agencies
IAEA
FOE
ICSU
IUCN
OPCW
CTBTO
WA
UN programmes
International
Criminal
Court
UNEP
WMO
GICHD
ICBL
Main UN
organs
Security
Council
General Assembly
Secretary-General
International Court of Justice
IWC
ICRC
IOM
UNHCR
OHCHR
IMO
ICAO
ICCA
ISA – ITLOS – ISO – ITTO
INTERPOL
UNESCO
UNICEF
ECOSOC
IMF
WIPO
ICS   IATA
ICCA
UNDEP
UNCTAD
ITU
CMI   INTELSAT
AI
HRW
UNFPA
WFP
UNDP
UPU
IASB BCBS
WHO
UNIDO
IAIS IOSCO FATF
IWHC
MSF
ILO
IFAD
World Bank Group
WTO
IOC
FAO
CCC ICC
Oxfam
Save the Children
OMT
ICANN
IFPMA
ICFTU
GFW

HUMAN WELFARE

ECONOMY

Key to abbreviations

AI	Amnesty International
BCBS	Basel Committee on Banking Supervision
CCC	Customs Cooperation Council
CMI	Comité Maritime International
CTBTO	Comprehensive Nuclear-Test-Ban Treaty Organization (not yet operational)
ECOSOC	UN Economic and Social Council
FAO	Food and Agriculture Organization
FATF	Financial Action Task Force
FOE	Friends of the Earth
GESAMP	Joint Group of Experts on the Scientific Aspects of Marine Environmental Protection
GFW	Global Fund for Women
GICHD	Geneva International Centre for Humanitarian Demining
HRW	Human Rights Watch
IAEA	International Atomic Energy Agency
IAIS	International Association of Insurance Supervisors
IASB	International Accounting Standards Board
IATA	International Association of Transport Airlines
ICANN	Internet Corporation for Assigned Names and Numbers
ICAO	International Civil Aviation Organization
ICBL	International Campaign to Ban Landmines
ICC	International Chamber of Commerce
ICCA	International Council of Chemical Associations
ICFTU	International Confederation of Free Trade Unions
ICRC	International Committee of the Red Cross
ICS	International Chamber of Shipping
ICSU	International Council for Science
IFAD	International Fund for Agricultural Development
IFPMA	International Federation of Pharmaceutical Manufacturers Associations
ILO	International Labour Organization
IMF	International Monetary Fund
IMO	International Maritime Organization
INTELSAT	International Telecommunications Satellites Organization
INTERPOL	International Criminal Police Organization
IOC	International Olympic Committee
IOM	International Organization for Migration
IOSCO	International Organization of Securities Commissions
ISA	International Seabed Authority
ISO	International Organization for Standardization
ITLOS	International Tribunal for the Law of the Sea
ITTO	International Tropical Timber Organization
ITU	International Telecommunication Union
IUCN	World Conservation Union
IWC	International Whaling Commission
IWHC	International Women's Health Coalition
MSF	Médecins Sans Frontières
OHCHR	Office of the High Commissioner for Human Rights
OMT	World Tourism Organization
OPCW	Organization for the Prohibition of Chemical Weapons
UNCTAD	UN Conference on Trade and Development
UNDCP	UN Drug Control Programme
UNDP	UN Development Programme
UNEP	UN Environment Programme
UNESCO	UN Educational. Scientific and Cultural Organization
UNFPA	UN Population Fund
UNHCR	UN High Commissioner for Refugees
UNICEF	UN Children's Fund
UNIDO	UN Industrial Development Organization
UPU	Universal Postal Union
WA	Wassenaar Arrangement on Export Controls for Conventional Arms and Dual-Use Goods and Technologies
WFP	World Food Programme
WHO	World Health Organization
WIPO	World Intellectual Property Organization
WMO	World Meteorological Organization
WTO	World Trade Organization
WWF	Worldwide Fund for Nature

Figure 16.1 Organizational infrastructure of global governance: a UN-centric view

Source: Koenig-Archibugi (2002), pp. 64–65

Environmental issues such as global warming, pollution and the development of genetically modified (GM) crops do not recognise or remain within national boundaries. Accordingly, governments, TNCs, NGOs, trade unions and even community groups and other social movements are increasingly directing political action to the global or international arena. This is certainly, although not exclusively, the case with anti-globalisation protesters who, in turn, have increasingly set the agenda for discussion if not the resolution of issues such as the indebtedness of developing countries and global poverty. One fascinating aspect of the development of these 'anti-globalisers' is the way in which they organise and act through the use of precisely the forms of ICT that are said to be facilitating many of the developments in capitalism they consider to be the 'evils of globalisation' (see, for example, websites such as www.protest.net; www.globalissues.org).

Economic globalisation

Arguments suggesting various forms of economic globalisation are by far the most numerous and common. They are also those most frequently linked to arguments about globalisation and social policy, so we shall concentrate on these at greater length than the arguments about social and political globalisation. We shall, nevertheless, return to the multifaceted economic *and* social *and* political character of globalisation when we attempt to identify the key features of globalisation for the analysis of social policy at the end of this section.

We are constantly told that governments and individual firms have to cope with the pressures of global economic competition and the problems associated with the interlinkage of the different economies of the world. The argument is that not only are we subject to a world capitalist economy that is increasingly competitive, increasingly dominated by large firms and/or trading blocs and within which national economies are less and less open to control by national agents such as governments, but also that this world economy is now so interdependent that changes in one part affect other parts with fundamental consequences that can be good or bad. Some say that the nature of the global economy, based on free markets and increasing trade, is essentially beneficial for all; others say that the system is unequal and benefits the developed economies most, generating a bigger and bigger gap between rich and poor both between countries (rich and poor nations) and within countries.

Those who argue for a global economy point to the unprecedented scale of world economic interaction. National economies, they argue, are enmeshed in what are now global patterns of production and exchange unlike any previous period. International economic integration is also at new levels both within and between different regions or economic blocs such as the USA, Japan and the EU. Ohmae (1990) is credited with suggesting that there is now a 'borderless world', where national boundaries are essentially irrelevant to what is, in essence, already a global economy.

> **Briefing 16.2** **Multinational corporations and transnational corporations**
>
> What is the difference between an MNC and a TNC? It is commonly suggested that MNCs have a clear national base, although they operate in more than one country. TNCs, by the same token, operate without any clear national 'home'. Thus a transnational corporation would produce and market its goods or services on a truly international scale.

According to this view, the current phase of economic globalisation is different from earlier internationalisation of the world's economies because now the system is essentially open (with no trade barriers, tariffs or such like) and integrated, with even the most marginal economies in some senses integrated in the world capitalist economy. There has been a parallel process of economic regionalisation in areas such as the single European market (a central feature of the European Community/EU), and the North American Free Trade Agreement (NAFTA). This form of regionalisation is an 'open' form of linkage, however, involving the liberalisation of national economies (for example, through loss of tariffs and rationalisation of production) rather than protectionism. As such, the modern economic regionalisation process has both been a response to and a facilitator of economic globalisation.

Although most economic flows are between the developed economies of the OECD (Organisation for Economic Co-operation and Development) member states, the share of world trade and investment flows has increased for developing countries too. If we look at long-term statistics we can see how the volume of world merchandise trade has increased very significantly in recent decades as compared with earlier periods of international trading (see Table 16.1).

Table 16.1 Export–GDP ratios, 1870–1998

Merchandise exports as % of GDP (1990 prices)

	1870	1913	1929	1950	1973	1998
France	4.9	7.8	8.6	7.6	15.2	28.7
Germany	9.5	16.1	12.8	6.2	23.8	38.9
Japan	0.2	2.4	3.5	2.2	7.7	13.4
UK	12.2	17.5	13.3	11.3	14.0	25.0
United States	2.5	3.7	3.6	3.0	4.9	10.1
World	4.6	7.9	9.0	5.5	10.5	17.2

Source: Maddison (2001), cited in Held and McGrew (2002)

Who or what are the agents of this globalising economy if it is not national economies or states? Multinational corporations (MNCs) and/or Transnational corporations (TNCs) are the central actors (Briefing 16.2).

As Held and McGrew (2002) point out, in 2000 there were some sixty thousand MNCs worldwide, with 820,000 foreign subsidiaries, selling $15.6 trillion of goods and services globally. Citing authorities such as UNCTAD (the United Nations Conference on Trade and Development), they also point out that the production of MNCs exceeds the level of all global exports and is now the primary means of selling goods and services abroad. MNCs now account for roughly 25 per cent of the world's production and 70 per cent of world trade and their sales account for about half the world's total GDP.

Spatially, these patterns of economic globalisation are creating changes in labour markets and the patterns of division of labour around the world. The deindustrialisation of the northern economies can be linked, according to this view, to increasing relocation of manufacturing activities to areas such as Latin America, East Asia and eastern Europe, as MNCs and others restructure production to the least expensive sites. Within countries too, the impact of

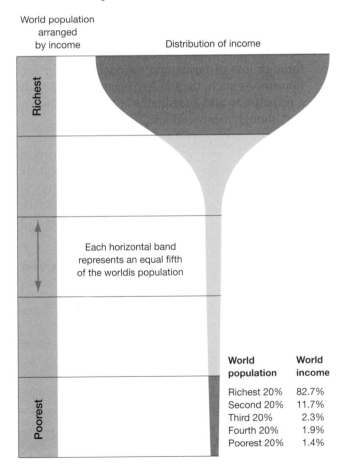

World population	World income
Richest 20%	82.7%
Second 20%	11.7%
Third 20%	2.3%
Fourth 20%	1.9%
Poorest 20%	1.4%

Figure 16.2 Wade's 'champagne glass' of world income distribution

Source: After Wade (2001). *Note*: National incomes are converted into US dollars at market exchange rates

economic globalisation is to create divisions between those with and those without jobs; those who live in areas that are integrated into the processes of economic growth and prosperity and those who do not. A new and more complex New International Division of Labour (NIDL) is developing and new patterns of wealth and inequality are developing to go with it (see Figure 16.2, p. 351).

Yet there are alternative, 'sceptical' views that suggest this 'hyperglobalist' account is essentially mistaken or, at least, overstates the case for a truly 'global economy'. We have used the terms 'interaction' and 'integration' when referring to the nature of economic globalisation earlier. Various measures exist to indicate that the capitalist economies around the world are now certainly interacting and trade measures are the most obvious example of this. The sceptics argue, however, that for a truly 'global economy' to exist it must also be integrated. The main measure used to consider the level of economic integration is that of capital flows expressed in terms of foreign direct investment (FDI). Here the picture is less supportive of an integrated global economy. The great majority (three-quarters) of FDI goes to developed economies. Indeed, the share of developing countries in global FDI flows declined from 38 per cent in 1997 to 24 per cent in 1999.

Hirst and Thompson have argued (1999) that examination of both trade and FDI measures indicates that the international economy has a degree of interdependency, but that it is not (yet) integrated into a single global economy. In fact, they suggest that the international economy was more integrated and interdependent in 1913 than it is today.

They and others also argue that the true cause of deindustrialisation and loss of (manufacturing) jobs in the north is only partially (around 10 to 20 per cent) explained by the shift of such jobs to cheaper developing economies. The main cause (up to 90 per cent), they suggest, is technological change in these developed economies, coupled with a shift in their nature from an industrial to a post-industrial character. Although these two trends are part and parcel of economic changes affecting the whole international economy, they were not caused by globalisation itself.

Key features of globalisation?

Clearly there is a very wide range of arguments about the various forms and dimensions of globalisation processes and we have only touched on a very small sample of these here. From this rather bewildering array of ideas we can, however, identify some key features and potential effects of globalisation from the point of view of social policy analysis.

The first and foremost notion is that globalisation involves an increasing interconnectedness between states, peoples and regions across the world. Increasingly, a range of social, economic and political processes operate at global rather than national or other local levels. What is more, these processes are occurring with increasing frequency and intensity at the global level – we communicate more frequently through email, telephone and fax across countries and regions; global financial transactions are now increasing in both volume and frequency; international organisations such as the EU and the WTO are responsible for more and more decisions and policies that affect both nation states and their citizens. Third, time and space have become compressed: world travel, whether for business or leisure purposes, is now more common and more frequent than ever before (SARS and AIDS became global health crises almost immediately they were discovered). There really are senses in which the world has now become smaller: we are now economically, physically and culturally 'closer together'. Through telecommunications, the spread of satellite television and other communications media, people are now more aware of the rest of the world and how developments in one part of it can affect their own lives. In short, these various aspects of globalisation may be said to link together the local and the global to such an extent that 'the impact of distant events is magnified while even the most local developments may come to have enormous global consequences. In this sense, the boundaries between domestic matters and global affairs may be blurred' (Held et al. 1999: 15).

If this summarises the key features of globalisation as a set of processes in overall terms, what can be said about the key economic, political and social dimensions in terms of their potential impact on governments as social policy makers? Although social issues are important – migration, health risks, world poverty – the main ways in which governments are affected by globalisation are in terms of economic and political challenges.

It may be said that the principal problems of economic policymaking are now at an international rather than a national level: exchange and interest rates, the prices of oil and other raw materials, the state of health of the world economy are all matters beyond the exclusive control of national governments. What is more, national governments must make policy decisions that broadly meet the criteria of other public and private economic players such as MNCs, the OECD, the WTO and credit agencies. If they do not, they risk losing credibility, MNCs may choose not to invest and private speculators can attack national currencies. Even national taxation levels can be seen as a factor influencing the world markets, such that overall governments will try to keep taxes low in order to make their economies as competitive as possible. Alongside tax policy, governments have generally sought to **deregulate** their financial systems as a result of pressures from the private sector and international bodies such as the WTO. Indeed, these international groups – WTO, G8, EU, NAFTA, etc. – all now heavily influence and constrain the economic policies of national governments. All in all, the key principle in attempts by national governments to meet the various economic challenges posed by globalisation has been to maximise competitiveness. Government politicians of every persuasion consistently argue to their electorates that various policy initiatives, whether in the economic or the social fields, are necessitated by the pressures of globalisation and the requirement for the nation's economy to be competitive.

If we look at these economic constraints overall, they may appear to suggest that the scope for national governments to manage their own economies and, by extension, the rest of their societies, is increasingly curtailed by the pressures of economic globalisation. This question of government autonomy or, as some writers would prefer to put it, of government sovereignty, is, of course, fundamental to an understanding of the political challenges posed by globalisation. Some argue that the nation state has now become almost an irrelevance in the age of the global economy and that 'in terms of the global economy, nation states have become little more than bit actors' (Ohmae 1996: 12). Yet most writers on globalisation and politics now argue that globalisation actually needs the state almost as much as states have to operate within the context of global political circumstances. It may well be, as Hirst and Thompson argue, that national governments are having to function 'less as sovereign entities and more as components of an international quasi-polity' (1999: 257), but as Weiss (1998) and others have persuasively argued, the notion of a completely powerless state in the face of globalisation is a myth. It is a myth that, to some extent, may be seen as a useful fiction to serve the interests of national politicians, since it shifts the blame for unpopular policy decisions away from them and to the impersonal forces of 'globalisation'. This important ideological dimension of globalisation cannot be underestimated – the very fact that it has been necessary here to try and clarify and demystify the character of globalisation is a testament to the powerful use of a vague and unspecific term by politicians all over the world. Nevertheless, it is clear that international bodies such as the EU, the IMF and the World Bank do now play an important role in policy debates and policy initiatives, although it is still national state governments that make policy in almost all areas.

To sum up, globalisation is not a unified 'thing' but rather a *range* of processes that may affect different countries and different peoples in different ways around the world. In order to consider how it is implicated in welfare issues and social policy developments we now need to move on to consider some of the major theoretical approaches to globalisation and welfare.

Globalisation and welfare

In this section we shall look at some theoretical perspectives for analysing the link between globalisation and social policy, followed by an assessment of the usefulness of such perspectives for understanding what actually seems to be happening in the world of globalisation and welfare.

Theories and perspectives

As Sykes has argued (2003), it is possible to identify three characteristic perspectives on globalisation and welfare: globalisation is causing welfare retrenchment; globalisation has had little effect on welfare states; the effects of globalisation on welfare states are mitigated by national politics (see Policy eye 16.1). Let us unpack each of these perspectives further.

Globalisation has a significant impact on welfare states through the increasing dominance of the (market) economy

In this perspective, the view of globalisation and welfare is closest to the apocalyptic version of the globalisation thesis summarised earlier. Among this group are those who argue that globalisation has a strong impact because internationalisation of the world economy implies the demise of nation state autonomy, a reduction of national governments' policy options (especially those of social-democratic governments) and a weakening of labour movements. Thus, the main foundations of the national welfare state, it is argued, are fundamentally weakened. Others explain that globalisation has an effect on welfare states in the sense that the expansion of trade is responsible for unemployment and rising inequality, which creates (new?) problems for the welfare states. Trade and technological change both create a significant decline in demand for the unskilled, semi-skilled and traditionally skilled workers for whom the traditional welfare states were designed.

Ramesh Mishra (1999) provides an example of this perspective. He premises his account on the proposition that the socialist alternative to capitalism has collapsed; indeed, this collapse is, for Mishra, the *cause* of globalisation. The major effect of globalisation is the decline of the nation state in terms of its autonomy. Mishra makes seven propositions regarding globalisation and welfare:

1 globalisation undermines the ability of national governments to pursue full employment and economic growth

2 globalisation results in increasing inequality in wages and working conditions

3 globalisation exerts downward pressure on systems of social protection and social expenditure

4 globalisation weakens the ideological underpinnings of social protection

5 globalisation weakens the basis of social partnership and tripartism

6 globalisation virtually excludes the option of left-of-centre policy options for national governments

7 the logic of globalisation conflicts with the 'logic' of national community and democratic politics.

Mishra argues that globalisation has empowered and privileged neo-liberal economics as a transnational force beyond the control of nation states and governments. Thus globalisation 'must be understood as an economic as well as a political and ideological phenomenon', and 'is without doubt now the essential context of the welfare state' (1999: 15).

The problem with this perspective is that accounts of national economic, political and welfare state changes do not, in fact, support such apocalyptic conclusions. At the overall economic and political level, various writers have

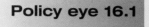

Policy eye 16.1   Three perspectives on globalisation and welfare

1   Globalisation causes welfare retrenchment through capitalism's dominance:

● Internationalisation of the world economy implies the demise of nation state autonomy, a reduction of national governments' policy options and a weakening of labour movements – i.e. the main foundations of the national welfare state are fundamentally weakened.

● Development of global capitalism is responsible for unemployment and rising inequality, creating worsening problems for the welfare states.

● Both international trade and technological change create a significant decline in demand for unskilled, semi-skilled and traditionally skilled workers.

● Need for national economies to compete in the world market exerts pressure for reduction in social expenditure by governments and private firms.

● All of these create pressures to shift from social-democratic and collectivist to neo-liberal and individualist welfare ideologies leading to *overall retrenchment and decline of welfare states*.

2   Globalisation has little effect on welfare states:

● Changes in the world economy are less widespread, smaller and more gradual than the full-blown globalisation thesis suggests.

● Even if globalisation has occurred, welfare states remain compatible with this process – globalised economies need to provide some sort of social welfare and political counterbalance to the effects of economic change.

● 'Threat of globalisation' is more an ideological ploy of national governments wishing to restructure welfare than an unchallengeable economic force.

● Welfare states are changing, but this is due to factors other than globalisation (for example, population ageing, technology, changes in family structures and new risks).

3   Globalisation's effects on welfare states are mediated by national politics:

● External global forces are impacting on national welfare state changes.

● Certain types of welfare state are more compatible with economic competitiveness than others and can adapt better than others to the new environment.

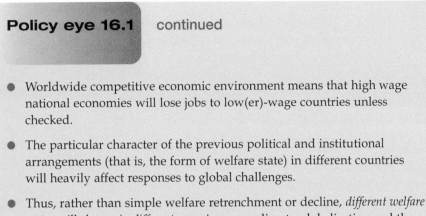

Policy eye 16.1   continued

- Worldwide competitive economic environment means that high wage national economies will lose jobs to low(er)-wage countries unless checked.

- The particular character of the previous political and institutional arrangements (that is, the form of welfare state) in different countries will heavily affect responses to global challenges.

- Thus, rather than simple welfare retrenchment or decline, *different welfare states will change in different ways* in responding to globalisation and the support of different constituencies (such as trade unions, politicians and voters) will ensure continuation of the welfare state in some form.

argued for the continuing autonomy of national economies and national governments (for example Hirst and Thompson 1996; Weiss 1998). At the level of welfare state change, other writers have challenged the assumption that (economic) globalisation represents the sort of direct, debilitating and homogenising impact outlined by exponents of this perspective.

Globalisation has relatively little impact on welfare states

In contrast to the previous view, some writers have argued that globalisation has no significant impact on welfare states. Some claim that there is no such thing as globalisation since trade is at the same level as it was at the beginning of this century and that the changes in the world economy are far less widespread, smaller and more gradual than the full-blown globalisation thesis suggests.

Others argue that, even if globalisation has occurred, welfare states remain compatible with this process and that it may even be a necessary feature of globalised economies to provide some sort of social welfare and political counterbalance to the effects of economic change. Such writers argue that the erosion of welfare states is due more to the ideological projects of governments seeking to restructure than to the impact of economic globalisation processes.

For others in this theoretical camp, the argument is that, while welfare states *are* changing, the cause is not globalisation: national welfare states are challenged by domestic factors (such as demography, technology, changes in family structures and new risks) rather than by globalisation. Pierson (1998, 2000) is probably the most influential proponent of this argument. He asserts that the welfare state, rather than facing fundamental retrenchment and decline, is likely to be sustained in almost all countries in the future. This is not to say that there are not pressures on welfare states. These are likely to lead to renegotiation, restructuring and modernisation, but not to dismantling of welfare states. What Pierson calls the 'irresistible forces' playing on welfare states are domestic forces, in particular the changed economies of advanced societies, the consequences of the 'maturation' of welfare states and demographic change. Globalisation as an exogenous set of forces is, at best, of secondary significance:

> The available evidence casts doubt on the claim that in the absence of growing economic integration welfare states would be under dramatically less pressure, and national policy-makers markedly more capable of addressing new public demands.
>
> (Pierson 1998: 541)

Pierson argues that three processes are largely responsible for the pressures on welfare states and are essentially unrelated to globalisation:

1 Advanced economies have witnessed a shift from manufacturing to services as their dominant sector along with slower economic growth. The low productivity associated with service employment means that such economies have a fundamental and growing fiscal problem in paying for welfare.

2 Such economies have, nevertheless, seen a tremendous expansion in the coverage and complexity of welfare state commitments because welfare states have come to 'maturity'. These present serious budgetary problems, plus a loss of policy flexibility.

3 The changing demographic balance, coupled with the growth of welfare programme commitments, presents two sorts of problems for welfare states. The first is that as the elderly increase as a proportion of the population, there a corresponding reduction in the proportion in work and thus in the fiscal base for welfare provision. Second, the increasing numbers of elderly people have direct effects in two areas of welfare provision where costs are thus likely to increase significantly: pensions and healthcare.

Pierson's approach is insightful, but it is focused mainly on the American and British welfare states. The argument that domestic factors in general, and the three factors just listed in particular, are more significant than globalisation regarding welfare state change remains to be tested in a broader range of countries. Evidence exists that service activities are not always associated with low or no productivity growth. If we are to understand why welfare states are experiencing 'permanent austerity' (Pierson 1998) then we must look beyond low productivity in services. Pierson's argument that globalisation is of very limited significance vis-à-vis welfare change is also debatable and seems to overlook the ideological and political dimensions of its role in welfare state change. Governments cite globalisation pressures as the external force compelling change and international organisations such as the World Bank provide both support for this view and a range of policy 'solutions' to the problems.

Globalisation is having an effect on welfare states, but these effects are mediated through (national) institutional structures and policy responses

In common with the two previous perspectives, proponents of this perspective focus on the effect of global forces on national welfare state changes. They argue, however, that certain types of welfare state (as well as certain types of labour market organisation) are more compatible with competitiveness than others and can adapt better than others to the new environment. Different welfare states are thus differently affected by globalisation. Esping-Andersen and his associates (1996), provide an account of the relationship between the global economy and welfare states that illustrates this approach. Esping-Andersen concludes that a nation's economic growth now appears to require economic openness, involving greater competition and vulnerability to international trade, finance and capital movements. Consequently, national governments are more constrained in their economic and other related policies so that 'Keynesianism, let alone social democracy, in one country is accordingly no more an option. It may even be that governments' freedom to design discrete social policies has eroded' (1996: 256). This worldwide competitive economic environment means that high wage national economies will lose jobs to low(er)-wage countries.

So far there are similarities between this perspective and the first perspective, but Esping-Andersen's analysis leads to quite different conclusions. First, he argues that Keynesianism in one country was, in any case, something of a myth: 'the most advanced welfare states tended to develop in the most open economies … the more residualistic welfare states in countries with relatively protected domestic economies' (1996: 257). Second, he argues that, in terms of labour costs, the real pressure from globalisation for advanced economies is on their low-skilled and labour-intensive mass production economic sectors: 'The most acute globalization problem that Europe and North America face may, indeed, be that the market for unskilled labour has become international' (1996: 258).

Esping-Andersen's key point here is that in responding to the dilemmas created by globalisation, different national systems can and do respond in different ways. As an example he points to different labour supply policies adopted by national governments in response to the pressures of globalisation. The continental European states opted mainly for an exit strategy enabling workers to leave the labour market; the USA and UK went for a wage-deregulation strategy to bring down relative wage costs; and the Nordic countries chose retraining and the provision of welfare state jobs (1996: 258).

Alongside the economic pressures, welfare states also face two other crises, according to Esping-Andersen. The first is the change for advanced welfare states from provision for the working classes to provision for all. The crisis rests in the fact that the principles on which such universal provision might be made no longer command broad consensus. The other crisis concerns the fact that neither the egalitarianism of the 'Swedish model' nor the targeted approach of the 'US model' seem, for different reasons, to support the sort of human capital improvement that contemporary economies require. In the first case, the system provides disincentives to work and to improve skills and education, whereas the second generates poverty traps and also disincentives to work.

Drawing on these two elements, far from foreseeing a system of 'competitive austerity', as Mishra does, Esping-Andersen concludes that 'the welfare state is here to stay ... The fact of the matter is that the alignment of political forces conspires just about everywhere to maintain the existing principles of the welfare state' (1996: 265). Within the advanced economies, although perhaps less so in the embryonic welfare states, existing political alignments of clients, welfare state workers, trade unions, political parties and others, imply that welfare state change will be limited and slow, even in the face of global economic changes and challenges. The particular character of the previous political and institutional arrangements in different countries will also heavily affect change. Accordingly, responses to globalisation and other pressures on welfare states are also likely to be differentiated.

This perspective is undoubtedly instructive, yet two criticisms may be made of it. The first is that even though such approaches differentiate welfare state changes, they do not differentiate the pressures of globalisation. Esping-Andersen points to the 'path-dependent' character of welfare state changes, but largely argues that globalisation and the internationalisation of economies occur everywhere with broadly the *same* characteristics. However, as we have seen earlier in this chapter, since globalisation has different dimensions, it can and does affect different welfare states in different ways, mediated by policy-makers. Different dimensions of globalisation create different 'pressure points' on different welfare states, according to their specific institutional features.

The second criticism concerns the view in this perspective that few important changes in welfare states have actually occurred, especially in continental Europe, for whatever reason. Esping-Andersen concluded that 'the cards are very much stacked in favour of the welfare state status quo' (1996: 267).

'Testing' the perspectives

What are the main propositions of these three perspectives that could be assessed in some way? The word 'testing' is placed in inverted commas here to signify that we are simply talking here about setting some empirical evidence alongside these theoretical assertions, not applying statistical or other specially developed tests.

From the first perspective we should expect the impact of economic globalisation to have led to various countries experiencing substantial, and essentially similar, welfare state changes, essentially those of retrenchment or at least significant 'cuts'. From the second perspective, we should expect globalisation to have had little or no clear or direct impact on welfare state changes in individual countries. Changes that may have occurred are likely to have been slow and incremental with a high degree of continuity with the past. Finally, from the third perspective, we should expect to see policy changes that are path dependent, but may be quite significant. The nature of change will depend on the pre-existing national welfare ideology and the institutional framework of the welfare state in each country, but with similarities in trends within the same type of welfare state regime.

In relation to the first perspective, there is in fact little evidence of a direct and essentially similar impact by globalisation on the world's welfare states or of overall retrenchment along similar lines. Changes that have occurred, although they may have been indirectly related to globalisation, have rather been mediated through national governmental policies and institutions, a process that has led to quite different outcomes.

There are similar problems with the second perspective, which links changes in welfare states solely to domestic factors. While the significance of factors, such as population ageing and the increasing cost of welfare systems should not be undervalued, it is clear that external factors, some of which were related to globalisation, have been part of the reason for changes in welfare states. Globalisation is not a monolithic exogenous force that impacts directly and with equal impact on nation states, but rather a complex set of ideological and practical processes, some of which are accepted, internalised and acted on by national governments. Within this broader view of globalisation, the argument of Leibfried and Rieger (1998), that welfare state change is due more to the ideological projects of governments seeking to restructure than to the direct impact of economic globalisation processes, seems closer to the evidence in various countries.

The third perspective seems closest to the evidence and experiences of different welfare states around the world. Esping-Andersen argues that existing institutional arrangements and welfare commitments constrain change in response to economic globalisation in 'path-dependent' ways. These arrangements and commitments, and the constituencies they created, coupled with the need for governments to sustain political support mean that welfare state responses and adaptations to globalisation will be slow and piecemeal. This 'path dependency' idea suggests that different types of *welfare state regime*, as proposed, for example, by Esping-Andersen elsewhere (1990), will respond in type-similar ways. Thus what he calls 'Liberal' welfare states (primarily the Anglo-Saxon welfare states such as the UK, the USA and New Zealand) have responded in one, broad sort of way. 'Conservative-Corporatist' states (such as Germany and France) have broadly responded in another way and 'Social-Democratic' welfare states (the Nordic states such as Sweden, Norway and Denmark) in yet another.

Various other studies also indicate that welfare state changes may also vary from country to country *within* similar types of welfare regime, because national governments may combine different sets of policy solutions. This can be seen, for example in Europe, in the variation within the social-democratic group between Swedish and Finnish developments, and within the conservative-corporatist group between French, German and Dutch developments.

This brings us to a fourth perspective as set out by Sykes, Palier and Prior (2001, especially pp. 198–206). The central feature of this perspective is that it treats globalisation not as a homogenous, exogenous force impacting on nation states and causing them to adapt their welfare states, but as a differentiated phenomenon, the character of which is constructed and interpreted differently in different types of welfare system. Furthermore, the relationship between globalisation and welfare state change is conceptualised as being two way and reciprocal, not unidirectional. From this perspective we should expect the following:

1   Welfare state changes to have occurred that can be linked with globalisation.

2   Differences between countries both in terms of their responses to globalisation and in terms of the forms that globalisation may take in different countries. A major pattern of differences may be expected between the more advanced and the less developed economies of the world in both these senses.

3   National politics and policies do matter, so they are likely to have had a significant effect on how globalisation is perceived and responded to in different countries.

4   Globalisation may not only have created problems for welfare states, especially pressure for cuts and retrenchment, it may also have provided opportunities that have sometimes been taken by certain governments to develop new social policies that are actually beneficial to their citizens.

Globalisation and the future of welfare

Using this final perspective on globalisation and welfare as a framework, how might we expect the relationship between globalisation and welfare to develop in the future? To begin with we can argue that the major players in setting and delivering social policies will continue to be nation state governments. Although there are clearly significant economic and political constraints on governments posed by globalisation in its various guises, it is clear that only national governments currently command the authority and support of their citizens to deliver various forms of welfare provision. Furthermore, given the 'path-dependent' character of such policies and their associated organisational and ideological underpinnings, it is unlikely that all welfare states will gradually converge around one form in the near or even quite distant future. The British, French and Chinese welfare systems, for example, are embedded in different political strategies and decisions, different systems for delivering services such as education and health and different ideas about, for example, 'welfare', 'citizenship' and 'poverty'.

Nevertheless, we can recognise a drift by welfare states around the world to a more neo-liberal approach to welfare. This approach, both ideologically and practically, prioritises economic competitiveness above welfare provision. Or, at least, it prioritises economic competitiveness above welfare provision that is seen to be excessively expensive and/or counter to the needs of economic flexibility and efficiency. What this means in practice is that social policies around the world are less and less focused on targets of 'equality' or redistribution, less related to ideas of collective as opposed to private and or market-based provision and fundamentally related to employment as the central feature of social policy. In this regard, the role of the various international organisations such as the WTO, the IMF and World Bank, as well as regional organisations such as NAFTA and the EU is proving to be increasingly significant. Somewhat paradoxically, while the World Bank, IMF and the EU, for example, have become more and more committed in recent years to having some sort of welfare role, that role is very much set in the context of employment rather than benefits, of economic growth rather than redistribution and of a commitment to the benefits of capitalist globalisation, increased international trade and low taxes.

Yet an increasing number of academics and others have questioned whether globalisation is inextricably linked with this neo-liberal project. Some have argued for a different approach, a 'socially responsible' globalisation that both permits the benefits of a truly global economy but also sustains and even develops the welfare of peoples around the world. They argue that capitalism continues to need the provision of some sort of welfare outputs as much in the global era as in the past. Without these provisions, economies, societies and governments around the world will become less and less legitimate in the eyes of their citizens and thus less stable. The worldwide anti-globalisation movement is a clear example of how many people are already challenging the unchecked growth of trade that benefits the rich much more than the poor, the actions of multinational corporations such as Nike and Microsoft in making decisions that appear to supersede or at best ignore national governments, and the environmental and public health costs of uncontrolled industrial development and dangerous work practices.

However, despite the suggestions of academic writers such as Deacon (with Hulse and Stubbs) (1997) and George and Wilding (2002) and of bodies such as the International Labour Organisation globalisation does not at present appear to be developing in a way that benefits the poor. Any realistic assessment of progress towards a globalised form of social policy to deal with global welfare issues such as poverty and social exclusion, unemployment and health would have to conclude that fine words have not yet been translated into much significant action. Does this mean that neo-liberal forms of global economic development are likely to continue unchecked and that the welfare of peoples around the world is likely to be less and less protected and provided by national welfare states to be replaced either by market-based provision or nothing? As with so many issues in the social policy field, we shall have to wait and see.

Summary

This chapter has examined the debates around globalisation and welfare and from these has argued that:

- Globalisation is essentially contested both as an idea and in terms of what it actually involves economically and/or socially and/or politically.

- Despite this controversy, it is possible to suggest that a central feature of globalisation is that it involves an increasing interconnectedness between states, peoples and regions across the world. Increasingly, a range of social, economic and political processes operate at global rather than national or other local levels.

- Most analysts of globalisation suggest that it is its economic characteristics that are primary and that the features of increased international competition, trade and the role of transnational corporations are challenging the power of nation states to make effective policy, not least in the economic policy and social policy fields. At the very least, the range of policy options open to national governments has become curtailed by the various features of the global economic context.

- In terms of the links between globalisation and social policy, there is also a dispute as to the character and effects of globalisation. Three theoretical perspectives have been outlined:

  1 that globalisation has little effect on national welfare systems

  2 that globalisation does have effects but does not prevent national governments from making effective policy choices

  3 that globalisation is causing wholesale retrenchment in welfare provision.

- A fourth perspective on globalisation and social policy can be outlined, suggesting that the linkage between globalisation processes and national governmental social policymaking should be regarded as a two-way process – globalisation does have the potential to limit policy choices, but the form globalisation takes is also affected by the choices that various national governments and international organisations such as the EU make.

- In the future the major players in setting and delivering social policies will continue to be nation state governments. Although there are constraints on governments posed by globalisation, only national governments currently command the authority and support of their citizens to deliver various forms of welfare provision. Furthermore, it is unlikely that, as a result of globalisation, all welfare states will gradually converge around one form in the near future.

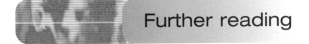

Discussion and review topics

1 What is the most important evidence that globalisation is occurring?

2 Consider which of the four perspectives on globalisation and welfare you find the most convincing and the reasons for this.

3 What examples are there of the ways in which national governments can seek to mediate the impacts of globalisation on social policy?

Further reading

Deacon, B. with Hulse, M. and Stubbs, P. (1997) *Global Social Policy*, Sage, London – this book is particularly useful on the role of international organisations such as the World Bank and the EU

George, V. and Wilding, P. (2002) *Globalization and Human Welfare*, Palgrave, Basingstoke – provides a good review of current trends and suggests future developments with regard to globalisation and social policy

Held, D. and McGrew, A. (2002) *Globalization/Anti-Globalization*, Polity, Cambridge – the best short introduction both to the various dimensions of globalisation and to its disputed character

Scholte, J. A. (2000) *Globalization: A Critical Introduction*, Macmillan, Basingstoke – this book provides a more sophisticated discussion and a more challenging read than those by Held and McGrew and Waters

Sykes, R., Palier, B. and Prior, P. M. (eds) (2001) *Globalization and European Welfare States: Challenges and Change*, Palgrave, Basingstoke – focuses on both theories and evidence concerning globalisation and social policy within a specifically European context

Waters, M. (2000) *Globalization*, Routledge, London – still one of the most readable and interesting books dealing with issues around globalisation

Some useful websites

http://en.wikipedia.org/ – the free Wikipedia online encyclopedia provides information and links on the whole globalisation debate including the anti-globalisation movement itself (type 'globalisation' in its search box and follow the links), but remember that all of this information is open to dispute and interpretation!

www.journoz.com/global/ – this Australian-based site contains a large number of links to other web-based information about globalisation

www.protest.net and www.wdm.org.uk – these sites provide a view of globalisation and its welfare impacts from various broadly 'anti-globalisation' perspectives

References

Collier, P. and Dollar, D. (2001) *Globalization, Growth and Poverty*, Oxford University Press/World Bank, Oxford

Deacon, B. with Hulse, M. and Stubbs, P. (1997) *Global Social Policy*, Sage, London

Esping-Anderson, G. (1990) *The Three Worlds of Welfare Capitalism*, Polity, Cambridge

Esping-Andersen, G. (ed.) (1996) *Welfare States in Transition: National Adaptations in Global Economies*, Sage, London

George, V. and Wilding, P. (2002) *Globalization and Human Welfare*, Palgrave, Basingstoke

Giddens, A. (1990) *The Consequences of Modernity*, Polity, Cambridge

Giddens, A. (1991) *Modernity and Self-identity*, Polity, Cambridge

Harvey, D. (1989) *The Condition of Postmodernity*, Blackwell, Oxford

Held, D. (1996) *Models of Democracy*, 2nd edn, Polity, Cambridge

Held, D. and McGrew, A. (2002) *Globalization/Anti-globalization*, Polity, Cambridge

Held, D., McGrew, A., Goldblatt, D. and Perraton, J. (1999) *Global Transformations*, Polity, Cambridge

Hirst, P. and Thompson, G. (1999) *Globalization in Question*, 2nd edn, Polity, Cambridge

ILO website: http://www.ilo.org/public/english/wcsdg/globali/facts.pdf

Koenig-Archibugi, M. (2002) 'Mapping global governance', in Held, D. and McGrew, A. (eds) *Governing Globalization*, Polity Press, Cambridge.

Leibfried, S. and Rieger, E. (1998) 'Welfare state limits to globalization', *Politics & Society*, 26(4), 363–90

Maddison, A. (2001) *The World Economy: A Millennial Perspective*, OECD, Paris

Mishra, R. (1999) *Globalization and the Welfare State*, Edward Elgar, Cheltenham

Ohmae, K. (1990) *The Borderless World*, Collins, London

Ohmae, K. (1996) *The End of the Nation State*, Free Press, New York

Pierson, P. (1998) 'Irresistible forces, immovable objects: post-industrial welfare states confront permanent austerity', *Journal of European Public Policy*, 5(5), 539–60

Pierson, P. (2000) *The New Politics of the Welfare State*, Oxford University Press, Oxford

Robertson, R. (1992) *Globalization: Social Theory and Global Culture*, Sage, London

Sklair, L. (2002) *Globalization: Capitalism and its Alternatives*, Oxford University Press, Oxford

Sykes, R. (2003) 'Social policy and globalization', in Alcock, P., Erskine, A. and May, M. (eds) *The Student's Companion to Social Policy*, 2nd edn, Blackwell/SPA, Oxford

Sykes, R., Palier, B. and Prior, P. M. (eds) (2001) *Globalization and European Welfare States: Challenges and Change*, Palgrave, Basingstoke

Wade, R. (2001) 'Inequality of world incomes: what should be done?', www.opendemocracy.net/themes/article.jsp?id=6&articleId=257

Wade, R. and Wolf, M. (2002) 'Are global inequality and poverty getting worse?', *Prospect*, 72, 16–21

Weiss, L. (1998) *The Myth of the Powerless State*, Polity, Cambridge

Conclusions

17 Hugh Bochel

Issues in Focus

This book has outlined some of the many areas of debate in contemporary social policy. This chapter reflects briefly on:

- trends in social policy since 1997
- changes that may affect the subject
- emergence of a possible new consensus on social policy.

As discussed in Chapter 1 of this book, social policy is an academic subject that is founded in the social sciences and that relates strongly to other social science subjects, such as economics, politics and sociology; it is a subject that continues to have relevance to a range of professions, such as social work and housing. Yet, at the same time, social policy is also something that goes on in the real world, affecting real people on a daily basis. It is sometimes therefore necessary to take all these different actualities into account when discussing 'social policy'. To some extent this chapter reflects this: its primary purpose is to focus on developments in the real world, but at the same time it seeks to point out a number of areas where there are implications for the academic subject and, where the two may come together, also to point this out.

Any reading of this volume will have made clear that social policy is continually developing and that there are inevitably a wide range of interactions with many other policy areas and with political and ideological imperatives (see, for example, Chapters 13 and 14). It is therefore not surprising that we can perceive a number of changes of direction in the development of governments' approaches to welfare over the past 100 years. Nevertheless, for three-quarters of the 20th century it was possible to argue that the key social policy development in the United Kingdom was the gradual extension of state welfare and the establishment of a welfare state. As noted in Chapter 1, this was closely linked with the rise of organised labour and, in particular, the 1945 Labour government, which was strongly influenced by social democratic and democratic socialist thinking, including the Fabian tradition. Following the Second World War there was a broad consensus on the idea of the welfare state, together with a commitment to full employment, and to a mixed economy managed by governments using Keynesian techniques.

However, by the 1970s, this consensus was coming to an end, shaken by a variety of criticisms from different parts of the political spectrum and by a recognition that the welfare state had not achieved all that many of its supporters would have wished. Indeed, from 1979, with the election of the Conservative government led by Margaret Thatcher, elements of previously widely accepted social policy were being seriously questioned, with a new emphasis on individualism, selection and the market replacing that on collectivism, universalism and the state. At the same time, within the academic subject of social policy, there was a much greater recognition of the diversity of the subject, with the development of a variety of critiques of past approaches and the incorporation of new ideas from both domestic and comparative approaches to the study of social policy.

Despite much of the rhetoric, and some significant reforms, after 18 years of Conservative government, substantial parts of the welfare state remained largely intact when Labour returned to power in 1997. However, by the late 1990s Labour's approach to social policy was not the same as it had been. There was now a much greater commitment to the use of a diversity of forms of provision, from public, private and voluntary sectors and a view from the New Labour government that what mattered was 'what works', rather than who provides services and benefits. Public opinion, which, as measured in opinion polls and surveys, frequently favours increased expenditure for improved public services, but does not always match this with a willingness to pay the higher taxes necessary for this, added to the difficult position for the government. In addition, the rising costs of welfare were encouraging governments to seek to control levels of expenditure and to spread the financial burden. To achieve this the government sought to use a variety of means including pressures for greater efficiency in public services, further use of targeting and encouraging people to make provision for themselves and their families, for example through insurance or pensions provision by the private sector.

One of the major questions for the future is, therefore, how welfare should be paid for. However, equally important is how resources should be used.

Questions of government income and expenditure therefore relate strongly to issues around the distribution and, potentially, the *re*distribution of resources. For much of the post-war period there had been a broad commitment, particularly from the political left, to a degree of redistribution from the wealthier in society to the poorer, to be achieved primarily through higher taxes on the former and the provision of benefits and services to the poorer. By the 1990s this had largely been replaced by a desire by New Labour to keep 'middle England' happy and, in particular, to do so by avoiding increases in income tax. Any attempts at redistribution under New Labour would therefore have to be very different from those of the post-war years (see Chapter 3).

Chapter 2 draws our attention to different issues, but ones that nevertheless have significant implications for the development of social policy in the United Kingdom, these being the importance of politics and decision making for social policy. Social policy is not technocratic: it is not simply a question of making minor adjustments to ensure the smooth running of mechanisms. As noted earlier, there are fundamental decisions to be made that affect society, including over how resources are raised and distributed. To these traditional social policy concerns have been added, as has been highlighted, particularly following the introduction of devolved administrations since 1997, an awareness of the importance of the mechanisms that are used to make and implement social policy and there is now the potential for even greater diversity within the United Kingdom. Yet, as has frequently been noted by commentators, Labour's apparent desire to devolve some aspects of decision making was matched by a high level of centralisation and control, including the many directions to schools and local education authorities that emanated from the Department for Education and Skills and the strengthening of the Treasury's role in directing and controlling social policy.

In addition to its governmental reforms, New Labour has also been, importantly for the subject of social policy, a government that has paid some attention both to policymaking and to engagement with academics and academic research. Academics have been drawn into advising government in a way and to an extent that they have not been since the 1960s, if then. And the amounts of money that government has been spending on policy research and evaluation have increased markedly. One example of this apparent commitment to 'evidence-based policy' and to evaluation is the creation of the 'Magenta Book', designed by the government Chief Social Researcher's Office to provide guidance on policy evaluation and analysis, which draws heavily on social policy approaches. Nevertheless, some critics might question the extent to which any of these have significantly impacted on the government's policies.

As Chapters 15 and 16 have shown, while the domestic agenda remains important, international developments, including the UK's membership of the European Union, are having a marked impact on social policy. Yet the discussions within these chapters also demonstrate that the same phenomenon can be interpreted very differently from different analytical or ideological standpoints. In the same way, the academic realm of social policy has been broadened by other debates, including those over the boundaries of the subject (Chapter 11) and by the impact of others, such as debates over 'risk' (Chapter 10).

Some of these have also been significant for decision makers. Given what it has seen as these uncertainties, New Labour has taken the view that the world is now very different and that an approach grounded in the provision of a range of state welfare services to passive recipient citizens is neither viable nor desirable. Rather, supporters of New Labour have argued that the role of governments is to work towards flexibility for governments and their citizens in their interactions with an increasingly complex society and economy. Citizens therefore have to take greater responsibility for themselves and the role of the state is becoming primarily that of an *enabler*, rather than a *provider*. It may, in some instances, continue to pay for services, but even in those areas there is to be a greater requirement for individual initiative than in the past.

One of the debates that has been important in social policy since 1997 is the extent to which the approach to social policy under New Labour has been similar to or distinct from that of the preceding Conservative governments. Some of the discussions in Chapters 3 to 9, in particular, demonstrate that it is possible to consider the answer to that question in different ways. Critics of the Labour government can support their arguments by pointing to a number of examples where there appears to be significant continuity, such as the commitment to a significant role for the private sector in the provision of welfare, the managerialist approach and the continuing use of performance measures and the use of targeting. There have been some apparently quite right-wing policies introduced by New Labour, such as the introduction of fees for higher education and cuts in entitlements to some social security benefits. Contrariwise, there have been commitments to eradicate child poverty and to expand the provision of childcare and it is possible to show that expenditure on welfare services, such as education and the National Health Service, has grown significantly under Labour and to argue that there has been some redistribution of wealth from the rich to the poor, in particular the working poor. This leads on to one of the fundamentals of New Labour's approach, the emphasis on work, with 'welfare-to-work' being a central part of its programme, so that people are expected to work where possible and there should be no reliance on benefits. Again, this can be interpreted as an attempt to return to a past position, where citizens had rights and obligations or as a shift to a point where governments are requiring people to work and blaming and penalising them if they are unable to do so.

Looking beyond New Labour to the broader political debate, some have argued that within the major political parties there is again something approaching a general consensus on social policy. This could be said to be founded in: a belief that there should be mixture of providers, drawn from across the sectors, but with regulation by the state; some commitment to public provision, but with a significant emphasis on provision by the private sectors, and to encouraging individuals to make provision for themselves; and a greater concern by the state with tackling social problems and exclusion through attempts to create more equal opportunities for individuals, rather than through financial redistribution from the richer to the poorer. However, the extent to which such a consensus actually exists, either within the parties or the wider public, is unclear. And, as is clear from a reading of some or all of this book, one of the few certainties about the subject is that social policy, and social policies, will continue to change and develop.

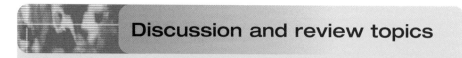

Discussion and review topics

1 Do you agree that there is an emerging political consensus on social policy?

2 What do you believe should be the balance of welfare provision across informal, public, private and informal sectors? Why?

Glossary

applied philosophy seeks to apply philosophical ideas and approaches to real problems and issues

benefit policing efforts to ensure that those in receipt of welfare are abiding by all rules governing entitlement

breadwinner a model of the family where the husband works (the breadwinner) and earns the family income while the wife provides care for the family

BSE crisis in 1996 fears over an epidemic of Bovine Spongiform Encephalopathy and over vCJD (new variant Creutzfeldt-Jakob Disease, the human equivalent of BSE) led to a crisis in British farming, with the slaughter of millions of cattle and the introduction of new regulations on the slaughter and consumption of beef

caseloading one-to-one relationship between a claimant and the state official assisting with the return to work

Children's Fund focused on developing services that support multi-agency working, the Fund is targeted at 5–13 year olds and is a key part of the Labour government's strategy to tackle disadvantages and inequalities that derive from child poverty and social exclusion

Class A drugs those drugs deemed by the government to be the most harmful when used. Conviction for possession of Class A drugs can lead to a maximum of seven years in prison and a fine; conviction for supply or intent to supply can result in life imprisonment and a fine.

commodity a good or service regarded as having no intrinsic merit. Its value is its exchange price as determined by the interaction between supply and demand

community care a term that can be understood in many different ways, but generally applicable to a range of policies applied to looking after people with particular needs in the community, including the movement of people from long-stay institutions to living in the community

Community Charge in 1989 (in Scotland) and 1990 (in England and Wales) the Conservative government replaced the existing system of local taxation, known as 'rates' with the Community Charge (also called the Poll Tax), a charge on each member of a household. Following widespread protests and significant problems with collection it was replaced by the Council Tax in 1993

comprehensive education a system of state secondary schools designed to ensure that all children receive similar education, thus increasing equality of opportunity

Comprehensive Spending Review introduced by Gordon Brown, this involves government departments justifying their expenditure plans to the treasury for a three-year period, rather than the previous annual spending allocations. It also gave the treasury a greater role in coordinating and controlling government expenditure

criminalisation   refers to a range of social and criminal justice processes (including policing, prosecution, punishment, penalisation, stigmatisation and blame) through which an individual or group is accorded the 'label' of criminal

dependency rates   dependency rates or ratios focus on the relative sizes of the economically active part of the population and those who are designated as dependent (primarily children and older people). Generally, a lower dependency ratio implies relatively more workers and less requirement to support dependent populations, while a higher dependency ratio suggests that a higher proportion of a population is dependent and a smaller proportion economically active

deregulation   the process by which governments have sought to reduce and remove regulations on businesses in order to improve the theoretical efficiency of markets. The theory is that deregulation will lead to greater competitiveness and efficiency

devaluation   when the rate at which one currency is exchanged for another is reduced

Earth Summit   an attempt to bring together participants, including heads of state and government, national delegates, non-governmental organisations, businesses and other major groups to focus upon improving people's lives and conserving natural resources

equal opportunity   the principle that everyone should have the same opportunity to succeed regardless of factors such as disability, gender, 'race' or social class

equity   the principle of treating individuals alike, but is linked to a recognition that the most equal outcomes are not always achieved by equal treatment so that individual needs must be taken into account

eugenics   can be interpreted as the view that society can be improved through the manipulation of genetic inheritance through reproduction

externality   a side-effect of an activity that affects other parties without being reflected in the price of the good or service involved

Fabianism   the Fabian Society has existed for more than 120 years. Fabians have believed that the free market system was inappropriate for the solution of social problems and that instead there should be collective provision. Closely linked with the Labour Party and with social democratic and democratic socialist thinking, Fabian ideas were influential in the development of the post-war welfare state

full employment   the achievement of a position where everybody who wants a job is able to find one. This was a generally accepted goal of British governments from 1945 to the late 1970s

further education   education often provided by further education colleges, sometimes available to children aged 16 to 19, but also aimed at adults. Although often linked to qualifications or careers, it can also be used solely to enhance knowledge and skills

generic social services   the use of a common pool of ideas and skills so that social work tasks could be applied regardless of the client and that distinctions between different client groups would be reduced and all would receive a similar level of service

genetically modified crops   these (GM) crops are from plants that have had their genes modified, for example, to make them more tolerant of particular conditions or resistant to certain herbicides

globalisation   while there are different perspectives, globalisation recognises that a variety of forces are leading to similar cultural, economic, social, political and technical developments around the world

GP fundholders   as part of the internal market within the Health Service created by the Conservatives in the 1990s, GP practices were able to opt to receive a budget (become fund-holders) with which they could then establish contracts with their chosen providers

grant maintained schools schools that opt out of local education authority control, are self-governing and receive their funding directly from central government

gross domestic product the total value of goods and services produced by a nation. GDP includes consumer and government purchases, private domestic investments and net exports of goods and services. It therefore measures national output

higher education more specialist provision through universities and colleges of higher education, including undergraduate degrees (BA (Bachelor of Arts), BSc (Bachelor of Sciences), LLB (Bachelor of Laws), etc.), taught postgraduate awards (such as MA and MSc) and research degrees (frequently a PhD, or Doctor of Philosophy)

housing association non-profit making body that specialises in housing and ploughs any surplus into maintaining existing homes and helping to finance new ones; provides homes to rent and also runs low-cost home ownership schemes

human genetics the understanding of human genes and their behaviour, a topic that has received greater attention with the unravelling of the human genome and the development of a greater ability to manipulate DNA

inelastic a good or service is inelastic if it is insensitive to changes in prices or incomes

intergovernmental organisations organisations that are generally created by treaties or agreements between states, such as the World Bank; these have a legal status and often have mechanisms for resolving disputes between members

internal markets the Conservative governments of 1979–1997 sought to improve the efficiency and responsiveness of services such as health and social care through the introduc-tion of internal markets, based on the separation of the functions of purchasing and providing of services

Keynesianism the economist John Maynard Keynes argued that governments could successfully intervene in the economy to stimulate demand (and therefore to achieve full employment) and to reduce demand (and therefore achieve lower inflation). Keynesianism provided the basis for economic policy in most western states from 1945 to the 1970s

Kyoto Protocol signed in Kyoto in 1997 this committed the industrialised nations to reducing worldwide emissions of greenhouse gases by an average of 5.2% below 1990 levels over the next decade

laissez-faire the economic doctrine that urges abstention by governments from interfering in the workings of the free market

local strategic partnership a single non-statutory, non-executive body, aligned with local authority boundaries, that brings together at a local level the different parts of the public sector as well as the private, business, community and voluntary sectors so that different initiatives and services support each other and work together; they are intended to operate at a level that enables strategic decisions to be taken and is close enough to individual neighbourhoods to allow actions to be determined at community level

'make work' schemes giving work experience that might not be available in the open market

'making work pay' policies creating financial incentives for claimants to enter paid employment

means testing the testing of a claimant's means in order to assess his/her entitlement to benefits. Only those whose resources fall below the eligibility level receive the benefits

modernising government one of the Labour government's aims following Labour's 1997 election victory, one of the government's aims was to 'modernise government'. This rather vague term can be seen as encapsulating

Labour's attempts to achieve a shift to more joined-up and strategic policymaking; a guarantee that users of public services, rather than providers, are the focus; the delivery of efficient and high-quality services

morality a term that is variously defined, but can be viewed as concern over the distinction between good and evil, or right and wrong and about right or good conduct

multiculturalism arising out of a recognition of ethnic diversity, multiculturalism has tended to emphasise how differences can create misunderstandings between different groups and to suggest that greater understanding of different cultures might reduce these. There is a concern with celebrating difference rather than with integrationist approaches

National Curriculum introduced by the Education Reform Act 1988 the National Curriculum specifies what subjects must be taught to children of compulsory school age in virtually all state schools

Next Steps agencies 'arm's length' bodies, sharing many of the characteristics of quangos, that are headed by chief executives who have responsibility for operational issues, but which also have responsibilities to their Whitehall department

NHS trusts created by the Conservative government in the 1990s as part of the internal market within the NHS, the trusts run hospitals as self-governing bodies, although their freedoms have been constrained by governments

non-governmental organisations organisations established by individuals or associations of individuals and not possessing governmental powers; NGOs vary widely in size and influence

nursery education pre-school education for children below the age of formal compulsory education

One Nation Conservatism a term that arose from a pamphlet produced by several prominent Conservatives in 1950, this is a view within Conservatism that was linked with the acceptance of the welfare state and the postwar consensus, but which differed markedly from the universalistic and egalitarian views of the Labour Party at that time, preferring selectivity as the means of delivering benefits and services

performance measurement the use of measures of performance for organisations, such as schools, hospitals or even local authorities, sometimes linked to the use of 'league tables'

pluralism a view that believes that power is or should be shared among the diverse groups and interests in society and that political decision making should reflect bargains and compromises between these groups

policy process the process of policy formulation, implementation and evaluation, which, while sometimes portrayed as linear, is in reality, generally dynamic and iterative

Poll Tax *see* Community Charge

predictive genetic testing the ability to test or screen using genetic tests that may suggest that individuals are likely to develop one or more particular condition, such as Huntington's disease

prices and incomes policy a policy that seeks to restrain increases in prices and incomes to achieve price stability

primary education education from the age of 5 to 11, designed to provide children with basic skills

Private Finance Initiative a method of injecting private capital into the provision of public services. It can take the form of an agreement between a public body and a private company for the supply of buildings or services over a period of time, often 30 years. The public body sets the standards and pays a fee to the private company for the services provided, such as a hospital or school building or the repair and improvement of local authority dwellings. Borrowing by the private company does not count as part of the Public Sector Borrowing Requirement

progressive taxation where the proportion of an individual's income paid in tax increases as their income increases, so that richer people pay relatively more than poorer people

public health the health of the population as a whole, initially concerned with issues such as sanitation, but more recently focused on areas around the prevention of illness, such as immunisation

public schools independent schools that charge fees; they do not have to teach the National Curriculum

Public Sector Borrowing Requirement (PSBR) the difference between government spending and its income. It is regarded as an important indicator of the chancellor of the exchequer's prudence in managing the economy

public service agreements established between the treasury and central government departments, public service agreements set out what the department aims to achieve with a given level of resources

quangos although not entirely accurate, the term quasi-autonomous non-governmental organisation (quango) is widely used to describe organisations that are not directly accountable to elected bodies, such as parliament or local government

racial harassment the most widely used definition of racial incident is that used by the Metropolitan Police and accepted by the Association of Chief Police Officers. 'Any incident in which it appears to the reporting or investigating officer that the complaint involves an element of racial motivation; *or*, any incident which includes an allegation of racial motivation made by any person.' (see www.racialharassment.org/about.htm and 'Statistics on Race and the Criminal Justice System 2000' (Home Office 2000: 49)

racism can be seen as in ideology or belief system that attributes negative qualities to some groups seen as inferior and that legitimises the unequal distribution of power and

resources as well as discriminatory and oppressive practices

rent control state determination of the rents charged by private landlords. The Conservatives attempted to phase out rent control in the 1930s and 1950s. By the 1970s, the major form of rent control was the determination of 'fair' rents by rent officers

secondary education education from 11 to the minimum school leaving age of 16 or to 18

security of tenure refers to the legal presumption that a tenant should remain in a dwelling unless the landlord can convince a court that there are very good reasons to evict the tenant

selectivity the targeting of benefits or services at particular groups, usually those considered to be in greatest need

social democracy this position has historically encompassed both socialism and democracy as essential components. Social democrats see capitalism as capable of transformation and reform through democratic action including the welfare state. However, from the 1980s some social democratic parties have adjusted their positions in response to critiques from the New Right and others

social housing defined by the Office of the Deputy Prime Minister as accommodation let at a rent below the market price. The term was invented in the 1980s as a way to blur the distinction between local authority housing and accommodation provided by housing associations

social inclusion being concerned with policies and measures designed to combat social exclusion. Government has sometimes defined social inclusion as the situation where people do not suffer from the problems associated with social exclusion. A socially inclusive society is seen by many as providing a more cohesive and harmonious social structure

social justice a concern with the extent to which social arrangements, and in particular the distribution of resources, are based on due process, impartiality and distribution according to appropriate criteria, with fairness being an important component of this

standardised attainment tests (SATs)   standard assessment tasks designed to assess the levels of attainment that pupils have achieved in core subjects, as defined by the Secretary of State for Education and Skills

stealth taxes   taxes where the population are supposedly unaware (or at least are only partially aware) of their existence and function

supply-side approach   policies focusing on what individuals and employers can do to overcome shortfalls in the economy

Sure Start   a programme introduced by the Labour government designed to address the social and health needs of children and families, including the availability of childcare

think tanks   arguably a special type of pressure group that often has close (usually informal) links with a particular political party (such as those of the Adam Smith Institute, the Institute for Economic Affairs and the Social Affairs Unit with the Conservatives, particularly from 1979 to 1997, and the Institute for Public Policy Research with Labour)

'underclass'   often used to denote a class of people dependent on welfare and in particular state assistance, for survival. It has been associated, by thinkers on the right, with dependency, while some on the left have made a link with social exclusion

universalism   the provision of public services, available to all, removing the need for means testing

wage subsidy   money paid by government, or agent of government, to supplement earnings

welfare state   where the state takes responsibility for providing at least minimal levels of economic and social security through the provision of public services (such as education, health, housing and income maintenance)

welfare-to-work   policies intended to move those reliant on the state for financial support (welfare) into a position of relative financial independence through paid work

'white-collar' offence   white-collar crime may be defined as those offences committed by people of relatively high status in the course of their occupation and so could include (for example) fraud, embezzlement, tax evasion and corporate crimes involving health and safety violations and pollution

work tests   requirements placed on welfare recipients to be available for, seek and take-up available jobs

'workfare'   the requirement to work or engage in other work-related activity in return for welfare

Index

Figures in **bold** indicate glossary entries